ALEXANDER'S VETERANS AND
THE EARLY WARS OF THE SUCCESSORS

The Fordyce W. Mitchel Memorial Lecture Series, sponsored by the Department of History at the University of Missouri–Columbia, began in October 2000. Fordyce Mitchel was Professor of Greek History at the University of Missouri–Columbia until his death in 1986. In addition to his work on fourth-century Greek history and epigraphy, including his much-cited *Lykourgan Athens: 338–322*, Semple Lectures 2 (Cincinnati, 1970), Mitchel helped to elevate the ancient history program in the Department of History and to build the extensive library resources in that field. The lecture series was made possible by a generous endowment from his widow, Mrs. Marguerite Mitchel. It provides for a biennial series of lectures on original aspects of Greek history and society, given by a scholar of high international standing. The lectures are then revised and are currently published by the University of Texas Press.

PREVIOUS MITCHEL PUBLICATIONS:

Carol G. Thomas, *Finding People in Early Greece* (University of Missouri Press, 2005)
Mogens Herman Hansen, *The Shotgun Method: The Demography of the Ancient Greek City-State Culture* (University of Missouri Press, 2006)
Mark Golden, *Greek Sport and Social Status* (University of Texas Press, 2008)

ALEXANDER'S VETERANS AND THE EARLY WARS OF THE SUCCESSORS

by Joseph Roisman

 UNIVERSITY OF TEXAS PRESS, AUSTIN

Requests for permission to reproduce material from this work should
be sent to:
    Permissions
    University of Texas Press
    P.O. Box 7819
    Austin, TX 78713-7819
    utpress.utexas.edu/about/book-permissions

♾ The paper used in this book meets the minimum requirements of
ANSI/NISO Z39.48-1992 (R1997) (Permanence of Paper).

LIBRARY OF CONGRESS CATALOGING-IN-PUBLICATION DATA

Roisman, Joseph
    Alexander's veterans and the early wars of the successors / Joseph
Roisman. — 1st ed.
        p.   cm. — (Fordyce W. Mitchel memorial lecture series)
    Includes bibliographical references and index.
    ISBN 978-0-292-75431-7

    1. Greece—History—Macedonian Hegemony, 323–281 B.C.
2. Greece—History—Macedonian Hegemony, 323–281 B.C.—
Historiography.   3. Greece—Kings and rulers—Succession—
History—To 1500.   4. Generals—Greece—History—To 1500.
5. Alexander, the Great, 356–323 B.C.—Friends and associates.
6. Veterans—Greece—History—To 1500.   7. Greece—History,
Military—To 146 B.C.   8. Babylonia—History, Military.   9. India—
History, Military.   10. Turkey—History, Military.   I. Title.
    DF235.4.R65   2012
    938′.08—dc23

                                                    2011035011

First paperback printing, 2013

To Hanna, Elad, and Shalev

CONTENTS

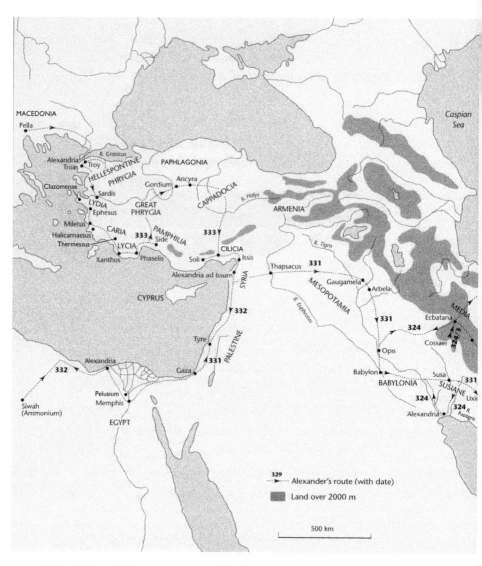

Map of Alexander's campaigns. Reproduced with the permission of Wiley-Blackwell.

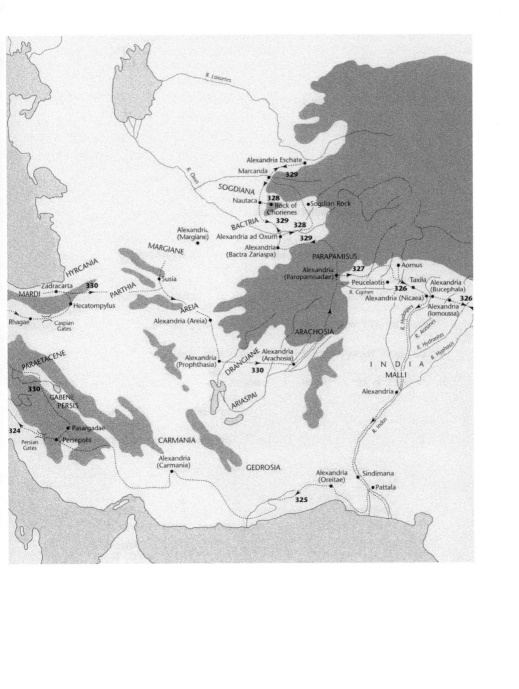

R. Laxartes

Alexandria Eschate
Marcanda
329

SOGDIANA

Nautaca **328**
Rock of
Chorienes ● Sogdian Rock

Alexandri ● BACTRIA **329** **328**
(Margiane) ● **329**
Alexandria ad Oxum

MARGIANE Alexandria
(Bactra Zariaspa)

R. Oxus

PARAPAMISUS
Alexandria **327** ● Aornus
(Paropamisadae)
Peucelaotis ● Taxila Alexandria
HYRCANIA **326** (Bucephala)
Zadracarta **330** ● Susia R. Cophen
MARDI PARTHIA Alexandria (Nicaea)
Hecatompylus AREIA **326**
Rhagae Alexandria
Caspian Alexandria (Areia) (Iomoussa)
Gates

R. Hydaspes
R. Acesines

PARAETACENE Alexandria Alexandria R. Hydraotes
(Prophthasia) DRANGIANE (Arachosia) R. Hyphasis
330 ARACHOSIA
330 ARIASPAI I N D I A

GABENE MALLI
PERSIS
Alexandria
324
Pasargadae
Persian Persepolis CARMANIA
Gates
Alexandria
(Carmania) GEDROSIA Alexandria Sindimana
(Oreitae)
325 Pattala

R. Indus

LIST OF ABBREVIATIONS

Aelian *VH*	Aelian, *Miscellaneous Histories*
App. *Mithr.*	Appian, *Mithridatic Wars*
App. *Syr.*	Appian, *Syrian Wars*
Arr. *or* Arr. *Anab.*	Arrian, *Anabasis*
Arr. *Succ.*	Arrian, *Successors*; or, *Events after Alexander*
Athen.	Athenaeus, *Deipnosophistai*
Curt.	Q. Curtius Rufus, *History of Alexander the Great*
Diod.	Diodorus of Sicily, *Library*
FGrHist	F. Jacoby, *Die Fragmente der griechischen Historiker* (Leiden, 2004).
Frontinus *Strat.*	Frontinus, *Stratagems*
IG	*Inscriptiones Graecae*
ISE	L. Moretti, *Inscrizione storische ellenistiche*, 2 vols. (Florence, 1967–1976).
Just.	Justin, *Epitome of Pompeius Trogus*
Nepos *Eum.*	Cornelius Nepos, *Eumenes*
Ox. Pap.	*Oxyrhynchus Papyri*
Paus.	Pausanias, *Description of Greece*
Phot.	Photius, *Library*
Plb.	Polybius, *Histories*
Pliny *NH*	Pliny the Elder, *Natural History*
Plut. *Alex.*	Plutarch, *Alexander*
Plut. *Demtr.*	Plutarch, *Demetrius*
Plut. *Eum.*	Plutarch, *Eumenes*
Plut. *Moral.*	Plutarch, *Moralia*
Polyaenus	Polyaenus, *Stratagems*
PSI	*Papiri greci e latini*
SEG	*Supplementum Epigraphicum Graecum*

FREQUENTLY CITED MODERN WORKS

Anson 2004 — E. M. Anson, *Eumenes of Cardia: A Greek among Macedonians* (Boston, 2004).

Berve 1926 — H. Berve, *Das Alexanderreich auf prosopographischer Grundlage*, 2 vols. (Munich, 1926).

Billows 1995 — R. A. Billows, *Kings and Colonists: Aspects of Macedonian Imperialism* (Leiden, 1995).

Bosworth 1980–95 — A. B. Bosworth, ed., *A Historical Commentary on Arrian's History of Alexander*, 2 vols. (Oxford, 1980–1995).

Bosworth 2002 — A. B. Bosworth, *The Legacy of Alexander: Politics, Warfare, and Propaganda under the Successors* (Oxford, 2002).

Briant 1972 — P. Briant, "D'Alexandre le grand aux Diadoques: Le cas d'Eumene de Kardia (1er article)," *REA* 74 (1972): 32–73.

Briant 1973a — P. Briant, "D'Alexandre le grand aux Diadoques: Le cas d'Eumene de Kardia (suite et fin)," *REA* 75 (1973): 43–81.

Briant 1973b — P. Briant, *Antigone le Borgne* (Paris, 1973).

Heckel 1992 — W. Heckel, *The Marshals of Alexander's Empire* (London, 1992).

Heckel 2006 — W. Heckel, *Who's Who in the Age of Alexander the Great* (Malden, MA, 2006).

Hornblower 1981 — J. Hornblower, *Hieronymus of Cardia* (Oxford, 1981).

Landucci Gattinoni 2008 — F. Landucci Gattinoni, *Diodoro Siculo. Biblioteca storica libro XVIII* (Milan, 2008).

Schäfer 2002 — C. Schäfer, *Eumenes von Kardia und der Kampf um die Macht im Alexanderreich* (Frankfurt am Main, 2002).

Vezin 1907 — A. Vezin, *Eumenes von Kardia: Ein Beitrag zur Geschichte der Diadochenzeit* (Münster, 1907).

PREFACE

This book originated in an invitation to participate in the conference on the origin of the Hellenistic world that took place in Edinburgh in 2006. By most ancient and modern accounts, the Hellenistic world was the creation of Alexander's great successors. Without denying these individuals' contribution, I try to focus in this study on their soldiers' input into and view of the post-Alexander era. The case of Alexander's veterans calls for special attention both because they played a significant role in the early wars of the Successors and because they exemplified the veteran experience, which has been a neglected topic in Greek history.

Teaching obligations and the beckoning of other projects created their usual impediments on the long journey to the final product. I was helped by many kind people and benefited from the comments and suggestions of different audiences at talks based on this project. I am especially indebted to Greg Woolf and the School of Classics at the University of St. Andrews; Hans van Wees and the Institute of Classical Studies, London; and Franca Landucci Gattinoni and the Università Cattolica di Milano and the School of History, Classics, and Archaeology at the University of Edinburgh for giving me the opportunity to present the results of my research. I wish to express my deep gratitude to Douglas Cairns, Andrew Erskine, and Lloyd Llewellyn-Jones for their kind hospitality and help, and to the Institute of Advanced Studies in the Humanities at the University of Edinburgh for the opportunity to work on the manuscript as a spring 2009 Senior Research Fellow. I am equally grateful to the Department of Classics at the University of Cincinnati, the helpful staff of the Blegen Library, and especially Getzel Cohen for enabling me to take full advantage of a fall 2009 Tytus Fellowship. Ian Worthington and the Department of History at the University of Missouri at Columbia privileged me with an invitation to deliver the 2010 Fordyce Mitchel Memorial lectures, which were based on this book. Brian Bosworth, who read a portion of the manuscript, and the readers of the University of Texas Press, who read it all, made valuable suggestions. Mel Regnel helped with the illustration and the map, and Jay Karden with the editing process. Thanks are also due to Jim Burr of the University of Texas Press for shepherding the manuscript through the process.

Earlier versions of parts of the book were published elsewhere and have been revised here to varying degrees. I thank Anton Powell and the Classical Press of Wales for granting me permission to use "The Silver Shields, Eumenes, and Their Historian," published in A. Erskine and L. Llewellyn-Jones, eds., *Creating a Hellenistic World* (Swansea, 2010), 61–82; Stefan Vranka and Oxford University Press for permission to use "Hieronymus of Cardia: Causation and Bias from Alexander to His Successors," published in E. Carney and D. Ogden, eds., *Philip II and Alexander the Great: Father and Son, Lives and Afterlives* (Oxford, 2010), 135–148, 285–286; and Leon Mooren for permission to use "Perdiccas' Invasion of Egypt," published in H. Hauben and A. Meeus, eds., *The Age of the Successors (323–276 B.C.)* (Studia Hellenistica) (Leuven). Haze Humbert and Wiley-Blackwell kindly allowed me to use a map of Alexander's campaigns. I thank Maria Tsimibidou-Avloniti and Lilian Acheilara of the 16th Ephorate and the Ministry of Culture of the Hellenic Republic for giving me permission to use the image on the book's cover.

ALEXANDER'S VETERANS AND
THE EARLY WARS OF THE SUCCESSORS

INTRODUCTION

In the spring of 319 BCE, Eumenes of Cardia and Antigonus the One-Eyed—both former commanders under Alexander the Great—fought at Orcynia in Cappadocia over the control of Asia Minor.[1] Antigonus won the battle and Eumenes fled in the company of Macedonian troops who had served with Alexander.

Eumenes' biographer, Plutarch, relates that in the course of his flight Eumenes came across Antigonus's rich baggage but decided not to seize it. He feared that the heavy booty would slow down his men and make them too spoiled (lit. "softer," *malakoteroi*) to endure the wanderings and the long recovery required before he could defeat Antigonus in a second round. Knowing, however, that it would be hard to stop the Macedonian veterans from taking property within their reach, Eumenes told them to rest before attacking the enemy. He then sent a messenger to Menander, the man in charge of Antigonus's baggage, advising him to move it to a place inaccessible to cavalry. Menander heeded his advice, and Eumenes, feigning disappointment with the news, went away with his men. Plutarch adds that when the Macedonians in Antigonus's camp learned that Eumenes had spared their belongings and families, they were filled with gratitude and praise for him. But Antigonus quipped that Eumenes had acted not out of concern for the Macedonians but because he did not want to tie up his legs when in flight (Plut. *Eum.* 9.6–12).

We shall reexamine this incident in its historical context later in this book (chapter 6). Here I wish to draw attention to how the story is told. The focus is on the generals and their perspective, and even when Antigonus's troops think that they and their affairs are important, Antigonus has-

---

1. For the battle, see chap. 6 below. For the date, see Boiy 2007, 148.

tens to bring them back to reality. Generally, the role of Eumenes' veterans in Plutarch is to highlight the merits of their general. The narrative contrasts Eumenes' foresight with the Macedonians' shortsightedness, his self-control and superior manliness with their corruptibility and almost Pavlovian greed at the sight of potential gain. For Plutarch the incident illustrates (once again) Eumenes' brilliant resourcefulness, which resulted in his duping both his own troops and those of Antigonus.

But the troops' point of view and interests are ignored by both the generals and the biographer. The Macedonian veterans expected to be given booty, both as an important supplement to their irregular wages and as their due reward. Moreover, Eumenes' veterans had just lost their possessions to Antigonus, and capturing his baggage would have allowed them to recover their losses. Eumenes' plan to wage a prolonged war against Antigonus also typically assumed that his interests overrode the veterans'. Yet Plutarch approves his cheating of his troops of their reward and options. This biographer is known for focalizing his heroes, but other authors share his viewpoint. When the troops and their leader are in conflict, the sources as a rule take sides with the latter.

The history of the events following Alexander's death is in many respects the history of the leaders who succeeded him. This circumstance is the legacy of our sources, which deal primarily with prominent individuals, as well as of the scholarship that is dependent on these sources. Indeed, many historians of the Hellenistic age focus on the careers, ambitions, and points of view of Alexander's great successors. This book endeavors to deal with the Macedonian masses rather than the elite of the post-Alexander era. By tracing the histories of Alexander's Macedonian veterans in the armies of his successors, I hope to illuminate their experience, along with the military, political, social, economic, and cultural conditions that shaped it.

Such an examination is justified, because modern investigations of the period tend to give only cursory attention to the veterans' story or to treat it as an addendum to their leaders' careers, except when the troops earn the generals' and the sources' reprimand (and many scholars') by disobeying orders.[2] In addition, scholarly analysis of the troops' conduct tends to adopt the ancient sources' elitist view of them as primarily interested in ma-

---

2. Among the notable exceptions are M. Launey's commanding work on Hellenistic armies (1949–1950; addenda 1987) and P. Briant's discussion of the Macedonian soldiers of the early Diadochs (1972–1973 [repr. 1982]).

terial gains or guided by basic needs while denying them moral and other nonmaterial considerations. In an attempt to go beyond the sources' tendentious depictions, this book examines the veterans' behavior in the army assemblies, on the march, and on the battlefield, as well as their volatile relationships with their generals and other related themes, all from the troops' perspective. I hope that such a "bottom-up" view of early Hellenistic history will shed new light on the period. To the best of my knowledge, no attempt has yet been made to examine this era from the viewpoint of the soldiers who had served with Alexander and later fought for his successors.

There is an additional advantage to investigating Alexander's veterans. Like the Athenian fighters at Marathon, Alexander's former troops were deemed the standard-bearers of martial heroism and patriotism. They stood for military experience and success as well as for Macedonian pride and identity, and they were even accorded the right to grant power to leaders. Their importance justifies an examination of their image and the reality behind it. The veterans' story also shows how soldiers responded to the demands of marching and battle, how they transferred loyalty from one authority to another, and how, in spite of their minority status, they dominated a much-larger army.

The bulk of this book deals with the Macedonians who served in Alexander's infantry and then with his successors. It is hard to extend the investigation to Alexander's non-Macedonian veterans, because they largely disappear from the record after his death, and even his Greek troops have been called a "silent majority."[3] Alexander also used Macedonian cavalry, the Companions (*hetairoi*), who played a crucial role in his campaign. Yet they retained their separate group identity only for a short time after his death, and are seldom mentioned afterward, probably because of their relatively small initial numbers (ca. 1,700–2,000 men), which facilitated their disappearance into the Successors' armies.[4]

I largely avoid two tangential scholarly controversies. One concerns the total number of veterans who survived Alexander, and the other revolves around the dating of key events in the years after his death. Oddly, the

---

3. Greek veterans: Wirth 1984. Bosworth (2002, 80), however, suggests that Asian troops who fought Macedonian-style in the Successors' armies might have gotten their training during Alexander's time.

4. The size of Alexander's cavalry: Diod. 17.17.4; Arr. 6.14.4; Curt. 10.2.8; Bosworth 1988a, 261–263, 266–270; Billows 1995, 188n10. See also chap. 3 below.

count of Alexander's Macedonian veterans has generated more recent interest than their careers, perhaps because of historians' disagreement over how much Alexander's campaign had depleted the human resources of his homeland. A. B. Bosworth launched the debate in 1986 by claiming that Alexander's expedition seriously reduced Macedonian manpower and left a relatively small number of veterans. Subsequent reassessments of the evidence by N. G. L. Hammond and R. Billows, with their more generous head count estimates, did little to dissuade Bosworth, who reiterated his basic assertions in 2002.[5] I shall not join the debate between the minimalists and maximalists concerning the veterans' numbers. In spite of much scholarly ingenuity, no new evidence on the subject has been brought to light. Moreover, the ancients' difficulties in accurately counting or even estimating large numbers of men are practically ignored in the discussion.[6] This book deals with the question of the veterans' number only when it is relevant to reconstructing their history.

The story of Alexander's veterans spans the period from his death in 323 to their last clear attestation in 316. The chronology of this period is as controversial as the question of the veterans' numbers. Since the publication of Eugenio Manni's challenges to the commonly accepted chronology of early Hellenistic history, scholars have been divided between the advocates of the traditional "low chronology," which gives later dates to the events after Alexander, and a smaller group of historians who argue for the earlier "high chronology." The differences may range from months and seasons up to a year. Fortunately, this controversy has little effect on the issues discussed in this book, which adopts a recent attempt at compromise between the rival chronologies.[7]

Somewhat less controversial than the veterans' number and chronology is the nature of their weapons and deployment. Here too the evidence is quite scanty. Written sources on the troops' arms and organization are much richer for earlier and later periods, while artistic and archaeological evidence informs us mostly on leaders and elites. The sources for Alexander's veteran rank and file tend to lump them in large groups, ignoring their equipment or smaller units and saying little about their battle or camp

---

5. Bosworth 1986; Hammond 1989b; Billows 1995, 182–217; Bosworth 2002, 64–97.

6. See esp. Rubicam 1991; 2003, 462.

7. High chronology: Manni 1949 and 1953, 67–81; Bosworth 1992b; Wheatley 1998; Bosworth 2002, 278–284. Low chronology: Errington 1970; 1977; Landucci Gattinoni 2008, xxiv–xlvi. The compromise: Boiy 2007.

experiences. Such limitations justify settling for only a brief survey of the veterans' likely equipment and organization.[8]

The Macedonian infantrymen of the period served mostly in the phalanx, and in battle wore helmets of the "Phrygian," the "Boeotian," and possibly even the *pilos* (conical) types. All three helmets left the face exposed, with the Phrygian protecting the cheeks and the *pilos* offering the least protection. It is not entirely clear if all infantrymen wore metal body armor, of which some versions were more protective (and heavier) than others. Leather or other nonmetal body armor was also used, although soldiers at the front and the back of the phalanx, as well as officers and high commanders, probably wore metal protective gear that distinguished them from the rank and file. Metal greaves and/or leather boots complemented the body armor. The infantryman's defensive weapon was the bronze shield. The phalangists may have used the "Macedonian shield," which was somewhat concave and about 65 cm in diameter; this relatively small shield allowed the soldier to hold the infantry pike (*sarissa*) by both hands. Enough evidence survives, however, to suggest they used shields of different sizes and shapes, including the larger hoplite shield, when the infantry fought either in hoplite formation or in individual combat. The phalanx's major offensive weapon was the sarissa, which consisted of an iron head and a butt spike connected by a two-part shaft that was joined by a metal collar. The length of the sarissa could range from perhaps 4.5 to 5.5 m and even longer. For hand-to-hand combat the warrior used a thrusting or slashing sword or a dagger. The shields, body armor, and plumed helmets were painted and sometimes decorated with gold and silver. It is likely that the soldiers received their arms from their commander.

The sarissa gave the phalanx an advantage over troops with smaller spears, and staggered rows of sarissas made for an effective and intimidating attacking front. The infantry was arranged in rows of various depths, with sixteen men deep being the recommendation of ancient tacticians. The smallest unit, the *dekas* (decade, or file), normally consisted of sixteen men, with the leader and the more experienced soldiers standing at the front or end of the unit and earning more money for their trouble. A number of decades formed the *lochos*, and a number of *lochoi* formed the *taxies*, a battalion of around 1,500 men, identified by its commander. The sources rarely

---

8. For the following see, e.g., Markle 1982; Bosworth 1988a, 259–277; Heckel and Jones 2006; Lush 2007; Hatzopoulos and Juhel 2009.

mention units of veterans smaller than a battalion in the post-Alexander armies. The phalanx inflicted the most damage and provided the best protection for its members when it remained in a compact formation. When the formation broke, the soldiers faced the enemy in hand-to-hand combat that did not discriminate among types of soldiers. One panel on the so-called Alexander sarcophagus (now in the Istanbul Archaeological Museum) provides a clue to the face of battle in spite of its artistic license. It depicts individual battles between Macedonians and Persians over a ground covered with fallen bodies, where cavalrymen, infantrymen, and archers fight soldiers of their kind and others.[9]

When the infantrymen fought as the more traditional hoplites, they wore body armor, greaves, and (usually) Phrygian helmets. Their shield was larger than the phalangists', and they also carried a ca. 2–2.5-m spear and a sword.[10]

The Macedonian cavalry plays only a secondary role in the history of Alexander's veterans, although as a fighting unit and a higher class of troops it enjoyed greater prestige and pay than the infantry. They wore Boeotian or Phrygian helmets, body armor, and leather boots, and carried the *xyston*, a spear shorter than the sarissa. It seems that they fought without a shield, and they probably got their horses from their commander. The operational cavalry unit was the *ile* (squadron) of probably 200 men, and generals might be accompanied by an *agēma* of 300 cavalrymen. During Alexander's time, two squadrons (*ilai*) made a hipparchy. A common offensive formation was the wedge, and the cavalry might find shelter during trouble behind the sarissas of the phalanx.[11]

The evidence for the history of Alexander's veterans comes from a variety of sources, but especially from Diodorus of Sicily's *Library*, books 18–20. To different degrees and with varying levels of immediacy, Diodorus and other sources most likely relied on the Hellenistic historian Hieronymus of Cardia. Hieronymus accompanied some of the major actors in the early Hellenistic period and knew the veterans personally from his service at their side. He enjoys high repute among modern scholars, who have

---

9. For an image see, e.g., Stewart 1993, fig. 102.

10. Heckel, forthcoming, argues that the elite unit of the hypaspists and their heirs, the Silver Shields, fought as hoplites, but his earlier view that they fought thus only on occasion (Heckel and Jones 2006, 32) is preferable.

11. For the cavalry, see Sekunda 2010, 452–454, 467–470 in addition to note 8 above.

largely overlooked his elitist approach of underplaying the contribution to Hellenistic history of ordinary soldiers and non-Macedonians. Hieronymus seems also to prioritize utilitarian considerations in his treatment of events and historical actors, even when such a preference is unwarranted. My first chapter discusses Hieronymus's bias and methods and their impact on ancient and modern depictions of Alexander's veterans. Similarly problematical for the veterans' story are Plutarch's and Cornelius Nepos's biographies of Eumenes of Cardia, whose career is intertwined with those of the veterans. Biography's tendency to exaggerate its subjects' power to shape events warrants a reassessment of the troops' and leaders' contributions to the history of the period.

After Alexander's death, the veterans' service with him defined much of their identity and their relations with others. Less discussed are the patterns of behavior they exhibited in their confrontations with Alexander and the lessons they learned from them during his reign and its aftermath. In 326 the veterans opposed Alexander's wish to march farther into Indian territory, and in 324 they mutinied in Opis when he planned to discharge the unfit and send them home. These experiences influenced the veterans' later group behavior and taught them and their leaders how to conduct themselves in confrontations. Chapter 2 offers an analysis of the troops' clashes with Alexander, the similarities and differences between the two conflicts, the difficulties of reconstructing the veterans' positions, and the nature of their relationship with the king, including its emotional dimension.

The veterans made their greatest impact on Macedonian political history after Alexander's death in Babylon. Thanks to their intervention in the succession controversy, Philip Arrhidaeus, Alexander's half-brother, became a co-king of the realm. Chapter 3 examines the role of the veterans and the army assembly in the events attending Alexander's death and the reasons their achievement failed to give them significant political power in the affairs of the kingdom.

The rest of the book follows the diverse histories of the veterans in the armies of Alexander's successors. Chapters 4, 5, and 6 investigate the disintegration of Alexander's army into groups that served in the royal army led by Perdiccas till his death in Egypt, in Craterus's and Antipater's armies in Asia Minor and Europe, in the force of Eumenes of Cardia in Asia Minor, and in Antigonus's army in the same region. Of all Alexander's veterans, the 3,000-strong unit of the Silver Shields (Argyraspides) occupied the most prominent role. Chapters 7 and 8 deal with this unit's character, its service with Eumenes in Asia, and its fate. We shall examine the Silver Shields as the Macedonian group par excellence and look at how they and their leaders defined their identity vis-à-vis other troops. These chapters also reassess the Silver Shields' claim to distinction and the way the sources privilege their military performance at the expense of other units. I conclude with the circumstances attending the Silver Shields' surrender of Eumenes to his enemy and the universal condemnation they received for this act. I hope that my investigation will shed useful light on men who were often overshadowed by the great individuals of the Hellenistic age.

CHAPTER I

MOTIVES AND BIAS IN THE HISTORY OF HIERONYMUS OF CARDIA

One is reluctant to begin an investigation by lamenting the sorry state of the evidence, but the case of Hieronymus of Cardia justifies this not-uncommon complaint. Too little is known about the career of this historian, whom many scholars regard as the bedrock of early Hellenistic history, and whose account arguably included our most valuable information on Alexander's veterans.

The known facts about Hieronymus are few and discontinuous. He came from the city of Cardia in the Thracian Chersonese, and is said to have died at the age of 104, perhaps ca. 270–260.[1] Around 319 he represented the general Eumenes—his townsman, companion, and likely employer—in negotiations with Eumenes' opponents, the generals Antipater and Antigonus Monophthalmus. About two years later, after being wounded in Eumenes' defeat in the Battle of Gabene, Hieronymus moved with most of Eumenes' followers to the camp of Antigonus. In or about 312, Antigonus sent Hieronymus to take over the collection of bitumen from the Dead Sea, where he was soundly defeated by the local Arabs, who held the monopoly over this profitable resource. Hieronymus fared only slightly better in 293, when he served as the governor (*harmost*) of Thebes for Antigonus's heir, Demetrius. The Thebans rebelled and Demetrius had to recapture the city by a costly siege. The last factual testimonies about Hieronymus's life refer to an intellectual exchange between him and Antigonus Gonatas, Demetrius's son and king of Macedonia, who may have been his patron.[2]

As if to compensate Hieronymus for his less than illustrious political

---

1. [Lucian] *Macrobii* 22 = *FGrHist* 154 T 2 says that Hieronymus died at the age of 104, and *Ox. Pap.* 4808 seems to say that he was over 90. He may even have served in Alexander's campaign: Beresford et al. 2007, 35.

2. Although often speculative, Hornblower 1981, 5–17, is still the best account of Hieronymus's career. See also Jacoby 1929–1930, IIB no. 154, 544–545; Brown 1947; Bosworth 2002, 25–26, 172–173, 188–189, 206–207.

and administrative careers, many scholars are inclined to credit him with a superior historiographical product. His repute is exemplified by the following wish regarding uncertain evidence: "We may like to have Hieronymus's name as a guarantee of good faith and reliable reporting."[3] Ancient views, however, are not so encouraging. The erudite first-century literary critic Dionysius of Halicarnassus thought that readers of Hieronymus would likely give up on his work because of its bad style. The first-century CE historian and Jewish patriot Flavius Josephus faulted Hieronymus for not mentioning the Jews, and the second-century traveler and antiquarian Pausanias believed that the historian had fabricated information and disliked kings, except for Antigonus (probably Gonatas).[4] The extant fragments of Hieronymus's work, which hardly constitute a representative sample, suggest that it was wide in scope, perhaps beginning from Alexander's campaign and extending at least to Pyrrhus's death in 272. They also indicate the inclusion of histories of places and peoples mentioned in the work, and of information that ancient readers might consider wondrous. These remnants of the evidently digressive narrative show an interest in ethnography, geography, and data ranging from measurements to casualty figures.[5]

These uninspiring characteristics stand in contrast to the great promise of Hieronymus's work. The author was a contemporary and eyewitness of many of the events he describes, and a personal acquaintance of some of their major participants, thus qualifying as potentially better informed and more knowledgeable than competing historians. To a large extent it is this promise—and the lack of a better candidate—that have led scholars to recognize Hieronymus's lost history of Alexander's successors as the main source for the best extant ancient histories of the period. This is especially true for books 18–20 of Diodorus Siculus's universal history, the *Library*.[6] Diodorus wrote his work in the first century BCE, and books 18–20 are an invaluable resource for reconstructing early Hellenistic history. Al-

---

3. Badian 1968, 190. For the following cf. Asheri 2006.

4. Dionysus Halicarnassus, *De compositione verborum* 4.112 = *FGrHist* 154 T 12; Josephus, *Contra Apion* I, 213–214 = *FGrHist* 154 F 6; Paus. 1.9.9–10 = *FGrHist* 154 F 9. Dionysius's criticism of Hieronymus's account of the Romans is designed to showcase his own historical investigation: *Roman Antiquities* 1.5.4–6.1, 7.1.

5. Billows (2000, 303–306) identifies Hieronymus also as an Alexander historian, but the ancients suggest that his focus was the Diadochs: Diod. 18.42.1; *Ox. Pap.* no. 4808. Hieronymus's fragments: Jacoby 1929–30; Hornblower 1981, 16–17, 238–262. It is unfortunate that a papyrus that apparently discussed Hieronymus's history extensively is so lacunose: *Ox. Pap.* vol. 71 (2007), no. 4808. But it seems clear that the author faults the historian for his bias.

6. E.g., Fontana 1957–1958, 151–237; Hornblower 1981, passim; but see Asheri 2006.

though the idea that Diodorus relied heavily in these three books on additional sources (especially on Duris of Samos) has been recently reinvigorated, the majority opinion, to which I subscribe, still views Hieronymus as Diodorus's chief informant. In any case, there is no doubt that Hieronymus was more knowledgeable about the Macedonian veterans than Duris.[7] Hieronymus is also identified as the direct or ultimate source of a number of other accounts of the period, such as Arrian's history of events after Alexander, Plutarch's and Nepos's biographies of the Diadoch (Successor) Eumenes, and even Justin's epitome of Pompeius Trogus.[8] Because of the meager number of fragments that survive from Hieronymus's history, any investigation of this historian must rely on the authors who used him. Yet rather than regarding the latter, especially Diodorus, as mere copiers of Hieronymus, it is important to recognize their contribution to the narrative while trying to tease Hieronymus's share out of it.[9]

In this chapter, my approach will be more thematic than chronological. I shall focus on events related to the Greek general Eumenes, about whom his fellow countryman and companion Hieronymus is the likeliest chief source. My goal is to draw attention to two characteristics of Hieronymus's history that have been either ignored or insufficiently recognized. The first is Hieronymus's tendency to seek and find causes in ulterior motives. The search for hidden agendas has appealed to historians of all ages, but it carries the risk of reaching simplistic conclusions or of rejecting other, equally valid explanations. My second concern is Hieronymus's elitist approach, which often privileges the perspectives and interests of leaders while devaluing those of their followers. I shall enumerate these characteristics and their impact on his history.

ULTERIOR MOTIVES AND HIDDEN AGENDAS

Jane Hornblower, the author of the most detailed study of Hieronymus to date, has noted that most of the generals who vied for power after Al-

---

7. Earlier literature on Diodorus's use of sources other than Hieronymus: Goukowski 1978, ix–xx; Seibert 1983, 2–11, 32–36. For his reliance on Duris, see Landucci Gattinoni 1997, 194–204; 2005; 2008, xii–xxiv. On the vexed and probably irresolvable question of whether Duris's history preceded Hieronymus's or vice versa: Geiger 1995, 176–177 with n8.

8. See, in addition to the previous note, Seibert 1983, 42–43; Geiger 1995, 178–181.

9. Among the growing number of scholars who protest against viewing Diodorus as a slave to his sources are Sacks (1990) and Green (2006, 23–24).

exander (the "Diadochs") are depicted in Diodorus's narrative as acting or thinking in their own interests, except for Hieronymus's patron, the general Eumenes.[10] Admittedly, there are other ambitious individuals who are guided by self-interest in Diodorus's *Library*, before and after Alexander. Yet it is surely significant that the verb *idiopragein* ("to pursue one's own interests") and its verbal family appear only in book 18, which is largely based on Hieronymus. A few examples will illustrate its use. The general Pithon, described as a man of high ambitions and grand plans, was given the command against rebellious Greeks in the upper satrapies in 323. He hoped, however, to reach an agreement with them *in his own interests* in order to become the satrap of these provinces (Diod. 18.7.4). Another instance is Eumenes' observation that he could benefit from the fact that many ambitious men who obtained military commands after Alexander were inclined to act *in their own interests* and hence would require his services (Diod. 18.42.2). Similarly, the death of Antipater, the regent of the kingdom, in 319 is said to have induced each potentate to work *in his own interest* (Diod. 18.50.1).[11]

Although "working in one's own interest" can at times characterize more than explain an action, the following example suggests Hieronymus's partiality to explanations based on self-interest or expediency.[12] In 324 Alexander issued a decree that allowed Greek exiles to return home and instructed their native *poleis* to accept them. My interest is not in assessing his motives but in how they are reported in the sources.[13] Apart from epigraphic and other evidence, the four major historical accounts of this decree come from Diodorus's book on Alexander's campaign (17.109.1–2), Curtius Rufus's history of Alexander (10.2.4–7), Justin's summary of Pompeius Trogus on Alexander (13.5.2–5), and Diodorus's book on Alexander's successors (18.8.2–5). Diodorus 17, Curtius, and Justin all report on the decree and the reactions to it, but say nothing about Alexander's reasons for issuing it (cf. also Orosius 3.23.14). Only Diodorus (book 18) explains that Alexander ordered the return of the exiles not only in order to gain fame (*doxa*) but also because he wished to have in each *polis* many people who would entertain

---

10. Hornblower 1981, 159.

11. See also Diod. 18.39.7, 52.7, 62.3–7 and Hornblower 1981, 168–169.

12. It should be mentioned that after Diodorus's interest in Sicilian and Roman affairs increases (especially in 19.70–20.81), his account of the Diadochs becomes sketchier and shorter on explanation of actions or events, perhaps because of space constraints.

13. For a recent discussion of the exiles decree, see Dmitriev 2004.

goodwill (*eunoia*) toward him and so allow him to curtail revolutions and stases among the Greeks. In response to the proclamation of this decree at the Olympic Games, the crowd shouted their approval, welcomed Alexander's favor, and praised his benefaction (*euergesia*).

The wording of the last report is probably Diodorus's own, and so is the reference to the reciprocal power of doing good to others.[14] Our interest is not in Diodorus's style or motifs but in his explanation of the decree. The reasons given for Alexander's actions, regardless of their validity, are absent from the other sources and, most important, from Diodorus's book 17. Because book 17 was based mostly on Cleitarchus, and because it is highly unlikely that Diodorus, after reporting on the decree in book 17, decided to add his own explanation of it in book 18, it is right to recognize here the contribution of his source, Hieronymus, who detected utilitarian motives and self-interest behind the royal decree.[15]

While the explanation of Alexander's decree in terms of its utility is not improbable, the attribution elsewhere of utilitarian motives to the satrap of Persis, Peucestas, is hardly adequate. In 318/7 the Diadoch Antigonus Monophthalmus campaigned against a coalition army representing the kings of Macedonia, led by Eumenes. According to our sources, Eumenes faced frequent challenges to his command from fellow generals, especially Peucestas. After Eumenes' victory in the competition with this satrap over who would be the supreme commander, we are told that Eumenes and Antigenes, the commander of the Macedonian elite unit of the Silver Shields, planned to stop Antigonus's advance at the Pasitigris River in Iran, and therefore asked Peucestas to draft and bring there 10,000 Persian archers. At first Peucestas ignored their request, feeling wronged in not having been awarded the supreme command himself. But then he realized that he would lose both his satrapy and his life if Antigonus won. Agonizing about his own situation, and thinking that he would probably get the command if he had a large number of troops, he brought the requested 10,000 men.[16]

---

14. Diodorus in praise of *euergesia*: e.g., 13.27.1; 20.93.6–7; 31.3.1–3; Sacks 1990, esp. 43n82, 68–70, 78–79, 103. See Hornblower 1981, 209–210, 269, for his language, although she thinks that in this passage Diodorus borrowed the concepts of *euergesia* and *eunoia* from Hieronymus.

15. Cf. Diod. 18.55.1–2, 20.102.1; Rosen 1967, 51; Flower 2000, 127. I am not persuaded by Sordi's argument that Diodorus did not use Hieronymus as a source for his account of the Lamian War: Sordi 2002, 433–443, 463–475; Landucci Gattinoni 2008, 55–56.

16. Diod. 19.17.5–6 erroneously calls the river the Tigris. For the episode, see further chap. 7 below.

This is hardly the only time when Peucestas is portrayed negatively in the sources, thanks most probably to Hieronymus, Eumenes' friend.[17] In the case of the plan to meet Antigonus on the river, however, this bias puts Peucestas's significant contribution to the coalition's war efforts in the worst possible light. If we look at what the satrap actually did, as opposed to his purported motives and thought process (to which Hieronymus could hardly have been privy), we see that Peucestas fully honored Eumenes' request for troops. Rather than showing an ambition for supreme command, he obeyed the instructions he was given and helped Eumenes and Antigenes. Moreover, what is described here as a period of delay and hesitation on his part was probably the time needed for the mobilization of such a large force, not to mention that Peucestas, who had already contributed 10,000 archers to the coalition army, thus doubled his contribution with this new contingent.[18] The source also never mentions that Peucestas could easily have eliminated his alleged fear of Antigonus by changing to his side, but chose not to. By ascribing to Peucestas ulterior, selfish motives, the source distorts his cooperative conduct, as does subsequent scholarship that follows Diodorus.[19]

Akin to attributing unworthy and selfish motives to individuals is Hieronymus's search for a hidden agenda, which is not always depicted negatively, and which the historian attributes on occasion to the Diadoch Antigonus. Although Hieronymus enjoyed the continuous patronage of Antigonus, his son Demetrius, and his grandson Antigonus Gonatas, I see little difficulty in ascribing Diodorus's criticism of the former two to Hieronymus. The criticism is never harsh, and if, as is likely, Hieronymus's history was published under Gonatas, it was hardly damaging to that king, whose reaction (or even strong interest in Hieronymus's publication) is a matter of conjec-

---

17. See Bosworth 1992a, 68 (although he thinks that Plutarch exaggerates Peucestas's negative portrait in his *Eumenes*); Schäfer 2002, e.g., 156; Anson 2004, 9. Diodorus gives different estimates of the distance between Susa and the river Pasitigris, an indication that he uses in book 19 a source different from the one in book 17 (probably Cleitarchus): Diod. 17.67.1 (correct distance); 19.17.3 (incorrect).

18. Peucestas's original force: Diod. 19.14.5. In 323 Peucestas arrived at Alexander's camp in Babylon with 20,000 men whom Diodorus—who dates their arrival to 324 *and* at Susa—identifies as archers and slingers: Arr. *Anab.* 7.23.1; Diod. 17.110.2.

19. Schäfer (2002, 138–139) and Anson (2004, 167) accept Diodorus's account. Schäfer stresses Eumenes' military vulnerability at this point, a circumstance that actually puts Peucestas's action in an even better light. For more instrumental and selfish motives in Diodorus, see, e.g., 19.21.1–2, 43.9; cf. 18.11.4, 19.94.1. Diod. 20.93.6 regards the utilitarian motive favorably.

ture.[20] I shall mention only two examples of Antigonus Monophthalmus's alleged hidden agenda. After Perdiccas was assassinated in Egypt, the old general Antipater succeeded him as guardian of the Macedonian co-kings Philip III (Arrhidaeus) and Alexander IV, and in 321 he redistributed imperial commands to various generals at Triparadeisus in Syria. Diodorus or his source is convinced that Antigonus, who was assigned to fight the Perdiccan forces left in Asia Minor, was at that time already pursuing his own interests and grand ambitions.[21] Thus we are told that, after his victory over the Perdiccan general Eumenes in 320/19, Antigonus, rich in money and men, pretended to be loyal to Antipater, but actually strove to be independent of him and the kings. He tried to persuade Eumenes—then under siege at Nora, probably in Cappadocia—to side with him. Eumenes asked in return for restoration of the satrapies he had lost and dismissal of the charges made against him after Perdiccas's assassination. Antigonus referred this request to Antipater and proceeded to fight the other Perdiccan general, Alcetas.[22]

Clearly Antigonus's actions belied the intentions ascribed to him. Rather than acting behind Antipater's back in the negotiations with Eumenes, he deferred to the former and informed him of Eumenes' unreasonable requests. The fact is that Antigonus was loyal to Antipater as long as the regent lived, and Plutarch dates Antigonus's imperial ambitions to the time following Antipater's death. It is probably Hieronymus who saw here a hidden agenda and selfish motive.[23]

About two years later (317), Antigonus is said to have acted under false pretences again. By that time he had already defeated and killed Eumenes and incorporated into his army the Macedonian veterans known as the Silver Shields, who had traded Eumenes to him in return for their captured baggage. Diodorus says that Antigonus sent the most seditious of the Silver Shields to the Arachosian satrap Sibyrtius soon thereafter, supposedly (*men logōi*) so that the satrap could use them in war, but in fact (*d'ergōi*) to destroy them: he even told the satrap in person to send them on suicide mis-

---

20. Cf. also Hornblower 1981, 228–232; Simonetti-Agostinetti 1997; *contra*: Landucci Gattinoni 2008, xv–xxii. Antigonus's hiding his true purpose elsewhere: Diod. 18.41.5, 54.4.

21. Diod. 18.39.7, and generally other contenders (except for Eumenes): 18.42.2, 50.1; cf. Arr. *Succ.* 1.43.

22. Diod. 18.41.4–7; Plut. *Eum.* 10.3; and see chap. 6 below.

23. Plut. *Eum.* 12.1; cf. Diod. 18.47.4, 50.1–2; Briant 1973b, 233; Billows 1990, 77n47; Simonetti Agostinetti 1997, 217–220; but also Engel 1978, 31–32.

sions. Diodorus sees in the Macedonians' fate the workings of retribution for their betrayal of Eumenes, and he goes on to philosophize briefly on the difference between impious acts committed by powerful leaders and those committed by ordinary men (19.48.3–4). Plutarch similarly regards the veterans' last assignment as divine retribution and says that Antigonus sent the Silver Shields to Sibyrtius with instructions to eliminate them because he considered them impious and savage (Plut. *Eum.* 19.3). Lastly, Polyaenus reports that Antigonus wished to get rid of these troops as a precaution against their untrustworthiness. He sent 1,000 Silver Shields to Sibyrtius and the rest on remote garrison duties, so that they all disappeared (Polyaenus 4.6.15; cf. Justin 14.4.14).

Of special interest are the sources' descriptions of Antigonus's action. While Plutarch and Polyaenus give different reasons for Antigonus's treatment of the Silver Shields—disgust in Plutarch, distrust in Polyaenus— Diodorus leaves Antigonus's behavior unexplained. For this historian, Antigonus was an instrument of vengeance against the Macedonians for their betrayal of Eumenes. Diodorus is the only historian, however, to claim a hidden agenda for Antigonus, making a distinction between his ostensible goal, helping Sibyrtius militarily, and the real one, destroying the Silver Shields. But there is no reason to look beyond Antigonus's "pretended" reason of aiding Sibyrtius. The latter needed soldiers to deal with the rising power of the Indian ruler Chandragupta, and eliminating a valuable elite unit just to gratify Antigonus would have made little sense. Indeed, why would Sibyrtius wish to take soldiers described as the most rebellious of the Silver Shields (Diod. 19.483)? Attributing a hidden purpose to Antigonus, however, confirms for the reader his cunning intelligence and strengthens the retributive element in the story, for Antigonus violated the pledge he had made to the Macedonians when they joined his army, just as they had violated their pledge to Eumenes.[24]

Looking for hidden motives was hardly a novel historiographical practice. Dionysius of Halicarnassus praises the fourth-century historian Theopompus of Chios for surpassing all other historians in his "ability to see and to say in connection with each event not only the things that were obvious to the majority, but to scrutinize the secret causes of events and the motives of the actors and the passions of the soul (things not easy for most men to

---

24. Hieronymus as the source for this affair: Engel 1972, 122; Hornblower 1981, 156, 192. Sibyrtius and Chandragupta: Schober 1981, 86, 93; Bosworth 2002, 164–165. Antigonus' pledge: Diod. 19.43.9. His cunning: e.g., Diod. 18.23.4. For the Silver Shields' violation of their oath to Eumenes, see chap. 8 below.

know), and to unveil all the mysteries of seeming virtue and undetected vice."[25] Hieronymus, perhaps a less-moralizing author and less-motivated detective than Theopompus, seems nevertheless to have taken a page from his book, as evidenced by his attempts to explain actions through the actors' hidden agendas and ulterior motives. A man's hidden agenda, however, did not always discredit him, especially not when he was favored by Hieronymus. Even Alexander's ulterior motives for the Exile Decree or those of Antigonus for sending the Silver Shields to their deaths do not make them appear villainous. Yet I hope it has been shown here that Hieronymus's fondness for utilitarian explanations could be misleading.[26]

ELITIST APPROACH

The history of the period following Alexander's death is in many respects the history of individual leaders who fought each other over power and territory. This focus privileges the story of the dynasts at the expense of those who followed them. Two stories involving trickery and breach of faith by the army and its commander can illustrate the sources' double standard in their treatment of each.

After Eumenes' victory over Craterus in 320, Eumenes surrounded Craterus's defeated Macedonians and exacted from them a pledge to join him. At night, however, they fled to Antipater, Craterus's colleague. Diodorus describes them as faithless men who broke their oath to Eumenes (Diod. 18.32.2–3), but he spares Eumenes a similar reproach for later breaking his oath to Antigonus. Diodorus also failed to commend the fleeing Macedonians for sticking with their original leader and cause in spite of their defeat, an example of loyalty rather remarkable in the time of the Diadochs (Diod. 18.53.5, 58.1–4). It was not just Diodorus's or his sources' pro-Eumenes bias that informed his negative depiction of the Macedonians; equally influential was the notion that it was fine for generals to deceive the troops but not vice versa. For example, Photius's summary of Arrian's history of events after Alexander, which probably relied on Hieronymus and some additional

---

25. Theopompus *FGrHist* 115 T 20a = Dionysius of Halicarnassus, *Letter to Pompey* 6; Flower's translation 1994, 170.

26. For other cases of ulterior motives see also Diod. 18.58.3 (Olympias on the royal regents), 65.3–66.3 (Alexander, son of Polyperchon); 19.15.5 (Eumenes), 23.1 (Eumenes on Peucestas); 51.2–3 (Cassander), 61.4 (Antigonus). Hieronymus also allowed for other kinds of explanations: e.g., Diod. 19.53.2, 54.1.

sources, relates that Antipater's army mutinied and demanded money before crossing back to Europe from Asia in the winter of 320/19. Antipater promised the troops that he would pay them in three days at Abydus, allowing him to get there in peace, but then he sneaked away under the cover of night to Thrace. The empty-handed troops followed him the day after. Clearly, it was justified and even admirable for a general to get out of trouble by a stratagem, even if it meant cheating the troops out of their wages (Arr. *Succ.* 1.44–45).[27]

The legitimization and delegitimization of actions and agendas described above were based on a broadly elitist approach toward actors and history. According to this view, individual leaders were the makers of history, which their followers had little part in shaping. It regarded the leaders' concerns and interests as more worthy than those of their subordinates and sided with the former whenever the interests of the two classes were in conflict. It condoned conformity to well-established aristocratic values, such as self-control and the competitive pursuit of good repute, and held the military elite to higher standards of conduct than the masses. But it also ranked Macedonians (and Greeks) above Asians, who were portrayed as their inferiors and their natural victims in war and plunder. This was hardly a novel outlook, anchored as it was in traditional Greek or conquerors' mentalities, and in the political, social, and economic hierarchies of the Macedonian state. In Macedonia, the king and his elite used the masses to sustain and enhance their positions and policies, and although kings such as Philip and Alexander deemed themselves their subjects' benefactors, they were no less primarily their exploiters, as some Macedonians told Alexander in tears or in resentment (Curt. 9.3.1–3; Arr. 7.8.1–10.7). For Hieronymus, who made his career rubbing shoulders with such dynasts as Eumenes, Antigonus, Demetrius Poliorcetes, and Antigonus Gonatas, it came naturally to privilege the elite's role and perspective. In the following I wish to examine how Hieronymus's elitist approach affected his history.[28]

Diodorus—himself no friend of popular democracy—painted a negative picture of democratic Athens in the post-Alexander era. We do not know to what extent Hieronymus contributed to his description, but there

---

27. For this and the previous episode, see chaps. 4 and 5 below. Cf. Eumenes' stratagem of preventing his troops from capturing Antigonus's baggage: Plut. *Eum.* 9.6–12. Arrian's sources: e.g., Simonetti Agostinetti 1993, 16–19.

28. See, however, Hornblower 1981, 194–195. Given Diodorus's interest in great men, whom he used to educate his readers, he must have found Hieronymus's account appealing: cf. Sacks 1990, 23–36; Anson 2004, 12, 21.

was nothing in Hieronymus's background and record to suggest sympathy for the city. His place of origin, Cardia, had a history of enmity with Athens, and his intimate association with potentates and monarchs bespeaks little appreciation for democratic politics. As Diodorus's primary source for book 18, Hieronymus may have inspired—or at least offered nothing to contradict—Diodorus's hostile portrayal of the Athenian demos and its leaders when they decided to join the Hellenic (or Lamian) War against Macedonia, or in the trial of the oligarch Phocion. In both cases the demos is depicted as governed by passions, swayed by belligerent speakers, and behaving like an uncontrolled mob, while Phocion's trial and execution are presented as an unmitigated travesty.[29]

Hieronymus's elitist perspective comes through more clearly in our sources' description of generals' relationships with their troops. Plutarch's biography of Eumenes, describing Antigonus's siege of Eumenes at Nora in 319–318, provides one example. Since Hieronymus was involved in the negotiations between these two generals as well as with Antipater, he is Plutarch's most likely direct or indirect source.[30]

We are told that after Eumenes had fled to Nora, Antigonus followed with the intention of putting him under siege, but first offered to meet him. Following preliminary negotiations, in which the author allows Eumenes both a moral and a rhetorical superiority, Eumenes left his shelter to meet Antigonus at his camp. Plutarch says that the two commanders embraced and greeted each other like old, intimate friends. As the conference and the negotiations went on, many Macedonians rushed to catch a glimpse of Eumenes, the most talked-about man in the army since his earlier battle with Craterus in which that highly respected Macedonian general had found his death. Fearing that Eumenes would suffer some violence, Antigonus shouted at the soldiers not to come closer, threw stones at them, and fi-

---

29. Diod. 18.10.1–4, 64.1–67.6. Admittedly, Duris shared Hieronymus's unsympathetic view of democratic regimes and of the masses' conduct, as well as his emphasis on individuals in history: cf. Kebric 1977, 32–33, 58. Diodorus on demagogues and the many in democracies: 11.77.6, 11.87.1–5, 19.1.18; Sacks 1990, 167. Hieronymus as Diodorus's source here: Hornblower 1981, 60–61, 171–177; Lehmann 1988, 753; but see Green 2003, 3; 2006, 241. Mossé 1998 suggests a source other than Hieronymus for the Phocion affair. See also note 15 above.

30. Hieronymus's involvement: Diod. 18.42.1, 50.4; Plut. *Eum.* 12.2. The differences between Plutarch's description of the following episode in *Eum.* 10.3–8 and Diodorus's account of it in 18.41.6–7 are not significant enough to justify the assumption that Plutarch consulted another source for it, perhaps Duris: Anson 1977, 254–255; 2004 131n54.

nally embraced Eumenes and kept the crowd (*ochlos*) away with his body-guards until he could get him to a safer place (Plut. *Eum.* 10.3–8).

Even if only the gist of the story comes from Hieronymus, it still shows his elitist perspective. Clearly, the Macedonian troops were hostile to Eumenes, who had been outlawed in Egypt two years earlier and was charged with responsibility for Craterus's death and a Macedonian civil war. In short, they were not attracted by his celebrity status or a wish to admire him, but sought to lynch him.[31] Antigonus's staunch defense of Eumenes probably had less to do with friendship than with the presence in Nora of Ptolemy, Antigonus's nephew, who had gone there before the nego-tiations to serve as a hostage and ensure Eumenes' safety (Plut. *Eum.* 10.5). All this is ignored in the episode, which centers instead on the generals' no-ble and collegial manner. The Macedonian troops, on the other hand, are relegated to the role of providing these leaders with an opportunity to dis-play their friendship, code of honor, and superior rank and character. The author largely disregards the encamped soldiers' feelings and motives, em-phasizing instead their mob behavior, which obstructs and threatens the dealings of the generals.

Conversely, when the sources describe the troops positively, it is often to show how they liked and esteemed their generals. Diodorus's account of the eve of the Battle of Gaza in 312 (fought between Demetrius, son of An-tigonus, on one side and Ptolemy and Seleucus on the other) illustrates this perspective on general–troops relations, but with a twist. The author draws a portrait of Demetrius that is rare in its rich details about a command-er's personality and the troops' attitudes toward him (Diod. 19.81.1–6). Jane Hornblower has persuasively identified Diodorus's source here as Hierony-mus, who focused his narrative on Demetrius and appears to have accom-panied him during this period.[32] In the following I am more interested in the way the author presents leader–follower relations than in the accuracy of his statements. Hence the anachronistic references to Antigonus and De-metrius as kings (a designation official only from 306) have little bearing on the analysis.

---

31. Charges against Eumenes: Plut. *Eum.* 8.1–3 and chap. 4 below. Cf. Nepos *Eum.* 11.2, where Eumenes, as a captive in Iran, became an object of curiosity for Antigonus's troops; but then he was under arrest.

32. Hornblower (1981, 12, 232) is more convincing than Seibert (1969, 170–171), who identifies in Diod. 19.81 two different sources. Hornblower also speculates that Hieronymus might even be one of the advisers reported to have (wisely) warned Deme-trius against going into battle. Cf. Diod. 20.92.1–5 and Hornblower 1981, 58–60, 228.

Diodorus's report begins with subdued criticism of Demetrius for confidently going into a major battle against his advisers' recommendations and in spite of his youth and the absence of his father. Demetrius convened an army assembly and was ill at ease when facing it, but the audience unanimously called upon him to take courage and then fell silent of its own accord. The author opines that because Demetrius was a new commander, he was free from the troubles that characterize long-standing generalship, such as the cumulative burden of minor resentments that soldiers feel toward a veteran general and the increasing difficulty of pleasing them. He was also liked by those who felt that their previous general had deprived them of something and were looking for a change. As heir to the kingship of Antigonus, who was now elderly, Demetrius enjoyed the goodwill (*eunoia*) of the people and became the focus of their hopes. The fact that he was a handsome and imposing figure, especially in his royal armor, induced men to respect and expect much of him. His youthful mildness gained him universal support and sympathy in his intimidating task of fighting experienced and apparently invincible generals such as Ptolemy and Seleucus.

Diodorus's sensitive description of the troops' psychology shows them reacting to this general with a mixture of hope, empathy, and even paternalism. Such sentiments explain why, instead of doubting the ability of their new commander to lead them into battle against such formidable enemies, they wished to help this young, handsome, and promising general and were anxious to hear what he had to say. The historian's extensive treatment of the soldiers' hopes and mood leads the reader to anticipate an equally detailed description of Demetrius's view and expectations of the troops or how he took advantage of the favorable atmosphere. Instead we get a disappointing general statement about his emboldening the troops and promising them the usual rewards of gifts and booty.

Perhaps Diodorus epitomized a longer speech by Demetrius in the original.[33] But it is no less likely that he was loyal to his source, because the depiction of the troops and their general is infused with irony, which is hard to find elsewhere in Diodorus's work and thus suggests another authorial hand. He shows us a Demetrius who owed his command solely to the fact that he was Antigonus's son, but who was liked by the troops because they hoped that Antigonus would die and that Demetrius would prove different from him. The rest of his popular appeal consisted of his good looks,

---

33. For Diodorus's (selective) reluctance to include speeches in his history, see 20.1.1–2.2. Cf. Simpson 1959, esp. 374.

his royal demeanor, and the protective impulse excited by his vulnerability. These were not credentials that could justify either Demetrius's self-confidence before the battle or the soldiers' trust in him. In reality, many troops must have felt relieved to know that the experienced general Pithon, son of Agenor, was Demetrius's co-commander, and that there were other veteran commanders in the camp.[34] But this factor is not mentioned among the considerations that moved the soldiers to follow Demetrius into battle. Instead, we have troops who centered their false hopes on an unqualified commander, and who, in spite of their good feelings toward him, would desert him in droves after his defeat in battle. After the defeat in Gaza, one wonders how many soldiers were still looking for a change in command and a leader milder than Antigonus. Neither the general nor the troops acquit themselves well here, but when one reads how at the end of the battle Demetrius was left standing with only a few cavalrymen, and that he unsuccessfully begged his soldiers not to flee (19.84.5), sympathy goes to him rather than to the troops.

A different kind of sentiment involving the troops and their general is presented in connection with Eumenes' illness and its effect on the troops during their march through Iran in 317. Both Diodorus (19.24.5–6) and Plutarch (*Eum.* 14.3–15.2) report on this incident, Plutarch proving the better storyteller and Diodorus offering the more sober account. Once again, their most likely source is Hieronymus, who was an eyewitness to the events.[35]

Eumenes and his opponent Antigonus were marching with their armies not far distant from each other, and were looking for a suitable battlefield. Eumenes became seriously ill after a drinking bout (so Diodorus) or from some disease (Plutarch). According to Diodorus, the march halted for some days and the army lost its spirit because its most competent general was incapacitated (19.24.5; cf. Plut. *Eum.* 14.3). When Eumenes had somewhat recovered, he was carried in a litter at the rear, out of sight and away from the tumult of the marching army, which was being led by Peucestas, the satrap of Persis, and Antigenes, the commander of the Silver Shields.

Plutarch relates that while Eumenes' army was on the move it suddenly

---

34. Pithon: Diod. 19.82.1, 85.2; other generals: Billows 1990, 127 (omitting Boeotus: Diod. 19.85.2).

35. Plutarch perhaps overstresses Eumenes' virtues in his biography (see Bosworth 1992), but I see no compelling reason to attribute his account here to Duris or a source other than Hieronymus, as does Fontana 1960, 231–232; Hornblower 1981, 69. For the following, cf. Vezin 1907, 101–102; Schäfer 2002, 148–149.

saw Antigonus's force descending onto the plain in all its might and splendor. The troops at the front of Eumenes' column stopped and shouted their refusal to go on and risk battle without Eumenes in command. This message was delivered to the rest of the army, and Eumenes, quite pleased, rushed forward in his litter and stretched out his hand. The soldiers hailed him in Macedonian, raised the battle cry, and challenged the enemy to fight. Plutarch then artfully shifts his narrative to the enemy's reaction. Antigonus, who knew about Eumenes' condition, was amazed to see Eumenes' army ready for battle, the litter moving from one wing to another. He even joked that his army was facing a litter, and then he withdrew his forces. Plutarch ascribes Antigonus's retreat to Eumenes' appearance at the front, an explanation consistent with his flattering portrait of the latter. According to Diodorus's more level-headed account, both armies withdrew because they did not like the terrain.

Both descriptions use the soldiers' reactions to emphasize Eumenes' prominence and his popular leadership, thereby betraying the elitist perspective of the source. Let us look at what happened from the soldiers' rather than their leaders' point of view. Earlier, Eumenes had invested great effort in ensuring that no one else could hold the supreme command. He demonstrated to the troops that he could reward them with gifts and provisions as richly as his alleged rival to leadership, Peucestas. He forged letters that reported the victory of his European allies in the fight over Macedonia and claimed they were marching with an army to help him. Significantly, these were allies and friends of Eumenes himself, not of the other generals. He also intimidated Peucestas through a failed attempt to get rid of his friend Sibyrtius, the satrap of Arachosia (Diod. 19.23.1–4).

In short, the troops demanded that Eumenes take charge because he had succeeded in making the alternatives to his leadership appear weak and unappealing. Scholars have also noticed Eumenes' efforts to draw similarities between himself and Alexander—among them, his greeting the soldiers from his litter in illness, just as Alexander had done in 325 after being seriously wounded in an attack on an Indian town.[36] From the soldiers' perspective, Eumenes' gesture might have enhanced his stature, but the situation also triggered unpleasant memories and fears. The ailing Alexander had made an effort to come and greet his soldiers in order to prove that he

---

36. Bosworth 2002, 126–127; cf. 1992, 60. I found the similarities he detects to Alexander's illness in Babylon less persuasive. Eumenes' showing up in a litter was intended also to signal Antigonus that he was in charge; cf. Polyaenus 8.4.1.

was not dead (Arr. *Anab.* 6.12.1–13.3). Since Eumenes was seriously ill and was being carried in a litter away from the marching army, fear for his life must have been on the minds of his troops as well. This involved more than concern for the fate of a dearly loved commander. Imagine soldiers who faced battle against a strong army in a foreign land, under a general who had presented himself as their caretaker and the sole link to potential allies: a commander who had weakened every other leader in the camp, but who was not in sight. I suggest that the Macedonians' refusal to march on without Eumenes in the lead meant that, before risking their lives in battle, they wanted to know if he was alive, because his death would have required them to reassess their situation and even the rationale for fighting Antigonus. The description of the love fest between Eumenes and the troops surely flatters him, but it is a dubious compliment if it reflects the difficult situation of the soldiers and their dependence on their general.

A similarly elitist perspective can be detected in Diodorus's description of the aftermath of the Battle of Paraetacene between Eumenes and Antigonus in 317. The battle was indecisive, because although Eumenes' cavalry and infantry were victorious over their respective enemy counterparts, Antigonus defeated Eumenes' left wing. The two armies regrouped, but by the time they were ready to offer a second battle it was midnight and the troops were exhausted from the marching, fighting, and lack of food. Each side went back to its camp, but Eumenes wanted to return to the battlefield to bury the dead, an act tantamount to a declaration of victory. We are told that his soldiers refused and shouted that they wished to go back to their own baggage, which was at a distance. Eumenes had to comply with their demand and was unable to punish them when so many leaders disputed his command; nor was this an opportune time to discipline the troops. But Antigonus, who had a firm grip on his command and did not have to resort to *dēmagōgia* ("popular leadership"), forced his army to camp next to the battlefield, where he could declare victory by burying the dead (Diod. 19.31.1–4).

Immediately after this report, Diodorus records the greater number of losses that Eumenes had inflicted on his opponent (19.31.4). There is an authorial motive at work here: regardless of the battle's indecisive outcome, Diodorus and his source aim to show that Eumenes was the real victor, robbed of his victory by no fault of his own. The culprits were the disobedient troops and Eumenes' rivals to command, who prevented him from punishing the soldiers. The language used to describe Eumenes' constraints is likely Diodorus's own, since he elsewhere criticizes demagogues and unruly masses. Yet several aspects of this story show him sharing with his source the privileging of the commanders' distinction and agenda, as well as a clear pro-Eumenes bias.[37]

First, here and elsewhere the soldiers express themselves by making a commotion, either by shouts or by banging their spears against their shields, while their leaders speak in individual, articulate voices. Second, the contrast between Eumenes' difficulties in controlling the army and Antigonus's easier task is problematic, both because it is designed to exonerate Eumenes' failure to possess the battlefield and because it does not tell the whole story.[38] While Antigonus's army was made up of relatively fresh recruits, who probably had little baggage, the Macedonians in Eumenes' army carried baggage accumulated since Alexander's campaign, and hence had a greater incentive to go back for it. In addition, Eumenes' army fought the battle after a hurried meal and a quick march, while Antigonus's army, except for the cavalry, reached the battlefield at a regular pace (Diod. 19.26.3–10). The claim, then, that *both* (*amphoteroi*) armies were hungry and exhausted (Diod. 19.31.2–3) underestimates the greater distress of Eumenes' troops.[39] A good general knows when to push his men beyond their capability and level of motivation. It was not his soldiers' fault, nor to Eumenes' credit, that he had failed to appraise correctly their low morale and physical condition.

Furthermore, although the source ranks the two commanders' goal of declaring victory above the soldiers' concerns, this does not make the former more legitimate or justified. Eumenes' soldiers wished to recuperate and were anxious about the welfare of their baggage, which included their families and dependants. The Silver Shields would demonstrate the importance of this concern again after the subsequent Battle of Gabene, moving to Antigonus's side when he had captured their baggage. In any case, it was the generals who needed to assert victory, not the troops, who had little reason or ambition to make sacrifices and expend extra effort so that Eumenes could win his battle of prestige with Antigonus. In the eyes of the source, however, this was a shortsighted, petty, and selfish attitude. Only an author who focused on the general's perspective and needs, and who was

---

37. See above for criticism in Diodorus of the many and their leader. His support of social ranking: Green 2006, 24.

38. Antigonus's reportedly more secure command does not mesh well with Pithon's disobeying his orders in the Battle of Paraetacene: Diod. 19.29.7–30.1; Bosworth 2002, 134–137.

39. See Schäfer 2002, 153–154, for additional possible reasons for Antigonus's advantage.

convinced that the soldiers' interests should be subordinated to those of their commander, would produce such a tendentious report.

This belittling and unsympathetic appreciation of the troops' needs recurs in other accounts of Eumenes' campaign. Diodorus tells that during the winter of 317, Eumenes' army was widely scattered over unplundered Gabene. According to Plutarch and Nepos, this was not done by Eumenes' design.[40] Plutarch says that Eumenes' troops acted once again as if they were led by popular leaders (*edēmagōgounto*) and, mocking their commanders, spread themselves wide in their winter quarters. Nepos states that Eumenes distributed his soldiers according to their wishes, not his own. This inspired the Roman biographer to comment on the insubordination of Alexander's phalanx, its aspiration to rule rather than obey its commanders, and the possible lesson of this bad example for those commanding Roman veterans. He adds that Eumenes' troops were dispersed in search of winter quarters not for any military purpose but for their own luxury or pleasure.

Diodorus's failure to mention any conflict over the winter camps between Eumenes and his troops is probably due to his abbreviating his source, for it appears that Diodorus, Plutarch, and Nepos all relied on a common author,[41] following the above episode with similar reports on Antigonus's failed attempt that winter to catch Eumenes' forces by surprise, and on Eumenes' successful countermeasures (Diod. 19.37.2–39.1; Plut. *Eum.* 15.4–13; Nepos *Eum.* 8.4–10.1). Each historian links Antigonus's stratagem to the dispersion of Eumenes' army, and concludes the description of the generals' maneuvers with the almost identical comment that Eumenes outgeneraled Antigonus. Hieronymus is their most likely direct or indirect source.

The description of Eumenes' mutinous soldiers is one-sided at best. We cannot be certain how many of Eumenes' 36,700 infantry and 6,000 cavalry (the numbers reported to have participated in the Battle of Gabene shortly afterward) actually wintered in the region. Some may have gone home to their nearby satrapies for the winter, while others may have joined him just before the battle (cf. Diod. 19.40.4; cf. 19.39.1–2). Yet it is fair to as-

---

40. Diod. 19.34.7, 37.1, 39.1. Plut. *Eum.* 15.4; Nepos *Eum.* 8.1–4. Polyaenus uniquely asserts that Eumenes himself distributed his army along a 1,000-stade road, but the distance alone is confirmed by the other sources: Polyaenus 4.6.11; cf. 4.8.4.

41. Cf. Bosworth (2002, 142n158), who confuses Plutarch with Nepos, however, when he says that the former highlights the troops' luxuriousness. Plutarch's 15.1 *tois hegemosin entruphōntes* is best translated as "mocking the commanders."

sume that more than half of his force stayed at Gabene. There was no one camp that could have accommodated and provisioned so many troops and their companions. More important, locating good winter shelter was necessary for the survival and comfort (both legitimate goals) of the soldiers, some of whom had families with them.[42] Moreover, even if Eumenes' army covered 1,000 stades (ca. 185 km) from end to end, as the sources tell us, its bulk could not have been far removed from Eumenes' camp, since he himself estimated that it would take (only) three to four days to assemble his and his fellow commanders' forces.[43] Indeed, when he needed his troops for battle, they all showed up, indicating that the ill effects of the troops' insubordination were exaggerated by the sources, who adopted Eumenes' view of it, and that their criticism of the soldiers for pursuing their own interests was both unjustified and unfair.

Finally, the sources' elitist attitude comes out clearly even in Diodorus's digression (most likely derived from Hieronymus) on *sati*, the Indian practice of burning widows along with their dead husbands.[44] In the past, he tells us, the Indians had allowed young men and women to marry each other freely and without parental matchmaking. This practice resulted in many disappointed couples and even in wives poisoning their husbands so they could live with their lovers. To discourage such murders, the Indians instituted a law ordaining that wives must join their dead husbands on the pyre or else become religious outcasts and lifelong widows. Recently A. B. Bosworth has analyzed this account and argued with great ingenuity that Hieronymus's discussion of the Indian custom and its origins was possibly a reworking of Indian traditions or a criticism of some of Diogenes the Cynic's followers, who advocated free choice of partners in marriage. I believe he is correct in saying of Hieronymus's digression that "there was on occasion an implied message, moral or political, which the reader might detect beneath the plain text of the excursus."[45] In the following I wish to show that the excursus gains added significance when viewed as a comment on events in Eumenes' war against Antigonus.

The digression on the Indian custom and the funeral is placed in the

---

42. Cf. Bosworth 2002, 142; Anson 2004, 182; Loman 2005, 360–361.

43. Distance covered by the army: Plut. *Eum.* 15.4; Polyaenus 4.6.11. Eumenes' mastering the troops: Diod. 19.38.2; cf. Plut. *Eum.* 15.9–19.

44. Diod. 19.33.1–34.7. For the source, see Bosworth 2002, 174–176, who argues that Strabo's (15.1.30; cf. 62) very similar account may also come from Hieronymus. See also Szczurek 2009.

45. Bosworth 2002, 173–187; quotation: p. 173.

context of the aforementioned contest between Eumenes and Antigonus over who would bury the dead of the Battle of Paraetacene and so claim the right to victory. Eumenes, who first wished to possess the battlefield, was denied the privilege by his tired and hungry troops: they shouted that they wanted to go back to their personal baggage, and he was unable to punish them. Antigonus, who began the burial, failed to finish the job because he was anxious to retreat and give some relief to his army. This allowed Eumenes to come back and give a splendid burial to the dead (Diod. 19.32.1–3; cf. Polyaenus 4.6.10).

The digression comes next. It tells of the Indian general Ceteus, who died in battle, and who was married to two loving wives. After explaining the origins of the custom of burning living widows with their dead husbands on the pyre, the source comments that the introduction of this law reversed the former lawlessness of Indian women, and made them face death willingly, care about their husbands' safety, and compete with each other to gain a great reputation (*megistēs eudoxias*). We hear of rivalry between Ceteus's wives over the right to die with him, as if they were competing for excellence and honor (*hōs hyper aristiou symphilotimoumenai*). When the younger wife wished to disqualify the older, pregnant wife because of her condition (the law forbade cremation of pregnant wives), the older woman claimed seniority, which placed her higher in respect (*entropē*) and honor (*timē*). The generals in Eumenes' army decided in favor of the nonpregnant wife, and the other left the scene as if she had suffered a catastrophe, while the younger woman went to her death as full of joy in her victory as if she were going to a wedding, with her kin singing her virtue (*aretē*). She gave away all her precious jewelry (enthusiastically itemized by the source), climbed the pyre, and ended her life heroically (*herōikōs*), making no ignoble sound (*oudemian phonēn agennē*). We are told that some of the spectators were moved to pity, some to extraordinary praise, but that some Greeks viewed the custom as savage and cruel. The next sentence reports on Eumenes' completing the burial of the dead and leading his army to the well-supplied environs of Gabene.[46]

The description resembles, perhaps by intention, Herodotus's description of the Thracian wives, who also competed for the honor of joining their dead husbands. It might even have been partly informed by Indian

---

46. Diod. 19.33.1–34.7. Diodorus reports on a range of reactions also to the death of Caranus (in fact, Calanus), the Indian sage who accompanied Alexander and climbed the pyre to die in flames: 17.107.4–5. But there the reactions were quite different: he was deemed mad and vain but also worthy of admiration.

tales. I wish to draw attention here, however, to the Greek rendering of the story.[47] Hieronymus reports Hellenic criticism of *sati*, but the descriptors used for the wives' conduct leave no doubt about his admiration. They behaved *piously, courageously, nobly, honorably, heroically,* and *without a thought for themselves*. Such terms suggest a stark contrast with the troops in Eumenes' army, who a few days earlier had prevented their leader from burying the dead because they wanted to return to their baggage. In the Indian widows, we are shown enthusiastic conformity and strict obedience to the law, exemplary self-control, a noble victory over fear and pain, and the highest form of self-sacrifice. In Eumenes' troops, we see defiance, lack of discipline, an inability to overcome bodily wants, and an unwillingness to serve others. Ceteus's wife paid her dead husband the ultimate honor and gave away all her precious belongings. The troops would not even return to give the dead their last honors, because they wished to be reunited with their personal belongings, presumably far less valuable than those of the widow. Thus two Indian women, who in Greek elitist fashion competed for a good name in deference to societal norms, put to shame the selfish, inconsiderate, and lawless troops. That the contrast was not coincidental is indicated by the context in which the Indian story is set (the burial at Paraetacene) and by the two sentences that introduce and conclude the digression, both referring to Eumenes' magnificent burial of the dead.

This is not Diodorus's first contrast between noble barbarians and inferior Macedonians. When the body of Alcetas, Antigonus's opponent, was surrendered to him by local Pisidians in 319, Antigonus abused it for three days before throwing it away unburied. But the young men of the Pisidian city of Termessus, whom Alcetas had greatly benefited in the past, gave him a magnificent burial. Diodorus was sufficiently impressed to insert a remark on the power and rewards of benefaction (*euergesia*; 18.47.3). The contrast between the young Termessians and Antigonus could not be clearer, and such a contrast is equally clear in the case of the burial at Paraetacene.[48]

The fact that barbarians behave better than Macedonians in both ep-

---

47. Herodotus's influence: Hdt. 5.5; Bosworth 2002, 178–179; Szczurek 2009, 137–140 (indirectly); but see the reservations of Heckel and Yardley 1981, esp. 306. Szczurek (2009, 124–143), who mentions additional studies of the incident, convincingly argues for an eyewitness account, likely by Hieronymus, and for its historical reliability. But I am not convinced by his rejection of Hieronymus as the source of 19.33 on the grounds of Hieronymus's supposedly incontestable credibility. Indian influence: Bosworth 2002, 179–184.

48. A tomb in Termessus with a relief of a cavalryman has been identified as Alcetas's burying ground: Perdikou 1986.

isodes does not necessarily contradict the author's elitist attitudes. In Hieronymus, positive depictions of barbarians show them conforming to traditional Greek ideals. This is true for the Indian wives and the Pisidians discussed above; for the Isaurians whom Perdiccas fought in 322 and who were willing to sacrifice themselves, their families, and their possessions for the sake of liberty (Diod. 18.22.1–8); and for the Nabatean Arabs in Hieronymus's famous digression about them.[49] The last-named were resourceful, manly, and eager to fight for their freedom, which they enforced through laws carrying the death penalty. The source grants them the exceptional privilege of a speech reproaching Demetrius, son of Antigonus, for senselessly fighting them and for trying to change their steadfast attachment to their way of life.[50] Barbarians who validated Greek values thus demonstrated where the Macedonians and their leaders went wrong.

Hieronymus was hardly unique among the ancients in his search for ulterior motives or in constructing his history around the stories of prominent individuals. While the motives and causes he ascribes to actions are not in themselves unlikely, they may, together with his elitist focus and perspective, produce distorted and biased accounts. It is unfortunate that many scholars of the Hellenistic age have followed Hieronymus in identifying the military and political history of the period with the careers, ambitions, and points of view of Alexander's great successors. I hope this chapter has shown the benefits of a different perspective and approach.

---

49. Diod. 19.94.1–99.3. Hieronymus as Diodorus's source: e.g., Jacoby 1929–1930, IIB, 559; Hornblower 1981, 144. It is an indication of the impact of the sources on Diodorus that a similar story of a barbarian mass suicide—also by fire and also for the cause of freedom—in Diod. 17.28.1–5 (and based probably on Cleitarchus) lacks the praises accorded to the Isaurians in 18.22.1–8.

50. Diod. 19.94.2–8, 96.1 (*andrōdōs*; uniquely in Diodorus), 97.3–5.

CHAPTER 2

ALEXANDER AND DISCONTENT:
THE KING AND HIS ARMY IN
INDIA AND OPIS, MESOPOTAMIA

The chronological starting point for the history of Alexander's veterans is the king's death at Babylon in June 323. Yet there is something to learn about their conduct and ambitions in the post-Alexander era from two episodes of their conflict with him while he lived. The first took place in 326 on the River Hyphasis in India, and the second in 324 at Opis in Babylonia. Modern studies of these events tend to deal with their impact on the king and his policies, or to focus on the power relationships among the king, his commanders, and the army. This chapter will look at how the troops handled themselves on both occasions, highlighting elements that resurfaced in the veterans' later history. My investigation deals with the nature of the troops' wishes and grievances, how they expressed them, the reasons for their success and failure, and what they learned from these experiences. I shall also consider the largely ignored emotional dimension of the relationship between the king and his army.[1]

The ancient sources are not always helpful to our analysis. They differ in details, and some seize the opportunity to write speeches for the protagonists—speeches whose historical basis is at best controversial, and at worst impossible to verify. In addition, the ancient historians show much more interest in what Alexander did and said than in the actions and words of his soldiers. Nevertheless, enough has survived to allow the reconstruction of the troops' behavior in these affairs.[2]

---

1. Cf. Berve 1926, 1:213–214; Carney 2000a, 284.
2. Cf. for Arrian: Austin 2003, 128. For the speeches, see conveniently Bosworth 1980–1995, 2:344–345 and Carney 1996, 33–34, both disputing the authenticity of the speeches; *contra*: Hammond 1999. My use of the speeches here is limited to what I consider their least controversial contents.

THE CONFLICT ON THE HYPHASIS

The conflict between Alexander and his army near the Indian river Hyphasis (Beas) was a turning point in his campaign. The king wished to continue marching deep into India but was stopped short by his reluctant soldiers and commanders. The sources largely agree on the reasons for this event, the soldiers' first and only successful opposition to their king's plan. They were exhausted physically and especially mentally after their long service, which for some old soldiers stretched as far back as Philip II's wars. The army had won a recent victory over the Indian king, Porus, but it was not an easy one. The hot summer and the ceaseless monsoon rain deteriorated equipment, bodies, and morale. Towering above all concerns, and heightened by their mental fatigue, was the fear of having to cross large rivers and fight enemies who were reported to be stronger in warriors, chariots, and elephants than any they had encountered before.[3]

It should be said, however, that, except for the mental fatigue, many of the above difficulties were more immediate than cumulative. The soldiers endured hard fighting and difficult terrain for the next three years—and many of Alexander's veterans even beyond—and at the conclusion of this conflict Alexander ordered the army to build twelve huge altars and held equestrian and athletic games (Arr. 5.29.1): physical exertions for which the worn-out and water-soaked army found both the will and the strength. Nevertheless, on the Hyphasis, present and expected hardships must have appeared formidable.[4]

Arrian, the most detailed source for what happened on the Hyphasis, uses these hardships to stress how differently the king and his Macedonian troops saw the future. Arrian's hero, Alexander, was eager to meet the next danger, but the army had had enough of the continuing toil and dangers (Arr. 5.25.2). The disparity does not flatter the soldiers. The Roman historian Quintus Curtius Rufus draws a similar contrast but is also critical of Alex-

---

3. Arr. 5.25.1–3, 6, 26.1, 27.6; Curt. 9.2.1–3, 12–25, 3.1, 10–11; Diod. 17.93.1–94.3 (most informative about the wear and tear on the troops); Plut. *Alex.* 62.1–3; Strabo 15.1.27, 32. Diod. 2.37.2–3; 18.6.1, perhaps based on Hieronymus (Bosworth 1980–1995, II:340), says that Alexander did not wish to fight the Indian Gandaridae across the Ganges because of their many war elephants, but see Diod. 17.93.4.

4. This point is ignored by Spann (1999), who revives the unlikely thesis that Alexander tricked the army into opposing his advance so that he could save face (cf. also Heckel 2008, 120–125). The assumption that only Alexander could control events underplays the troops' role in the affair and their fear of what awaited them across the river.

ander in presenting him as more ambitious than reasonable (Curt. 9.2.9–
12). Generally, the so-called vulgate sources—Curtius, Diodorus, Plutarch,
and Justin—are more sympathetic to the plight of the troops in India than
Arrian and presumably his source, Ptolemy. It is a pity that the presumed
common source of the vulgate tradition, Cleitarchus, did not write a history of the Diadochs.[5]

Alexander was aware of the soldiers' concerns, which he discussed in
his speech (below). Diodorus claims that Alexander, before addressing the
army, tried to gain the gratitude of his exhausted soldiers and induce them
to follow him by allowing them to plunder the country and by giving subsi-
dies to their wives and children (Diod. 17.94.4). (That no other source provides this information is an insufficient reason for dismissing it. In fact, the
tradition that Alexander burnt his own and the army's baggage, including booty, before entering India suggests that his license to plunder was
timely.)[6] Alexander's incentives failed to achieve their objective, but his action was significant for two reasons. First, it foreshadowed similar attempts
by his successors to induce their troops to follow and obey them by giving
them a license to plunder. Second, his premise that he would be able to exact obedience through booty and provisions showed his misreading of the
troops and of his relationship with them. Alexander's Macedonians were
not typical mercenaries. His attempt to bribe them evinced a failure to appreciate the magnitude of their distress, their mental state, and their expectations of him, which were greater than they would have of a paymaster and benefactor. While for Alexander and his historians the expedition
was about Alexander, for the veterans it was a joint enterprise in which he
was supposed to recognize the limits of the troops' debt to him as king and
commander, extending their partnership beyond the sharing of danger and
even riches. They could clearly see that behind his permission to plunder

5. For Curtius, see, however, Bosworth 1988b, 130–133. Ptolemy is mentioned as
Arrian's source for the end of the conflict on the Hyphasis: Arr. 5.28.3–5 = Ptolemy
FGrHist 138 F 23, but it is unclear how much or how exclusively he was used for the entire affair: Holt 1982, 42–47; Brunt 1983, II:532; Hammond 1993, 257–280; Bosworth
1980–1995, 2:344–345. For Cleitarchus as Curtius's possible source here: Atkinson 1998–
2000, 2:534–535.

6. *Pace* Spann 1999, 74n52. Burning the baggage: Plut. *Alex.* 57.1; Polyaenus 4.30.10;
Curt. 6.6.14–15 (who places the episode in Parthia). Briant (2003, 361–365) rejects the
story, but see Bosworth 1980–1995, 2:343–344, in defense of Diodorus's version, and cf.
the king's speech in Curtius, where he tries to lure the soldiers across the river by promising them a plundering campaign: 9.2.27; cf. 9.3.21.

there was no real goodwill. Besides, they had reached a breaking point and they wanted the king to realize it.[7]

The sources differ about how and where the troops expressed their opinions. The vulgate sources state or indicate that Alexander and the troops faced each other in a general assembly, where the soldiers displayed their distress and where, according to Curtius, the veteran general Coenus opposed Alexander's wish to march on. Arrian describes a meeting in council of allied and Macedonian commanders headed by the king, where he and Coenus spoke, respectively, for and against pressing the campaign onward. The historian reports on the soldiers' and the commanders' reactions only before and after this debate. Despite some differences, the two versions do not vary greatly. Arrian alludes to an assembly meeting too: not the one in which Alexander addressed the reluctant troops, but a later one where he announced to the army that he had decided to go back (Arr. 5.28.4). It is likely, then, that both the council and the assembly met in the course of this affair, probably more than once, and that it was the primary or secondary sources who decided where to place the opposition to the king. If that is true, the differences in the sources concerning the *soldiers'* reactions are of less importance than they might otherwise have been.[8]

Nonetheless, it made sense for the king to deal with the soldiers' unrest by first calling the commanders to a council meeting. While dependent on the king, the officers were sufficiently close to the soldiers to serve as an effective conduit of his wishes to the army and to enforce discipline on the troops. The commanders also formed a smaller and more manageable group than the army, and thus were easier to control and persuade. Moreover, getting the officer class on his side would have left the rank and file leaderless in case of a conflict. Indeed, the troops regarded their commanders as their spokesmen: after Alexander had urged the troops in the assembly to continue the campaign, Curtius reports that the soldiers waited in silence for their commanders to tell him that they were not mutinous but worn out (Curt. 9.3.1). The troops were fortunate, then, in the attempt by their general, Coenus—either in the assembly (Curtius) or in the council (Arrian)—to convince the king to discontinue his push onward.[9]

---

7. Grainger (2007, 83–84) thinks, however, that for the Macedonians Alexander's empire "was still a long raid for booty, after which they would go home rich"; cf. Austin 1986, 454.

8. Cf. also Errington 1978, 110–111; Bosworth 1980–1995, 2:34–45; Carney 1996, 34. Hammond (1983b, 63), however, denies any opposition in the assembly.

9. For the chain of communication, rank, and personal bonds among generals, lower-rank commanders, and the troops, see Berve 1926, 1:25–42; Briant 1973a,

Calling the council or the army together was the king's prerogative.[10] Yet Arrian reports on independent gatherings of agitated and despondent soldiers before the king's reaction. He describes meetings (*xyllogoi*) in camp where the most moderate speakers lamented their lot and the more radical said that they would not follow Alexander farther (Arr. 5.25.2; cf. Curt. 9.2.12). Focused as they are on Alexander and the Macedonian elite, Arrian and his sources obscure the identity of these speakers and the nature of the meetings themselves. These were likely spontaneous, informal gatherings in which the soldiers tried to establish a common ground for their discontent—never an easy task for the masses. The reported range of reactions, from complaints to defiance, suggests that the soldiers were unsure how far they could go beyond confirming to themselves that they had suffered enough. From Arrian's report on subsequent developments and from the other sources, it can be gathered that the troops' wishes became more concrete when they expressed unwillingness to meet the next danger and to advance beyond the Hyphasis. Generally the assembled army found it easier to agree on what it didn't want than on what it did, as in later meetings of a similar nature at Opis in 324, in Babylon in 323, and at Triparadeisus in 321/0 (below). Even the soldiers' positive wish to return home was a form of opposition to Alexander's plan of continuing the campaign.[11]

The other sources—Diodorus, Plutarch, and Justin—describe the troops' condition and sentiments but are unclear about exactly who voiced them. For example, Justin impossibly depicts the entire army as begging the king to end the campaign, producing proofs of their long service and distress, and raising other points.[12] In contrast, both Arrian (5.25–28) and Curtius (9.2.12–3.13) give no speaking parts to the rank and file, offering instead an exchange of speeches in the council (Arrian) or the assembly (Curtius) between Alexander and his general Coenus, who tried to dissuade the king from advancing farther on account of the troops' poor physical and mental condition.

In spite of differences about who articulated the troops' wishes, most of

55–57 (repr. 1982, 67–69); Errington 1978, 113; Griffith in Hammond and Griffith 1979, 2:392.

10. For the character of the army assembly and the scholarly debate over its powers, see chap. 3 below. It is generally agreed that the assembly was convened at the king's will.

11. Reluctance to advance: Arr. 5.25.2, 27.7; Curt. 9.2.26; Just. 12.8.11. Wish to go home: Arr. 5.25.3, 26.3, 27.6, 8, 28.1; Curt. 9.2.26; Justin 12.8.11–14.

12. Just. 12.8.10–17; Diod. 17.94.1–5; Plut. *Alex.* 62.1–4; cf. *Metz Epitome* 69. See Adams 1986 for the Macedonians' right to speak their mind to the king, and esp. 49–50 on the Hyphasis episode.

the sources, including those that situate the resistance to Alexander in the assembly, agree that they kept a relatively low profile in confronting the king. Only Plutarch reports their strong opposition to his pressure to fight across the river (Plut. *Alex.* 62.2). According to Arrian, the soldiers complained or defied Alexander among themselves but did not challenge him directly (5.25.2). Diodorus says that the Macedonians did not give their assent when the king spoke about the future campaign, and Justin describes the soldiers entreating Alexander to take account of their plight, stop his advance, and go back.[13] The army's preference for a nonconfrontational approach is best attested by Curtius, who describes a fairly passive and taciturn audience. In his account, the troops reacted to Alexander's speech of exhortation and reproach with subdued silence and downcast eyes, waiting for one of their commanders to take courage and explain to the king that they did not wish to disobey him but were simply exhausted. When no one spoke, there was a disgruntled murmur before weeping engulfed the entire assembly, culminating in Coenus's decision to risk speaking against marching on.[14] Although neither Curtius nor Arrian allow the troops to speak at this point, Curtius's portrait of them is the more sympathetic (cf. Justin 12.8.10–16). He indicates that the crisis was forced upon the army by the king's unreasonable ambition, which put them in a painful situation. They did not want to be disloyal (Curt. 9.3.5) but felt physically incapable of following him, and they could not, or would not, say so to his face. Although the scene of the silent and then weeping soldiers is fraught with drama, Curtius and his source well describe less a mutiny and more a rupture between king and army involving significant emotional strain on the troops.[15]

In a speech attributed by Arrian to Coenus, the veteran general claimed that the officers, unlike the "majority of the army," would follow Alexander anywhere (Arr. 5.27.2). The authenticity of Coenus's speech aside, his statement was clearly disingenuous. The king's hope of advancing deeper into India was frustrated because the military elite and the troops were of one

---

13. See the previous note. Diod. 17.108.3 conflates this story with the mutiny at Opis.

14. Curt. 9.3.2–3, 15. In Arrian, the troops give Alexander the silent treatment not out of despair but in defiance. They weep only after he finally gives up: Arr. 5.28.4, 29.1. I share Bosworth's opinion (1980–1995, 2:351) on the historicity of the silence. As these sources show, nonverbal behavior is open to different interpretations.

15. Many scholars suggest that it is wrong to call the soldiers' reaction here a mutiny: e.g., Errington 1978, 110–111; Holt 1982, 49; Carney 1996, 19n4, 33–37; Spann 1999, 67 with n38; but see also Worthington 2004, 237n15.

mind against it.[16] Alexander grew angry but did not give up. Seeing the favorable reaction to Coenus's speech from his fellow commanders, the king convened a second meeting the next day, where he moved from reasoned persuasion to indignation and shaming. He told his audience that he would not force the Macedonians to go with him but would continue with volunteers. When his outburst moved no one, he shut himself up in his tent for three days.[17] If Alexander's self-secluding gesture was Achillean, it was misplaced. Unlike Achilles, who abandoned the Greek army and refused to fight, Alexander was eager to fight but complained of being deserted by his own army.[18] Arrian suggests that he was waiting for the Macedonians and allies to change their minds, "as is often the way of a crowd of soldiers" (Arr. 5.28.3). Quite apart from the historian's condescending characterization of the troops' conduct, his account shows that Alexander changed his tactic. After being disappointed with his commanders, he tried through emotional blackmail and display of anger to move the masses to reconsider their position.

Alexander had acted similarly after killing his general Cleitus in Samarkand in 328. There the remorseful king first threatened to kill himself and then shut himself in his tent for three days until the Macedonians' entreaties persuaded him to resume the campaign. Scholars have assumed that in India, as in Samarkand, Alexander expected the army to fear doom without him and to entreat him to come out of his self-seclusion.[19] The comparison is problematic for a number of reasons. According to most sources, it was Alexander's friends and not the troops who pleaded with him to emerge from seclusion at Samarkand. Strictly speaking, then, Alexander could not have predicted the troops' reaction in India by this alleged precedent. Justin is the only source who describes the troops' begging the seemingly suicidal Alexander in Samarkand not to abandon them in a barbarian country.[20] Yet even if Justin's account is accepted, the situation was quite the reverse in India, where Alexander complained of the troops' deserting *him* in enemy territory (Arr. 5.28.2). At Samarkand the king was angry at himself, but in India at the troops. Finally, in Samarkand a repentant Alexan-

---

16. Errington 1978, 111; Müller 2003, 189.

17. Arr. 5.28.1–3, and see also Curt. 9.3.16–19; Plut. *Alex.* 62.5–8. In Curtius 9.2.31–34 Alexander complains about being deserted by the army and threatens to continue his march in a second speech to the assembly.

18. Alexander's imitation of Achilles: e.g., Carney 2000a, 282–283.

19. E.g., Errington 1978, 110–112; Badian 1985 2:457, 466–467.

20. Just. 12.6.15–16, but see Arr. 4.9.2–8; Curt. 8.2.11; Plut. *Alex.* 52.1–7.

der waited to be persuaded to change his mind, but on the Hyphasis he waited in anger for the army to change *its* mind. In sum, there was little in the events in Samarkand to teach Alexander to predict the troops' reaction to his barricading himself in his tent. Indeed, his attempt to evoke regret, guilt, or even fear among the troops backfired, making them resentful of what they perceived as his unjustified anger (Arr. 5.28.3–4).

Ever adaptable, Alexander changed his tactics once again. According to Arrian, who bases his narrative on Ptolemy, the king made sacrifices to ensure the safe crossing of the Hyphasis, but when the signs proved ominous, he called in his friends, and later made it known to the army that he had decided to go back (5.28.2–29.1). The fact that the soldiers played no part in the resolution of the crisis reflected their relative passive conduct in the entire affair.

Scholars have viewed the conflict on the Hyphasis as a power struggle between Alexander and his army that resulted in the king's single defeat. Among the opposing parties, perhaps only the king shared this view.[21] It is true that (according to Arrian) some soldiers called against going any farther at the beginning of the conflict, and others approached Alexander's tent at its conclusion and blessed him profusely for being vanquished by them alone (Arr. 5.25.2, 29.1). But this dubious compliment was intended to comfort the king and to reassure him that his yielding was legitimate, that it involved no loss of face, and that he was still in control. Even if some soldiers deduced from the affair that Alexander was dependent on them for waging war, none of them acted upon this realization. The varied accounts of their nonconfrontational behavior throughout the episode are proof that, for many soldiers, the crisis had little to no political meaning, and that they did not see it as a victory over the king. During the crisis they let the king use the army assembly for his ends, and their weeping and shouts of joy at its conclusion were not for defeating the king but rather were expressions of distress, of relief, and of celebration at their reconciliation with him.

No source fails to mention the soldiers' and even the officers' weeping, although ancient historians place the scene at different times. In Arrian, the commanders react tumultuously to Coenus's speech, and many shed tears. The author thought they were expressing their despair at the prospect of new dangers and their delight in retreat (Arr. 5.28.1). Later, when Alexan-

---

21. Hyphasis as a power struggle: Badian 1961, 20; 1964, 199–200; 2000, 73–74; Carney 1996, 35–37; cf. Müller 2003, 189. Badian sees here also an attempt by Coenus to make political capital of the popular discontent against the king. See, however, Holt 2000, 49–55.

der publicly declared that he would go back, the mixed Macedonian and allied crowd shouted in joy, and many wept, approaching Alexander's tent and showering him with blessings because he "allowed himself [*henescheto*] to be defeated by them alone" (Arr. 5.29.1). This hardly sounds like a declaration of victory. Curtius has the army weep twice: first after Alexander's speech, in their frustration that no commander would tell him how frail they were, and then after Coenus's speech, when some shouted and wept and others called Alexander their "king," "father," and "lord."[22] Justin describes a tearful army begging Alexander to conclude his Asian campaign and take into consideration their miserable condition (Just. 12.8.10–11). Plutarch says that Alexander gave up only after his friends reasoned with him, and emerged from his tent to the sound of loud crying and lamentation from the troops who surrounded the entrance (Plut. *Alex.* 62.5–6).

Such unanimity among sources regarding the soldiers' emotional reaction cannot be attributed to mere sensationalism, literary effect, or the wish to present Alexander in a favorable light. The soldiers' weeping had more than one meaning. Before Alexander retired to his tent and announced his decision to reverse the march, the weeping displayed their discomfort and served as an alternative to riots as a means of pressure. Once he had announced his decision, the troops wept and shouted to express their delight with the prospect of ending the campaign—shouting being an expression of collective joy as well as a common element in the sources' descriptions of mob behavior.[23] Yet in the course of the conflict the wish to stop the march onward became inseparable from the soldiers' desire to mend their relationship with Alexander. Explicitly or implicitly, all the sources agree that the troops were not eager to quarrel with their king. They wanted to be on good and preferably personal terms with him, and to show that they were loyal, respectful, and appreciative. It was their emotional neediness and the wish to pressure but also gratify the king that led to tears when they could not abide by his wishes (in the vulgate sources). It was also the troops' emotional neediness and attachment to the king that Alexander hoped to manipulate by his speeches and by shutting himself up in his tent. His tactics did not work because the soldiers' desire to please their king was weaker than their displeasure with him for prolonging their sufferings. Once he relented, the old relations between king and army could be restored. This was

---

22. Curt. 9.3.3, 16. It is possible that these invocations were added by Curtius because they ironically mirrored Alexander's flattering the crowd by calling himself the soldiers' comrade and foster son, "not to say your king" (9.2.28).

23. Cf. Lateiner 2009, 107; Lane Fox 1974, 370.

an occasion both for joy and for tears of relief, though not for Alexander, who felt frustrated, betrayed, and wounded in his ego. He tried to comfort himself by building monumental riverside altars to the gods in gratitude for his far-reaching conquest and in memory of his toils. The sources give no indication that he shared the credit with the Macedonians.[24]

PAYING THE TROOPS' DEBTS

In the summer of 324 Alexander's troops mutinied at Opis after his announcement that he intended to send veteran soldiers back home. It appears that their reaction took the king by surprise, partly because they must have known of his plan to dismiss them since 326, if not earlier, and partly because the king thought that he was doing the discharged soldiers a favor (Arr. 6.17.3; 7.8.2). It was not the first time that Alexander's goodwill, real or alleged, failed to be appreciated. In the spring of that year, Alexander paid the soldiers' debts at Susa, but the gratitude he received was belated and mixed. The affair illustrates that the royal benefactor and his beneficiaries saw such liberality differently.[25]

It seems that Alexander, before dismissing the veterans, had an acute attack of generosity. While in Susa, he gave wedding gifts to 10,000 Macedonians who had married Asian women.[26] Afterward he paid his soldiers' debts at a total cost ranging between 20,000 and a little less than 10,000 talents. Around this time he also rewarded courage in battle with gifts and golden crowns. Arrian mentions only elite recipients of these honors but implies that others received them too. Did Alexander try to win the army's favor in anticipation of dismissing the veterans?[27]

---

24. Arr. 5.29.1; Diod. 95.1–2; Curt. 9.3.19; cf. Plut. *Alex.* 62.7–8; *Metz Epitome* 69; Strabo 3.5.5; Pliny *NH* 6.62. Philostratus (*Vit. Apoll.* 2.43) and Suda (s.v. *Brachman*) purport to know the text of the dedication. See Bosworth 1980–1995, 2:356, on the unlikely traditions that Alexander also built a giant camp. For the altars see also Badian 1961, 20.

25. Paying the debts: Arr. 7.5.1–3; Just. 12.11.1–4; Diod. 17.109.2; Plut. *Alex.* 70.3–4; *Moral.* 181a, 339c, 343d.

26. Arr. 7.4.8. Plutarch (*Alex.* 70.3) lowers the number of recipients to the 9,000 guests of the wedding banquet (which included Asians), but Arrian's figure has more official credibility because he ties the gifts to the registration of the marriages.

27. Cf. Lane Fox 1970, 419–421. Cost of defraying the debts: 20,000 (Arr. 7.5.3; Just. 12.11.1); 10,000 (Diod. 17 *Contents*; cf. 109.3); 9,870 (Curt. 10.2.8; Plut. *Alex.* 70.3). Honors: Arr. 7.5.4–6.

The sources' explications of the king's motives are unsatisfactory. They mention his (sudden?) discovery of the troops' indebtedness (Curt. 10.2.9; Diod. 17.109.1; cf. Plut. *Alex.* 70.3) or his seizing of the occasion of the Susa weddings to pay the debts (Arr. 7.4.8–51). Arrian actually implies the weakness of the link between the payment in Susa and the dismissal of the veterans a few months later in Opis on the Tigris by separating these events in time and place (Arr. 7.4.4–5.3, 7.1). All the other sources, who put them in close chronological proximity and in the same place (probably Susa), imply that Alexander tried to soften the blow of discharge with monetary compensation. Justin comes closest to establishing a causal link when he says that Alexander told the assembled army, before the mutiny, that he had paid their debts to allow them to take their earnings home from the campaign intact.[28]

Ultimately, the sources' lack of clarity about Alexander's motives is rooted in his failure to explain them adequately, which led the soldiers to suspect them. Scholars, in turn, have suggested that Alexander wanted to compensate the soldiers for overdue payments and the loss of belongings during the march in the Gedrosian desert in 325. But Alexander is reported to have given overdue wages to the soldiers he sent home after, rather than before, the Opis mutiny (Arr. 7.12.1). Among those compensated by the king were soldiers, including veterans, who did not march through Gedrosia but took the main road to Carmania with Craterus (Arr. 6.17.3). It has also been conjectured that Alexander tried to mollify an army resentful of his orientalism. According to Curtius, however, Alexander tried to bribe the army that disliked his "going Persian" not in 324 but in 330 (Curt. 6.6.11).[29]

I suggest that the payment of debts was related to the discharge of the veterans, but that Alexander's considerations were no less pragmatic than political. Justin claims that both creditors and debtors were grateful to Alexander for solving the problems of paying and collecting debts, respectively (Just. 12.11.2). Indeed, sending many troops home and keeping others with him, including the camp's bankers, created a need for the immediate settling of accounts between soon-to-be-separated creditors and debtors in either group. To prevent a credit crunch and potential conflicts, Alexander

---

28. Just. 12.11.1–4; cf. Curt. 10.2.25. Diodorus (17.109.1–2), exceptionally and probably wrongly, places the payment of debts after the veterans' dismissal; cf. Atkinson and Yardley 2009, 121; Olbrycht 2009, 237.

29. Overdue wages and compensation for Gedrosia: Badian 1985, 480 with n2. Mollifying Alexander's orientalism: Green 1991, 446–448; Franz 2009, 131.

paid the soldiers' debts.[30] The king may also have wished to make the debtors more dependent on him and less on the lenders, and he surely expected his action to reaffirm his status as the troops' benefactor and patron. But if he was looking for appreciation, the soldiers showed that this could not be taken for granted.

Three authors report on the soldiers' reactions to Alexander's offer to pay their debts. Justin, as we have seen, notes the creditors' and debtors' gratitude for Alexander's generosity (Just. 12.11.2), but Arrian and Curtius, especially the former, report that the soldiers' initial reaction to Alexander's offer was unappreciative. Arrian says that Alexander ordered each debtor to write down how much he owed, so that the king could pay his debt. Many did not register because they suspected that Alexander really wanted to know who was living extravagantly or beyond his means. Alexander then reproached the soldiers, perhaps in an assembly, for doubting his truthfulness. He dispelled their suspicions by giving them money when they showed proof of debt, without taking down their names (Arr. 7.5.1–3). For Arrian, then, the story of paying the soldiers' debts is more about royal trust and honesty than generosity.[31] Arrian is also much more sympathetic to the king, depicted as well meaning and frank, than to the troops, whose distrust and fear of the king were misplaced (cf. Arr. 7.10.3).

Curtius's version is similar. Alexander decided to discharge the debts even though they had been accumulated through extravagance. The troops, suspecting a wish to know who lived extravagantly, did not report their debts. But Alexander, who understood that they were more embarrassed than obstinate, placed money on tables in camp, and the soldiers reported their debts and took the money. Curtius thus highlights the soldiers' awareness of their misconduct, an awareness that led to their misinterpretation of Alexander's purpose. He may even imply that the king should have been clearer about his intentions (Curt. 10.2.8–11).

Curtius and Arrian agree that the troops were mistaken but do not explain why they were suspicious of Alexander or so ashamed of an extravagant lifestyle. Later in his narrative, Curtius's Alexander denounces extravagance as morally reprehensible and harmful to military performance. Personal extravagance, often regarded as resulting in debts, was perceived in Philotas as an affront to others, and was associated with political subver-

---

30. The major source of credit in camp was banks (e.g., Plut. *Alex.* 70.3), but there were surely also noncommercial lenders and issuers of loan security. For wages paid to Alexander's troops, see Le Rider 2007, 62–64, 73–77; Franz 2009.

31. Cf. Arr. *Preface* 2 with Bosworth 1980–1995, 1:43.

sion in the case of Harpalus and in democratic Athens.[32] Yet unlike Philotas and Harpalus, who were high-ranking members of the elite, the troops were mostly apolitical. Furthermore, the king's failure ever to discipline his soldiers for their lifestyle makes their suspicion of him on this account puzzling. Was it a symptom of their general mistrust of him? Probably not, both because there is little evidence for a collective distrust of the king in the army and because this particular suspicion is like no other grievance against him.

I suggest that Alexander alone is to blame for the troops' reaction. His failure to explain himself suggests that, as in India, he thought that he could predict their reaction because he knew what they wanted and because they would do as they were told. He probably believed they would simply be glad to take the money and that royal patronage would sufficiently account for his motives. Yet his act of registering the debts, which was designed to prevent double-dipping into the treasury or other frauds, made the troops suspect that he wanted to know something in which he had never shown an interest before, namely, who was in debt. It was also the first time that he offered to pay their personal debts. This was suspicious enough in itself, especially as debt was considered the outcome of wastefulness: they could not see why he would reward them for wrongdoing. Alexander's recent punishment of satraps charged with various kinds of maladministration may have contributed to a general nervousness and anticipation of disciplinary action in camp.[33]

The impact of the king's generosity on the soldiers, even after the misunderstanding was cleared up, should be put in perspective. To begin with, the troops were not overly concerned about their economic situation. Although Curtius wondered how so many of them could be in debt while serving in a victorious army in rich lands (Curt. 10.2.11), the troops never complained of inadequate compensation or poverty.[34] Arrian even states

---

32. Alexander's denouncing luxury: Curt. 10.2.22, 26–27; cf. Arr. 7.9.9; Curt. 6.6.14–16. Extravagance and Philotas: Plut. *Alex.* 49.1–3; and Harpalus: Diod. 17.108.4; Plut. *Alex.* 35.15; *Moral.* 648c–d; and Athens: Davidson 1997, 213–308. In Curt. 6.2.4 the troops are said to mutiny because of Alexander's decline into luxury, and, in 6.6.9–10, to have resented extravagance as a symptom of Persian decadence.

33. Rogers (2004, 253) links the soldiers' suspicion to their dissatisfaction with the Susa weddings (cf. Sisti and Zambrini 2001–2004, 2:590), but the link is forced. Alexander and the satraps: esp. Arr. 6.29.1–3, 11, 30.1–2, 7.4.1–4; Badian 1961; Cartledge 2004, 199–200.

34. For Alexander's prodigious spending on his army, see Franz 2009, and cf. Millett 2010, 499–500.

that they preferred concealing their names to canceling their debts (Arr. 7.5.3). Despite Justin's statement that both debtors and creditors were grateful to Alexander (Just. 12.11.2), the creditors must have been the happier of the two groups, since Alexander's money would ultimately reach them (Plut. *Moral.* 329b). Those who were free of debt may have envied their indebted fellows and felt discriminated against by the king's generosity.[35] Finally, though Curtius says that Alexander thought the troops concealed their debts out of shame (*pudor*), not defiance (10.2.10), the initial embarrassment was the king's when few soldiers accepted his offer. In any case, the soldiers showed the limits of his power over them, both before and after Alexander decided to pay their debts without registering their names.

An anecdote in Plutarch may be illuminating in this regard. The biographer reports that a certain Antigenes the One-Eyed, a man whose distinguished record went back to service with Philip II, was remunerated for debt on false pretenses. When the fraud was discovered, Alexander punished him by taking away his command and expelling him from the court. Humiliated, Antigenes sought to kill himself, but was pardoned by the king and allowed to keep the money (Plut. *Alex.* 70.3–6). Although the identity of this individual is in dispute, we may assume that he was not the only soldier to abuse Alexander's generosity, but among the few to be caught.[36] Antigenes' abuse of royal favors showed that gratitude did not sum up the subordinates' attitude toward the king. Finally, Alexander's acts of generosity, including the paying of debts, were in one respect counterproductive, because they gave the soldiers the economic freedom to focus on issues other than their need during the mutiny at Opis.

THE OPIS MUTINY

Among the questions that complicate the reconstruction of the army mutiny at Opis is the puzzling conduct of the troops. Although Arrian locates the mutiny at Opis and the vulgate sources probably at Susa, all agree that the incident was occasioned by Alexander's announcement that he was going to discharge and send home the old, weak, and disabled soldiers. Ex-

---

35. Some probably resorted to false claims of debt: see Antigenes below.

36. Tarn (1948, 2:314n1) thinks that Plutarch, or his copier, confused Antigenes with Antigonus the one-eyed Diadoch. Billows (1990, 27–28, based on Plut. *Moral.* 339c) identifies him with the veteran soldier Atarrhias, but Heckel (2006, 31 "Antigenes" [1b]) stresses the sources' confusion. Cf. Hammond 1993, 133–134.

cept for Justin, they also concur in stating that all the troops demanded to be sent home. What, then, were the already-discharged soldiers doing among the rebels?[37] It is to Curtius's credit that he is the only source to raise this question, although he does so in a rhetorical context. In Alexander's speech to the seditious soldiers, the king claims that those discharged are just the first ones to go home, and then wonders: "I see as much opposition from those who are going to leave as from those with whom I have decided to follow the advance party. What is going on? You all join the uproar, but for different reasons. I should dearly like to know whether the complaints about me are coming from those leaving or those being kept back."[38]

What indeed was going on? Not that it is difficult to come up with explanations of the inclusive character of the mutiny, such as soldierly camaraderie or even crowd psychology. But the sources do not take this tack. In fact, they offer a variety of reasons for the troops' conduct, probably because they, or their sources, were typically much better informed about Alexander than about the troops, and therefore had to figure out what stood behind their mutiny. This can be discerned even in Arrian, who gives the most detailed account of the affair.

Arrian reports on the troops' grievances in two passages, one in relation to events in Susa, and the other, later, when the story reached Opis. After describing the payment of the soldiers' debts and the honoring of various commanders in Susa, he narrates the arrival of the so-called *Epigoni*, or Successors: about 30,000 young Asians, trained in Macedonian-style arms and combat, who now joined Alexander's force. Arrian says that their arrival distressed the Macedonians,[39] and then goes on to list the Mace-

---

37. Olbrycht (2009, 238) correctly points out that it is far from certain that the vulgate sources locate the mutiny in Susa. Yet Diodorus 17.110.2 (Peucestas's arrival to Susa) and 110.4 (the march out of Susa after the mutiny) and Arrian 7.10.7 (locating the mutiny in Susa in an apparently unintentional concession to the other tradition) make Susa the likeliest alternative locale of the mutiny. For the following see Carney 1996, 38–42. Her concerns about the proper use of the term "mutiny" for this incident (and other incidents) are addressed in part by Worthington 2004, 237n15. The inclusive nature of the mutiny: Arr. 7.8.3; Curt. 10.2.12, 16, 18; Plut. *Alex.* 71.3; cf. Diod. 17.109.2 (members of the hypaspist bodyguard excepted: Arr. 7.8.3); Polyaenus 4.3.7.

38. Curt. 10.2.16–17; Yardley's (1984, 242) translation.

39. Arr. 7.6.1–2. Arrian introduces his report with "it is said," but see Brunt (1976–1983, 2:219n2) and Hammond (1983a, 143 [repr. 1994, 3:91]) for the possibility that, in spite of this qualifier, much of Arrian's report goes back to his chief sources. For the following, cf. Brunt 1963, 42–44; Griffith 1963; Badian 1965, 160–161; 1985, 481–483.

donians' other, related grievances. They thought Alexander was using every ploy to reduce his future need of them. They disliked his pro-Iranian tendencies, evinced by his Median dress, the Persian-style weddings, and his approval of his satrap Peucestas, who also imitated Persian customs. They resented the incorporation of Asians—under their own commanders but with Macedonian equipment—into the Macedonian cavalry of the Companions (*hetairoi*). Finally, they thought that Alexander was turning completely barbarian and treating Macedonians and their customs with disrespect (Arr. 7.6.1–5). One might expect the historian to describe the expression and outcome of this manifold dissatisfaction. Instead, he abruptly cuts off his account of the disgruntled troops to tell about various operations led by the king in and around the Persian Gulf (inserting a digression on the Tigris and Euphrates rivers), before he brings the story up to Opis on the Tigris (7.7.1–8.1).

Clearly, the account of the soldiers' grievances in Susa is a departure from the story line of the events of the campaign. Since the soldiers did not protest, riot, or even complain in Susa, according to Arrian (who keeps referring to what they felt or thought), one wonders who articulated these detailed grievances. I suggest that this passage belongs to the explanatory rather than to the descriptive part of the history. It shows Arrian's or his sources' effort to understand the troops' behavior and is probably designed to prepare the reader for the later mutiny at Opis.

Once the narrative reaches Opis, Arrian reports on Alexander's discharging of the old and disabled, his promise to reward the troops he kept, and the soldiers' belief that he now disdained them and thought them useless for war. This later account credits the troops who were sent home with good reasons to be upset, but it is unclear why those who were to stay took offense and felt useless if the king discharged only the unfit and even promised to reward those he kept. Arrian does not clarify this point or let the soldiers spell out their complaints against the king. Instead he takes a retrospective look when he says that Alexander's speech vexed them again, and he goes on to recap the soldiers' aforementioned discontents, which he alleges they felt throughout the campaign. These revolved around Alexander's Persian dress, the Macedonian-look-alike Epigoni, and the incorporation of foreigners into the cavalry. These grievances resulted in the troops' demand for a general dismissal and their sarcastic advice to Alexander to carry on the war with his father, Ammon (7.8.1–3).

The two breaks in Arrian's narrative where he reports on the troops' grievances, once in Susa and the other in Opis, are thus revealed to be the author's analysis of the troops' behavior rather than his description of what they actually did or said. Indeed, when Arrian gives the troops a voice, they insult or defy Alexander but make none of the complaints he attributes to them (Arr. 7.8.3). In other words, Arrian and his sources depend mostly on conjecture in reporting motives for the mutiny, chiefly because they were much more interested in the king than in his troops.[40]

Whatever the historicity of the complaints reported by Arrian, it is impossible to determine their impact, if any, on the troops' motivation to rebel at Opis, because they were not voiced during the mutiny. The vulgate sources are no better in this regard. According to Justin, the unfavorable reaction to Alexander's discharge came from the younger soldiers who were meant to stay in Asia. They too wanted to go home and felt unfairly treated, since all the veterans had served from the outset of the campaign. Later, when the conflict heated up, they told Alexander to go fight with his father, Ammon, since he slighted his own soldiers.[41] As in Arrian, the troops felt dishonored, and their contemptuous reference to Ammon indicates both their wish to insult Alexander and their confidence in his need of them. Justin narrows down the rioters to the troops whom Alexander intended to keep in Asia, thus excluding from the mutiny those already discharged and solving the puzzle of their demand to go home; but the other sources make the mutiny more inclusive. It is worth noting that Justin mentions no long-term grievances that culminated in this mutiny, and omits even the Macedonians' fear of and resentment toward being replaced by Asians. The causes were more immediate: the discriminatory discharge of troops and their feeling that Alexander was treating them unfairly and disrespectfully.

Although the manuscript of book 10 of Curtius's *Histories* has many gaps, the surviving portions adequately convey his version of the troops' grievances.[42] He relates that Alexander planned to send home the older soldiers and keep 13,000 infantry and 2,000 cavalry in Asia, defraying the soldiers' debts before choosing those to be retained (10.2.8–11). When the troops learned that some were being sent home and others not, they surmised that Alexander wanted to establish the royal seat permanently in Asia. They ri-

---

40. Wüst (1953/4a) and Badian (1965; cf. 1985, 482) speculate, however, that the above narrative structure is due to Arrian's sifting his way through different sources. See also Sisti and Zambrini 2004, 2:592, 597. Olbrycht (2009, 239) thinks that the soldiers' complaints in Susa and Opis were identical.

41. Just. 12.11.4–6. Müller (2003, 208) suspects that the demand to be discharged for years of service instead of age reflects Roman usage. *Pace* Heckel in Yardley and Heckel 2003, 274, Just. 12.11.5 indicates that the "younger men" in 12.11.5 were Macedonians rather than the Epigoni.

42. Curt. 10.2.8–4.3. See Olbrycht 2009 in defense of Curtius's account.

oted and abused him, and all demanded to be discharged, displaying their scarred faces and gray heads.[43] Unlike Justin's characterization of the rioters as younger, Curtius's broader version of the mutiny includes even the old and wearied. Like Justin, however, Curtius does not record the soldiers' simmering complaints or their envy of the Asians among the reasons for their conduct. Even the troops' protest against the transfer of the center of government to Asia seems to have had less to do with Macedonian nationalism than with their concern that they would have to stay in Asia.[44]

Plutarch's account contradicts this version. Like Arrian, he makes the appearance of the Epigoni a cause for Macedonian resentment, but he does not distance their arrival from the mutiny in time. In Plutarch, the mutineers are not men wishing to go home, but the discharged veterans and others who dread going back and living as dependents on their families. The soldiers interpret Alexander's delight in the Epigoni and his dismissal of the infirm as an insolent humiliation of men on whom he once depended. Therefore they ask him to discharge them all and tell him with bitter irony that he can now think them useless and conquer the world with his military dancers, i.e., the Epigoni (Plut. *Alex.* 71.1–3). Plutarch thus shares Arrian's view that the Macedonians believed Alexander thought less of them after the arrival of the Epigoni. But, unlike Arrian, he does not link the mutiny to such cumulative grievances as Alexander's Asian manners and his integration of Iranians into the cavalry. At the root of the conflict lay the issue of honor and respect: the Macedonians mutinied because they felt used and abused by their king.

Diodorus's account of the affair is the least useful. After reporting the arrival of the Epigoni in Susa and Alexander's warm welcome of them, he launches a digression on the origins of the Epigoni. He claims they were intended as a counterforce to the Macedonian phalanx, which was unruly in assemblies and mocked Alexander for believing that Ammon was his father (Diod. 17.108.2). Diodorus's brief notice makes no mention of a riot or any other Macedonian reaction to the Epigoni's arrival, and, at best, shares implicitly Plutarch's and Arrian's view that they irked the Macedonians. When he returns to the narrative of Alexander in Asia, he reports that the king discharged the old Macedonians and paid the soldiers' debts. Diodorus then says that the soldiers Alexander kept with him grew disobedient,

---

43. Curt. 10.2.12. Atkinson (Atkinson and Yardley 2009, 124–125) thinks that Curtius wrongly attributes to the troops what were, in fact, Roman fears of losing the center of the empire to the east.

44. See, however, Carney 1996, 40; Müller 2003, 209–210.

creating a tumult when called to a meeting, but he adds nothing about the nature of their complaints or demands (Diod. 17.109.1–2).

These differences among our historians are a matter more of interpretation (perhaps in their sources) than of their knowledge of what moved the soldiers to mutiny or of the mutineers' exact identity. This is why the troops in Arrian and Plutarch defy Alexander to manage without them, suggesting that they do not really wish to leave, while Curtius and Justin think the troops have simply had enough of the campaign and want to go home. While we may concur with or elaborate upon these speculations about the troops' motives, we must acknowledge them as speculations and no more. Although Arrian's analysis of and historical perspective on the affair are valuable, the other sources and the pattern of Arrian's own narrative suggest the wisdom of deemphasizing the effect of long-term grievances at Opis. As with the Hyphasis incident, the cause of the mutiny lay in recent events, possibly the appearance of the Epigoni and surely Alexander's discharge of the old and infirm, the event that led to the crisis, according to all sources.[45] There is less unanimity among the sources, but not outright disagreement, about whether the troops felt slighted by the king, called upon Alexander to discharge them all, and probably taunted him to go on fighting alongside his father, Ammon. From this more safely limited viewpoint, the dismissal of the veterans was not, as often described, the last straw that broke the soldiers' backs, but the real cause of the mutiny; Alexander's Asianization was not a major factor at first, but played a central part only later, after his response to the soldiers' outburst.[46]

As at the Hyphasis, the army found it easy to agree on what it did not want. Both the discharged veterans and those who would stay in Asia were united in their opposition to what they regarded as the king's unfair and disrespectful treatment of them. In spite of the variant accounts of this episode, this theme's recurrence in Arrian (7.6.5, 8.2), Plutarch (*Alex.* 71.1–2), and Justin (12.11.6) shows its centrality to the affair. The veterans may have felt slighted and aggrieved for different reasons: some for being dismissed, some for being kept, and others for Alexander's seeming ingratitude in dis-

---

45. Brunt (1963, 43–44) thinks that the Macedonian grievance about the incorporation of orientals in the cavalry was recent, dating this military reorganization to 324, after the march in Gedrosia. But see below for the complaints regarding the Asians.

46. See below. Olbrycht (2009, 234–236; cf. Green 1991, 453–454) believes that Alexander actually provoked the confrontation at Opis in order to break the Macedonians' resistance to his Iranian policy, but his best evidence, Arr. 7.6.2, does not really confirm it.

carding them (or planning to do so) after using them throughout the campaign. If Alexander felt betrayed by his army on the Hyphasis, in Opis it was the Macedonians, loyal to him throughout the campaign, who felt betrayed and abused by an ungrateful king. Alexander seems to have been aware of the latter sentiment, since both Arrian and Curtius make him countercharge the troops with ingratitude for all the benefits he and his father had bestowed upon them.[47]

It is doubtful that the Macedonians were united in their desire to go home. There were certainly some who wanted to go back, but the veterans' behavior after leaving Opis must qualify our belief in the strength and prevalence of this wish. They waited with Craterus in Asia Minor for almost two years before he took them to Europe—not home to Macedonia, but to Thessaly to fight the Greeks with Antipater. The reasons for Craterus's delay do not concern us here; the significant point is that we hear of no opposition to his stay in Asia, and that the number of his troops there and in Europe remained constant, at around 11,500, suggesting no desertion during the wait. Apparently the desire to return home varied over time or among the individual Macedonians.[48]

Finally, the Macedonians' taunting Alexander to fight with his father, Ammon, or with his "war dancers" (the Epigoni) suggests primarily their belief that Alexander was unable to pursue his war without them: a lesson that they must have deduced from the Hyphasis affair. Alexander would soon prove them wrong, but it is noteworthy that their daring him to fight with his divine father and the Asians showed not fear of being replaced but contempt for the Epigoni who would replace them. At this stage of the mutiny it appears that the Macedonians were less upset about Alexander's "going Asian" than about his treatment of them.[49]

Showing typical crowd behavior, the soldiers complained and made demands by shouting and raising tumult. Justin observes an escalation in their conduct. At first the troops entreated Alexander to send them all

---

47. Arr. 7.9.1–9, 10.2–3, 7; Curt. 10.2.20–29; Wüst 1953–1954b, 185–186; Bosworth 1988b, 105.

48. See, however, Wüst 1953/54b, 419; Errington 1970, 57, 61; Briant 1972, 55–56 (repr. 1982, 36–37); Hammond 1980, 469–470 (repr. 1994, 3:79–80). The troops' wish to go home after Darius's death in 329/8 yielded readily to the king's ambition to continue the campaign: Curt. 6.2.15–4.1; Diod. 17.74.3; Plut. *Alex.* 47.1–5; Justin 12.3.2–3. See also chap. 4 below.

49. I should make clear that I do not deny that the Macedonians were angry with Alexander for trying to equalize their status and honor with that of the Asians; see Roisman 2003, 292–293. But this grievance was not prominent at the outset of the revolt.

home; later they proceeded to insult him, an expected reaction of men who felt dishonored to begin with. Curtius, on the other hand, describes out-of-control soldiers from the very beginning. They paid no heed to military discipline, spoke mutinously, insulted the king, ignored their officers' rebukes, and, for a while, interrupted Alexander with tumultuous shouts and violence. They also declared that they would go nowhere but home. Eventually they fell silent, but only because they thought that Alexander had grown amenable to their demands (Curt. 10.2.12–14). Curtius's vivid account describes a military nightmare in which all mechanisms of control collapse and the common soldiers invert the decision-making process.[50] He may exaggerate the riotous behavior to emphasize the effectiveness of Alexander's countermeasures and to highlight, by contrast, the troops' later transformation into submissive followers who sought to placate him. In any case, it is hard to imagine that the troops demanded to be sent home, charged Alexander with planning to settle in Asia, or made all the complaints against his abusing and slighting them mentioned by Plutarch, speaking in unison throughout (Curt. 10.2.12–14; Plut. *Alex.* 71.2–3). Their spokesmen must have been the so-called ringleaders, anonymous in the sources, whom Alexander would soon arrest and execute.

After an unsuccessful attempt to calm the soldiers by persuasion, Alexander reasserted his authority by employing three of his favorite weapons: surprise, violence, and psychological pressure. The sources disagree on the order of his actions, but not on their substance. According to Arrian, whom I follow here, a highly agitated Alexander jumped from the podium into the midst of the crowd. Accompanied by his officers, he directed the hypaspists (his shield-bearing bodyguards) to arrest thirteen of the most conspicuous agitators and lead them to execution. Curtius's lacunose account indicates that there may have been multiple rounds of executions: one on the day of the mutiny and at least one more, by drowning, on the day after.[51]

The sources agree that the king's action stunned the troops, who made no move to oppose it. Curtius and Justin ascribe their paralysis to their fear of the king, to their veneration of royalty and of Alexander in particular, and to his self-confidence. We may add another reason: Alexander's swift

---

50. For the claim that Curtius here borrows motifs from Livy, see Rutz 1983. See also Atkinson 1998–2000, 2:563–564; 2009, 126–133. Spencer (2002, 201–203) draws attention to Curtius's engagement with depictions of Roman mutinies.

51. Curt. 10.3.4–5, 4.1–2; Arr. 7.8.3; Just. 12.11.8 (who states that Alexander seized the leaders with his own hands). On the small unit of hypaspist bodyguards, see Bosworth 1980–1995, 2:59–61. Curtius's account: 10.2.30, 3.4, 4.1–3.

strike had deprived them of their leaders, and therefore of their voice.[52] The appearance of ringleaders here was an anomaly, because normally the troops looked to their immediate commanders for leadership and direction. But the fact that the military leaders helped Alexander to put down the mutiny indicates that the soldiers had difficulty finding sympathetic ears among their superiors, as they did not on the Hyphasis. It does not mean that the camp was divided along lines of class and rank. Arrian's report on one cavalry officer, Callines, who spoke later for the troops (see below), suggests that some of the discontented were cavalrymen of relatively high standing.[53] But Callines spoke only after the troops gave up; before Alexander's disciplinary action they had no advocate like the prominent general Coenus, who spoke for the army on the Hyphasis. This created a vacuum, which was filled by men from the rank and file (Curt. 10.3.4). The troops, however, had no experience of following popular leaders instead of men of rank and the king's appointees.

Indeed, there was nothing in the past that prepared the troops for this mutiny.[54] They learned from their semi-passive resistance in India how to get together in camp and vent their frustrations, but they had never before confronted the king directly, made demands of him, or insulted him. This was their first test of his authority, and they were unsure how far they could go, or if they should trust the more vocal among them with leadership against an angry and threatening king. Their failure to oppose the arrest of the ringleaders meant not just that Alexander took them all by surprise but also that they were not ready to support the speakers. After the arrest and Alexander's angry speech (whose contents cannot be safely ascertained), the Macedonians stood around the empty podium in silence (Arr. 17.11.2). A lacuna in Curtius's text ends with an unknown speaker's remonstrating with the king against the execution (especially by foreign, i.e., Asian executioners) of additional popular leaders without a trial. The speaker's identity is unknown, but his advice was disregarded and only strengthened the resolve

52. Arr. 7.8.3; Curt. 10.2.30–3.3; Justin 12.11.8–9; Diod. 17.109.2–3 (who is exceptional in arguing that Alexander's action increased the soldiers' hostility toward him; *contra*: Curt. 10.3.4). Adams (1986, 151) argues that the troops were shocked because they were entitled to a royal hearing. However, they had already yelled their piece.

53. Officers helping Alexander: Curt. 10.2.13, 4; Arr. 7.8.3, 11.2; 3. Callines: Arr. 7.11.6–7. Carney (1996, 40) thinks that lower-ranking officers shared the troops' resistance; cf. Berve 1926, 1:217, on the higher officers. It is impossible to tell how representative the troops who arrested the leaders were of their fellow hypaspists.

54. See, however, Carney 1996, 40–42.

of the furious king. It is fair to say that Alexander found the mutiny at Opis easy to quell.[55]

Following his exercise of power and authority, Alexander shut himself up in his residence for two days, neglecting his bodily wants and excluding even his companions from his presence (Arr. 7.11.1; cf. Plut. *Alex.* 71.7–8). The king was surely furious and disappointed, and probably contemplating his next move, but his mental state is of less interest to this study than the effect of his seclusion on the troops,[56] for whom it meant that they now had no one to guide them, neither mutinous leaders nor the king and his generals. Curtius well understands the soldiers' predicament when he makes Alexander scold and then challenge them: "You will soon know how strong an army is without a king" (Curt. 10.2.29; cf. Polyaenus 4.3.7).

To prove the point, the king moved to scare, humiliate, and defeat the Macedonians. If they had thought that Alexander could not fight without them, he now convinced them that they had lost their exclusive status in camp and their special bond with him: that they were both replaceable and dispensable. He incorporated Iranian units and commanders into the army and drove the point home by giving them good old Macedonian titles. He strengthened the Persian character of his court by incorporating 1,000 young Asians into his Macedonian bodyguard and by allowing only Asian troops into his presence. He recreated the elite Persian unit of the Kinsmen, who had the exclusive privilege of kissing him. (Alexander often used proximity to his person to honor and rank individuals and groups.) He also called a separate assembly of Asian soldiers, away from the Macedonian camp.[57]

Since all these actions were taken after the riot broke out, I suggest that it was largely at this point, rather than earlier, that the Macedonians' fear, resentment, and envy of the Asians came into play (esp. Curt. 10.3.5; Just.

---

55. Curt. 10.4.1–2. Wüst (1953–1954b, 425; cf. Atkinson 2009, 139) identifies the speaker as a Macedonian soldier, and Olbrycht (2009, 245) as one of the leaders, speaking before his execution; cf. Badian 1965, 160. Alexander's speech: Arr. 7.9.1–10.8 and Curtius (10.2.15–29, 3.7–14), who has two speeches, one to the Macedonians and another to his Asian troops. For arguments against the authenticity of the speeches, especially the one in Arrian, see Wüst 1953–1954a; Brunt 1976–1983, 2:532–533; Bosworth 1988b, 101–113; *contra*: Hammond 1993, 287–291; Nagle 1996; Olbrycht 2009, 240–245.

56. For Alexander's conduct see Carney (2000a, 283–285), who thinks that he was "most calculatingly manipulative."

57. Arr. 7.11.1–3; Curt. 10.3.5–14; Just. 12.12.1–5; Plut. *Alex.* 71.4–5; Diod. 17.109.3; cf. Polyaenus 4.3.7. For these actions: Bosworth 1980, 16–17. Alexander's person and honor: Roisman 2003, 297–306.

12.12.5; Diod. 17.109.3). On the Hyphasis, the king is said to have threatened his audience with dismissal, vowing to continue his campaign with volunteers. At Opis, with the Asians at his disposal, he planned to show that the threat was real. This was something of a bluff, because the Macedonians still constituted the best element in Alexander's mixed army, despite their numerical inferiority.[58] But the troops were disoriented, scared, and without leaders to enlighten them about the realities of power. They believed simply that they had committed a misdeed meriting the king's wrath and punishment. If the king disciplined them, the mutiny would boil down to a case of indiscipline rather than a deeper crisis, thus allowing both sides to go back to the *status quo ante seditionem.*

To reach this goal, the troops made a show of weakness and submissiveness. This was not conscious role-playing, because they really believed in the role, as is evident in spite of the sources' almost perverse keenness to describe the troops' humiliation. We are told that the Macedonians mobbed the closed doors of Alexander's residence as his two-day confinement continued to raise the price of his emergence. They showed their vulnerability by standing unarmed and by assuming supplicating positions. They begged Alexander for pity, asked him to let them in, and expressed a willingness to sacrifice more leaders and even themselves to royal punishment. All of this was done through weeping and shouting, including self-accusations of wickedness and ingratitude, along with acknowledgments that Alexander was their master. Things were back to normal when units of soldiers appealed to their commanders and to Alexander's friends (i.e., their traditional leaders) to mediate between them and the king, giving him permission to kill anyone he suspected of involvement in the mutiny. The soldiers had shown a similar psychological need to restore their close bonds with Alexander on the Hyphasis, but there it did not involve giving him an almost-free hand to punish them.[59]

Both Arrian and Plutarch say that when Alexander finally came out of his residence, he cried on seeing the weeping, pitiful, and humble troops (Arr. 7.1.5; Plut. *Alex.* 71.8). Mass crying can be infectious, and Alexander probably wished to suggest to the army that he was a victim too. His tears

---

58. Thus even later, in 323, when Alexander mixed Macedonians and Persian infantry in the phalanx, the numerically inferior Macedonians still commanded and formed the head and back of each file, with the Persians manning the middle: Arr. 7.23.1–4; cf. Diod 17.110.2 (erroneously predating it to 324); Bosworth 1980, 18–19.

59. Arr. 7.11.3–5; Curt. 10.3.5, 4.2; Just. 12.12.6; Plut. *Alex.* 71.6–8; Diod. 17.109.3; cf. Griffith in Hammond, Griffith, and Walbank 1979, 2:392.

also suggest that he sympathized with their distress (of which he had been the cause), that he was no longer angry, and that he did not seek to humiliate them. But they were still unsure of their standing in camp and in the king's affections, as compared to the Asians. Arrian dramatizes the scene by making Callines, an old cavalry commander who appears to represent the Macedonian salt of the earth, complain that Alexander made Persians instead of Macedonians his kinsmen and gave them the exclusive honor of kissing him. If authentic, this depiction is a testimony to the sorry morale of the troops, who now asked not to be ranked *above* Asians in honor but merely to be their equals. In response, Alexander is said to have named all Macedonians his kinsmen and to have permitted first Callines and then anyone to kiss him (Arr. 7.11.5–7). For a man who monopolized the distribution of honors in camp, this was a small price to pay. His gestures also meant different things to the different constituencies in camp. For the Persians, the title of Kinsmen and the right to kiss the king signaled royal appreciation but also the inferior status of the honoring person in relation to the one honored. For the Greeks and presumably the Macedonians, the term "Kinsman" and the kissing gesture denoted an intimate and more equal relationship. Alexander could tolerate these different interpretations as long as they all acknowledged his authority.[60]

We are told that the now-happy troops picked up their arms and went back to the camp, clamoring and singing a paean (Arr. 7.11.7). Even if the Macedonian repertoire of group singing was limited to paeans, it is still striking that they celebrated their defeat with a victory song. Things had been very different in India, where the Macedonians are reported to have comforted Alexander with the notion that he had been defeated by them alone!

Yet Alexander's victory was not total, because the soldiers got some of their wishes. The mutiny was followed by a banquet in which the theme of partnership between Macedonians and Persians in the empire played a prominent role, and for obvious reasons: it was important for Alexander to ease the tension that he had just heightened by playing one group against the other. Very few, if any, readers today subscribe to W. W. Tarn's view that Alexander's prayer for harmony between Macedonians and Persians articulated his vision of the brotherhood of mankind. Many instead concur with A. B. Bosworth's thesis that Alexander's policy toward the Iranians rested

---

60. See Fredricksmeyer 2000, 157; Roisman 2003, 299–301. Olbrycht suggests that Alexander forced the Macedonians to perform *proskynesis* to him: 2009, 247–248.

on principles more of separation than of equality and unity.[61] In the context of the mutiny, however, the banquet aimed to show the Macedonians that they had regained their superior status after Alexander had thrown it into doubt. Each guest among the reported 9,000 banqueters could see the king surrounded first by the Macedonians, then by Persians, and lastly by other nationals picked for their worth and excellence.[62] Both the reconciliation scene outside the king's doors and the display of descending order in the banquet compensated the Macedonians for Alexander's insults before and during the mutiny.

The troops' other gain was more tangible. All sources agree that Alexander had planned to send back the old, the weak, and the disabled. The force that eventually left Opis under Craterus's command numbered 10,000 infantry and 1,500 cavalry. Diodorus adds that of the 10,000 foot soldiers, 6,000 had fought with Alexander since the beginning of the campaign and 4,000 had joined him during the march (18.16.4).[63] Regardless of the scholarly controversy over the number of Alexander's Macedonians at this point, it is improbable that all or even most of the 11,500 men who left Opis were old and infirm.[64] Their later participation in the Diadochs' wars, both in Europe and in Asia, shows that these groups included many men still fit for service and younger than those Alexander had originally intended to dismiss. Alexander sent these men away because he expected new reinforcements from Macedonia and planned to increase his reliance on the Asians (Arr. 7.8.1; cf. Curt. 10.2.8). He may even have lost his trust in the veterans after the mutiny.[65] It is no less likely, however, that he finally yielded to the troops' pressure. Justin characterizes their tearful supplication of Alexan-

---

61. Tarn 1948, 2:399–440; Bosworth 1980; cf. Badian 1958. See, however, Hamilton 1987, 482–484, and especially Olbrycht (forthcoming) who argues that Alexander had already started to prefer Iranians in central Asia.

62. Arr. 7.11.8–9. Olbrycht (2009, 250–251) denies, however, the ethnic hierarchy in the banquet.

63. The numbers of the discharged: Arr. 7.8.1, 10.5, 12.1; Curt. 10.2.8; Just. 12.11.4–5; Plut. *Alex.* 71.2, 8; Diod. 17.109.1–2, 18.4.1, 12.1. Justin 12.12.7 mentions 11,000 veterans, not far from the aforementioned total of 11,500 infantry and cavalry; cf. Billows 1995, 188. For this reading of the text of Diod. 18.16.4, see Bosworth 2002, 73n31.

64. Curtius (10.2.8) states that Alexander aimed to keep with him 13,000 infantry and 2,000 cavalry, but these could include non-Macedonians. For ca. 25,000 Macedonians in camp before discharge: Hammond 1989b, 64; Billows 1995, 188. For ca. 13,000: Milns 1976, 112. For Alexander's retaining ca. 15,000: Billows 1995, 192. For retaining 8,000 or fewer: Bosworth 1988a, 267; 2002, 73–75.

65. See also Schachermeyer 1970, 16; Wirth 1984, 21; Bosworth 1988a, 272–273. Alexander also kept older soldiers: Curt. 10.7.18.

der not to dishonor them as a moderate request that made the king release 11,000 veterans (12.12.6–7). I am aware that, according to Justin, Alexander gave in to the troops both here and on the Hyphasis (12.8.16) because they asked politely, but this looks like putting the best face on yielding to pressure. The veterans who wanted to go home, for whatever reason, could look back on the mutiny with satisfaction in the effect of their defiance.

There were additional rewards for the veterans, both material and symbolic. Alexander paid each departing soldier his overdue wages and the expenses of the trip home, with a bonus of one talent. He also instructed Antipater, his deputy in Macedonia, to honor the returnees with front seats and garlands at public contests and in the theater.[66] There was more than one reason for this generosity. Alexander had paid his soldiers' debts earlier, in Susa, but since the money went presumably to the creditors and for travel expenses (Curt. 10.2.25), the veterans were going home with little to show for their long campaign in rich lands. This was poor advertisement for the new recruits Alexander was anxious to bring to Asia. Moreover, Arrian reports that in a speech to the Macedonians before the breakup of the mutiny, Alexander promised to reward those who stayed with him in a way that would evoke the envy of people at home and motivate new recruits to share their danger and toils (Arr. 7.8.1–2).[67] Yet he made no such promise to the men he was going to discharge. In discharging the Greek allies from Hecatompylus in 330, Alexander paid a talent to each cavalryman, one-sixth of a talent to each infantryman, and due wages and travel expenses to all (Diod. 17.74.3; Curt. 6.2.17). The veterans who left Opis must have expected similar compensation, and by paying them their wages and bonuses Alexander corrected his mistake of ignoring them or failing to promise their reward. Finally, there was the royal duty to play the benefactor, which Alexander took seriously. But the usual scholarly focus on Alexander's motives and actions should not distract attention from the men affected by them. After all, the beneficiaries of Alexander's generosity were the veterans, not just himself, and even if they were aware of his agenda it is doubtful that they cared about it. Furthermore, the departing troops could have correctly concluded that their mutiny, by forcing Alexander to realize

---

66. Material rewards: Arr. 7.12.1; Plut. *Alex.* 71.8; Just. 12.12.10. Symbolic rewards: Plut. *Alex.* 71.8 with Hamilton 1969, 199. Even the appointment of Craterus and other veteran generals to lead the veterans home was presented as a token of Alexander's appreciation: Arr. 7.12.3.

67. For the reading of Arr. 7.8.1 as a promise to those who stayed in Asia: Hammond 1980, 469–467 (repr. 1994, 79–81).

that they deserved compensation for their service, had made them richer in money and honor.

There remained the issue of the veterans' families in camp. Arrian reports that more than 10,000 Macedonians registered their marriage to Asian women in Susa and received royal gifts (Arr. 7.4.8; cf. Plut. *Alex.* 70.3). The registration was not designed, as is often thought, to legalize pre-existing unions or make them official.[68] Nowhere in the Greek (or presumably the Macedonian) world was it the custom for couples to register their marriages. The purpose was to record the wedding gifts that Alexander gave the veterans, just as he intended to record his payment of their debts.

The evidence concerning Alexander's plan for the veterans' children from these unions is more complex, and raises questions about when he first conceived it, the number of children affected, and even his intentions. According to Justin, Alexander had allowed his Macedonians to marry captive women as early as 330. He subsidized and trained their children, including orphans, as future replacements for their fathers, thereby easing the pressure of the draft on Macedonian manpower. He even paid soldiers by the number of sons they had fathered (Just. 12.4.1–11). Yet Justin's account has its share of problems. He calls these children "Epigoni," which was also the name given to a force of young, local recruits. Moreover, since the Macedonians could not have fathered children from captive women before 333, the oldest of these children could not have been more than three years in age in 330 and nine in 324. These could hardly be the young men (*juvenes*) who, according to Justin, received weapons and horses from the king for their training (Just. 12.4.8).

Arrian's and Diodorus's dating of the program to 324 is preferable, and the most that can be said for Justin is that he confirms Alexander's plan to use the children as future substitutes for their fathers.[69] Diodorus adds that after Alexander had released the veterans, he conducted a census of their sons from captive women and came up with a figure of almost 10,000. The king then allocated money for their education (Diod. 17.110.3; *Contents*). This figure would earn more confidence if the ancients had been better at counting large numbers in general, and if this number in particular less re-

---

68. So, e.g., Milns 1968, 240; Lane Fox 1973, 418–419.

69. Dating the plan to 324: Arr. 7.12.2; Diod. 17.110.3; cf. Plut. *Alex.* 71.9. Epigoni: Curt. 8.5.1; cf. Heckel in Yardley and Heckel 2003, 208. The first likely opportunity for the Macedonians to capture women was after the Battle of Granicus in the summer of 334. Bosworth (1980, 18), however, finds Justin's account largely credible.

sembled the 10,000 discharged veterans and the "little less than 10,000 talents" Alexander paid for their debts (Diod. 17 *Contents*).

We come now to Arrian's report on these children, which the author links to the veterans' discharge. By this account, Alexander told the veterans that if they took their children home they would cause friction with their Macedonian families. He assured them personally that he would give the children Macedonian education and military training, and that he would reunite them with their fathers in Macedonia when they reached manhood. It is significant that even Arrian, Alexander's great admirer, doubted the king's sincerity in playing the double role of benefactor and troubleshooter (7.12.2–3). Indeed, if the purpose of leaving the children in Asia was to prevent domestic conflicts in Macedonia, what difference did it make if they went now, with their fathers, or later, with Alexander? As has been long recognized, Alexander wanted these children to enlarge his pool of prospective military recruits.[70]

Arrian and the other sources (and, following them, many modern scholars) are silent about the effect of Alexander's action on two other groups. One was the veterans' Asian women. It is highly likely that they stayed in Asia to care for their sons until the children would be sufficiently mature for training. As captives of mostly Asian origin, occupying the lowest rungs in the hierarchy of the camp, these mothers and their daughters must have been accorded the least of the king's attention. The sources, who say nothing on their fate, are equally silent about the reaction of the discharged veterans to Alexander's plan. Were all the veterans happy to leave their home in camp behind? According to Justin, Alexander believed that marrying his Macedonians to captive women would lessen their longing for home by giving them something of a domestic experience in camp (Just. 12.4.3). And in 317, about 3,000 of Alexander's veterans known as the Silver Shields cared enough about their dependents to surrender their leader Eumenes to his enemy Antigonus in return for their captured baggage, which included their camp families. At Opis, some may have been indifferent to the fate of their foreign companions and their children, while others possibly considered Alexander's wages and bonuses a fair exchange for their children. Still others may have appreciated Alexander's care for their children, recognizing it as better than what they themselves could afford to provide. Whatever they felt about Alexander's offer, however, they all understood that re-

---

70. E.g., O'Brien 1992, 208.

fusing it was not an option. I hope it is not too sentimental to think that when Alexander and the departing veterans wept together for the last time (Arr. 7.12.3), some of the tears were shed for those left behind.[71]

The clashes and reconciliations between the troops and Alexander were emotionally charged because, for the veterans, issues such as pressing on with the campaign (in Hecatompylus or India) or being sent home called for reassessment of their relationship with the king, including its affective aspects. The troops looked at these strategic decisions in terms of the future, but also through the prism of whether the king respected and cared for them, held them close to him, and treated them fairly. It is no wonder that there was so much crying when feelings were hurt and mended and, for those who left involuntarily, hurt again.[72]

---

71. It should be noted that not all veterans had families or children, and some might have lost them to flash floods in the Gedrosian desert the year before: Arr. *Anab.* 6.26.5.

72. See also Lateiner 2009, 120–121.

CHAPTER 3

THE VETERANS AND THE MACEDONIAN INTERNAL STRIFE IN BABYLON (323)

THE DELIBERATIONS OVER ALEXANDER'S SUCCESSION: SOURCES, INSTITUTIONS, AND DEBATE

On June 11, 323 BCE, Alexander died in Babylon without leaving an heir.[1] The question of who would replace him as king and as the ruler of the empire led to dissension both within the elite and between the elite and the masses. The crisis also provided the rank and file with an opportunity rare in Macedonian history: the chance to participate meaningfully in the politics of the kingdom.

In investigating the events immediately after Alexander's death, scholars have tended to focus on source analysis and especially on the nature of the Macedonian political institutions, such as the council and the assembly, that played an important part in them. I do not have much to contribute to the debate over the sources' relative credibility or the character of the Macedonian institutions, but I shall make clear in which scholarly camp I stand on those issues.

The sources for the events in Babylon consist chiefly of the narrative—poorly preserved, but still rich in details—of Curtius Rufus (10.6.1–10.20) and the briefer account of Justin (13.2.1–4.25). There are also highly abridged reports by Diodorus (18.2.2–4), Arrian's history of events after Alexander as summarized by the Byzantine Photius (Arr. *Succ.* 1.1–4), and the *Heidelberg Epitome* (*FGrHist* 155 F 1).[2] As might be expected, the sources differ in their details, especially the chronological order of the events they record.

---

1. For the date, see Depuydt 1997. For the events discussed in this chapter, see, in addition to studies cited in the following notes, Schachermeyer 1970; Errington 1970, 72–75; Anson 1992.

2. Other narratives—such as the *Liber de Morte Testamentumque Alexandri Magni*, the *Alexander Romance*, and non-Greek accounts—are tainted with propaganda and invention or have little relevance to the story of the veterans.

While trying when possible to reconcile the various versions, this chapter mostly follows Curtius's account, because it is fuller, at times supported by the other sources, and inherently sensible. Among the scholarly suggestions for Curtius's ultimate source, I prefer Cleitarchus of Alexandria to Hieronymus, especially because Cleitarchus is Curtius's likely direct or indirect source for much of his history of Alexander. For Curtius's speeches, the prudent scholar will accept as historically valid only the speaker's identity and his core argument. The focus of my investigation, in any case, is more on the audience's reactions to a speaker's ideas than on the speaker's agenda or mode of expression.[3]

In the days following Alexander's death, the troops gathered a number of times to decide weighty issues, including who would inherit the Macedonian throne. Some historians grant considerable power to the Macedonian popular assembly, which they identify with the army assembly; I side with those others who regard this institution as a minor player in Macedonian politics. As we shall see, however, the assembly could attain greater power when the elite and the king became weak.[4]

According to Curtius, the choice of Alexander's heir took place in the royal quarters. Though the original intention was to limit the discussion to members of the elite (Alexander's close circle of bodyguards, marshals, and members of the officer class), the troops did not wait passively to hear their decision but rushed in.[5] It is worth noting that the crowd at the meeting could easily have included non-Macedonians. There was no one at the gate to check admission, and Curtius, significantly, identifies the troops as Macedonians only after the meeting was over and the troops became upset with Meleager over his attempt to eliminate Perdiccas (Curt. 10.8.5, and below). Indeed, non-Macedonian troops had as much of a stake in the delib-

---

3. For a strong criticism of Curtius's account, see McKechnie 1999; *contra*: Bosworth 2002, 38–43; 2003, 177–181. Curtius's sources: Bosworth 2002, 35–44; and esp. Atkinson 2009, 19–28, 172–175. See also Meeus 2008, 39–46.

4. Among recent studies of the Macedonian assembly, see Briant 1973b (who distinguishes, however, between the army and the people's assemblies when in Macedonia); Hammond 1989, 58–64; Hatzopoulos 1996, 1: esp. 261–332; cf. Müller 2003, 17–21; and Rzepka 2005, who all grant it significant powers. Among the scholars who largely deny the assembly such powers are, e.g., Lock (1977); Errington (1978); Anson (1991, 2008). Mooren 1983, esp. 210–221, occupies a middle ground. For a summary of scholarship on the assembly and monarchical succession, see L. Mitchell 2007, 61–63.

5. Curt. 10.6.1–2. See Schachermeyer (1970, 134–135), who argues that the meetings could not have taken place in the limited space of the throne room of the royal palace. Justin restricts the participants to Alexander's friends (13.2.4), but Curtius's version is preferable: Errington 1970, 50–51; Meeus 2008, 44; Atkinson 2009, 175.

erations as anyone else, and their presence was tolerated even in Philotas's trial for treason to Alexander in 330 (Curt. 6.9.34–35). Nevertheless, it can be reasonably assumed that speakers aimed their words chiefly at the veterans, who were also the most active in reacting to them.[6]

Several factors could account for the troops' taking the unprecedented liberty of barging into the meeting. Of course they had a strong desire to find out who would be their leader, and they knew that there was no one in charge to prevent them from intruding. But there was justification for another motive, which was suspicion of the elite's agenda and integrity at this time of uncertainty. In 326/5 Alexander was severely injured in an attack on the Indian city of the Malli and was taken away for treatment. A great fear seized the camp, and there were rumors of his death. Few believed the report that he was alive, and when a letter arrived later, announcing his coming to camp, it was thought to be a forgery created by Alexander's bodyguards and generals (Arr. *Anab.* 6.12.3). A similar suspicion surfaced shortly before Alexander's death in Babylon. According to Arrian, many soldiers wished to see their king before he died, but some thought that he was already dead and that the bodyguards did not want the army to know about it (Arr. *Anab.* 7.26.1; cf. *Liber de Morte* 104; Plut. *Alex.* 76.8). It is likely, then, that the troops at the succession conference wanted to avoid being deceived by the elite and to understand fully the plans that would affect their future.

The troops' presence turned the forum of decision-making from a council into an informal assembly in which they could show their approval or disapproval of suggestions made by elite speakers. It did not make the meeting into a constitutional assembly, because the people could not vote on who would inherit the throne but could only listen and react to the generals' ideas.[7] The troops' eventual promotion of Alexander's half-brother, Arrhidaeus, to the throne in opposition to the elite was due to divisions within the high command, the dynamics of events, and the soldiers' naked power—they came with their weapons (Curt. 10.6–12)—rather than their predetermination to exercise constitutional prerogatives.

Perdiccas, Alexander's second in command, was the first to realize the

---

6. See also King 2010, 388. Hammond (2000, 159–160), however, makes no distinction among the terms that the sources use to describe the attendants: e.g., *contio* (informal assembly), *vulgus* (crowd), *populus* (people), and *plēthos* (many), but sees them all as synonymous with the Macedonian assembly. In 315 Antigonus called a joint assembly of soldiers and visitors, whose decisions were perceived as having been made by the Macedonians (Diod. 19.61.1–3, 62.1).

7. See also Errington 1978, 94–96; Anson 1991, 236–137.

changing circumstances. He displayed Alexander's empty throne, regalia, and weapons to the crowd, ostentatiously placing on the throne the ring that Alexander had given him on his deathbed—a gesture telling the army, but even more his fellow marshals, that he was making no claim to the empire or to its custodianship.[8] Scholars have argued that Perdiccas tried to manipulate these symbols of authority to advance his claim to power. Whatever his ambitions or tactics may have been, the troops showed not the slightest interest in them or in the marshal himself. Instead, the sight of the empty throne reportedly triggered renewed grief about the dead king.[9] The empty throne and the objects on it were also visual proofs of an absent authority and of the need for a new ruler. Yet because Alexander's generals disagreed on who should succeed him, they sought support for their positions outside their ranks, giving the army a role in the proceedings and justifying their proposals in the name of the interest or needs of the troops and the Macedonians (Curt. 10.6.8, 11, 14).

The first to speak was Perdiccas, who proposed that they wait for the birth of what he hoped would be a son to Alexander's widow, Roxane, and in the meantime that they choose an interim leader.[10] No source reports on the troops' reaction, probably because they waited to hear what other speakers had to say and because they were not of one mind about Perdiccas's plan. Generally, as we have seen, it was easier for the rank and file to agree on what they did not want than on what they wanted, as became apparent in their response to the proposal of Nearchus, Alexander's former admiral.

Like subsequent speakers in this debate, Nearchus criticized rival sug-

---

8. Curt. 10.6.4. For the Macedonian royal throne, see Picard 1954, 1–4; Paspalas 2005, esp. 87. Ring and custodianship: Plut. *Alex.* 9.1. Hammond's (1989a, 158–160) arguments against the historicity of Alexander's giving his signet ring to Perdiccas are too one-sided. Badian (1987–1988, 608–609) is uncommitted, while Rathmann (2005, esp. 16–17) defends the tradition but denies its significance for Alexander's succession. See also Meeus 2008, 46n30.

9. Curt. 10.6.4. Justin's claim (13.1.7, 2.1) that the troops were happy about Alexander's death is both unlikely and irreconcilable with his description of their teary reaction to the sight of the dying king: 12.15.2–3; Meeus 2009, 237. Perdiccas's motives: among others, Errington 1971, 50; 1976, 139; Schäfer 2002, 34; Rathmann 2005, 22–26. I adopt the sources' inconsistent designations of the person who looked after the kingdom (as *prostates*, *epimeletes*, and *epitropos*) by calling him "regent" or "guardian." See Meeus 2009c, and cf. Anson 1992, 41; 2009, for their essential synonimity.

10. Curt. 10.6.4–9; Just. 13.2.5. According to the *Liber de Morte* 112, 118 Alexander willed Roxane to Perdiccas. See Billows (1990, 53) and Rathmann (2005, 32–50) for an attempt to divide the marshals into factions.

gestions before advancing his own, which was to crown Heracles, the son of Alexander by the Persian Barsine, whose daughter Nearchus had married in Susa. The troops showed their displeasure with this proposal by banging their spears against their shields, and they almost rioted when Nearchus refused to give up (Curt. 10.6.12). Curtius, who allows speakers to state the logic of their recommendations, accords no such privilege to the audience and does not bother to explain why they were so hostile. Except for a handful of occasions, it is typical of our sources to describe the troops' conduct rather than its causes, giving them mostly a reactive role and showing them evincing crowd behavior. In regard to Nearchus's suggestion, the soldiers possibly shared the prejudicial sentiments attributed to Ptolemy, who would soon oppose it in the name of the superiority of Europe over Asia and of conquerors over the conquered. In addition, Nearchus had suffered a greater loss of authority from the death of his patron Alexander than did the other, more-independent Macedonian generals. Therefore popular opposition was enough to put his initiative to rest.[11]

According to Justin's different account, it was the infantry commander Meleager who advocated Heracles' accession to the throne. Meleager also named Alexander's half-brother, Arrhidaeus, as a possible heir if an older candidate was preferable. Justin's report is problematic, both because he likely confused Meleager with Nearchus as Heracles' champion and because he and Curtius date the controversy over Arrhidaeus's candidacy and the troops' active support of it to a later stage. The most that can be said for Justin's version is that Arrhidaeus's name was now possibly added to the list of candidates for the first time, although evoking no reaction from the audience.[12]

Ptolemy was the next to speak. He argued in favor of giving the rule to a small group of Alexander's close advisers and chief generals, who would meet in the presence of Alexander's throne to discuss public policy and to make decisions by a majority vote (Curt. 10.6.13–16). While Perdiccas, Nearchus, and Aristonus (below) discussed the need to find an heir to Alexander, Ptolemy essentially contended that no heir was necessary because the king was still there by virtue of his throne, and that the old council could

---

11. Curt. 10.6.13–15; Bosworth 2003, 179. Cf. also Green 1990, 7; Ogden 1999, 47; Anson 2004, 53. Around 309, Polyperchon and possibly Antigonus temporarily resurrected Nearchus's idea of making Heracles king, only for Polyperchon to kill him later: Billows 1990, 140–141.

12. Just. 13.2.6–3.1, but see Bosworth (2002, 34–45), who favors Justin's version over Curtius's.

continue to function as in the past. Ptolemy's suggestion was not without its appeal, because it created a fiction of continuity from the past, even if in actuality it gave the council powers it never held. Yet it was too vague about who would be the real or even titular leader. The veterans, some of whom had served since Philip's day, were accustomed to the presence of a dominant king in their midst, and were unlikely to accept an empty throne as a substitute. In any case, the sources fail to report on the troops' reaction.[13]

Aristonus, Alexander's bodyguard, countered Ptolemy's proposal with the statement that Alexander had already elected to give Perdiccas supreme power by giving him his ring. Curtius says that everyone (*universi*—probably referring to the crowd) called upon Perdiccas to pick up the ring (10.6.4, 16–18; cf. Just. 13.2.3). The army had heard enough to judge this proposal more attractive than Nearchus's unpopular choice of heir, or Ptolemy's attempt to prevent a single leader from taking charge, which went against the Macedonians' experience and desire. Aristonus's proposal, on the other hand, purported to respect Alexander's wish and gave supreme command to Perdiccas, who had promised to retain it for the king's prospective heir.[14] Perdiccas hesitated—perhaps sincerely, perhaps not—and then retreated without the ring, although he made sure to stand close to the throne and the other symbols of power (Curt. 10.6.18–19). Whatever his motives were, it is certain that the soldiers did not know or try to learn them.[15] His behavior was a mistake, because real or pretended indecision invited alternative suggestions and also told the troops, who had urged Perdiccas to take the ring, that he was willing to ignore their wishes.

This allowed the infantry general Meleager to take center stage. According to Curtius, Meleager forcefully opposed the idea that Perdiccas should occupy the throne. He also called for plundering the royal treasury because of the people's entitlement to it, and indeed went on to loot it in the company of the troops. With Meleager now surrounded by armed men, the meeting became more seditious and discordant. At this point a

---

13. Curtius's remark that more men concurred with Ptolemy's suggestion than with that of Perdiccas refers most likely to other speakers than to the audience: Mooren 1983, 233. In Justin's much-less-attractive version, the main thrust of Ptolemy's speech is an attack on Arrhidaeus's candidacy, concluding with a suggestion to choose instead a general or a governor who stood close to Alexander in *virtus* (13.2.11–12).

14. Bosworth claims (2002, 43) that the story of Aristonus's proposal was the product of later hostile propaganda against this bodyguard, but a hostile source would not say that everybody liked his plan. Justin skips over Aristonus's speech.

15. See conveniently Meeus (2008, 51), who also rightly rejects the view that Curtius anachronistically transplanted to Babylon the emperor Tiberius's hesitation before ascending the throne.

man of the lowest status, unknown to most of the Macedonians, reminded the assembled people that Alexander's half-brother, Arrhidaeus, the somewhat mentally challenged son of Philip II, deserved to rule by virtue of his birth. The troops shouted their approval for bringing Arrhidaeus over and vowed to kill those responsible for calling the meeting without him (Curt. 10.6.20–7.3).

Curtius's description of these events has met with skepticism. His portrayal of Meleager is drawn with a very broad brush and too easily fits the stock type of demagogic troublemaker. It has also been argued that the historian's inspiration for the scene of Arrhidaeus's almost accidental choice as heir was a Roman tradition about a Praetorian soldier who found another mentally challenged man, the future emperor Claudius, hiding behind a curtain.[16] One may also add that the independent initiative of the anonymous Macedonian soldier in naming Arrhidaeus to the throne was unprecedented; the assembly normally waited, as in this case, for the leadership to name the heir.

These circumstances make the story look like an effort to discredit the choice of Arrhidaeus, which was opposed by the elite: hence the presentation of his right to the throne as an afterthought, put forward by a man so lowly and obscure that even the Macedonians did not know him. Arrhidaeus's cause was then taken up by Meleager and the troops, who are stereotypically portrayed as emotional, bloodthirsty, greedy, corruptible, and generally out of control. That Justin's narrative shares some of these themes suggests that he and Curtius used common or like-minded sources. In a sweeping statement, Justin distinguishes between Alexander's generals, who were interested in attaining authority and the throne, and the rank and file, who were undisciplined, fickle, and interested in Alexander's treasure chests and riches (Just. 13.1.8, 2.1–2).[17]

Yet the hostility of this account does not make it a sheer fiction. Meleager is presented as a gang leader and demagogue, but he probably owed some of his influence over the phalanx to his service as an infantry commander under Alexander.[18] There is also nothing improbable in his leading

---

16. See Martin 1983 [1987]; Sharples 1994. Bosworth (2002, 35–37) thinks, however, that the story of Claudius was modeled after that of Arrhidaeus.

17. Bosworth (2003, 180–181; 2004, 38–43), who identifies the source as Cleitarchus, claims that he portrayed Arrhidaeus positively because it served Ptolemy's interest to do so. But the presentation of Arrhidaeus's later cooperation with Perdiccas against Meleager is hardly sympathetic: Curt. 10.9.7–21.

18. Heckel 1992, 165–170. Meleager in action is often mentioned with Perdiccas. Bennett and Roberts (2008, 1:4) overestimate his distinction.

the troops to plunder the treasury boxes: the generals who followed Alexander would try similarly to strengthen their bonds with their troops by providing for them, although normally at the expense of the defeated or of the local population. Meleager's claim that the people should inherit the royal riches must have appalled Curtius's audience, but it did not lack reason or justification (Curt. 10.6.23). An earlier episode involving Meleager and Alexander indirectly echoes this point. When Alexander displayed munificent generosity toward an Indian ruler, says Curtius, Meleager sarcastically congratulated the king on going all the way to India to find someone worthy of a thousand-talent gift, thereby suggesting that the financial rewards of the conquest went to undeserving people. It was a view that the troops in Babylon would have found easy to agree with.[19]

The looting of the treasury confirmed for the sources, and for the scholars who follow them, the greedy character of the troops.[20] Obviously, the rank and file sought material gains and were ready to attain them by force (often differing from their leaders in this regard only in their smaller share of the profits). Yet to say that they sought only money or that they were oblivious to nonmaterial considerations is to reduce their perspective and interests to mere basic needs. If they were greedy for profit alone, they would have retired to their tents after robbing the treasury instead of proceeding to protest the absence of Arrhidaeus. The looting of the treasury in fact empowered the troops and gave them the confidence to make other demands. Underlying both their plundering of the treasury and their support of Arrhidaeus was the wish to correct injustice, which they saw both in the unfair distribution of the wealth amassed by their efforts and in the elite's disregard of a member of the royal family (Curt. 10.7.10, 15). The soldiers did not oppose the elite instinctively or on principle, but looked to it for a solution that most of them could accept. Once Nearchus's candidate was universally rejected, Ptolemy's suggestion had received probably only lukewarm support, and Perdiccas appeared interested in pleasing his fellow marshals more than the troops, Arrhidaeus became an attractive choice.

It is unclear whether the man who proposed Arrhidaeus was Meleager's agent or, as seems more likely, an independent voice. In a riot situation, with the elite's authority being challenged, an ordinary soldier could

---

19. Curt. 8.12.17–18. For Meleager's freedom of speech there, see Roisman 2003, 320. Cf. also Bennett and Roberts 2008, 1:4; Atkinson 2009, 183.

20. Cf., e.g., Errington 1970, 51; Anson 1991, esp. 230–236; 2004, 118–119. See also Griffith (1935, 39) and Austin (1986, 464–465), who attribute to Hellenistic soldiers in general selfish, materialistic motives.

certainly have spoken and made a difference.[21] Once Arrhidaeus's name was put forward (or resurfaced), several factors combined to recommend him to the soldiers. He could have become a king then and there, obviating the unattractive alternatives of a vacant throne or the birth of a female heir. The veterans were attached to the Argead (ruling dynasty of Macedon) house and thought that Arrhidaeus was being unfairly excluded from consideration for the throne. In spite of his mental deficiencies, whose nature is unclear, he represented legitimacy, continuity, and the prospect of stability.[22] In essence, the troops' choice consisted of an unborn child (perhaps even a girl), Barsine's son, an empty throne, and an impaired adult. It was not a great choice, but it had a predictable result.

The general Pithon, son of Crateuas, still tried to prevent the growing rift between the elite and the veterans through personal attacks on Arrhidaeus, but his attempt backfired. Curtius then describes a tumultuous gathering, with Arrhidaeus being brought to the royal quarters, then exiting them, then being recalled. Although the historian changes his focus from the leaders to the soldiers, he limits his depiction to this mob behavior. He borrows a simile of a stormy sea from Homer's *Iliad* (2.142–46) in order to describe an unwieldy assembly, and goes on to describe the troops as unruly, emotional, inconsistent, and looking for blood. His account and Justin's much briefer one yield the following reasonably certain facts: that the troops acknowledged Arrhidaeus as King Philip (III); that he donned royal garb and was given royal bodyguards from among the soldiers; and that Meleager placed himself firmly next to him with a core of probably thirty supporters.[23] For the time being, the troops had gotten both a king and a general to lead them. This was better than the outcome at Opis, where Al-

---

21. *Pace* Schachermeyer 1970, 97; cf. Atkinson 2009, 184–186. Martin 1983 [1987] and Sharples 1994 offer conflicting analyses of this episode. Anson (2004, 54n17) defends this soldier's existence and points to another *ignotus* who spoke in Philotas's trial, but if he means Bolon (Curt. 6.11.1–7), the latter was neither unknown nor of low rank. Ober's use of "speech act" theory may be applicable here: 1998, 32–51, esp. 36–40.

22. Curt. 10.7.15. See also Errington 1970, 51. Errington's view (1976, 146–147, 152–153) that the troops preferred Philip's line of descent to Alexander's is belied both by their later agreement to accept Roxane's son (see also Curt. 10.7.10) and by the leaders' use of Alexander and his memory to attain legitimacy; see also Meeus 2009a, 238. Arrhidaeus's mental condition: Bosworth 2002, 30n9; Meeus 2008, 41–42 (but see infra). The Macedonians' expectations of their kings: Hammond 1989, 21–23.

23. Curt. 10.7.4–15; Just. 13.3.1. Plut. *Moral.* 337d–e; 791e has a slightly different but even-more-hostile coloring of the events. Meleager's supporters: Diod. 18.4.7, and see below. For possible echoes of Livy in Curtius: Atkinson 2009, 192–193.

exander had won the confrontation by making the troops leaderless, but it was also an unstable, temporary arrangement because it was based on an anomalous antagonism between the troops and their commanders. One of the reasons Meleager's leadership eventually faltered was that it drew its power from this antagonism. Nevertheless, it had been the elite, rather than the troops, who took the decisive step toward creating two distinct camps in Babylon. In defiance of the soldiers, the officers and their supporters threw in their lot with Perdiccas, appointing him and his old friend Leonnatus the guardians of Roxane's future child (and hence de facto rulers of the Asian empire) and giving Craterus and Antipater command over Europe.

This is Curtius's version of the events, which is preferable to Justin's, according to which the generals discussed the future of the kingdom in the commanders' council, where they resolved to support Perdiccas's plan and took an oath of allegiance to the guardians, as did the cavalry. Angered at being ignored, the infantry picked Arrhidaeus as king.[24] The richer details of Curtius's account favor his version, as does Diodorus's brief report, which also places the army's decision to support Arrhidaeus earlier than the elite's decision to oppose it (Diod. 18.2.2). In addition, the story of the infantry's indignation at being excluded from the discussion regarding who should rule the kingdom suggests a much more democratic process than is warranted by our understanding of Macedonian history and the evidence. Even the alleged populist Meleager did not justify the crowning of Arrhidaeus as the people's choice.[25]

Our sources also disagree about Meleager's involvement. While Curtius describes him as opposing Perdiccas's plan from the outset, both Justin and Diodorus say that he was first sent by the cavalry (with Attalus) to try to patch up differences with the infantry, but opportunistically switched sides and became their leader (Just. 13.3.2; Diod. 18.2.2–3). Although it is possible that this version was fabricated by a hostile source, it is no less likely that the troops welcomed generals whose changing sides constituted a victory for the latter. In this case, Meleager's assumption of leadership would

---

24. Curt. 19.7.8; Just. 13.2.4–3.1. Atkinson (2009, 190) thinks that the meeting in Justin included the soldiers, but that the officers are the subject of the narrative. For the appointment of guardians, see, e.g., Fontana 1960, 18–19; Errington 1970, 52–53; Mooren 1983, 234–235.

25. *Liber de morte* 115 has Alexander allegedly ordain that the assembly elect a king if Roxane's child proved to be a daughter. Even if such an eventuality was conceivable, it was still a far cry from the present circumstances.

have taken place (according to Curtius's scenario) shortly after the looting of the treasury.[26]

THE RIFT IN BABYLON

The sources are unanimous that the split in camp was between the infantry, which stood behind the new king, and the cavalry, which supported Perdiccas.[27] But they largely fail to explain the division, which probably depended on these groups' different sizes and compositions. The number of the Macedonian cavalry in Babylon is uncertain. In 344, when Alexander left for Asia, he took 1,800 Companions (*hetairoi*) and ca. 600 additional Macedonian horsemen—if the unit of *prodromoi* (Scouts) was not already included in these forces.[28] In the course of the campaign, the cavalry were reinforced and reorganized but also suffered losses. Probably after 328/7 Alexander incorporated a significant number of Asian cavalry into the Companions.[29] By 326 the *prodromoi* had disappeared and Alexander is recorded to have sailed down the Indian river Hydraotes with 1,700 "of the Companions" (Arr. 6.14.4). In 324, according to Curtius, Alexander intended to keep with him in Asia 2,000 cavalry after sending the veterans home (Curt. 10.2.8). In 322, Craterus, the leader of the discharged veterans, crossed to Europe with 1,500 cavalry (Diod. 18.16.4).

It is not easy to reconcile these figures. It is highly unlikely that Alexander had 3,500 Macedonian Companions (his 2,000 and Craterus's 1,500) before sending the veterans home, because such a number would almost double the horsemen he took to Asia and would ignore discharges and losses suffered during the campaign. We may assume, then, that the 2,000 horsemen he kept or intended to keep in Asia, and perhaps even Craterus's

---

26. Cf. Briant 1973b, 246–247; Heckel 2006, 318n417. It was claimed that the nobles would not send Meleager, who supported Arrhidaeus for the throne, to argue for their position in favor of Roxane's unborn child: Wirth 1967, 291; Meeus 2008, 44–45. It should be said in Justin's defense that the council concluded its discussion with a unanimous vote (i.e., including Meleager's) in favor of Roxane's child: 13.2.13. See Polyaenus 4.6.6 and chapter 6 for a case of a commander who pretended to change sides and was welcomed by the opposition.

27. Curt. 10.7.20; Just. 13.3.1; Diod. 18.2.2; Arr. *Succ.* 1.2. Cf. Wirth 1967, 289.

28. Alexander cavalry: Brunt 1963; Bosworth 1988a, esp. 266–271; Aperghis 1997; Hammond 1998; Rzepka 2008; Sekunda 2010, 452–454. Their number in 334: Diod. 17.17.4; Brunt 1963, 41–42; Heckel 1992, 344–345; and the studies cited in this note.

29. Olbrycht forthcoming; cf. Arr. *Anab.* 7.6.3–5, 8.2.

1,500 cavalry, included non-Macedonians. But we know that the Macedonian cavalry in Babylon exceeded 800 from the information that, after the crisis there was over, Perdiccas gave Pithon 800 Macedonian cavalry for his campaign in central Asia (Diod. 18.7.3). Perdiccas sorted the cavalry by lot, and it is unlikely that he gave Pithon most of his Macedonian horsemen. I would estimate their number in Babylon, then, to be at least double this number, i.e., ca. 1,600 men.[30] Scholarly estimates of the number of the Macedonian infantry in Babylon vary greatly, but Perdiccas now also gave Pithon 3,000 Macedonian infantry, also selected by lot, suggesting that their number was significantly larger than that of the cavalry.[31]

The cavalry's modest size, social prestige, and higher pay distinguished them as a more cohesive group than the foot soldiers. They were closer to the marshals and more amenable to their influence, and so found it easier to identify with the elite than did the larger and more diversified infantry. During the Opis mutiny, these social differences were overridden by the antagonism that the infantry and the cavalry felt in common toward Alexander. In Babylon and later, however, there was no shared resentment to unite them, and the cavalry stood with the elite. Moreover, in Babylon the infantry ignored the cavalry when they proclaimed Arrhidaeus king. Resentful as well as alienated, and probably fearful of losing their preferred status in camp, the cavalry distanced themselves from the infantry.[32]

The spark that would ignite the confrontation between the two groups originated with the elite. Perdiccas ordered the room where Alexander's body lay to be locked, and he stood guard over it with Ptolemy, 600 men of "proven valor" (likely bodyguard units), and the Royal Boys (pages) (Curt. 10.7.16).[33] Curtius thinks that Perdiccas acted in terror, but desperation seems a likelier motive. While Philip's son was donning Alexander's

---

30. The possibility that Perdiccas gave Pithon Macedonians who normally did not serve in the cavalry should not be discounted. See Brunt (1963, 38–39; 1976–1983, 2:484–490) for a different interpretation of these figures, including speculations on unrecorded Macedonian reinforcements.

31. Diod. 18.7.3. Estimates of infantry: chap. 2, note 64, above.

32. Cavalry and class, including in pre-Alexander Macedonia: Anaximenes: *FGrHist* 72 F 27; Curt. 6.11.20; 10.7.20; cf. Theopompus: *FGrHist* 115 F 225b. But the sources militate against a view of the present conflict as rooted in class differences. There might have been, however, a rival esprit de corps: cf. Curt. 7.6.8. For the following see also Schubert 1914, 180–181.

33. The identity of the 600 who fought with Perdiccas's men cannot be established with certainty. Schachermeyer (1970, 14) and Atkinson (2009, 194) think that they were hypaspists. If correct, this identification suggests that the dichotomy between infantry

cloak in the opposite camp, Perdiccas had only an unborn heir in his own, giving him and his supporters little to legitimize their choice of a ruler (and perhaps Perdiccas's own ruling pretensions) except for Alexander's corpse and the rites associated with its burial. The infantry was ready to move on and proclaim Arrhidaeus king, but the elite clung to Alexander's memory throughout the succession crisis in order to legitimize their self-interested solutions (Curt. 10.6.4–7.5).

Once Perdiccas took possession of Alexander's body in an arbitrary and confrontational fashion, he provoked a reaction in kind. Indeed, if anyone had a rightful claim to the royal corpse, it was Arrhidaeus, Alexander's half-brother. A large number of troops burst into the death chamber followed by the new king, who was surrounded by his attendants and his protector, Meleager. Using his only card against a superior force, Perdiccas called on the attackers to defend Alexander's body, presumably from Meleager and his gang. What ensued was the first recorded armed clash among Alexander's veterans, many of whom were wounded. Thanks to their numerical superiority, the infantry had the upper hand, and the older soldiers among them used their authority to plead with Perdiccas's men to give up. Despite Curtius's earlier statement to the contrary, the infantry was clearly not looking "to glut themselves with the blood" of the opposition.[34] At the same time, that they called for surrender only after many were wounded suggests that Macedonian camaraderie in arms had a limited inhibiting power.

Perdiccas stopped fighting first. He could recognize defeat, and his ambition to be regent counseled him to avoid antagonizing the infantry beyond repair. Meleager, who wanted to ensure that the opposition would stay in town, where he could watch them, was equally conciliatory. He called Perdiccas's men to stay with Alexander's body, which was now symbolic of a united camp. But Perdiccas's followers distrusted his intentions and fled the city toward the Euphrates, where they were joined later by the entire cavalry force. The latter would not accept an infantry-based monarchy and knew that they were at a disadvantage in the city, especially in urban combat. Perdiccas stayed in town in the hope of stealing the phalanx away from Meleager.[35]

Curtius and Justin give different accounts of what happened next. Ac-

---

and cavalry lacks nuance. But the possibility that they were cavalry, given their support of Perdiccas and their probable youth (Curt. 10.7.18), should not be discounted.

34. Curt. 10.7.14. Just. 13.3.3–5, who is equally hostile to Meleager and to the phalanx, claims that they wanted to eliminate the cavalry.

35. Curt. 10.7.16–21; Diod. 18.2.2–3; Just. 13.3.3–5.

cording to the former, Meleager, with the tacit agreement of the king, sent men to bring Perdiccas over on charges of conspiracy, with orders to kill him if he refused to come. But Perdiccas intimidated Meleager's men, who went back empty-handed, and he later appeared on the plain to join the cavalry and his ally Leonnatus. When the Macedonians learned what had happened, they intended to use their arms to punish Meleager, thinking it a disgrace that Perdiccas had been put in mortal danger (Curt. 10.8.5). Here the manuscript breaks off, resuming with Meleager asking the king in the assembly if he had ordered the arrest of Perdiccas. Philip responded that he had, but only because Meleager led him to it, adding that there was no need for rioting, because Perdiccas was alive. The meeting was disbanded, leaving Meleager in terrified uncertainty about what to do regarding the cavalry's departure (Curt. 10.8.1–7, 11).

Justin, on the other hand, claims that Attalus (who in Justin's version had deserted earlier to the infantry with Meleager) sent men to assassinate Perdiccas, but that Perdiccas courageously scared them off. Perdiccas then called the infantry to a meeting and eloquently rebuked them for fighting their kinsmen and brothers-in-arms to the delight of their enemies. Impressed by his rhetoric, the assembly voted to make Perdiccas their general, and the infantry subsequently reconciled with the cavalry (Just. 13.3.6–4.4).

The two accounts are similar, but Curtius's version is preferable where they differ. Justin seems to confuse Attalus with Meleager or to omit the latter's name, while Curtius's story that Perdiccas left Babylon after Meleager's failed attempt to arrest or kill him makes more sense than the idea that Perdiccas left the city after gaining the leadership of the infantry.[36] It can be said in favor of Justin's version, however, that the arguments he attributes to Perdiccas in the assembly (which resemble thoughts and words attributed to other individuals in Curt. 10.8.10, 16–19) appealed to the soldiers' desire to avoid a civil war and their fear that the conquered population would take advantage of the crisis.

Nevertheless, Curtius's report of the phalanx's anger at Meleager and their sympathy for Perdiccas is puzzling in the light of their previous support of the former and opposition to the latter. Indeed, A. B. Bosworth, who prefers Justin's account, argues that it was the cavalry, not the infantry, who were upset with the news of the assassination attempt against Per-

---

36. See Atkinson 2009, 196–197, for a summary of scholarly opinions for and against Justin's account, and for the identity of Attalus. Bosworth (2002, 46–49) dates Perdiccas's appearance in the assembly to a later stage, but Just. 13.3.8 unambiguously ties it to the assassination attempt, both causally and temporally. See below.

diccas, and that they decided to punish Meleager. Bosworth suggests that Meleager then called an assembly, but that someone—perhaps Perdiccas's brother, Alcetas—made it clear by interrogating the king that Meleager was behind the assassination attempt.[37] However, Bosworth's identification of the angry Macedonians in Curtius 10.8.5 with the cavalry moves the narrative away from Babylon, where it is firmly located. It also goes against Curtius's use of the ethnic term "Macedonians" to describe the infantry to distinguish them from the cavalry in this conflict (10.8.14).

I suggest that it was the infantry who were upset with Meleager, because he tried to use their support of Philip III and the king himself in his personal power struggle against Perdiccas.[38] The infantry was less interested in which general would prevail than in whether he backed their king and did not intensify the conflict, as the commanders had done so far. While Meleager thrived on the division among the Macedonians, Perdiccas's staying in Babylon after the cavalry had left was seen (or could be presented) as an expression of disagreement with those who were resolved to divide the camp. But Meleager's clumsy attempt to get rid of him justified Perdiccas's departure and made him look unfairly treated.

RÉCONCILIATION MANQUÉE

In technical terms, Perdiccas and the cavalry were deserters and rebels. The seat of power and legitimacy was Babylon, the residence of the king with his court and the repository of Alexander's body. Like other deserters and rebels, the cavalry adopted harassment tactics. Taking advantage of their greater mobility, they distressed the infantry and the local population by blocking grain supplies to the city and possibly engaged in pillaging as well. Hunger and fear of food riots and disorder moved the Macedonians in the city to meet and discuss their options. Negotiation and truce were more attractive than fighting the cavalry, who enjoyed a clear advantage on the Babylonian plain, while the infantry had already shown a desire to stop the conflict before it turned too bloody, both in the struggle over Alexander's body and in the aftermath of the attempt to get rid of Perdiccas.

We do not know who called the assembly or moved to send three dele-

---

37. Bosworth 2002, 46.

38. See also Briant 1973b, 249–250. Briant thinks that the assembly flexed its political muscles here, but according to Curtius the meeting was informal and the assembly made no decision. Bauman's suggestion (1990, 152–153) that the assembly was upset with Meleager for bypassing its jurisdiction overrates the Macedonians' legal territorialism.

gates to Perdiccas and the cavalry. They went as the king's envoys, perhaps not just as a matter of protocol but also because they were more Philip's men than Meleager's. They were also all or mostly Greeks.[39] Even if their ethnicity suggests a wish to pick men who were seemingly neutral and without a personal stake in this intra-Macedonian conflict, their dispatch indicates a policy closer to Philip's than to Meleager's. Indeed, the choice of such envoys shows Meleager's failure to consolidate his position through alliances with other Macedonian commanders who were present in court (Curt. 10.8.8) but were unwilling to represent him in the negotiation with Perdiccas. The king, who had blamed Meleager for the Perdiccas affair, could not be counted as his loyal ally either.

Something should be said about the role of Eumenes of Cardia in these events. We have discussed Hieronymus's portrayal of him during later stages of his career, when he commanded Macedonian veterans (chap. 1 above). Before the rift in Babylon, Eumenes served as Alexander's chief secretary and, from 324, as a hipparchy commander.[40] Plutarch claims that Eumenes, as a Greek, maintained neutrality in this Macedonian feud, siding with the cavalry but also staying in Babylon to placate the infantry and work toward reconciliation (Plut. *Eum.* 3). Scholars have questioned this depiction of Eumenes as nonpartisan and as contradicted by Arrian's epitomizer, who describes Eumenes as a cavalry commander (Arr. *Succ.* 1.2). They have argued that Eumenes in fact served as Perdiccas's agent in Babylon.[41] But Eumenes had reason to believe that neutrality would make him attractive to both sides and serve his cause better than joining what could be a losing party. He appears later as Perdiccas's ally, but this need not

---

39. Curt. 10.8.8–15; cf. 10.8.22. For the envoys as Meleager's men: e.g., Rathmann 2005, 33, 49. Curtius names them as Passas of Thessaly, Amissus of Megalopolis, and Perilaus. Bosworth (2002, 47n67) speculates that Perilaus could have been Cassander's brother, but Heckel (2006, 202–203 s.v. *Perilaus* [1]) surmises that he was a Greek. Niese (1893, I:245) and Heckel (2006, 102 s.v. *Damis* [2]) are also in favor of emending the manuscript from "Amissus" to "Damis"; cf. Bosworth (2002, 47n68), who suggests emending "Pasas" to "Pasias." Both Damis (Diod. 18.71.2) and a Perilaus (Diod. 19.64.5–8) were later involved in land operations in the service of Megalopolis and Antigonus, respectively. Schachermeyer (1970, 101–102) thinks that they were members of Eumenes' circle (although Damis later fought Polyperchon, Eumenes' ally), and Anson (2004, 55) that they were Greek mercenary generals.

40. Eumenes under Alexander: Heckel 1992, 346–347; Schäfer 2002, 47–52; Anson 2004, 35–49.

41. Eumenes as Perdiccas's agent: e.g., Schachermeyer 1970, 101–102; Anson 2004, 55–57. Waterfield (2011, 24) goes beyond Plutarch's testimony when he ascribes to Eumenes the authorship of the eventual compromise between the camps.

mean that he played that role consistently. On the present occasion the se-cessionists' leadership was much too crowded, including generals such as Perdiccas, Leonnatus, Ptolemy, Lysimachus, Aristonus, Pithon, and Seleu-cus, while Philip's court may have offered more opportunities.

The fact that the Macedonians in the city asked for a settlement was first interpreted by Perdiccas and his men as a sign of weakness. The marshal, who had seen in Opis how Alexander subdued the veterans after eliminat-ing their leaders, demanded that "the king should surrender the authors of the discord" in return for a cessation of hostilities (Curt. 10.8.15). The ad-dress to the "king" could appeal to Philip and the troops because it sug-gested the cavalry's recognition of his royal status. It also separated Philip from Meleager and his core supporters, relieving him and the masses of re-sponsibility for the conflict and putting the blame on Meleager's group.

The reaction in Babylon, however, was a spontaneous call to arms (Curt. 10.8.16). Perdiccas's message showed that he differed little from Meleager in striving primarily to destroy his rivals, although the phalanx preferred Me-leager, who tied his fate to Philip's. There was also indignation against Per-diccas and the cavalry, who behaved like victors in a contest they had not won, and who rejected the troops' wish for universal appeasement, thus prolonging the phalanx's plight. At the same time, the troops' readiness to fight showed that the infantry's aversion to civil war was not unconditional. It was probably now that those labeled by the cavalry as the authors of the discord demanded and received Philip's personal guarantee of safety (Curt. 10.9.16).

Curtius goes on to report Philip's speech to the troops, which recom-mended calm and reconciliation as opposed to civil war. The king sug-gested sending a second embassy and conducting a funeral for Alexander as a unifying event, and concluded by offering his resignation if it was nec-essary to prevent bloodshed. The assembly urged him to pursue his plan, and Philip sent the same envoys as before with an offer to make Meleager a third general, probably in addition to Perdiccas and Craterus or Leon-natus (Curt. 10.8.15–22). Although there is ample evidence to support the common scholarly view of Philip as a feeble-minded tool in the hands of more powerful generals, it would be wrong to assign him that role under every circumstance.[42] On this occasion, he was attuned to the mood of the troops and indispensable to their purposes. The veterans in Babylon were

---

42. Cf. Sharples 1995, 53–60 (too forceful in trying to rehabilitate the king); Car-ney 2001; *contra*: Meeus 2008, 41–42.

prepared to fight Perdiccas and his men, but they were even more interested in resolving the conflict and retaining their king. The offer to give Meleager high command was appealing, because a division of power between him and Perdiccas was a way to achieve peace. Yet it was the troops' readiness to fight that must have convinced Perdiccas to agree to a compromise.[43]

The compromise called for universal acknowledgment of Arrhidaeus as King Philip III and for making Roxane's future child, if a son, his partner on the throne. It also included the distribution of commands and powers in the empire, placing Perdiccas at the head of the royal army, with Meleager in a similar or slightly inferior rank.[44] The reconciliation scene was carefully staged. Meleager and the infantry came out to meet Perdiccas and the cavalry, with Alexander's body in their midst to give his seal of approval to the new power arrangement and to proclaim Macedonian unity (Curt. 10.8.23; Just. 13.4.2–4). This was Philip's agenda, and it is likely that he both possessed Alexander's body after the fracas in the chamber and now volunteered it for the occasion. But the infantry also got what they wanted, which was reconciliation and recognition of Philip's royal status—both unlikely without their resolute show of power. Some troops might have calculated that Philip had a fair chance of remaining sole king if Roxane's child turned out to be a girl, yet the prospect of shared kingship with a son was also acceptable, because both rulers would be Argeads. Indeed, the troops later acknowledged the baby as Alexander IV. The cavalry who made their cause with Perdiccas should have been mollified as well. Habicht has rightly defined the co-kingship compromise as "ein Novum und eine Anomalie."[45] It also showed that the elite and the masses could unite in discarding the tradition of a single king.

The compromise satisfied the troops but not their commanders, espe-

---

43. Bosworth (2002, 47–49) suggests that Perdiccas orchestrated the entire affair. First, his agents among the infantry (including Eumenes) moved to send the ambassadors to the cavalry. Then the envoys returned with harsh demands for the surrender of the leaders but also with Perdiccas, who attained reconciliation. The king was entirely passive, and his favorable portrayal in Curtius goes back to a pro-Cassandric and pro-Ptolemaic source (yet see 10.9.16, 19; Carney 2001; and above). The reconstruction has a diabolic charm, but the alleged plan was too delicate to succeed.

44. See the variant versions of Just. 13.4.2–6; Diod. 18.2.4; Arr. *Succ.* 1.3; Dexippus *FGrHist* 100 F 8, and the analyses of Bosworth (2002, 49–53) and Meeus (2008, 54–59). The positions of Antipater and Craterus are beyond the scope of the present analysis.

45. Habicht 1973, 376, but see also Carney 1995, 367–376. Only the *Heidelberg Epitome* 1 argues that Philip's kingship was a stopgap measure till Alexander's son came of age.

cially Perdiccas, who now turned to engineering Meleager's removal. What followed is an ugly story of double-crossing by both leaders and troops. According to Curtius, Perdiccas lulled Meleager into a false sense of security, instructing his men to protest against giving Meleager a position equal to Perdiccas's, and then consenting to their arrest to show his support of Meleager. The two then decided to use the ritual of purifying the army—from the pollution either of Alexander's death (Justin) or of the discord (Curtius)—as a public stage for displaying their reconciliation and for punishing those who wished to renew the stasis. The idea must have appealed to Philip because it was akin to his earlier motion to use Alexander's funeral to unify the army.[46]

The ceremony involved dividing a plain with two halves of a bitch and placing the infantry on one side and the cavalry on the other. Such positioning was hardly a show of unity, but it was conducive to Perdiccas's plan. The marshal stood with the king, the cavalry, and the elephants across the field from the infantry and Meleager, but all eyes were on the king, who was in charge of conducting the ritual.[47] The cavalry moved toward the infantry, which (according to Curtius) became suddenly fearful of foul play in light of the recent conflict. They considered retreating to the city, but decided to stay so as not to damage the reputation of their co-combatants for fidelity, remaining ready to fight if necessary (Curt. 10.9.13–15).

The phalanx was probably restrained less by concern for their image than by a wish to avoid a fight, but there could have been an additional reason for their hesitation. According to Curtius, the infantry was seized with fear not when the cavalry began to move forward but only after they had already made their advance (10.9.14). This suggests that the cavalry's advance was expected and even scripted, for otherwise the infantry would have been more concerned and much less hesitant earlier about the horsemen's intentions or about impugning their name. Livy's description of a similar purification ritual involving the Macedonian king and army may be helpful in accounting for their reaction. He reports that after the ritual, the army divided into two sections and conducted a mock battle between them. It is

---

46. Curt. 10.9.11–21, which is preferable to Just. 13.4.7–8, whose condensed and at times inaccurate version makes no mention of the king's participation. See Atkinson 2000, 322–324, for Curtius's highlighting of Perdiccas's deceit here. For the time separating this episode from the earlier reconciliation: Bosworth 2002, 55.

47. Some in the audience had already seen Philip participating in sacrifices and rituals under Alexander: Curt. 10.7.2; Greenwalt 1984, 77; but see also Bosworth 1992b, 77–78.

possible, then, that the phalanx decided to wait in spite of their suspicion, because they expected the cavalry to join them in a sham battle.[48] The infantrymen soon found out, however, that they had been betrayed by their king. At Perdiccas's behest, Philip reiterated the general's earlier demand for the surrender and punishment of those responsible for the conflict, even though he had guaranteed their safety. Philip also threatened to use the cavalry and the elephants if the infantry rejected his request. This may have been an expression of the king's feebleness, his political realism, or (with no less likelihood) his wish for unity. In any case, he took both Meleager and the infantry by surprise.

Since the cavalry and elephants stood close by and had an advantage on the plain, the phalanx could do little but remain immobile. Their leader, Meleager, proved useless when he failed to find a way out of the showdown, and the king's switching sides meant that he was no longer dependent on the infantry and that legitimacy moved to Perdiccas's side. Many troops must have felt despondent, confused, and betrayed. At the same time, the royal demand to surrender the instigators was also a call for inaction, because it freed most of the troops from punishment. The infantry had learnt this lesson in Opis, where Alexander had settled for punishing their leaders. This explains the "general approval" of Perdiccas's choice of Meleager's core supporters as culprits (Just. 13.4.8). As the king stood aloof, Perdiccas threw them to the elephants to be trampled to death. Curtius says that those taken for execution numbered three hundred, but Diodorus's figure of thirty is likelier, both because it better fits Arrian's description of them as the most conspicuous of the rioters and because Perdiccas would have found it hard to identify 300 men who went with Meleager to plunder the treasury (Curt. 10.6.24, 9.18). In any case, it was a horrifically brutal scene, with neither Meleager nor the troops lifting a finger to defend those who had acted on their behalf.[49]

Meleager was murdered shortly thereafter.[50] It should be said in his favor that his leadership faced a greater challenge than Perdiccas's, since it was easier for the elite and the cavalry to communicate with each other

48. Livy 40.6. See also Plut. *Alex.* 30; cf. Plb. 23.10.17; Pritchett 1979–1991, 3:196–199, 201–202; Martin 1987, 174.

49. Curt. 10.9.18; Just. 13.4.8; Arr. *Succ.* 1.4; Diod. 18.4.7.

50. Curt. 10.9. 19–21, Arr. *Succ.* 1.4–5, and Diod. 18.4.7 all place Meleager's death in different times. Shortly after the ritual makes the best sense; see Meeus 2008, 58–59. For the possibility that Meleager was executed following a trial: Diod. 18.4.7; Briant 1973b, 253–254; Hatzopoulos 1996, 1:281–282, 301.

and to take common action than it was for the more numerous and hetero-geneous masses. Indeed, the king and Perdiccas could not have effectively threatened the infantry on the plain unless the entire cavalry (and the el-ephant force) had been privy to the scheme and acted in concert. Another impediment to Meleager's leadership was its basis in camp disunity, which meant that it could rely on the troops' support only as long as they were in a pugnacious mood. Fundamental to his failure were his weakness and in-effectiveness as a leader, which our awareness of the sources' bias against him must not obscure. Alexander, who never gave him an important high command, had already seen that he was not the peer of his other lieuten-ants. Meleager died alone after losing Philip, his main asset, to Perdiccas and after leaving his close supporters in the lurch, allowing the soldiers to see that he could not be relied on. His death left a leadership vacuum, which Perdiccas hoped to fill by endearing himself to the army.

DECISION BY VOTE AND BY THE SPEAR

Once Perdiccas had consolidated his power, he and his fellow generals turned to distributing military commands and provinces amongst them-selves.[51] The distribution directly affected the veterans, who now received new commanders or new assignments, and their lack of influence on either choice was a sign that things had returned to normal.[52] Their passive role ostensibly changed when Perdiccas presented Alexander's future plans to the army for approval, or more accurately, for disapproval.

According to Diodorus, Perdiccas found in Alexander's memoranda plans for projects that Perdiccas deemed too expensive and unprofitable. Concerned that he might be seen as detracting from Alexander's glory, Per-diccas brought them before the Macedonian assembly. Diodorus, who em-phasizes the costliness of the plans, says that they included (unspecified) in-structions to Craterus, who was then with 11,500 veterans in Cilicia, as well as the following projects: the completion of Hephaestion's pyre (or tomb); the building of a huge navy for a campaign in the western Mediterranean, along with coastal roads and ports on the way there; the erection of six tem-ples in various places; the founding of cities in Europe and Asia, accompa-

---

51. I follow here Diodorus's order of events (18.3.1–4); see Errington 1970, 57n59; Bosworth 2002, 57–60. Badian (1968, 202n62) dates the distribution of the satrapies before the rejection of Alexander's plans, but see Meeus 2008, 77.

52. Diod. 18.3.1; *Heidelberg Epitome* 1.2; cf. Plut. *Eum.* 3.3; *pace* Billows 1990, 54.

nied by a population exchange between the continents and encouragement of unity through intermarriages; and the building of a pyramid-style tomb for Alexander's father. The Macedonians rejected the plans.[53]

In debating Alexander's last plans, scholars have focused mostly on their authenticity and on Perdiccas's motives for opposing them. I agree with those who regard the plans as largely authentic, but my focus on the veterans makes me interested primarily in their role in the affair.[54] I shall note only the problems with the claim that Perdiccas might even have misrepresented the plans to the assembly in order to prevent an ambitious colleague, especially Craterus, from claiming supremacy by calling for their realization.[55] If the plans were wholly or partly doctored to make them unappealing, Craterus could have protested that the army was deceived, and might have gained ground by advocating the "real" projects. If the plans were authentic, on the other hand, they could not have served Craterus or any other leader in garnering popular support, because the army did not care for them. Finally, it would have been too optimistic to expect Craterus to abide by the army's decision to shelve the plans if had he disapproved of it (which, I suspect, he did not). As Perdiccas and other generals knew well, Craterus never followed Alexander's instructions to go to Macedonia and replace Antipater there, and he had 11,500 Macedonians to back him up.[56]

There is merit in Diodorus's suggestion that Perdiccas presented the plans to the troops so as not to detract from Alexander's glory, but Perdiccas probably had additional reasons to get them involved. After the settlement of Alexander's succession and the distribution of commands, there remained one central issue to resolve: the future of the campaign and the empire. The expected and legitimate course was to seek guidance from Alexander, some of whose plans, especially for the western campaign, were not new or unknown.[57] It was the elite who made such a preference inevitable. From the beginning of the debate over Alexander's succession, speakers repeatedly invoked and manipulated his memory in order to justify their positions, either by using his regalia and body or by asserting what the dead king would have wanted. The cumulative effect was to make Alexander and

53. Diod. 18.4.1–6; cf. Arr. *Anab.* 4.7.5, 15.6; 5.26.2; 7.1.2–4; Plut. *Alex.* 68.1; Curt. 10.1.17–19.

54. Tarn (1948, 2:378–398) denies most of the plans' historicity, but see, e.g., Schachermeyr 1954; Bosworth 1988b, 185–211.

55. Thus, among others, Badian 1968, 200–204; Errington 1970, 59; Bosworth 2002, 59–60, 63; but see also Rathmann 2005, 26–32.

56. See, however, Bosworth 1988b, 210–211; 2002, 52–53.

57. For the history of the idea of a western campaign, see Bosworth 1988b, 191, and for the following: Bosworth 2002, 59–60, 63.

his legacy a living presence. It did not mean that the army and its generals were bound by his vision and plans, only that they could not ignore them. Moreover, after the recent discord with the infantry, Perdiccas could not discard the plans solely on the strength of the elite's opinion or his own. By presenting them to the army, he gained credit for including the troops in the decision process. At the same time, the discussion in the assembly made the troops, no less than the elite, the guardians of Alexander's memory and legacy.

Diodorus's reasoning that both Perdiccas and the troops considered the plans too expensive, impractical, excessive, and unattainable sufficiently accounts for their decision to reject them (Diod. 18.4.2, 6). Perdiccas may even have helped the army reach this conclusion. The same probably held true for Alexander's projected Arabian campaign, which is not mentioned in this context, but which must also have appealed to no one.[58] Yet the scholarly view that the troops rejected the plans because they were more preoccupied with immediate concerns than with long-term wishes unjustly denies them both the motivation and the ability to think on behalf of the good for the kingdom, beyond their basic needs.[59] The result, in any case, was that Perdiccas, the other generals, and the troops agreed to disregard the dead king's wishes, even though "they praised him." It was a break with the past, with grand imperialistic ambitions, with monumental projects— in short, with everything Alexander represented. Fittingly, this decision followed the one about conveying Alexander's body to its final rest.

Scholars have described the assembly that voted against the plans as the first decision-making assembly in Macedonian history and ascribed to the army a new sense of its own authority.[60] But the sources indicate that the troops played only a passive role in the affair. Unlike their active involvement in the dispute over Alexander's heir, their stance here involved no initiative and expressed no independent opinion. Instead, it resulted from Perdiccas's invitation to adopt the resolution he favored. Perdiccas's task was hardly challenging, because it was easy to get the masses to agree on what they did not want and because the troops and their assembly grew powerful and defiant only when the elite was divided. In this case, Perdiccas, the generals, and presumably the cavalry were of one mind in their opposition to the plans (Diod. 18.4.1). Therefore there was nothing in this

---

58. For Alexander's Arabian campaign and plans, see Högemann 1985; Potts 1991, 2:1–10.

59. Errington 1976, 139; cf. Austin 1986, 464–465. For the troops' reasoning see also Badian 1968, 200–201.

60. Anson 1991, 237–238.

assembly that the veterans could regard as a milestone or as a precedent-setting exercise of constitutional power. As always, the powers of the Macedonian armed assembly fluctuated with the circumstances rather than evolving over time.

If the Macedonian veterans learned anything in Babylon, it was that they could influence the course of events not by popular decrees but by the power of their spears. This became apparent in a campaign designed to put down a revolt in the upper satrapies toward the end of 323. The Greek soldiers left by Alexander in the upper satrapies rebelled once more against the central government and mobilized a force of 20,000 infantry and 3,000 cavalry. Perdiccas sent against them Pithon, the son of Crateuas and one of Alexander's bodyguards, with 3,000 infantry and 800 cavalry selected by lot from the Macedonians. He also gave him letters for the Asian satraps, instructing them to add 10,000 infantry and 8,000 cavalrymen to Pithon's force. Diodorus, probably following Hieronymus, attributes to Pithon the trademarks of Alexander's veteran marshals—skilled generalship, energy, and great ambitions—as well as a hidden personal agenda, saying that Pithon planned to draw the rebels to his side and then to use the enlarged army to rule over the upper satrapies.[61] But Perdiccas suspected Pithon's intentions and told him to kill all rebels and divide their possessions among the troops.

Next came a double breach of faith. Before clashing with the rebels, Pithon bribed a commander of 3,000 of them to withdraw from the battle. The desertion contributed to his victory, which he followed by promising the rebels a safe return to their satrapies in accordance with his plan. Assured of their safety, the unarmed Greeks mingled with the Macedonians, who remembered Perdiccas's instructions and killed the rebels by surprise and plundered their property, in violation of the oaths given to them. Disappointed, Pithon returned with his army to Perdiccas (Diod. 18.7.1–9).

Diodorus's account has its share of problems.[62] It is unclear why Perdiccas would entrust Pithon with such a large force if he suspected him of plotting to take over a great chunk of the empire. In addition, since Pithon's plan was unlikely to remain secret after the affair, one wonders how he jus-

61. The revolt: Diod. 17.99.6; 18.4.8, 7.1–9; Trogus *Prologue* 13; Babylonian Astronomical Diaries in Del Monte 1997, no. 12. For the date, see Del Monte, ibid.; Walsh 2009, 75–82. Neither Diodorus's language in 18.7.3 nor the Babylonian evidence well accommodates Bosworth's suggestion that Pithon was in Media when he got his command: 2002, 61–62nn119–120. Pithon: Diod. 18.7.3; cf. 18.36.5.

62. For the following see also Anson 2004, 239–240, and Rathmann 2005, 54–56, some of whose conclusions I share independently.

tified it to Perdiccas upon his return, or why he appears never to have been punished for his alleged treason. I would suggest that Hieronymus's search for an ulterior motive, fortified by Pithon's later rivalry with his patron, Eumenes, moved the historian to credit Pithon with anachronistic intentions (attested about seven years later) of taking over the upper satrapies (Diod. 19.46.1–4; cf. 19.14.1–2). This description of Pithon and his dealings with Perdiccas also conveniently encapsulates much of the subsequent history of the Diadochs, which features powerful, distrustful individuals, frustrated ambitions, undisciplined armies, and treason on both sides.

An examination of the actions instead of the supposed designs behind them, however, shows that Pithon did not ask to go on this mission but was chosen for it by Perdiccas, surely because Perdiccas trusted him and his military skills, not because he suspected him. Indeed, as the satrap of Media, Pithon was directly affected by the rebellion. His return to Perdiccas with the army similarly suggests that he had intended to do so all along instead of planning to carve out an empire for himself in the upper satrapies.[63]

After defeating the Greeks, Pithon opted for a peaceful solution that served both sides. Sending the Greeks back was a small cost for the revolt, and Pithon was able to restore order and return the colonists to the satrapies instead of losing them or having to contest a second battle with their comrades, who had been trained in hard fighting under Alexander (cf. Diod. 18.9.3). There is no reason to think that Perdiccas would have opposed Pithon's agreement with the rebels or been averse to a different way of compensating his troops. Bloodthirsty as Perdiccas may have been, even he would have found it excessive to eliminate an enemy force that originally included around 23,000 troops, and he knew that it would not be easy to replenish the satrapies with new settlers.[64]

It was the Macedonians who spoiled this sensible arrangement. Perdiccas had arranged to give them the enemy's possessions, not in order to spoil Pithon's plan, but to motivate the troops to go to war, to make himself pop-

---

63. See Anson 2004, 240n27, against the claim that Pithon got his command from the army assembly. Billows (2000, 300–301) argues that in the distribution of commands before the campaign, Perdiccas reduced Pithon's satrapy of Media by giving part of it to Atropates, Perdiccas's father-in-law. If there were hard feelings, however, they should have been on the part of Atropates, who had lost to Pithon much of the satrapy that Alexander had given him; cf. Berve 1926, 2:92n180; Heckel 2006, 61.

64. Eliminating all Greeks in camp: Diod. 19.7.9. Their number included more than 23,000 soldiers, minus those who died or fled the battle and possibly the 3,000 deserters. Schober (1981, 35–36) and Holt (1988, 88–90) argue for fewer Greek casualties, but the dead must still have numbered in the thousands. See also Anson 2004, 239–240 with n26.

ular with the army, and especially to seize upon the most cost-effective way of compensating them for their service. We do not know what Pithon offered the troops in return, but clearly it did not match Perdiccas's original offer. Feeling cheated of their reward, the Macedonians took matters into their own hands, just as they had done in Babylon.

Diodorus depicts them as breakers of the oaths and trust that stood between them and the booty,[65] yet their action was telling for other reasons. First, it took leadership, planning, and organization to surprise, kill, and rob so many men simultaneously, even if they were unarmed. Clearly the infantry, presumably the cavalry, and their immediate commanders could cooperate harmoniously after all, at least in slaughtering and plundering. Furthermore, in a sign of things to come, the Macedonians dominated the mixed army. There were only 3,800 of them in an army of 21,800 men, but they decided the outcome of the campaign, and even though they broke an agreement reached by their general, they were not punished for it. Perdiccas's original order may have served to legitimize both their insubordination and Pithon's lack of power and will to discipline them.[66] Finally, though the campaign culminated in the Macedonians' killing of Greeks, this was not a case of ethnic animosity. The Greeks suffered because they lost, because they were defenseless, and because they had what the troops wanted. Local communities in Asia Minor and elsewhere that were treated similarly by the Macedonians, and for the same reasons, could attest that the veterans did not discriminate among victims on the basis of their ethnicity.[67] Conversely, ethnic solidarity did not prevent the Macedonians from almost killing each other in Babylon, and they would soon fight their former comrades when they served in opposite armies. All in all, the veterans would have seen Pithon's campaign as short, profitable, and fought for a worthy cause. Some of them must have been looking forward eagerly to the future.

---

65. Diod. 18.7.8. The description bears some resemblance to his account of Alexander's treacherous massacre of Indian mercenaries under truce in 327: Diod. 17.84.1–6; cf. Plut. Alex. 59.3–4.

66. Heckel (1992, 154) suggests that Perdiccas may have been blamed for the Macedonians' conduct. But Briant (1973a, 62–63 = 1982, 74–75; 1973b, 166–167n9), followed by Will (1984, 25), thinks that the Macedonians behaved as they did because they wished to go home, not to the upper satrapies. Neither wish is mentioned in the sources.

67. For the Macedonians' anti-Greek animosity here, see Launey 1949–1950, 1:294; Fraser 1996, 193–195. For massacres under Alexander see Bosworth 2000a, 38–39, 48–49; Holt 2005, 117. For treatment of locals in Asia Minor, see chaps. 4 and 5 below.

CHAPTER 4

THE DISSOLUTION OF THE ROYAL ARMY, I:
THE VETERANS OF PERDICCAS AND CRATERUS

At the time of Alexander's death, the two largest concentrations of veterans were in the royal army in Babylon and with Craterus in Asia Minor. Soon the Macedonian core of the royal army would shrink. Every general who left Babylon for his satrapy must have wanted to take with him at least a Macedonian guard unit and, if he could get it, a piece of the phalanx. The number of veterans each took depended on Perdiccas and on the deals made with him, about which we know nothing. But we do hear of Macedonians who fought under different commanders in the ensuing years. This chapter and the next track their paths—sometimes divergent, sometimes intersecting—as they followed their generals' ambitions and fortunes. The resulting history of the period is fragmentary, like the soldiers' knowledge of it.

PERDICCAS'S VETERANS

As the commander of the royal army, Perdiccas probably had more Macedonian veterans than any other commander except Craterus. Their number accounts for the relatively prominent role they played in his campaigns.

The first attested campaign led by Perdiccas was in 322, against Ariarathes, the local ruler of Cappadocia in eastern Asia Minor. Ariarathes, who managed to survive Alexander's conquest with his dominion relatively intact, succeeded also in preventing Eumenes of Cardia from taking over Cappadocia as his province. Failing to obtain help from neighboring satraps, who had other plans for their troops, Eumenes went back to Perdiccas. Needing all the loyal governors he could get, the regent resolved to help Eumenes, and this is why Perdiccas, the royal court, and the royal army with its Macedonian veterans found themselves in Cappadocia in the summer of 322.[1]

Ariarathes' wealth reportedly allowed him to muster a local and mercenary force of 30,000 infantry and 15,000 cavalry. Nevertheless, Perdiccas won the battle, his first military victory since Alexander's death, killing 4,000 enemy troops and capturing more than 5,000. According to one version, the captured Ariarathes was first tortured and then crucified.

After securing Cappadocia for Eumenes, Perdiccas launched a punitive expedition into Pisidia against two cities that had killed the local strap, Balacrus, during Alexander's reign. Perdiccas took the first Pisidian city, that of the Larandians, by storm, killed all men of fighting age, enslaved the rest, and left the city in ruins. This harsh punishment suggests that he was treating them as rebels, just as he had dealt with Ariarathes.[2] His actions moved the second Pisidian city—of the Isaurians—to fight him to the bitter end. For two days the locals successfully withstood the attacks of the royal army and inflicted many losses on it. But they also suffered many casualties and resolved to deprive the enemy of the fruits of victory by setting their houses on fire and destroying their families, slaves, and goods. We are told that Perdiccas was astonished at their conduct and ordered the soldiers to break into the city. The defenders kept fighting and killed many Macedonians, forcing the yet-more-wonderstruck Perdiccas to call the Macedonians off. At last the Isaurians threw themselves into the flames. When the invaders entered the city in the morning, they extinguished the fires and, with Perdiccas's permission to plunder, found much gold and silver.

This account of Diodorus's, which likely follows Hieronymus, highlights the Isaurians' display of such Hellenic ideals as valiant courage, heroic sacrifice in the name of liberty, and refusal to allow the enemy to decide one's fate.[3] Perdiccas, whose treatment of the Larandians was partly responsible for the Isaurians' opposition, is depicted as both cruel and unable to com-

---

1. For Eumenes' mission, see chap. 5 below. Perdiccas's campaigns in Asia Minor: Diod. 18.16.1–3, 22.1–8; 31.19.4; Just. 13.6.1–3; Plut. *Eum.* 3.3, 12–14; Arr. *Succ.* 1.11 (uniquely reports two battles against the Cappadocians); Appian *Mithridatic Wars* 8 = Hieronymus *FGrHist* 154 F 3; *FGrHist* 154 F 4; Briant 1982, 15–17; Heckel 1992, 155–156. Ariarathes' career and policy: Hornblower 1981, 214–243; Anson 1988a; Briant 2002, 743, 1024–1025.

2. Ariarathes' fate: Diod. 18.6.3; cf. Arr. *Succ.* 1.11; Plut. *Eum.* 3.13, although elsewhere Diodorus says that he fell in battle: 31.19.4.

3. Diod. 18.22.1–8; cf. Just. 13.6.1–3 (who confuses and combines the Pisidian and the Cappadocian campaigns). See also chap. 1 above.

prehend their noble conduct. As is often the case, we hear nothing of the Macedonians' sentiments.

But those sentiments can be reasonably reconstructed. In spite of initial setbacks and losses, the siege of the Isaurian city lasted only three days and ended in its capture. Like their commander, the soldiers preferred the short, triumphant campaigns on which they prided themselves. Though Perdiccas was brutal in victory, the Macedonians had every reason to be pleased with a general who had led them to three consecutive victories in Cappadocia and Pisidia.[4] Furthermore, the sources do not make it clear if the Macedonians profited in any meaningful way from their victories over the wealthy Ariarathes and the Larandians in Pisidia. Diodorus mentions the capture of 5,000 Cappadocian troops and the mass enslavement of noncombatant Larandians, but he also says that Perdiccas gave the defeated Cappadocians back their security, implying that he set limits on the Macedonians' profits.[5] It was apparently with the intention of using the Isaurian city to compensate the troops more substantially that Perdiccas ordered his army to attack it when he saw the defenders setting their goods and families on fire. Indeed, if (as was likely) Pithon had joined Perdiccas in Pisidia with an army laden with booty from the campaign against the Greek settlers, Perdiccas may have felt a need to reward his own troops on a similar scale.[6]

Finally, the war that the Macedonians waged was just. The Cappadocian king and the Pisidian cities had been regarded as rebels against the throne since Alexander's time, and the presence of King Philip in camp legitimized the campaign. The troops, then, had every reason to be satisfied with their general and the war. They had fought to secure the empire and were generously rewarded for their service.

We are ill informed about the history of Perdiccas's royal army until its invasion of Egypt in the spring of 321. The sources indicate that it marched from Pisidia to Cilicia, and then back to Pisidia and Cappadocia, probably in order to stabilize Macedonian rule in these territories.[7] The sources also report on Perdiccas's matrimonial schemes, which revolved around marry-

---

4. Cf. Briant 1973b, 259.

5. Diod. 18.16.2–3, 22.1–2. For mass enslavement, see generally, Austin 1986, 457–466; Pritchett 1971–1991, 5:223–245; Volkmann 1990, esp. 61–64, 110–119; Ducrey 1999, esp. 74–92, 131–140.

6. Pithon's campaign: chap. 3 above. His joining Perdiccas: cf. Bosworth 2002, 62n121. For the policy of distributing booty in late Hellenistic Macedonia: Juhel 2002, and more generally, Chaniotis 2005, 129–137.

7. Plut. *Eum.* 4.1; Diod. 18.25.6; Just. 13.6.10; Bosworth 1978, 232.

ing Antipater's daughter, Nicaea, and simultaneously courting Alexander's sister, Cleopatra. The Macedonian veterans were at best passive spectators of these intrigues.[8] Perdiccas may have intended a more active role for his soldiers in his planned trial of the governor Antigonus, possibly in the army assembly. But Antigonus's escape to Greece frustrated his plan.[9]

Sometime earlier, the Macedonian veterans spoiled another of Perdiccas's schemes, this one involving Alexander's half-sister, Cynane. Cynane was Philip's II daughter from his Illyrian wife, Audata-Eurydice. She was also the mother of Adea and the widow of Amyntas, Philip's II nephew, killed by Alexander on the eve of the Asian campaign. After Alexander's death, the women of his house scrambled to preserve their prominence by trying to attach themselves to powerful generals. Cynane, who did not rank as highly as Alexander's mother, Olympias, or his sister, Cleopatra, set her sights on the less-powerful King Philip III as a prospective husband for her daughter Adea. Cynane was a formidable woman who, in good Illyrian fashion, led men to battle, claimed credit for military victories, and trained her daughter in the arts of war.[10] When Cynane left Macedonia for Perdiccas's camp, Antipater tried to stop her, but she overcame his opposition and continued on her way to Asia, presumably with a Macedonian retinue.

Like Antipater, Perdiccas would have much preferred for Cynane and her daughter to stay at home. As his relations with Antigonus, Antipater, and Craterus grew more tense and the loyalty of his governors became uncertain, he did not need a queen and a queen mother competing with him over the control of the king and the army. After all, Philip was the Macedonian veterans' choice, and if Perdiccas were to go to war against other Macedonian generals or over Macedonia, he needed Philip's full coopera-

---

8. For Perdiccas's marriage plans, see, conveniently, Carney 1988, 398–400; Meeus 2009b, 73–80.

9. Diod. 18.23.4; Arr. *Succ.* 1.20. "Arrian" uses the term *dikastērion* for the court, which could equally mean the assembly or the regent's council. Cf. Wilson, who advises caution in accepting Photius's summaries of nonextant works (1994, 5). See Briant 1973b, 153–157 (arguing for a trial in council); Engel 1978, 5–10; Hatzopoulos 1996, 1:281 (assembly's trial). Just. 13.6.8 uniquely reports on a war between Perdiccas and Antigonus before Perdiccas went to Egypt, but this likely refers to the quarrel that led to Antigonus's flight to Antipater and Craterus.

10. For Cynane and the following episode, see esp. Polyaenus 8.60; Arr. *Succ.* 1.22–24; Diod. 19.52.5; Heckel 1983–1984 (arguing for Duris as the source for her story); Carney 1987, 498; 2000b, 69–70, 129–131; 2004, 184–185. I find no evidence for Bennett and Roberts's claim (2008, 24) that Adea had been designated as Philip's wife years earlier.

tion and legitimacy along with the troops' loyalty. There was also a danger that a male child born to these two Argead royals would seriously threaten the claim of Roxane's son (who was Perdiccas's protégé) to the throne.[11]

The sources are not very clear about what happened next, but it appears that Perdiccas and his brother Alcetas characteristically tried all options before finding the right one. According to Polyaenus 8.60, the most detailed source for the affair, Alcetas was the point man in dealing with the problem. He met Cynane with his Macedonian troops, an act which proved a mistake because it enabled Cynane to use her impressive appearance and Argead credentials to shame them into inaction and perhaps defiance. She may also have claimed that she came to save the royal line, perhaps even from Perdiccas (cf. Polyaenus 8.60). Instead of resorting to negotiation, Alcetas killed her, possibly in battle. Her daughter, Adea, was spared, likely by the intervention of the Macedonians, who would not be placated until Perdiccas arranged for her to marry Philip Arrhidaeus. Adea then took the reginal name Eurydice, which strengthened her legitimacy and the continuity of the royal house.[12]

The Macedonians reacted as they did because they saw themselves as loyal followers and protectors of the Argead royal house. Yet these sentiments cannot be separated from another powerful motive that has been observed in their previous protests: their sensitivity to injustice. The veterans were probably ignorant of Perdiccas's and Cynane's ulterior motives, or indifferent to them. But Cynane's wish to join the army and marry her daughter to her half-brother Philip appeared to them both legitimate and desirable, because it fitted the pattern of royal marriages and strengthened the dynastic character of their court by creating a tightly knit Macedonian royal house. In addition, the martial Cynane must have appealed strongly to the soldiers, as did the prospect of the feasting and banqueting occasioned by royal weddings. (The veterans could recall Alexander's mass marriage of soldiers at Susa, and some even the festivities attending the marriage of his sister Cleopatra to Alexander of Epirus in 338.)[13] For all of these

---

11. See also Carney 2000b, 130; Rathmann 2005, 65–66.

12. Cassander would later honor Cynane with a royal burial: Athen. 4.155a. Errington (2008, 19) makes the attractive suggestion that Adea incited the troops after Cynane's death. Badian (1982a) denies, however, that Eurydice was a dynastic name. For the following, cf. Errington 1970, 64; 1976, 146. Briant's (1973b, 260–263) and Bauman's (1990, 154–155) reconstructions of the episode far exceed the evidence.

13. Feasting in Susa: Plut. Alex. 70; and in Aegae: Diod. 16.91.5; cf. Carney 2000, 205–206.

reasons, the Macedonian troops would have felt it wrong to refuse her request, and even more so to kill her solely in order to serve the general's personal goals, especially in a way that raised concerns about the security of the royal house. As at Babylon, the veterans united in opposition to the generals' wrongdoing and around the future of the royal house and their king.

The troops' protest forced Perdiccas to yield in the matter of Philip's marriage, but because Alcetas was held chiefly responsible for Cynane's death, the damage to Perdiccas's authority was limited.[14] Nevertheless, the episode suggests that the veterans of the royal army had greater power to bend their leader to their will than did the soldiers in other satrapal armies. It is not surprising that Antipater dispersed many of the royal veterans a few months later in Triparadeisus, and then separated the rest from the kings, whom he took with him back to Macedonia.

In 321 Perdiccas lost an important asset in the form of Alexander's body. Until early that year, Alexander's body was kept in Babylon under the supervision of the Macedonian general Arrhidaeus (not to be confused with King Philip III), who watched over the building of the elaborate funeral carriage. There are conflicting traditions about where Alexander was supposed to be buried, and I agree with the view that, in spite of his desire to be buried in Libyan Siwa and an apparent agreement among the generals in Babylon to honor his wish, Perdiccas planned to bury him at Aegae in Macedonia. But Perdiccas's confidants Attalus and Polemon failed to prevent Arrhidaeus from handing the body over to Ptolemy, who took it to be buried at Memphis in Egypt (later the body was moved to Alexandria).[15] Perdiccas and Ptolemy competed over the royal corpse primarily because possessing and burying it enhanced the reputation and authority of the man who had it. In short, it legitimized his position, and might even indicate his ambition to inherit the dead man's power.[16]

At some time between the murder of Cynane and Perdiccas's invasion of Egypt, the regent sent the Macedonian Docimus with an armed force to

---

14. *Pace* Briant 1973b, 177–181, who ties Perdiccas's demise to Cynane's murder. It could be significant that Adea/Eurydice turned troublemaker only after Perdiccas's death and that she cooperated with his brother-in-law in Triparadeisus (chap. 5). Alcetas's responsibility: Diod. 19.52.5.

15. The main sources for the affair are Diod. 18.26.1–28.6; Paus. 1.6.3; Strabo 17.1.8; Arr. *Succ.* 1.24.1, 25; Ps. Callisthenes 3.3.4; *Liber de morte* 119. See also Badian 1968, 185–188; Stewart 1993, esp. 221–223, 369–375; Errington 2008, 15–16; Erskine 2002, 170–171; Landucci Gattinoni 2008, 129–139.

16. Meeus 2008, 67–68 with n134, 70; 2009a, 242–243. The talismanic power of the body and tomb should not be discounted: Aelian *VH* 12.65.

replace the satrap of Babylon, Archon. Docimus accomplished the mission after a battle with Archon, who died of a wound. If the garrison that Alexander had left in Babylon in 330 still included its 700 original Macedonian troops (this is uncertain), the battle may have involved veterans fighting on both sides.[17]

In 320, Perdiccas faced a momentous decision: should he march west against Craterus and Antipater on his way to take over Macedonia or turn south to fight Ptolemy over Egypt and the body of Alexander, now in Ptolemy's hands? Diodorus and Justin report that when Perdiccas called his friends and generals to a meeting to discuss the question, they recommended going to Egypt.[18] We can be certain that the Macedonian veterans were not asked for their opinion, but their reaction to the news probably entered the council's considerations. The veterans were unlikely to favor a war against any of these generals, but they probably preferred an Egyptian campaign because of the much smaller number of Macedonians in Ptolemy's army. Diodorus, the most detailed source for Ptolemy's army at this point, mentions that Ptolemy had mercenaries, "many friends," garrisons and unspecified others, none of whom can be readily identified as rank-and-file Macedonians. He may have left Babylon for Egypt with a group of Macedonians, though they were clearly fewer than the many more veterans and compatriots in Craterus and Antipater's army.[19]

Avoiding Macedonian fratricide was both insufficient and improper as an official reason for fighting Ptolemy. Equally deficient in legitimacy were the causes that the sources, rightly or wrongly, suggest for the Egyptian

---

17. Docimus's mission: Arr. *Succ.* 1.24.3–5. Alexander's garrison in Babylon: Diod. 17.64.5; Curt. 5.1.43; cf. Arr. *Anab.* 3.16.4.

18. Diod. 18.25.6; Just. 13.6.10–13. Arr. *Succ.* 1.24.1 states that Ptolemy's seizure of Alexander' body in 321 only strengthened Perdiccas's resolve to go against the satrap, but this does not negate his reexamining the question later.

19. Ptolemy's army: Diod. 18.14.1, 21.7, 28.5, 33.3–4. His (relatively small) Macedonian contingent in the Battle of Gaza in 312 was very likely a later acquisition: Diod. 19.80.4. See also Hammond 1996, 106–108, although he does not substantiate his claim that Ptolemy took from Babylon to Egypt a detachment of *epigoni* and later 1,000 Macedonian guards who accompanied Alexander's body. Bosworth (2002, 82n59) thinks that Ptolemy had no veterans. In 331, Alexander left behind in Egypt 4,000 soldiers (probably mercenaries) and 30 triremes: Arr. 3.5.3–6; Curt. 4.8.4, but, *pace* Seibert (1969, 64–65), there is no telling how many of them remained there in 320. See also note 59 below. The number of Macedonians in Perdiccas's invading army has been estimated between over 9,000 (Billows 1995, 192) to ca. 5,000 (Bosworth 2002, 84–85), and in Craterus and Antipater's army between 25,000 (Billows 1995, 194) and 15,000–20,000 (Bosworth 2002, 85).

campaign, such as Perdiccas's wish to clear the way before going to fight over Macedonia, his and Ptolemy's fear of each other's power, their personal ambitions, and Perdiccas's wish to remove Ptolemy from office and regain Alexander's body.[20] Of all these goals only repossessing Alexander's body could dissociate the campaign from Perdiccas's personal agenda, but how much did it impress the Macedonian veterans? Undoubtedly, Perdiccas's plan to bring the corpse to Macedonia appealed to them both because it restored Alexander's Macedonian identity, which the king had increasingly blurred since his occupation of Egypt, and because it meant that they would return home with the body. Beyond that, holding the body did not necessarily translate into meaningful popular support or serve as a magnet for Macedonian troops. According to Diodorus, people were attracted to Ptolemy and willing to take risks for him because of his admirable character (one of the traits of his monarchy), which he demonstrated by paying respect to the dead king.[21]

The fact is that the sources largely ignore how Perdiccas justified the war to the troops, probably because these sources adopt the generals' perspective rather than that of soldiers, for whom the war required moral or ideological justification. The commonest charge against Alexander's former generals at this time was that they aspired to be king of the Macedonians. In 322 Eumenes told Perdiccas that Leonnatus, the satrap of Hellespontine Phrygia, was invited by Alexander's sister, Cleopatra, to come to Pella and marry her and that Leonnatus intended to lay claim to Macedonia; later that year Antigonus impressed upon Antipater and Craterus that Perdiccas had royal ambitions.[22] At the least, such ambitions meant going up against the reigning heirs of Alexander (Philip III and Alexander IV), and it would not have

---

20. See respectively, Diod. 18.25.6; Strabo 17.1.8; Paus. 1.6.3 (adding that Ptolemy killed Egypt's former governor and Perdiccas's friend Cleomenes); Arr. *Succ.* 1.24.1. Replacing Ptolemy fitted the pattern of Perdiccas's replacing Antigonus (above) and the satraps of Cilicia (Arr. *Succ.* 1.24.2) and Babylonia (above).

21. Diod. 18.28.4–6. Ptolemy and Alexander: e.g., Bosworth 2000b. See, however, Bingen 2007, 18–24, and Lianou 2010, esp. 127–128, for Ptolemy's use of the body for domestic purposes. Diodorus undoubtedly added something of his own to his sources' praises of Ptolemy: cf. Hornblower 1981, esp. 55–56; Green 2006, 7, 38, 241.

22. Leonnatus: Plut. *Eum.* 3.8–10; Sprawski 2008, 12–14. Perdiccas's ambitions: Diod. 18.23.1–3, 25.3; cf. Arr. *Succ.* 1.24, 26. Cleopatra as a means for attaining rule over the Macedonians and the empire: Diod. 20.37.4; Nepos *Eum.* 2.3–4; Meeus 2009b. Craterus too is said to have dressed like Alexander except for the diadem: Suda s.v. *Craterus* (K 2335 Adler). Even Antipater was allegedly suspected by Alexander of having royal ambitions: Curt. 10.10.14.

been difficult for Perdiccas to make similar allegations against Ptolemy. In expanding his domain to Cyrenaeca and his influence to Cyprus, as well as in taking over Alexander's body, Ptolemy could be seen as serving ambitions that did not acknowledge the sovereignty of Alexander's heirs.[23] This was also a good time to remind the troops of Ptolemy's proposal in Babylon to leave the royal throne vacant (Curt. 10.6.13–16.), or (according to another tradition) of his savage personal attack on King Philip III when Philip's candidacy to the throne was put forward (Just. 13.2.10; cf. Paus. 1.6.2–3). The second-century CE traveler Pausanias says that Perdiccas took the kings along to Egypt to give his campaign a decent face, and this may explain why Ptolemy made a point of being solicitous to them after Perdiccas's assassination (Paus. 1.6.3; Arr. *Succ.* 1.29).

Before coming to Egypt, Perdiccas sent forces to Cyprus, but we do not know if they included veterans.[24] According to Arrian, the kings, the army, and their general marched from Damsacus to Egypt, where Perdiccas made accusations against Ptolemy. The satrap defended himself in front of the troops (*to plēthos*), who regarded the charges as unjust and, the source adds, did not wish to fight (Arr. *Succ.* 1.28). This-much-too-brief account, exclusive to Arrian, has been supplemented by scholarly reconstructions of Perdiccas's charges, of Ptolemy's defense, and of the context and the forum in which their confrontation took place. It has even raised (unjustified) doubts regarding the historicity of the entire episode.[25] The meagerness of the available information, however, should discourage elaborate speculation. The most that the sources imply about the charges against Ptolemy is that they involved his appropriation of Alexander's body and, probably, his alleged challenging of the kings' authority (Arr. *Succ.* 1.24.1; Paus. 1.6.3). Arrian's epitomator uses legal terms to describe the verbal argument between the two commanders, but the radical abbreviation of the source makes it difficult to say whether the reference is to a trial or to an informal assembly.

Scholars have wondered why Perdiccas would grant Ptolemy the oppor-

---

23. Cf., in addition, Seibert 1969, 107.

24. Arr. *Succ.* 1.24.6. The chief sources for Perdiccas's invasion of Egypt are: Diod. 18.33.1–36.7; Arr. *Succ.* 1.24, 28–30; Paus. 1.6.3; Strabo 17.1.8. For discussion, see Schubert 1914, 190–201; Seibert 1969, 114–128; Briant 1973b, 263–272; Ellis 1994, 37–39; Rathmann 2005, 72–77; Landucci Gattinoni 2008, 148–165.

25. Both Schwahn (1930, 1931) and Seibert (1969, 118–120) doubt the report. Fontana (1960, 218–219) and Briant (1973b, 263–266) unconvincingly redate the episode to an earlier and later occasion, respectively; but see Anson 1991, 240–243, and the next note.

tunity to defend himself; some think it unlikely that the satrap of Egypt exposed himself to danger either from Perdiccas or from a potentially unsympathetic crowd. These difficulties have led them to dismiss the story altogether, or to suggest that Ptolemy spoke through envoys or from a safe distance, even though the text says nothing of the sort.[26] In fact, it appears that both speakers risked little. Perdiccas allowed Ptolemy to speak because he believed he (Perdiccas) could control the result of the meeting, as he had shown he could do earlier (for example, when he persuaded the Macedonians to reject the so-called last plans of Alexander), and because he was on good terms with the soldiers, whom he had rewarded in Asia Minor before the campaign. He had also planned to put Antigonus on trial when he was in Asia Minor, and Antigonus's refusal to show up indicated that he shared Perdiccas's view about the regent's ability to decide the results of the trial (see above). It is true that the troops protested the elimination of Alexander's half-sister, Cynane, in Asia Minor, but the blame for her death fell chiefly on Perdiccas's brother Alcetas, and Perdiccas's conceding to the Macedonians the marriage of Cynane's daughter, Adea-Eurydice, to Philip III could have been positively construed; Arrian says that it was Perdiccas who brought the marriage about (Arr. *Succ.* 1.23). In addition, the verbal exchange with Ptolemy happened too late to change the course of the expedition. Perdiccas had already sent forces to fight Ptolemy's allies in Cyprus, and the royal army would not have turned back after marching as far as Egypt simply because Ptolemy made a better case.[27] Finally, the royal army had disagreed with its commander's decision about the objective of the campaign only once, when Alexander wished to advance beyond the River Hyphasis in India, and even then there was no open rebellion. Ever since Babylon, the veterans had protested actively just in matters regarding the throne and its occupant. Perdiccas knew that he had little to lose.

It is unknown how Ptolemy secured his safety, but that is no good argument against the most natural reading of the text: that he came in person to the meeting.[28] The satrap took the chance of speaking to the troops

---

26. Ptolemy on trial: Hammond 2000, 153. Risk to Ptolemy: Schwahn 1930, 1931; Seibert 1969, 118–120. Anson (1991, 240–243) suggests that the troops met in an informal assembly against Perdiccas's wishes and that Ptolemy spoke through envoys or from a boat in the river. Briant (1973b, 264–266) argues for a hearing in the commanders' council, and (less likely) that Ptolemy's speech to the troops should be postdated to a time following Perdiccas's assassination.

27. See also Briant 1973b, 264.

28. Did he request hostages from Perdiccas before his arrival, just as Eumenes did before his meeting with Antigonus in Nora (Plut. *Eum.* 10.5)?

in order to justify his conduct and to gain support with his persuasive powers, his past joint service with the veterans, and his appeal to their wish to avoid what could be presented as civil war. Indeed, it was the first time that the veterans in the invading army were going to fight another Macedonian general, whose position had been duly confirmed by his fellow commanders and probably by the veterans as well (cf. Diod. 18.55.3). Whatever argument swayed the troops to favor Ptolemy's cause, their reaction revealed patterns of conduct and thought that occurred elsewhere when they weighed their general's policies and actions against their notions of fairness. They also found it easier to agree on what they were against—in this case, a war against Ptolemy—than on what they favored. We may conclude from this incident that when a leader such as Perdiccas unwisely convened the Macedonians and gave them a chance to voice their opinion, they did. Yet the significance of the affair should be put in proportion. It showed that the veterans' opinion mattered little when, as in this case, they lacked the energy or motivation to back it up with riots. Soon afterward they obeyed Perdiccas's order to march against the man whose cause they thought more just.[29]

The most detailed account of the Egyptian campaign comes from Diodorus. Its almost shameless bias in favor of Ptolemy evinces his reliance on a pro-Ptolemaic source, although Diodorus probably supplemented it with details from Hieronymus and his own lexicon of praise.[30] The historian begins his story of the invasion with a report on Perdiccas, who first camped not far from Pelusium. He adds that after Perdiccas had failed to clear out an old canal and the river destroyed his work, many of his "friends" (*philoi*) deserted to Ptolemy. Diodorus does not explain Perdiccas's purpose in cleaning the canal; he may have wished to allow his fleet, anchored in Pelusium under Attalus's command, to join him.[31] Nevertheless, it is not clear why the failed canal project led to the desertion of Perdiccas's men, and Diodorus, perhaps sensing the weak causal link between these events, moves on to contrast Perdiccas's brutal authoritarianism with Ptolemy's considerate and benevolent leadership, which allowed his commanders

29. Perdiccas's error here: Errington 1978, 118n139, but cf. Hammond in Hammond, Griffith, and Walbank 1972–1988, 3:121. Anson thinks the episode "represents an advance in the authority of the army" (1991, 243).

30. Diod. 18.33.1–36.7. Pro-Ptolemaic source: Seibert 1969, 69–71, 82–83; Hornblower 1981, 40–43, 50–52, 92–97 (Cleitarchus?); Landucci Gattinoni 2008, 138, 149–150; but also Merker 1988 (Hieronymus as a source); cf. Hornblower 1981, esp. 55–56, and Green 2006, 7, 38, 241, for Diodorus's own contribution to the portrait of the satrap.

31. Diod. 18.33.1–2. Attalus's fleet: Diod. 18.37.3. When Alexander invaded Egypt, he instructed his fleet at Pelusium to join him in Memphis: Arr. *Anab.* 3.1.3–4.

to speak their minds and elicited goodwill from many (18.33.2–4). Yet even this account of the desertion is problematic, both because of the tendentious and too-perfect contrast between the two leaders and because those who left Perdiccas had not yet experienced Ptolemy's courteous style of command, and hence can hardly have been attracted to it.

More likely, Ptolemy lured Perdiccas's officers to his side with promises and rewards. In this period it was a common practice to encourage enemy troops and their immediate commanders to desert or betray their generals. That this was Ptolemy's *modus operandi* here is suggested by Perdiccas's countermeasures, which involved reasserting his control and raising morale with gifts and promises to his commanders and friendliness to all.[32] Moreover, Perdiccas's treatment of his followers on this occasion shows that Diodorus's depiction of him as a "murderous man . . . who wished to rule over all by force" (18.33.3) does him an injustice and ignores his style of leadership, which changed according to circumstances. Finally, those who were dissatisfied with Perdiccas, or who were induced to obey him by material gains, were his close associates and not the rank and file, who remained loyal to him after Babylon.[33]

It was poor generalship, not lack of fighting spirit or lackluster effort on the troops' part, that lost the campaign for Perdiccas. Ptolemy was well prepared for the invasion, but Perdiccas had more and better soldiers. Instead of building on this advantage, he opted for surprise attacks that failed twice.[34] After the failure near Pelusium, Perdiccas set out to capture the "Fort of Camels," probably not far from Memphis, since it took him one night to march from the fort (after failing to capture it) to an island opposite Memphis. (It has been estimated that an army with elephants could march about ten miles in a day, and probably moved more slowly in the

---

32. Diod. 18.33.5; and see also Bennett and Roberts 2008, 32. Desertions and enticements to desert: e.g., Pithon's collusion with rebel settlers: Diod. 18.7.5–6; Craterus and Antipater inviting Eumenes and Neoptolemus to join them: Plut. *Eum.* 5.6–8; Diod. 18.29.4; Antigonus's luring Eumenes' cavalry: Diod. 18.40.5; Antigonus's and Ptolemy's appeal to Eumenes' men: Diod. 18.62.1–63.6; Ptolemy's appeal to Laomedon, the satrap of Syria: App. *Syr.* 52; Antigonus's appeal to Macedonians and satraps in Eumenes' camp in 317: Diod. 19.25.2–4.

33. *Pace* Briant 1973b, 269–272; and see also Anson 1991, 240–241. For the "friends" (*philoi*) of a ruler, see Herman 1980, esp. 111–113. On Perdiccas's character, see in addition Just. XIII 8.2; Suda s.v. *Perdiccas*, and Rathmann (2005), who questions his depiction in the sources.

34. Ptolemy's preparation: Diod. 18.33.3–4; Paus. 1.6.3; Just. 13.6.18–20. Perdiccas's advantage: Diod. 18.34.5.

dark of night.)[35] We are not told why Perdiccas chose the fort as his target, but it may have defended a convenient crossing to the west bank of the
river. From there Perdiccas could reach his ultimate goals, the city of Memphis and the body of Alexander that it contained. Indeed, Perdiccas's army
found no difficulty crossing the river here, as it later did upstream (*infra*).

Perdiccas told no one about his intention to attack the fort. The desertion of some of his associates earlier confirmed his generally suspicious attitude toward others and made him worry that his plan would be leaked
to Ptolemy.[36] Before the attack, the army marched all night at a hurried
pace and camped on the river across from the fort. Although the troops
must have been tired, Perdiccas attacked at dawn in order to take the fort
by storm, before Ptolemy could come to the rescue. The first to cross the
river were the elephants, whose mission was to destroy a variety of physical
obstacles that defended the fort. They were followed by the shield-bearers
(hypaspists) and ladder carriers, who were to scale the walls, as well as by
other troops. In the rear came an elite cavalry unit, whose task was to stop
Ptolemy if he showed up (Diod. 18.33.5–6).

The attackers must have included veterans, even among the shield-
bearers. Recently it has been argued that Diodorus used the term "hypaspists" generically for shield-bearers rather than for a specific group of
Macedonian veterans who had served as, or modeled themselves after, Alexander's hypaspists, a famous infantry unit. If true, this interpretation
should not be understood to mean that there were no Macedonians or veterans of Alexander's hypaspists among the shield-bearing soldiers. Perdiccas
had used his veterans to attack the walls of an Isaurian city in Pisidia, where
the defenders, before committing suicide, successfully defended themselves
from the walls and killed many Macedonians (Diod. 18.2.6–7). Alexander
too had used his famous hypaspists to attack fortified sites. These precedents make it highly likely that there were Macedonian veterans among the
"hypaspists" who marched against the Fort of Camels.[37]

Yet Perdiccas's plan of attack failed: Ptolemy succeeded in entering the

---

35. Diod. 18.34.6; cf. Huss 2001, 113 with n139. Engels (1978, 155) estimates a day's
march at less than 10 miles (ca. 16 km), but see the more generous estimate of 22–
23 km by Proctor (1971, 34). The distance from Pelusium to Memphis was 136 miles (ca.
219 km): Anson 2003, 385n49.

36. Arr. *Succ.* 1.5; cf. Goukowsky 1978, 49n1.

37. Hypaspists as "shield-bearers": Bosworth 2002, 82–83. Heckel (forthcoming,
esp. n15) rejects Bosworth's interpretation on linguistic grounds. Alexander's use of
the hypaspists against fortified places: Arr. *Anab.* 1.20.5–7, 2.22.6–24.2; cf. e.g., 1.8.3,
4.23.1–4, 26.6; 6.9.1–4, and see Anson 1988b; 1991, 242n52.

fort with his men ahead of the attackers and before the arrival of the cavalry meant to stop him. Diodorus's statement that this setback did not discourage Perdiccas's troops attests to their resolve and to their trust in their leader and in their own ability. The historian goes on to sing the praises of Ptolemy, whose heroic feats inspired and taught his men to resist a more numerous enemy. One moment he is wounding an elephant and its rider, the next he is striking enemy troops and sending them tumbling down ladders into the river. This last detail suggests that conditions for the attackers were not ideal: between the front wall and the river there was apparently only a narrow strip of land on which the ladders could be placed. Perdiccas is not accorded the authorial attentiveness given to Ptolemy, but we learn that his troops continued to attack the fort in waves, that they made every effort to accomplish the mission, and that both they and the enemy suffered many casualties. But Perdiccas was the first to cease fighting, realizing either that his efforts were futile or that his troops were exhausted by hard combat after a hurried night march.[38]

We do not know why Perdiccas abandoned the siege of the fort and the opportunity to capture Ptolemy there after only a single day's effort. In Pisidia he had succeeded in capturing a walled city with no-less-determined defenders after a three days' siege (Diod. 18.22.1–8). Perhaps he hoped to quickly overwhelm Memphis, Egypt's capital and repository of Alexander's corpse. In addition, keeping the army on the move toward Memphis turned the failure at the fort into a mere temporary setback. Concerned that Ptolemy would try to prevent him from reaching the city, he left secretly under cover of night. This was the second night in a row that the troops were deprived of sleep.[39] They marched toward an island in the river opposite Memphis, which was intended as Perdiccas's new base.

The regent was anxious to get there before Ptolemy, and believed that the army could cross the river on foot, as at the Fort of Camels. Laden with weapons, the soldiers had to wade through chin-deep water and contend with a strong current. To prevent their being swept away, Perdiccas positioned a line of elephants on the left to weaken the current and a parallel line of cavalrymen on the right to catch and bring to the island troops who had lost their footing.[40] The number of men who made it to the is-

---

38. Diod. 18.33.5–34.5. Landucci Gattinoni (2008, 152) observes in Ptolemy's battle with the elephant an imitation of Alexander's fighting the Indian king Porus.

39. Diodorus strongly suggests that the night march immediately followed the failed attack: 18.34.5–6.

40. Hannibal (Livy 21.47.4) and Caesar (*Gallic War* 7.56) used similar techniques. Cf. Echoles 1953, esp. 216–217.

land exceeded 2,000, but we do not know by how much. Soon the water rose where the army was crossing, either because of flood or because, as Diodorus or his source surmise, the movement of the elephants, men, and horses disturbed the sand on the bottom, which was then carried down the river, making it impossible to cross without being submerged.[41] The correct reaction would have been to move the crossing point; but perhaps the river was even deeper elsewhere, and it is only fair to grant that Perdiccas (and probably everyone else) did not know what was causing the water to rise. He also had to deal with what looked like an imminent danger to the men on the island. Two late sources, Polyaenus and Frontinus, report that Ptolemy approached the scene with cavalry and used herds of domestic animals and horses to raise a great cloud of dust that tricked his enemies into believing he would be joined by a large army.[42]

Although Diodorus fails to mention this incident, it adds urgency to his statement that Perdiccas ordered the soldiers to return because he did not wish to expose them to an enemy attack. The result was disastrous. Only those who could swim were able to return to safety, after abandoning their weapons in the water. The rest drowned or were carried to the opposite bank, where Ptolemy's men captured them. Many others were swept away and eaten by the river animals, that is, crocodiles and maybe even hippos. Diodorus estimates that Perdiccas lost more than 2,000 men, half of them to the animals.[43]

---

41. Diod. 18.34.6–36.1. The phenomenon of sand being disturbed and washed downstream is too common to require a proof. Anson (2003, 380) interprets one of Diodorus's other theories that the river flooded because of a rainfall as a reference to the Nile's inundation. But it would have been an extraordinary coincidence for the river to flood just after the crossing had begun. Heckel (forthcoming) attractively suggests that perhaps Ptolemy opened the floodgates. Landucci Gattinoni (2008, 155) explains the phenomenon by means of the so-called *barathra* (pits), or marshy sinking sands, that are described in several ancient accounts. But the ancients locate the "pits" on the way to or around distant Pelusium, and in places where the surface is covered with sand. Landucci Gattinoni is right, however, to note that swimming was not the Macedonians' strong suit: Diod. 19.18.7.

42. Polyaenus 4.19; Front. *Strat.* 4.7.20. Aelian's (*VH* 12.64) story that Ptolemy tricked Perdiccas into stopping his march by letting him capture a fake of Alexander's corpse is fantastic: Erskine 2002, 170–171.

43. Diod. 18.34.6–36.3; Polyaenus 4.19. Diod. 18.35.5. Strabo (17.1.8), Aelian (*VH* 4.19), and Frontinus (*Strat.* 4.7.20), cf. Polyaenus 4.19, credit Ptolemy with responsibility for the losses, and the *Babylonian Chronicles* mention the killing of the king's (i.e., Perdiccas's) troops in Egypt: *ABC* 10, obv. 4–5. But Diodorus, pro-Ptolemaic though he is, explicitly asserts in his fuller account that the losses were self-induced. Hippos can be carnivorous: Dudley 1998. For their presence in Lower Egypt: Pliny *NH* 8.15.

The disaster at the river sealed the fate of Perdiccas, who was assassinated shortly afterward. From the troops' perspective, he had failed to meet a cardinal expectation of a commander when, instead of leading them to victory, he was responsible for three consecutive failures. The Macedonian veterans in the army, who were used to a winning general and an almost uninterrupted series of successes, had never experienced such a chain of events. They were equally unused to losing so many troops in the course of one operation.[44] Perdiccas had made great demands on their endurance and fighting skills, and they gave him all they had, only to risk or lose their lives for nothing.

The fiasco at the Nile was exacerbated by Perdiccas's inability to take care even of his dead soldiers. After a military operation, a general was expected to ensure the proper burial of those who had died in his service and to return the dead to the enemy. Besides fulfilling a religious duty and a moral obligation to the troops, the practice demonstrated the general's rank and his power to distribute honors. When he buried the dead on the battlefield, it constituted his claim to victory. It was probably to show Perdiccas's failure in all these regards and to claim victory for himself that Ptolemy gave proper death rites to the enemy's dead soldiers, whom he had found and whose remains he then sent to their friends and relatives in Perdiccas's camp. It gained him gratitude and appreciation among Perdiccas's troops and put Perdiccas in an impossible position. The marshal could not oppose Ptolemy's gesture, even though it drew a sharp contrast between him and the satrap, highlighting his own responsibility for exposing his dead soldiers to the (cultural) horror of being eaten by animals. These were the wages of being the kings' guardian, who in the post-Alexander era (and unlike the kings) was expected to perform well militarily and to care for the soldiers.[45]

The troops grieved for their comrades, and their pity and fear, as Aristo-

---

44. Diodorus's figure of 2,000 dead in one day may not be inflated. Napoleon's victory over local Egyptian forces in the so-called Battle of the Pyramids (July 1798) resulted, according to one of his generals, in 2,500 men killed or drowned: Schom 1997, 130.

45. Diod. 18.36.1–2. Pausanias links Perdiccas's death to his decline in military reputation: 1.6.3; cf. Arr. *Succ.* 1.28. Seibert (1969, 72), who is too skeptical of the accounts of the campaign, questions also the story of Ptolemy's gesture, but this ignores the politics of burial, for which see Roisman 2003, 311–312, and chap. 8 below. On the injunction to bury the dead, see Curt. 5.4.3 (a sacred duty) and Garland 1985, 101–103, and cf. the Homeric threat of exposing an enemy warrior to the birds and the dogs: Redfield 1975, 168–189, 184–186. Burial and claiming victory: e.g., Diod. 19.31.3.

tle observes of these emotions, were likely projected onto themselves (*Rhet.* 2.5.12, 8.13). The protest that led to Perdiccas's death was on behalf of their superiors as well. Among those lost in the river were distinguished commanders (Diod. 18.36.1), and their peers must have been equally mournful and angry with Perdiccas. Thus, for the first time since the crisis on the Hyphasis in India, the troops and their commanders found common ground in opposition to their chief commander.

It has been claimed that the protest and its outcomes, including Perdiccas's murder and his replacement by the generals Pithon and Arrhidaeus, were orchestrated by Ptolemy with the help of Pithon. Yet these developments appear more spontaneous than guided by furtive hands.[46] First there was a night of mourning and recrimination, neither of which needed stirring up. Diodorus says that the Macedonians "raged savagely" against Perdiccas and became more sympathetic toward Ptolemy, but by his own account it was the former mood that clearly dominated the camp (Diod. 18.36.2). Then many commanders, apparently emboldened by the hostile atmosphere, made charges against the regent in what looked like an informal gathering, which they convened. As in the past, discontent with the leader, articulated by the soldiers' shouts and threats, gave the phalanx a common cause. Because the rank and file had been loyal to Perdiccas up to the recent fiasco, and because Perdiccas had supporters among the elite as well as the masses, it was important for both groups to find out if they were indeed united in opposing him. Nevertheless, the assembly seemed to make no decision except for confirming that those who wished to confront Perdiccas could do so without alienating the Macedonians.

One hundred commanders now openly rebelled against him. Among them was Pithon, son of Crateuas, whom Diodorus (18.36.5) describes as the general who put down the Greek rebellions among the upper satrapies and as a man equal to Alexander's friends in valor. The rebels probably also included two generals identified elsewhere as Perdiccas's killers: Seleucus, who had received from Perdiccas the command over the camp and the most distinguished hipparchy of the Companions (chilarchy), and Antigenes, a veteran infantry commander. It was a collection of commanders with much clout, and the fact that Pithon was "inferior to none of Alexander's friends in excellence and fame" (Diod. 18.36.5) made him Perdiccas's equal and added legitimacy to the plot.[47]

---

46. *Pace* Errington 1970, 65–66, followed by Anson 2004, 112.

47. Nepos *Eum.* 5.1; Diod. 18.39.6; Arr. *Succ.* 1.35; cf. *Heidelberg Epitome* 1.3. Seibert 1969, 125–126; Heckel 1992, 257, 311.

Diodorus, our chief source for the affair, is silent about Perdiccas's reaction, but Arrian's and Justin's brief accounts suggest that he did not help his own cause. In contrast with his conduct near Pelusium, where he regained the commanders' and the troops' favor through positive reinforcement, he now sought to reassert his control by intimidation, and proceeded to punish severely those he suspected of wishing to move to Ptolemy's side. These were most likely officers rather than rank and file. Perdiccas's action stirred memories of his earlier intolerance and arrogant treatment of those under him.[48] It was probably his reaction, the hostile climate, and the influence of Pithon, Antigenes, and the cavalry commander Seleucus that persuaded some of Perdiccas's own cavalry (his mainstay of support in Babylon) to join in the betrayal. They and the officers went into his tent and killed him. The contrast with another attempt on Perdiccas's life, at Babylon in 323, is instructive. There the general Meleager had sent agents to kill Perdiccas, but the marshal scared them off and the Macedonians were upset by the assassination attempt. In Egypt the conspirators were not as easily intimidated, both because of their bolder character and higher rank and because they knew that the phalanx was behind them. Indeed, we hear of nothing resembling the hostile reaction from the troops that Melaeger's attempt had elicited in Babylon.[49]

Clearly, the most active opponents of Perdiccas were now members of the Macedonian elite and not the veterans. In general, his authority was stronger with the troops than with their officers. The soldiers might protest and show their discontent, but they lacked political ambition and never claimed for themselves the elite's privilege of choosing or replacing commanders. Furthermore, in the period under discussion, the troops seldom resorted to violence against their chief general, recognizing that the right to use force during a mutiny belonged either to the commander against the rebels or to the officers against him.[50] This does not mean that they disap-

---

48. Arr. *Succ.* 1.28; Just. 13.8.2; Suda s.v. *Perdiccas.*

49. Diod. 18.36.1–5; cf. *Heidelberg Epitome* 1. Paus. 1.6.3 says that Perdiccas was killed by his own bodyguards. There are also traditions that he was killed in combat with Ptolemy by his own cavalry (Arr. *Succ.* 1.28) or by his sarissa-wielding troops (Strabo 17.1.8), and that his death was foretold (Arr. *Anab.* 7.18.5). Nothing in these versions justifies rejecting Diodorus's account. For the claim that one frieze on the so-called Alexander Sarcophagus depicts Perdiccas's murder, see von Graeve 1970, 138–142, followed by Stewart 1993, 301–302.

50. The only exception is the veterans' violent threats against Antipater in Triparadeisus, for which see chap. 5 below. The fighting over Alexander's body in Babylon occurred when no one was in charge.

proved of the officers' coup. The phalanx's conduct in the assembly before Perdiccas's murder and the lack of popular protest afterward suggest that they agreed with their superiors. The veterans' main contribution to the affair, however, was to show that a general who lost the army's goodwill was vulnerable to attacks from other Macedonians of rank.[51]

The sources' descriptions of the hectic two days that followed differ in details but agree that Ptolemy visited the camp of the royal army; that Pithon, son of Crateuas, and Arrhidaeus, who was the general formerly in charge of Alexander's hearse, became the new regents; and that Eumenes of Cardia, Perdiccas's general in Asia Minor, and other Perdiccans were condemned or put to death. The scholarly claim that Ptolemy managed all that took place in camp, directly or behind the scenes, relies too heavily on Diodorus's one-sided account.[52] Diodorus, following his pro-Ptolemaic source, focuses his attention exclusively on Ptolemy and, in addition to lavishing praise upon him, grants him sole power to shape events, much as in his account of Ptolemy at the Fort of Camels, where the satrap almost single-handedly repulses the royal army's attack. Ptolemy's influence is undeniable, but it is advisable to allow other generals and even the troops a role in the events after Perdiccas's death.

Because of our interest in the troops, we shall focus on their actions and reactions. Diodorus reports that Ptolemy crossed to the royal camp the day after Perdiccas's assassination and spoke in the assembly in his own defense, but the historian also suggests that the satrap did not call this assembly (18.36.6). Apparently it was a spontaneous meeting, like the ones that took place in Babylon following Alexander's death, which the troops attended in order to find out who was in charge and if they liked him. When Ptolemy arrived he needed all the goodwill that he could get from both the troops and the officers, both to avoid personal harm and to persuade the army to leave Egypt peacefully.[53] His honoring of Perdiccas's dead soldiers was a good start, but there were still Perdiccan supporters in camp, and the anti-Ptolemaic propaganda, which must have been reinforced throughout the campaign, had to be addressed. Ptolemy defended himself in the assembly and strengthened the legitimacy of his cause by paying court and giving presents to the kings and ranking Macedonians (Diod. 18.36.4; Arr.

---

51. Cf. Anson 1991, 241. Errington (1970, 66–67) assumes, however, that the troops did not necessarily approve of Perdiccas's murder.

52. See Errington 1970, 65–66; cf. Anson 1991, 243–244.

53. Cf. Diod. 18.43.1. For Ptolemy's other considerations, see Will 1984, 36–37; Billows 1990, 67.

Succ. 1.29). Perdiccas had invaded Egypt in the kings' names, and it was important for the satrap to acknowledge his loyalty to Alexander's heirs. Moreover, the kings had always enjoyed the veterans' support, and in the temporary absence of a regent they were more than ever the source of legitimate authority.

After securing the friendship of the kings and the officers, Ptolemy attended to the troops' immediate needs. There was a shortage of grain and supplies because the camp of the royal army was originally designed to serve not as a viable base but only as a temporary post before the abortive crossing of the river. Perdiccas had been too preoccupied with his own survival to take care of the army's needs, and Attalus and his ships could not help because they were anchored at distant Pelusium. Diodorus says that Ptolemy filled the camp with donations of grain and supplies (18.36.6), but provisioning such a large army required time and preparations, and the result could not have been achieved until sometime after he had promised the assembled Macedonians that he would provide for them. In this way Ptolemy put the Macedonians in his debt, ensuring that no ambitious general could revive the campaign against him.

Photius's summary of Arrian ignores the assembly and Ptolemy's role in it, ascribing to the commanders' council (*synedrion*) the appointment of Pithon and Arrhidaeus as temporary joint regents. But Diodorus gives Ptolemy sole credit for the election of the new regents in the assembly. Whether or not Ptolemy participated in the council's meeting before the assembly or concurred with its decision afterward, his contribution to the process should be put in perspective.[54]

Diodorus's description of the effects of Ptolemy's speech and generosity on the army is confusing. He says that the response was highly favorable and that although Ptolemy was able (*dynamenos*) to assume the guardianship of the kings because of his popularity with the troops, he did not reach out for it. Instead, in gratitude to Pithon and Arrhidaeus, he recommended them to the Macedonians for the supreme command, to which they were elected with unanimous enthusiasm (Diod. 18.36.6–7). Was the guardianship actually offered to Ptolemy? Not necessarily, for Diodorus can be equally understood to mean that Ptolemy merely resisted the opportunity to become a guardian. This interpretation is likely for two reasons. It serves the main agenda of Diodorus's description (to show Ptolemy's self-

---

54. Arr. *Succ.* 1.30; Diod. 18.36.6–7, and see Errington 1970, 60; Goukowsky 1978, 145–146; Billows 1990, 67 with n30.

lessness, moderation, and friendship), and it better fits the historical record, according to which the troops never proposed anyone to this office, before or after the meeting. They might approve or disapprove the generals' choice of a guardian, but they did not arrogate to themselves the right to propose their own candidate. We should consider the possibility, then, that no one moved to make Ptolemy the new guardian.[55]

Indeed, Diodorus's glorification of, and focus on, Ptolemy comes at the expense of other prominent Macedonians. The historian shows him acting and speaking alone, with the audience merely reacting to his initiatives. Yet Diodorus's statement that Ptolemy recommended the new guardians while the Macedonians "deliberated the command [i.e., guardianship]"— *boules protetheises peri tes hegemonias*—suggests that he was only one of several speakers in the meeting. We may expect that at least Pithon and Arrhidaeus addressed the public too. Diodorus's assertion that the troops elected them as new guardians unanimously and enthusiastically, thanks to Ptolemy's endorsement, relegates both men to the status of silent bystanders. It also ignores the fact that Pithon, at least, was an ambitious man of action and a veteran general who had just led the plot against Perdiccas—all of which indicates that his need of patronage to obtain the guardianship was exaggerated. If the Macedonians so badly wanted Ptolemy to be the guardian, their reception of his substitutes was too warm to be appropriate for a second choice. It appears that the Macedonians were happy to support the elite's choice of guardians for several reasons: they got familiar leaders with whom they felt comfortable; popular approval of these commanders strengthened their partnership with the elite; and the appointment marked the end of the Egyptian campaign, in which the royal army had fared poorly. The election of the new guardians picked by the commanders' council also showed, not for the first time, that the power of the assembly ebbed and flowed in inverse relation to the unity of the military elite.[56]

The next day the army learned that Eumenes had defeated and killed Craterus and Neoptolemus in Asia Minor. In response, the Macedonians

---

55. The evidence for the protocol of electing a regent is poor, and although the assembled people could have appointed one (cf. Curt. 10.6.9), they did not play a significant role in the process: Landucci Gattinoni 2003, 13–14. Hatzopoulos's discussion (1996, 1:276–279) fails to distinguish between regents and kings.

56. Huss (2001, 115n155) thinks that Arrhidaeus had remained with Ptolemy since handing Alexander's body over to him. The assumption is reasonable but also unattested. The possibility that Ptolemy and the new guardians made a deal, in which he gave them his support in return for their taking the army out of Egypt, should not be excluded.

and their kings condemned to death, *in absentia*, Eumenes and fifty of Perdiccas's followers, including his brother Alcetas. The exact charges are not reported, but they likely included the killing of Craterus and other Macedonians.[57] Both Diodorus and Plutarch state that if the news of Eumenes' victories in Asia Minor had become known in camp before Perdiccas's assassination and not (as it happened) shortly after, Perdiccas would have become the undisputed leader of all Macedonians instead of being killed.

This observation, originating probably with Hieronymus of Cardia, has received almost unanimous scholarly endorsement, but is of dubious validity.[58] The statement about the likely impact of the news on Perdiccas's fortunes is purely speculative, and therefore only as good as any other "what if" scenario. Furthermore, Plutarch's version shows that the point of this hypothetical construction is to glorify Eumenes. It concludes and enhances the description of Eumenes' victory over Craterus, giving it a momentous outcome that this battle never really had. It also undermines the justification for the assassination of Perdiccas, and for the army's subsequent decision to vilify Eumenes and condemn him to death, by attributing both actions not to these persons' perceived wrongdoings but to fortune and bad timing.

The decision to condemn the Perdiccans was followed by a purge in camp, which led to the death of Atalante, Perdiccas's sister and Attalus's wife, and of Perdiccas's close friends, although some managed to escape. An invitation was also extended to Antipater and Antigonus to join the kings and the army in Syria.[59] In this case it is likely that the Macedonians followed the lead of their new leaders and Ptolemy. The satrap was allied with both Antigonus and Antipater, and arranging their rendezvous with

---

57. Plut. *Eum.* 8.1–3; Diod. 18.37.1, 59.4; 19.12.2, 13.1.

58. Diod. 18.37.1; Plut. *Eum.* 8.2; and, e.g., Vezin 1907, 52–53; Schäfer 2002, 94. Hieronymus as the source: Hornblower 1981, 51. Diodorus, however, states elsewhere that Perdiccas already knew of Eumenes' victory at the beginning of his campaign (18.33.1). Hornblower (1981, 51) rejects this report, but Errington (1970, 127), followed by Anson (2003, 383–384n46), rightly defends it as a reference to Eumenes' victory over Neoptolemus, which preceded his defeat of Craterus.

59. Diod. 18.37.1–2, 4, 59.4, 62.1; Arr. *Succ.* 1.30; Plut. *Eum.* 8.2; Nepos *Eum.* 5.1; Just. 13.8.10; 14.1.1; App. *Syr.* 53; cf. *Mithr.* 8. The *Heidelberg Epitome* 4 states that Ptolemy took from Perdiccas's army as many troops as he wished. Unfortunately, the author mistakenly reports in the same breath that Ptolemy also captured and married Perdiccas's wife and Alexander's sister, Cleopatra. The evidence produced by Griffith (1935, 109) and Bagnall (2006, 15) for Ptolemy's acquisition of troops from the invading army is not much better; cf. also Waterfield 2011, 65.

the army in Syria both demonstrated his allegiance to them and removed the army from his land. It was no less in his and the commanders' interest to legitimize the outlawing and killing of the Perdiccan generals and friends through the army's decision and a royal sanction.

Plutarch states that Macedonians of the royal army angrily condemned Eumenes to death because his victory over Craterus earned him envy and hatred and because Eumenes, an alien, had used Macedonians (in his army) to kill Craterus, the most distinguished among them (*Eum.* 8.1–3). There are reasons, however, to believe that their reaction was not wholly spontaneous. Someone had to call the assembly and propose this resolution, to implicate Alcetas and the Perdiccans in camp in Craterus's death (even though they did not fight him in battle), and to conceal the fact that Eumenes' battles with Neoptolemus and Craterus were not good examples of Macedonian fratricide, in that no Macedonian force had fought on Eumenes' side.[60] In addition, if Arrian's report that Ptolemy showed sympathy to Perdiccas's friends and his fearful Macedonians is placed in this context, it suggests that the treatment of the Perdiccans was more discriminatory than impulsive. Arrian's claim that Ptolemy's act of kindness gained him a lasting good name makes sense if he helped the Perdiccans with more than soothing words.[61]

There is also no need to be deeply impressed by Plutarch's description of the Macedonians' strong reaction to the news of Craterus's death. As it happens, the evidence for Craterus's post-Alexander popularity comes chiefly from Plutarch's biographies and not from our other main sources.[62] This is not to say that the liking for him was unhistorical, for Craterus was surely popular among the veterans in *his* army. But it would be wrong to regard his popularity among other veterans as unaffected by time and cir-

---

60. Plut. *Eum.* 8.1–2; Diod. 18.59.4, 62.1; cf. Just. 13.8.10; App. *Syr.* 53; App. *Mithr.* 8. I follow Briant's (1973b, 273–274) and Engel's (1974) reconstruction of two assembly meetings, one to elect the guardians and another to condemn the Perdiccans. Hatzopoulos (1996, 1:285) argues for a regular procedure of a council preparing an agenda and decree and the assembly voting on it. The condemnations, however, were not necessarily the result of a formal trial: Anson 2004, 114n132.

61. Arrian (*Succ.* 1.29) dates Ptolemy's kindness toward the Perdiccans earlier than the decision to elect the new regents.

62. Plut. *Alex.* 47.9–10; *Eum.* 6.3, 7.1–2; 8.1–2; *Demetr.* 14.2–3. The only other source to mention Craterus's appeal after Alexander's death is Suda s.v. *Craterus*, which has been identified as Arr. *Succ.* F 19; cf. Arr. *Succ.* 1.27. Goukowski (1978–1981, 1:90–91) almost goes beyond Plutarch in describing the veterans' great admiration for Craterus; but cf. Hornblower 1981, 155; Bennett and Roberts 2009, 2:182n9.

cumstances. In the case of Perdiccas's veterans, it had been four years (or three, according to the "high chronology") since they had last laid eyes on Craterus. It was not just a case of "out of sight, out of mind"; there was also no one in the royal camp who made it his business to keep Craterus's memory alive. On the contrary, when Perdiccas arrived in Cilicia, he replaced the local satrap, Philotas, because he was known as Craterus's friend. An index of the wide range of goodwill toward Craterus was the fact that Perdiccas contemplated fighting him and Antipater before invading Egypt, a possibility that presupposed that the regent trusted his veterans to support him in this endeavor.[63] Although the Macedonians' resentment in Egypt of those presented as responsible for Craterus's and the other Macedonians' deaths should not be doubted, it cannot be separated from their anger about the recent losses in the campaign, anger which the anti-Perdiccan campaign allowed them to vent against persons associated with the man responsible for these losses.

There were additional reasons for the veterans' cooperation with the new leadership against the Perdiccans. They were eager to please their superiors, and they too could see that the coalition of Ptolemy, the new regents, Antigonus, and Antipater was stronger than its opponents (cf. Nepos *Eum.* 5.1). Yet those most enthusiastic about eliminating the Perdiccans were the generals and officers.[64] With the revenge concluded, both the veterans and the generals left for Triparadeisus in Syria, where, as we shall see, they would again find themselves at odds. We shall pick up their story there (chap. 5 below).

CRATERUS'S VETERANS

Before we turn to Craterus's veterans, something should be said about the possibility that the forces of the Macedonian marshal Leonnatus in-

---

63. Philotas's replacement: Arr. *Succ.* 1.24.2; cf. Just. 13.6.16. Craterus left Alexander's royal army in 324: Arr. *Anab.* 7.12.4; Heckel 2006, 98. I do not subscribe to the view that the Silver Shields left with Craterus and then joined Perdiccas's invasion of Egypt. For the controversial date of Perdiccas's invasion and death: Anson 2003 (favoring the "low chronology"). Fighting Craterus and Antipater: Diod. 18.25.6. Justin 13.6.11–12 indicates that those who advised Perdiccas to march on Macedonia were concerned about the reaction at home and not in camp.

64. Justin (14.4.11) has Eumenes later charging the veterans with killing Perdiccas, but the circumstances and the rhetorical context of this accusation cast doubt on its validity.

cluded Alexander's veterans as well. Leonnatus was one of Alexander's bodyguards and was closely associated with Perdiccas both during Alexander's campaign and later in the power struggles attending the king's death. For unknown reasons, the final settlement at Babylon gave him only the relatively middling position of satrap of Hellespontine Phrygia, but he was a sought-after ally. In 323 Perdiccas instructed him and Antigonus to help Eumenes conquer Cappadocia and Paphlagonia, but neither of them did.

Later, Antipater, who anticipated a war against a Greek coalition (known as the Hellenic or the Lamian War), also asked Leonnatus to come to his aid. This time Leonnatus accepted the invitation and, according to Eumenes, confided to him that he intended to use Antipater's request to take over Macedonia. In 322 Leonnatus crossed to Macedonia, where he acquired many Macedonians and increased his army to more than 20,000 infantry and 1,500 cavalry. He died, however, in a battle against the Greeks in Thessaly. The next day Antipater arrived on the scene and incorporated Leonnatus's army into his own.[65]

Scholars largely agree that Leonnatus took no veterans with him to his satrapy or to Europe.[66] Indeed, it is prudent not to postulate the veterans' presence where the sources fail to mention them. But the case of Leonnatus is different because there is both indirect and direct evidence for veteran Macedonians in his army. Leonnatus imitated Alexander in his royal practices and affluence, which would have been most effective when displayed to the veterans.[67] More telling is an explicit reference to Leonnatus's veterans in Plutarch's biography of Phocion, where the biographer mentions the Greeks' victory over Leonnatus, "who had joined forces with Antipater with Macedonians from Asia."[68] Yet because Plutarch's testimony is sparse, and because the number of Leonnatus's veterans is unknown, there is nothing to tell us about their role in Phrygia or Europe, apart from acknowledg-

---

65. Leonnatus in Asia Minor and Europe: esp. Diod. 18.14.5–15.5; Plut. *Eum.* 3.4–9; Schmitt 1992, 118–125; Heckel 2006, 147–151; Sprawski 2008.

66. Anson 1991, 239–240n43; 2004, 67–69 (persuasively argues against Briant's assertion [1973b, 166–167] that Leonnatus appropriated many Macedonians from Eumenes and took them to Europe); Bosworth 2002, 78–79 (who denies that Leonnatus had many Macedonians even in Europe); cf. Billows 1995, 193n24, but also Schmitt 1992, 122n24.

67. Arr. *Succ.* F 12; Plut. *Alex.* 40.1; Athen. 12.539c–d; Aelian *VH* 9.3: Heckel 2006, 150–151. Leonnatus had a personal cavalry *agēma* whose ethnic composition is unknown. Sprawski (2008, 14) thinks that they were Macedonians.

68. Plut. *Phocion* 25.4: *symmixantos Antipatrō(i) Leonnatou kai tōn ex Asias Makedonōn.* This phrase seems to have escaped scholarly attention.

ing their existence. Leonnatus's last battle, in any case, involved mostly the cavalry, while the phalanx's only attested contribution was to find shelter on high, difficult terrain, from which they successfully defended themselves.[69]

We are better informed about Craterus's veterans. This Macedonian marshal had enjoyed Alexander's special trust and was Perdiccas's equal in ambition and prestige. He had been away from the royal army since leaving Opis in the autumn of 324 with about 11,500 veterans and 1,000 Persian bowmen and slingers. His best-attested original mission was to bring the veterans home and replace Antipater as governor of Macedonia, Thrace, and Greece. However, following Alexander's death and Perdiccas's consolidation of power in Babylon, the Macedonians canceled Alexander's last plans as well as his instructions to Craterus. At first they appointed Craterus the guardian of Philip III, but eventually gave him a joint governorship with Antipater in Europe.[70] Throughout this time Craterus went no farther than Cilicia, where he received, still in 323, Antipater's request to come to his aid against rebel Greeks. He finally left Cilicia around the time Perdiccas entered neighboring Cappadocia, and he reached Europe in summer 322.[71]

Because Craterus did nothing remarkable between his departure from Opis and his arrival in Greece, and because he took no part in the drama of the Babylonian power struggles and their aftermath, the sources ignore his story, including what moved him to stay in Asia Minor for so long. I do not intend to add yet another explanation to the many that scholars have offered for his apparent inaction, although his reluctance to challenge Antipater in Europe or Perdiccas in Asia, and his looking for the right moment to make his move, seem likely motives.[72] I shall equally avoid speculating on how he justified the long absence from Macedonia to his veterans, who, in Opis, had quarreled with Alexander over their demand to go home,

---

69. Diod. 18.15.1–4 provides the most detailed description of the battle. For other sources and analysis: Sprawski 2008, 19–29. Diodorus's report on Lysimachus's Thracian campaign of 323 says nothing about the veterans' participation in it: 18.13.2–4.

70. Craterus's force: Diod. 18.16.4 and chap. 2 above. His different briefs: Diod. 18.4.1; Arr. *Succ.* 1.3, 7; Dexippus *FGrHist* 100 F 8.4; Badian 1967, 201–204. His career and positions: Anson 1992; Bosworth 2002, 52–53, 58–60; Heckel 2006, 95–99; Meeus 2008, esp. 62–63.

71. Diod. 18.12.1, 16.4; Schmitt 1992, 143–144; Heckel 1992, 130; Bosworth 2002, 60 (June at the latest).

72. See Badian 1961, 36–37; Ashton 1991, esp. 127–129; Heckel 1992, 125–129, for different suggestions regarding his possible motives and even how he occupied himself, although the stay was prolonged by any account.

and who had lost their camp families on this account. It is clear, however, that the veterans did not desert him—he returned to Europe with the same number of troops he took from Opis—and the sources' silence about any complaints against him should be taken at face value. As argued earlier, the veterans' conduct indicates that their desire to return home was not universal or unchanged.[73] At the same time, their staying with Craterus suggests their dependence on him, which only increased with the crises and uncertainty that followed Alexander's death. This dependence, as well as their political impotence, complemented their high regard for him.

On arriving in Macedonia, Craterus did not discharge the veterans to their homes but led them to Thessaly, where Antipater's army was stationed. We know that they followed him there in full force because Diodorus reports their size just before they entered Thessaly, and especially because the totals for the forces of Antipater, Leonnatus, and Craterus in the Hellenic war would not tally without including the veterans.[74] It should not have been difficult for Craterus to motivate the veterans to follow him to this war. In spite of recent Macedonian naval victories over Athenian fleets, Macedonia's hegemony in Greece was in danger after two consecutive defeats to a Greek coalition on land. Craterus showed up in Europe as the man who would reverse the Macedonians' fortunes, giving himself and his veterans the flattering role of saviors.

To ease Antipater's apprehension and (probably) to fulfill a prior agreement, Craterus yielded the chief command to the old marshal when the two joined forces in Thessaly (Diod. 18.16.4–5). His concession should have alerted farsighted veterans to what awaited them. By acknowledging Antipater's supremacy, Craterus effectively renounced the joint rule over Europe with Antipater that had been offered to him by Perdiccas and the marshals in Babylon. Since such a descent from equal partnership to a secondary position was incompatible with Craterus's ambitions and public persona, his move portended plans to carve out a rule for himself elsewhere. His deal with Antipater became public knowledge sometime after the Battle

---

73. See chap. 2 above. On their number and Diod. 18.16.4, see Bosworth 2002, 73n31. If Bosworth (2002, 51–53) is correct in believing that Craterus's financial power extended to the royal treasury in Cilicia, the veterans were presumably well taken care of.

74. Diod. 18.12.2–4, 14.5, 16.4–5. In fact, Diodorus's totals are higher than the sum of the numbers he gives for these individual forces, which suggests that, in addition to Craterus's veterans, unreported reinforcements reached Antipater in Thessaly or were drafted by Craterus.

of Crannon, when Craterus married Antipater's daughter, Phila, and made preparations to return to Asia.[75]

In his description of the Battle of Crannon between the Macedonians and the Greeks in July–August of 322, Diodorus properly does not distinguish the veterans' performance from others'. The Macedonian army won largely because of its numerical superiority, having more than 40,000 infantry and 5,000 cavalry against the Greeks' 25,000 infantry and 3,500 cavalry. The course of the battle suggests that the veterans' contribution to the victory was modest at best. At first the Greeks sent into battle the excellent Thessalian cavalry, which overcame the Macedonian cavalry. But then Antipater moved in with "his own infantry phalanx" (*tēn idian phallanga kai tois pezois*; Diod. 18.17.4), which inflicted heavy losses on the Greek infantry. The latter retreated to higher ground, where they were joined by their cavalry, and together they successfully defended themselves against Macedonian attacks. The battle ended in a Macedonian victory, with 500 Greek dead to the Macedonians' 130.[76] The role of the veterans in this battle was undistinguished. Their horsemen undoubtedly fought in the ranks of the Macedonian cavalry, who were beaten by their opponents. The veterans' phalanx, which must have been led by Craterus, either stayed put on their (left?) wing or tried to catch up with Antipater's phalanx, which led the attack and turned the battle around. Moreover, the victorious Macedonians were unable to prevent the Greeks from retreating in order, and when the Greeks reached high ground they had little difficulty holding the enemy off. The Battle of Crannon confirmed the veterans' invincible record but hardly justified their reputation for military excellence on foot or on horse.

In spite of their many casualties, the results of Crannon were not decisive enough to convince the Greeks to end their war of independence. Instead of returning home, the veterans had to stay in Thessaly, where the Macedonian army besieged and captured cities that refused to come to terms with Antipater and Craterus (Diod. 18.17.7; [Plut.] *Moral.* 846e). The Athenians also took their time deciding whether to sue for peace, a delay that led An-

---

75. Diod. 18.18.7. Joint rule of Europe: Arr. *Succ.* 1.7; Bosworth 2002, 58–60; cf. Kanatsulis 1968, 139–140.

76. The size of the opposing armies: Diod. 18.16.5, 17.2; cf. 18.17.6. The Battle of Crannon: Diod. 18.17.3–5; cf. Plut. *Phocion* 26.1; *Dem.* 28.2. Arrian (*Succ.* 1.12) gives Craterus credit for the victory, but Diodorus's more detailed account is preferable to his summarized report. It is possible, however, that Craterus's Macedonian veterans fought Alexander's Greek veterans, who had been recruited earlier by Leosthenes: Diod. 18.9.3.

tipater to apply pressure by marching into neighboring Boeotia. Plutarch reports that the Athenian general Phocion, who was a friend of both Alexander's and Antipater's, went to negotiate an agreement with Antipater in the Theban citadel of the Cadmea. When Phocion requested that the Macedonians not advance into Attica, Craterus, perhaps playing the "bad cop," told Phocion it was unfair for his army to live off the land of friends instead of destroying and looting enemy territory. But Antipater agreed to stay out of Attica, and the Athenians soon accepted his terms of surrender.[77] Some of the veterans, who had fought with Philip and Alexander in Greece, must have had a sense of déjà vu. Both kings had won victories over a Greek coalition, made demands of Athens from their camp in Boeotia, and stopped short of invading its territory, although neither king had imposed conditions on the city as harsh as Antipater's.

Antipater took the lead in the war and the negotiations, but there were no signs that Craterus's appeal and prominence suffered any decline. Even his threat to ravage Attica presupposed and displayed the concern to reward his soldiers that partly accounted for his popularity among them. Our sources, especially Plutarch, suggest that Craterus was universally liked by Alexander's veterans because of his Macedonian traditionalism, his opposition to Alexander's orientalism, his friendly attitude, his fame as a soldier and commander, and his visual fitness for the part of a warrior king, with his large physique and splendid, Alexander-like attire. Some of the reasons given for his popularity, such as his opposition to Alexander's "going Asian," must have lost their relevancy by now, and, as we have argued, Craterus was surely more popular in his own army than in other Successors' forces.[78] Yet there is little doubt that Craterus made a conscious effort to present himself to Macedonians and Greeks as kinglike, although he stopped short of wearing the diadem and claiming kingship outright. He dressed like Alexander and—according to the hostile testimony of the Athenian leader and intellectual Demetrius of Phaleron—he received Greek envoys sitting on an elevated golden couch and wearing a purple robe. Craterus's son and namesake dedicated at Delphi a monumental statue group (apparently commissioned by the senior Craterus before his death) showing his father coming to Alexander's rescue during a lion hunt. In such self-aggrandizement and advertisement of his link to Alexander, Craterus re-

---

77. Plut. *Phocion* 26.2–28.1; cf. Demetrius of Phaleron, *De elocutione* 289; Trittle 1988, 129–131.

78. For the sources on Craterus's post-Alexander popularity, see note 62 above.

sembled other Successors who emphasized their proximity or similarity to Alexander in order to legitimize their rule.[79]

The sources suggest that Craterus's veterans and companions willingly played along and even expected their general to act like a king (Arr. *Succ.* F 19). In this they differed from Perdiccas's Macedonians, who had not been exposed to Craterus's charisma since Opis and, more importantly, had two kings in their camp, to whom they were committed since rioting for Philip III in Babylon. Craterus's veterans, on the other hand, had been away from the royal court since 324 and did not witness or participate in the coronation of Alexander's successors. Their dependence on their beloved general moved them to respond favorably to his royal pretensions. Nor should we underestimate their wish to flatter him or to partake of his honor, since their prestige grew with his status. Honoring their commander like a king also distinguished Craterus from Antipater, who failed to meet the veterans' military and esthetic expectations of a commander. Antipater had fared poorly in the war against the Greeks before the veterans and Craterus came to save the day, and he carried himself unassumingly, was aloof, dressed plainly, and was shorter and older than Craterus. The troops' disobeying Antipater and preference for Craterus also signaled the veterans' special status in camp.[80]

We are not informed about Antipater's reaction to Craterus's and the veterans' conduct and aspirations, but he appears to have raised no objections, having no desire to quarrel with a man who both recognized his supremacy in Europe and meant to go to Asia in any case. By not wearing the diadem publicly, Craterus gave reassurance that he would not be the first to claim a royal title. Generally, it was a concern over their rivals' reactions no less than fear of the Macedonians that made the marshals reluctant to proclaim themselves kings (before Antigonus and his son Demetrius did so

---

79. Craterus's attire and audience: Arr. *Succ.* F 19; Demetrius *De elocutione* 289. The Delphian statues and dedication: *ISE* no. 73; Plut. *Alex.* 40.5; Pliny *NH* 34.64; Athen. 15.696e–f; Stewart 1993, 270–277, 390–391; Palagia 2000, 184–186, 203–204; cf. Roisman 2003, 302–303, 313–316. The marshals' invoking their connections to Alexander: esp. Suda s.v. *Leonnatus* = Arr. *Succ.* F 12; Bosworth 2002, 246–278 (on Craterus: 276–277); Meeus 2009a; 2009b, 66–70.

80. Arr. *Succ.* F 19; Plut. *Phocion* 29.2; *Moral.* 180e. The contemporary Demades of Athens called Antipater "a rotten, old thread": Plut. *Demtr.* 31.5; *Phocion* 30.5; Arr. *Succ.* 1.14. The veterans did not experience Antipater's moderate rule at home (Plut. *Demtr.* 37.2–4), and it is hard to separate the tradition about his moderation from the politics of the Antigonid claim to the Macedonian monarchy: Landucci Gattinoni 2009, 268–271.

in 306). In any case, it appears that the veterans' differing behavior toward Craterus and Antipater led to no rift between the two marshals, who decided on cooperation as their best course. When the Macedonian army returned home after the surrender of Athens, Antipater gave Craterus honors, gifts, and the hand of his eldest daughter, Phila (Diod. 18.18.7). This was also probably the right occasion for honoring Alexander's old instructions upon the discharge of the veteran at Opis (324) to reward them with garlands and front seats in dramatic and other contests once they returned home.[81]

Soon, however, events in Greece forced Craterus to postpone his departure for Asia. During the autumn and winter of 321/0, he and Antipater invaded the Greek rebel state of Aetolia, thereby extending Craterus's stay in Europe for almost a year. It is not certain that the veterans followed Craterus to Aetolia: Diodorus fails to mention them there, and the fact that the Macedonian army in Aetolia was smaller than the one in Crannon by 10,000 infantry and 500 cavalry suggests their absence (Diod. 18.16.5, 24.1). But if Craterus refused to give up on their service, their fighting in Aetolia was far from easy, because the invading army suffered many losses when it attacked fortified Aetolian places. The situation improved only after Craterus built covered buildings for his men and prevented the Aetolians from leaving their snowy mountain refuges to resupply (Diod. 18.25.1–2).

Then Antipater and Craterus learned from Antigonus Monophthalmus, now Perdiccas's enemy, that the regent had eliminated Cynane and plotted to get rid of Alexander's former generals, to marry Alexander's sister Cleopatra, and to take over Macedonia as its king.[82] The result was, according to Diodorus, that a council composed of Antipater, Craterus, and their officers made the following resolutions: to conclude the Aetolian campaign outright; to transport the armies quickly to Asia to make war on Perdiccas; to give the command of Europe to Antipater and that of Asia to Craterus; and to seek an alliance with Ptolemy, who was a fellow victim of Perdiccas's schemes (Diod. 18.25.3–4; cf. 14.2; Just. 13.6.9). It is fairly certain that the veterans contributed little to these decisions. According to Diodorus, it was the commanders, not the army, who received the news about Perdiccas's aims and made the decision to fight him. Their resolutions were

---

81. Plut. *Alex.* 71.8; Diod. 18.18.7. Le Rider (2007, 60–72) convincingly rejects the view that money brought by the veterans was responsible for a growth in coinage by the Amphipolis mint.

82. Diodorus and Arrian disagree on the way Antigonus delivered the news, but less on its essence: Diod. 18.24.1–25.5; Arr. *Succ.* 1.24–26; Billows 1990, 63–64.

brought to the assembly for approval after the fact and in Macedonia. A decree recording these decisions added a threat to reconquer Aetolia and to transport its people to farther Asia, and it is unlikely such a resolution attended the signing of the treaty with the Aetolians. It appears that the army merely rubber-stamped their motions.[83] The royal army in Babylon could influence the political process because the elite in camp was divided, but now, in Europe, Craterus's veterans and the other troops faced a solid command structure that discouraged potential opposition.

The sources accordingly ignore how the marshals justified the Asian campaign to their soldiers. In addition to charging Perdiccas with conspiring to remove Antipater and others from their duly confirmed positions in the Babylonian settlement, a likely accusation was that he intended to rob the reigning Argead kings of their throne. It should not have been difficult to present his tight control over the kings, his elimination of Cynane, and his marriage negotiations with Cleopatra, Alexander's sister, as proofs of his ambitions. Craterus too had royal aspirations, but there was no contest about whom his veterans preferred for the kingship. Another probable charge was that Perdiccas was fomenting a civil war (cf. Diod. 18.25.3–4, 14.2; Arr. *Succ.* 1.24). The fact was that Craterus and Antipater intended to start what might have become the greatest armed conflict between fellow Macedonians in more than a generation.

Before Antipater and Craterus's departure, Antigonus crossed with 3,000 infantry to Asia, where he was joined by the satraps of Lydia and Caria. He then tried unsuccessfully to ambush Eumenes with 2,000 infantry and a few cavalry. There is nothing in the sources about Antigonus's use of veterans in these operations. There is somewhat better evidence for their presence in the army that went with Antipater and Craterus to Asia in the spring of 320, but no report of how they fared before engaging Eumenes in the spring of 320.[84]

Before I discuss this battle, it will be useful to interrupt the story of Craterus's veterans in order to bring the history of other commanders' veterans—aside from those who had invaded Egypt with Perdiccas—up to this point.

---

83. Diod. 18.25.4–5. See, however, Hatzopoulos 1996, 1:286, arguing for a full legislative procedure here and citing similar views.

84. Antigonus's invasion: Arr. *Succ.* 1.25–26. Briant (1973b, 207–208) postdates the invasion to that of Craterus and Antipater, but see Hauben 1977, 93–95; Billows 1990, 62–63. Craterus and veterans: Hammond 1984, 55–60 = 1994, 3:135–140 (but see chap. 6 below); Billows 1995, 194, 196, 212; Bosworth 2002, 84–85.

CHAPTER 5

THE DISSOLUTION OF THE ROYAL ARMY, II: THE VETERANS OF EUMENES, NEOPTOLEMUS, AND ALCETAS, AND THE MEETING IN TRIPARADEISUS

THE VETERANS OF EUMENES, NEOPTOLEMUS, AND ALCETAS

Eumenes, Neoptolemus, and Alcetas were generals who supported Perdiccas and who operated in different territories in Asia Minor. Perdiccas later appointed Eumenes as his chief commander in Asia Minor, but seems to have allocated veterans only to Neoptolemus and Alcetas.

We have discussed Eumenes' earlier career and his role in Babylon in a previous chapter (chap. 3). After the Babylonian settlement in the summer of 323, Eumenes was given the governorship of Cappadocia and Paphlagonia, provinces that had mostly escaped Alexander's conquest. Perdiccas asked Leonnatus and Antigonus Monophthalmus, the satrap of Greater Phrygia, to assist Eumenes in taking over these lands, but Antigonus ignored the request, and Leonnatus preferred to join Antipater in Europe, where he found his death. With little gained, Eumenes returned to Perdiccas's camp with 300 cavalry of unknown nationality, 200 armed servants, and 5,000 gold talents.[1] In 322 he went back to his satrapy, this time accompanied by Perdiccas and the royal army that had defeated the Cappadocian king Ariarathes (chap. 4).

After subjugating the satrapy, Eumenes reorganized its administration, but then followed Perdiccas to Cilicia, well knowing where the real power resided. The regent, however, dispatched him back to Cappadocia with (according to Plutarch) the real mission of asserting control over neighboring Armenia, where Neoptolemus, who had commanded the hypaspists under Alexander, was holding operations in an apparent attempt to establish

---

1. Plut. *Eum.* 1.1–3.14. It is possible that Eumenes' 300 cavalry functioned as his *agēma* of bodyguards and as an elite attack unit, like similar units of other generals: Briant 1973b, 167n7; Billows 1990, 263.

Macedonian rule there (Plut. *Eum.* 4.1).[2] It was in this context, our sources tell us, that Eumenes and the veterans came into conflict for the first time. Plutarch says that Neoptolemus was given to ostentation and empty vanity, but that Eumenes tried to keep him in check through constant conversation. Finding the Macedonian phalanx to be insolent and brazen, Eumenes created a counter-unit (*antitagma*) of local cavalry, whose members he rewarded, trained, and provided with horses. When the Macedonians saw how quickly he put together a body of 6,300 cavalry, some were filled with astonishment and others were emboldened (Plut. *Eum.* 4.2–3).

Plutarch's purpose in recounting this episode is to demonstrate Eumenes' resourcefulness in overcoming difficulties. This is a leitmotif in the ancient accounts of this general and likely goes back to Eumenes' friend, Hieronymus. Yet the biographer's focus on Eumenes' ingenuity obscures many details that are significant for the history of the veterans. It is unclear exactly where Eumenes' clash with Neoptolemus and the phalanx took place and why they were hostile to him. Plutarch does not even specify if the Macedonians' commander at this time was Eumenes or Neoptolemus. It is easier to resolve some of these problems than others. The Armenian context of the conflict and Eumenes' plan to face Antigonus with Armenian allies later in 319 (Diod. 18.41.1) suggest that the men he drafted into his cavalry came at least partly from Armenia. It appears also that Neoptolemus commanded the Macedonians. In 320 Perdiccas gave Eumenes supreme command over forces in Armenia and Cappadocia, and later that year Eumenes defeated Neoptolemus in battle and captured many of his Macedonians. Both events suggest that Neoptolemus had commanded Macedonians already in Armenia.[3]

It is not surprising that Neoptolemus had Macedonian veterans but Eumenes hardly any. The veterans were needed more in unpacified Armenia, and Eumenes, unlike the noble and more-prominent Neoptolemus, was completely dependent on Perdiccas at this stage and therefore in a weaker position to bargain for such valuable troops.[4] Plutarch indicates

---

2. For Eumenes' career from Babylon to this point, see Schäfer 2002, 60–77; Anson 2004, 61–81. Neoptolemus's career and his Armenian mission: Bosworth 1978, 232–233; Heckel 2006, 174–175. He probably conducted operations in Armenia as a general rather than a satrap: Briant 1973b, 152n8.

3. Plut. *Eum.* 5.1; Diod. 18.29.4. Scholarly speculations regarding the number of these veterans ranged from three to five thousand: Billows 1995, 191; Bosworth 2002, 81, 84, 90.

4. Briant (1972, 54–55, 58–60 [repr. 1982, 34–35, 39–41]; 1973b, 166), however, thinks that both Eumenes and Neoptolemus had Macedonians in their armies, but see above

that Neoptolemus and his Macedonians faced difficulties in Armenia, but his depiction of both the troops and their leader as insolent also suggests that Eumenes' problems had less to do with their military performance than with their refusal to acknowledge his authority (Plut. *Eum.* 4.1–3, cf. 5.1–5). We do not know what fault the Macedonians found with Eumenes. It was not his non-Macedonian origin, because Plutarch, who frequently mentions Eumenes' difficulties on this account, fails to cite it here. More likely the Macedonians were demonstrating their personal loyalty to their leader, Neoptolemus, by showing their disregard of Eumenes, who threatened his authority. The Cardian's military record since Alexander's death did not inspire confidence, either. In any case, Eumenes' creation of the cavalry force illustrates how a general with substantial financial and administrative resources, including exemption from taxes, could decrease his dependence on the Macedonians and show them that they were not indispensable. Eumenes also saw in Babylon how the cavalry could stand up to the infantry. This experience may partly explain his playing power games with the Macedonians.

Plutarch's description of the Macedonian reaction to Eumenes' creation of the cavalry force is puzzling (Plut. *Eum.* 4.4). He says that the veterans were "amazed" or "emboldened": emotions that demonstrate the success of Eumenes' countermeasure but are hardly the response expected of men confronted with a unit designed to offset them. They had reacted very differently to Alexander's Epigoni, also created as what Diodorus calls an *antitagma*, a counter-unit, to the rebellious Macedonian phalanx.[5] It is evident that Neoptolemus's veterans did not come to admire Eumenes more or Neoptolemus less as a result of Eumenes' ploy, since a year or more later they followed Neoptolemus into battle against the Cardian, defeated his infantry, and joined him only under compulsion, after Neoptolemus had fled the battlefield. Clearly, the Macedonians were more upset than pleased by Eumenes' foregrounding of the cavalry at their expense.[6]

The available information about Eumenes and the veterans between this

---

as well as the counterarguments of Bosworth (1978, 233n6; 1980, 17n138) and Anson (1990; 2004, 67, 80–81). In addition, if both generals had had veterans here, the sources would not have passed over in silence the remarkable "fact" that Macedonians fought Macedonians in a later battle between Eumenes and Neoptolemus. Eumenes and Neoptolemus in Armenia: Bosworth 1978, 232–233; Anson 2004, 78–80, 95.

5. Diod. 17.108.3. For the concept of *antitagma*, see Briant 1972, 49–60 (repr. 1982, 30–41).

6. Diod. 18.29.4; Plut. *Eum.* 5.3–4, and below. Cf. W. Thompson 1984, 114–115n5. I date Neoptolemus's insult of Eumenes in Plut. *Eum.* 1.6 to a later occasion (below).

last-mentioned episode and his later battles with Neoptolemus and Craterus in the spring of 320 is meager, scattered over different sources, and not always consistent, leading scholars to offer different scenarios of their movements.[7] Before discussing the veterans' story in detail, I offer for the sake of clarity the following reconstruction, which includes only events that may be relevant to the veterans and are explicitly attested by the evidence.

Before marching to Egypt, Perdiccas put Eumenes in charge of the land operations against Antipater and Craterus. He sent him to the Hellespont and instructed his brother Alcetas and Neoptolemus to follow Eumenes' commands. Neither general obeyed Perdiccas's edict.[8] It is reported that Eumenes went to Lydia, that he foiled Antigonus's attempt to ambush him there, and that he retreated to Phrygia (Arr. *Succ.* 1.25.6–8). His failure to defend the Aegean coast and to prevent the defection of Perdiccan forces (probably including Perdiccas's fleet under Cleitus) to Antipater and Craterus allowed the latter two to cross to Asia and even to march inland unopposed (Arr. *Succ.* 1.26). Antipater and Craterus invited Eumenes and Neoptolemus to join them, but only Neoptolemus accepted their offer. Eumenes then won a battle against Neoptolemus, probably in Phrygia, and added Neoptolemus's Macedonians to his army. Ten days later he defeated Craterus near Cappadocia (320).[9]

What can be learned about the veterans from this synopsis? It is unlikely that Eumenes had many of them in his army before his acquisition of Neoptolemus's Macedonians. In reporting on Eumenes' force earlier, on the western front, the sources mention his friends, cavalry, light-armed troops, and relatively fresh recruits with deficient training, none of whom fit the description of Alexander's veterans.[10] Following Eumenes' retreat to central Asia Minor, Perdiccas renewed his request of his brother Alcetas and of Neoptolemus to put themselves and their armies under Eumenes' command (Plut. *Eum.* 5.2; Just. 13.6.15). According to Plutarch, Neoptolemus plotted secretly against Eumenes while Alcetas openly refused to have anything to do with the campaign, claiming that his Macedonians would be

7. Briant 1973b, 188–211; Hauben 1977, 91–110; Billows 1990, 59–65; Anson 2004, 90–103.

8. Diod. 18.25.6, 29.1–3; Plut. *Eum.* 5.1–5; Just. 13.6.14–15 (confusing Lydia with Lycia); Nepos *Eum.* 3.2–3. I do not consider Diod. 18.25.6 to be a doublet of 18.29.1.

9. Plut. *Eum.* 5.2–8, 8.1; Diod. 18.29.4, 37.1. For the location of the battle with Neoptolemus, see Anson 2004, 106n102.

10. The composition of Eumenes' army: Diod. 18.29.3; Arr. *Succ.* 1.25.6; Nepos *Eum.* 3.3. Its size: Diod. 18.25.6, 29.1; Nepos *Eum.* 3.3. Against Briant's assumption that Eumenes had Macedonians, see note 4 above.

ashamed to fight Antipater and were readys to welcome Craterus, to whom they were favorably disposed (Plut. *Eum.* 5.2–3).

We do not really know how many Macedonians Alcetas had or how long he had had them. The evidence up to this point mentions no satrapy or command that can be identified as his, and we learn about his independent operations in Phrygia, Caria, and especially Pisidia only later, after Perdiccas's death in the spring of 320. It is possible, then, that Alcetas got his veterans only for the purpose of repelling the invading force of Antipater and Craterus. And to judge by his claim that the Macedonians were reluctant to meet the enemy, they were sufficient in number to influence the result of the battle.[11] Yet how credible was Alcetas's assertion about his veterans' shaky loyalty? Alcetas's stated reasons for not cooperating with Eumenes cannot be dissociated from his personal and political rivalry with the Cardian. He was probably envious of Eumenes' supreme command. Earlier, when Perdiccas was wavering between keeping his alliance with Antipater and marrying his daughter Nicaia on the one hand and marrying Alexander's sister Cleopatra in preparation for his march on Macedonia on the other, Alcetas favored the former option and Eumenes the latter (Arr. *Succ.* 1.21). It is possible, then, that Alcetas refused to fight Antipater and Craterus because he was still hoping for reconciliation with them.[12]

Perdiccas's absence and consequent inability to enforce obedience to his directives (which he gave to Alcetas and Neoptolemus in writing: Plut. *Eum.* 5.2) made it easier for Alcetas to ignore his orders, as did Eumenes' weakened position after his failure to stop the march of Antipater and Craterus. Yet Alcetas's reluctance to fight the two marshals does not mean that he, or even his Macedonians, wished to transfer their alliance to them. Perdiccas, who gave Alcetas the veterans and told him to join the war, clearly trusted them to fight the invaders. Antipater and Craterus, who tried to entice Eumenes and Neoptolemus—but not Alcetas—to desert, appear to have shared this trust.[13] Indeed, if the veterans' reluctance to fight tied Alcetas's hands, how did he plan to stand up to the invaders if forced to do

---

11. Alcetas in Asia Minor following Perdiccas's death: Plut. *Eum.* 8.7–8; Arr. *Succ.* 1.41–42; App. *Syr.* 52; Diod. 18.44.1–47.5. For estimates of the number of his veterans, see Heckel 1992, 173, 175n52 (3,000); Billows 1995, 191 (1–3,000); Bosworth 2002, 81, 90 (ca. 2,000). Hammond (1984, 56 [repr. 1994, 3:136]) gives both Alcetas and Neoptolemus 4,000 veterans. There is no need for another speculation.

12. Errington 1970, 64n108; Anson 2004, 103–104; and esp. Meeus 2009b, 73–80.

13. As Perdiccas's brother, Alcetas was, *prima facie*, the least likely to desert him, but he was also upset with Perdiccas for preferring Eumenes as the supreme commander in Asia Minor.

so? It is true that Neoptolemus claimed, and Eumenes feared, that the veterans would join Craterus (Plut. *Eum.* 5.3, 6.1–7, 7.1–2), but this hypothesis was never tested. Without discounting the Macedonians' affection for Antipater and Craterus, Alcetas's assertion about its strength and impact is too tainted to be credible.

Yet even as a pretext, Alcetas's allegations provide valuable information. On the one hand, his and Neoptolemus's (later) statements that the veterans would refuse to fight Antipater or Craterus completely ignore the greater legitimacy of fighting on the side of the kings and their guardian, Perdiccas. Clearly the commanders understood the troops' loyalty only in terms of their relationship with individual generals. Because the sources reflect the generals' viewpoint, we cannot tell if the troops were equally unaware that their cause was just. On the other hand, Alcetas's words alluded to the predicament of generals who were still dependent on their Macedonian troops and who had to take into account what pleased and displeased them. In this respect, such leaders lived in the past. In contrast, commanders such as Eumenes and Ptolemy saw what Alexander had already realized in the later part of his career: that the future belonged to those who could recruit and train non-Macedonian troops.[14]

Alcetas's defiance of Eumenes went unpunished, but Neoptolemus's did not. Eumenes charged the latter with plotting against him and the Perdiccan cause, and the dispute led to a battle between them. Although Eumenes' infantry was defeated by Neoptolemus's larger force, which included Macedonians, Eumenes won the battle because of his well-trained local cavalry, who apparently far outnumbered Neoptolemus's cavalry. Eumenes then captured the enemy's baggage, called all his horsemen together, and attacked Neoptolemus's phalanx, which had scattered in pursuit of Eumenes' infantry. The phalanx surrendered and took an oath to follow Eumenes. In this way Eumenes acquired "many valorous Macedonians" and killed many enemy troops. Neoptolemus fled to the camp of Craterus and Antipater with 300 cavalry of unknown ethnicity.[15]

When Neoptolemus's veterans went to battle against Eumenes, they must have known that they were fighting on the side of Craterus and Antipater. Ironically, by later joining Eumenes' camp, they moved in exactly the

---

14. Alcetas himself would later be pushed toward this realization when he relied on local forces: Diod. 18.46.1–3.

15. Diod. 18.29.4–6; Plut. *Eum.* 5.4–5; Arr. *Succ.* 1.26–27; Just. 13.8.1–5. The quotation is from Diod. 18.29.5. See Vezin 1907, 44–45, for an attempt to reconstruct the battle.

opposite direction to that predicted by Alcetas. This is the first attested time that Alexander's veterans changed sides following a defeat. The infantrymen were at a disadvantage when they pursued the fleeing enemy and lost the cohesiveness that was their best defense against Eumenes' cavalry.[16] Thus the battle demonstrated the success of Eumenes' *antitagma* experiment, showing that while the veterans may have surpassed all other infantry in fighting, they could not decide a battle, and their success meant little against the offsetting effect of good cavalry. Eumenes also seized their baggage, which may have included their dependents. (We shall discuss the effect on their loyalty of capturing the soldiers' baggage in a later chapter. As proof of its deleterious potential, I cite here only the example of Antigonus's capture of the baggage of Eumenes' veterans in the Battle of Gabene in 317, a coup that moved them to change sides and to surrender Eumenes.)[17] The veterans' decision to join Eumenes in 320 was also influenced by their likely disappointment with their leader, Neoptolemus. They had played their part well in defeating the opposing infantry, but were abandoned by their losing commander, who fled the scene. The contrasting example of the victorious Eumenes must have impressed them favorably. The veterans liked their generals to be winners.

Neoptolemus, however, claimed that the veterans could be easily won back. He fled to Antipater and Craterus, who were deliberating the strategy of their campaign, and he told them that they should come to his aid with the entire army, or at least send Craterus against Eumenes, because the Macedonians in Eumenes' army missed Craterus so much that they would desert to him in droves once they saw his Macedonian hat (*kausia*) and heard his voice (Plut. *Eum.* 5.6, 6.1–2).

Before concurring with Neoptolemus's prognosis, as do many of Plutarch's modern readers, we should examine its context. Neoptolemus had just lost a battle and his army to Eumenes, and was desperate to undo both results. His only hope was to get help from Craterus and Antipater, but their aid could not be taken for granted because they were still undecided about how to proceed with the campaign (Plut. *Eum.* 6.1). Eumenes had declined their invitation to join them, but this did not necessarily mean an end to those negotiations, especially after his victory over Neoptolemus and acquisition of his veterans had made him an even more desirable ally. All of this meant that Neoptolemus had to convince both marshals that joining

16. I ascribe *PSI* 12: 1284 to Eumenes' battle with Craterus (below).

17. Baggage and loyalty: below, chap. 6. Loss of baggage in Gabene: Diod. 19.43.7–9, and my chap. 8. See also Bosworth 1978, 235; Schäfer 2002, 82–83.

him to fight Eumenes was their better choice. His promise that the veterans would quickly desert to Craterus made victory seem easily attainable and also flattered Craterus. Apparently neither Neoptolemus nor the marshals who took his advice had learned anything from Eumenes' recent victory, which was attained by cavalry against a force that included the veterans.

Two facts, however, are clear. First, Neoptolemus's assessment of the veterans' sentiments (whatever these may have been) was too tendentious and self-interested to be reliable. Second, Craterus knew better than to rely on his popularity for victory. He took into battle a large part of the invading army and tried to catch Eumenes by surprise.[18] In this way, Neoptolemus's defeat changed the later course of the invasion. Antipater was to go with a smaller force to Cilicia and wait there for Craterus, and then the two generals, in league with Ptolemy and Antigonus, were to go on to march against Perdiccas. Craterus and Neoptolemus marched against Eumenes with more than 2,000 cavalry and 20,000 infantry, many of them "Macedonians celebrated for their valor": presumably veterans in whom Craterus placed his hopes of victory.[19]

Early in his biography of Eumenes, Plutarch recounts an anecdote that fits well the eve of this battle. He identifies Neoptolemus as the commander of the hypaspists and reports that Neoptolemus said after Alexander's death that he had followed the king with a shield, but that Eumenes, Alexander's chief secretary, had followed him with a stylus and tablets. The Macedonians, however, laughed at Neoptolemus. They knew well that Alexander had honored Eumenes by his friendship, military commands, and giving him the hand in marriage of the sister of Barsine, the mother of Alexander's child.[20]

Neoptolemus's show of contempt toward Eumenes and his attempt to shape historical memory likely took place in an assembly, where the Macedonians could sound their approval or, as in this case, derision. Plutarch's dating of the episode to after Alexander's death, however, is too vague. It probably did not take place in one of the public meetings in Babylon fol-

---

18. Plut. *Eum.* 6.4; Just. 13.8.5–6. Schäfer (2002, 84) thinks, however, that Craterus and Antipater deduced from Neoptolemus's report that the veterans in Eumenes' camp suffered from low morale. Yet the source only reports on their alleged attraction to Craterus.

19. Diod. 18.29.6, 30.4; cf. Plut. *Eum.* 6.4. For identifying Craterus's Macedonians with the veterans, see chap. 4, note 84, above.

20. Plut. *Eum.* 1.6–7. The Macedonians' favoring of Eumenes here suggests the limited negative impact of his Greek origin on them.

lowing Alexander's death, because neither Neoptolemus nor Eumenes is mentioned in any account of them. This silence has led scholars to ascribe Neoptolemus's derogatory remark to his conflict with Eumenes during the Armenian campaign earlier in 322.[21]

I suggest that a likelier occasion is the prelude to Neoptolemus and Craterus's battle with Eumenes, perhaps the army assembly that Craterus is attested to have convened just before the battle (Diod. 18.30.12). The question of who was more esteemed by Alexander and better entitled to the distinction of service with him was less relevant to the dispute over Armenia than to the coming battle with Eumenes, the first between troops and commanders who had served with Alexander. (Craterus and Neoptolemus did not know that Eumenes would refrain from using his Macedonians.) This novel circumstance made it important for the general on each side to claim a higher place in the esteem of Alexander, which meant a greater entitlement to rule and lead the Macedonians after his death.[22] The dead king's favor could also contribute to victory. Indeed, the relevance of Alexander to this particular engagement (rather than to Armenia) is evinced by the warring parties' passwords and slogans: "Athena and Alexander" for Craterus and "Demeter and Alexander" for Eumenes. But while Craterus's record and proximity to Alexander needed no proof, Neoptolemus's recent loss to Eumenes drove him to highlight his earlier military record and association with Alexander and to denigrate these of Eumenes. The Macedonians, however, knew of Neoptolemus's defeat and put him in his place. The occasion also made them judges of the value of service with, and recognition by, Alexander. The duel between Neoptolemus and Eumenes in the ensuing battle was fueled by Homeric precedents, mutual antipathy, and the wish to conclude the battle by killing the enemy leader. Yet it also sought to decide—for the Macedonians and for the two protagonists themselves—the question of who was the worthier warrior.[23]

Thus, ten days after his victory over Neoptolemus, Eumenes faced a more formidable force. He had an advantage in cavalry—5,000 against Craterus's

---

21. E.g., Anson 2004, 81; cf. Bosworth 1978, 233n25.

22. Being judged worthy by Alexander was a mark of distinction and privilege following his death: Diod. 19.14.4–5, 15.1, 46.2, 51.1; cf. 18.7.3, 48.4; Plut. *Eum.* 18.1.

23. See below for the duel, and cf. Plut. *Pyrrhus* 7; Bosworth 2002, 253–255. Plutarch relates that Eumenes had a dream involving two warring Alexanders that foretold his victory against Craterus, but which he did not divulge to his commanders. Eumenes likely shared the story after the battle to enhance and legitimize his position. For Alexander in a dream presaging victory or rule, cf. Plut. *Demtr.* 29.1; *Pyrrhus* 11.2; Diod. 19.90.4.

2,000—while his ethnically diverse infantry of 20,000 matched Craterus's infantry in size (Diod. 18.30.4–5). But it was the disparity in the martial reputation of the opposing generals, as well as the quality and fame of Craterus's Macedonian phalanx, that made the conflict uneven. Fear of Craterus also accounted for Eumenes' lie to his army that they would be fighting not Craterus, but again Neoptolemus, who he said came to the battle with an unknown commander, Pigres, at the head of Cappadocian and Paphlagonian cavalry. Eumenes' deception was aimed less at his Macedonian veterans, whom he did not take into battle, than at the non-Macedonian majority of his army that was apparently hesitant to fight a general and infantry whose fame preceded them. Eumenes' concern about their resolve is shown also in his forbidding them to accept heralds from the enemy.[24] His ploy succeeded both because his military intelligence was far superior to his enemy's—he had learned of Craterus's attempt to catch him by surprise and knew the enemy's password—and because he kept the information to himself. Even his generals did not know the real identity of the enemy before it was too late (esp. Plut. *Eum.* 6.6–7.2).

For the veterans on both sides, the battle was an anomaly because they appear to have taken no part in it.[25] Eumenes would not have wanted to test the loyalty of his Macedonians, especially if he knew from his informants that Neoptolemus had confidently predicted they would change sides. No source reports on how he justified his tactic to the veterans, who presumably did not know that their opponents would be Craterus and their fellow Macedonians. Perhaps he told them that he would not use them because he wished to spare them fighting Neoptolemus, their former general. His lie that the enemy was composed mostly of cavalry may have also explained why their service was not required. Craterus, for his part, called his army to an assembly, but nothing survives from his exhortation speech but the promise to give the enemy's baggage to his soldiers (Diod. 18.30.2). Presumably the baggage of Eumenes' Macedonians was exempted because they were supposed to move to his side. Otherwise the promised reward responded to Eumenes' earlier capture of the baggage of Neoptolemus's army and demonstrated Craterus's concern for his soldiers' welfare, shown already in his meeting with Phocion in Greece ca. 322 (Plut. *Phocion* 26.4).

---

24. While Plutarch (*Eum.* 6.6–7, 7.1–2) stresses Eumenes' fear of Craterus's popularity, both Arrian (*Succ.* 1.27) and Nepos (*Eum.* 3.3–5) refer only to his concern about the Macedonians' fame. The suggestions of Bennett and Roberts that the battle took place on the Hellespont and that Eumenes led Macedonians to it are equally unattractive: 2009, 2:45–50.

25. Cf. Bosworth 2002, 86.

Craterus was the first to array his forces on the battlefield. He led the right wing, gave Neoptolemus the command of the left wing, and distributed the cavalry between them. Diodorus's statement that he put his main trust in the Macedonian phalanx suggests that he led most if not all of it, yet the sources' accounts of the battle action revolve chiefly around the cavalry. This emphasis is due to their greater interest in Eumenes, who relied on his superior cavalry for success, and to his outgeneraling of Craterus in the engagement. Eumenes used a small elevation to hide the force he sent against Craterus, who expected to engage Eumenes' infantry, including the veterans, but was surprised instead by two foreign cavalry units led by the Persian Pharnabazus and the Greek Phoenix of Tenedos, who charged the enemy in full force and without delay. These horsemen were meant to rout the enemy or, at worst, to hold off Craterus till Eumenes could join the fighting after (he hoped) winning over Neoptolemus's wing. Eumenes probably ordered his ethnically diverse infantry on both wings to assist the cavalry.

Eumenes and Craterus rode at a distance from their own infantries, Craterus expecting his appearance to induce Eumenes' veterans to defect. Although highly disappointed and angry with Neoptolemus when he realized that not a single Macedonian came to greet him, Craterus soon recovered and charged the enemy at the head of a crack unit of select warriors.[26] Plutarch says that Craterus's performance in battle did not dishonor Alexander. It was indeed fitting for an imitator of Alexander to display personal heroism in a battle over which the dead king's spirit hovered so prominently. Yet in spite of his personal courage, or because of it, Craterus was mortally wounded by the enemy cavalry.[27] In any case his fall, which emboldened the enemy to turn on his troops and to kill many of them, demonstrated the disadvantage of using his fame to intimidate the opposition. The survivors fled for shelter behind the Macedonian phalanx, which apparently had seen no action, but now assumed a defensive position (Diod. 18.30.6).

While this was going on, Eumenes led his right wing with 300 of his best cavalry against Neoptolemus. As usual, the sources focus on the gen-

---

26. Diod. 18.30.1–5; Plut. *Eum.* 7.1–4; Nepos *Eum.* 3.6; Justin 13.8.6. Craterus's disappointment: Plut. *Eum.* 7.4. It is hard to tell from the sources if Craterus's picked unit was made of infantrymen or cavalry. Justin, who confuses Craterus with Polyperchon, stresses more than Diodorus the element of surprise in Eumenes' attack.

27. Craterus in battle: Plut. *Eum.* 7.5–6. His fate: Diod. 18.30.5 (fell and was trampled down); Plut. *Eum.* 7.5 (wounded by a Thracian); Arr. *Succ.* 1.27 (killed by unnamed Paphlagonians). Arrian criticizes Craterus for his imprudent joy in combat, much as he criticized Alexander for exposing himself to danger against the Malli: Arr. *Anab.* 6.13.4. See below for Craterus's dying moments.

erals rather than their troops, describing in graphic detail the duel between Eumenes and Neoptolemus, which ended in Neoptolemus's death and injuries to Eumenes. Without discounting their personal motives, we can assume that both generals were also thinking about the effect of their contest on their followers, present and future. Their quasi-Homeric duel also illustrates the individual focus of the Macedonian wars, from Philip II to the age of the Successors.[28] Yet the troops and especially Eumenes' cavalry did not stop to watch the fight, being preoccupied with a hard battle against their opponents. Like Craterus's death, Neoptolemus's fall discouraged his followers and filled the opposition with confidence. Both sides also heard of the defeat of Craterus's wing, which moved Neoptolemus's troops to join Craterus's fleeing survivors behind the Macedonian phalanx.[29]

We are told that when Eumenes learned of Craterus's fall, he rode to him and found him dying on the battleground. The first to recognize the fallen marshal, however, was Gorgias, one of Eumenes' officers, who dismounted to watch over the dying man.[30] Eumenes took over when he arrived, weeping for Craterus, holding his right hand, blaming Neoptolemus for the fighting, and lamenting both Craterus's lot and his own, since they were forced to harm each other despite their friendship. He may also have carried Craterus off the field in an attempt to save his life. Later he gave him a magnificent funeral, kept his bones, and—shortly before his own death— sent them to Craterus's wife, Phila.[31] The famous marshal surely deserved a better fate than improving Eumenes' image or spending the last moments of his life as Eumenes' captive audience. Even if the feelings Eumenes displayed were sincere, he had a clear interest in portraying himself as Crater-

---

28. The duel: Plut. *Eum.* 7.7–12; Diod. 18.31.1–5; Nepos *Eum.* 4.1–2; Just. 13.8.8; Arr. *Succ.* 1.27; cf. Plut. *Pyrrhus* 7.4–5. Emulation of Homeric heroes by Hellenistic commanders: Lendon 2005, 148–149. The personal nature and heroism of Philip's and Alexander's leadership: Carney 1996, 28–31. Hornblower rightly identifies Hieronymus as the source of the duel's descriptions: 1991, 194.

29. Diod. 18.32.1. Plut. (*Eum.* 7.12), however, makes Eumenes ignorant of the victory on his left wing.

30. Plut. *Eum.* 7.6. Gorgias's identity cannot be safely ascertained. Berve (1926, 2:114n234) thought that he was one of the Macedonian recruits whom Amyntas brought to Alexander in 331 (Curt. 7.1.38). Yet his ability to recognize Craterus in the confusion of battle makes it more likely that he was the commander Gorgias, who left Opis with Craterus and the veterans (Just. 12.12.8). If these two men were one and the same, Gorgias had moved to the Perdiccan camp in the interval; cf. Heckel 1992, 327.

31. Eumenes and the dying Craterus: Plut. *Eum.* 7.13; Suda s.v. *Craterus* (K 2335 Adler). Eumenes' attempt to save Craterus's life, his funeral, and the dispatch of his bones: Nepos *Eum.* 4.4; Diod. 19.59.3. Nepos, however, suggests that Eumenes sent Craterus's bones after the funeral.

us's personal friend (an attitude attested for the first time in the pre-battle negotiations between Eumenes and the two marshals) and in making Neoptolemus the villain of the story. His treatment of Craterus and his remains also countered his enemies' charge that he was an alien who used Macedonians to kill the marshal (Plut. *Eum.* 8.1). Presumably the veterans in Eumenes' camp were among those who heard about his friendship and gestures of respect for Craterus.[32]

Eumenes presented himself as a reluctant victor, but a victor nevertheless. Despite Neoptolemus's disdainful remark about his poor military record, Eumenes had defeated the best of the Macedonian generals in the battle (cf. Plut. *Eum.* 8.1), coming away with many proofs of his victory and excellence, including the bodies of the two opposing generals and other dead, whom there was no one left from the other side even to claim. He also captured many prisoners, including men of high rank, and proclaimed his triumph by setting up a trophy and burying his dead and presumably the enemy's (Diod. 18.32.1; Nepos *Eum.* 4.3). Yet Eumenes' victory was not complete, because Craterus's Macedonian phalanx and those whom it protected were still unconquered. The sources report that he invited them to join him, promising that he would allow them to look for supplies wherever they wished. The veterans surrendered and gave Eumenes their oath after he had cornered them, but when they had recovered and obtained food, they fled to Antipater under the cover of night. Eumenes tried to capture them but gave up, weakened by injuries and apprehensive of their valor.[33]

A fragmentary papyrus, probably from Arrian's history of Alexander's successors, complements the story of these events. It describes the Macedonian phalanx advancing in close order in an attempt to frighten off the cavalry that attacked them. Behind the phalanx were cavalrymen who assisted it by throwing a constant barrage of javelins at the enemy. When Eumenes saw the densely packed phalanx and their readiness to face danger, he once again sent the Macedonian-speaking Xennias to them with the message that Eumenes would not fight them head-on but would follow them with his cavalry and light-armed troops to prevent them from getting provisions: even if they deemed themselves invincible, they would yield before long to starvation. The legible part of the papyrus stops here (*PSI* 12: 1284).

Scholars are divided in their dating of the incident, some placing it af-

---

32. Hornblower (1981, 69) and Anson (2004, 109n113) suspect that Duris might have been Plutarch's source for the scene of Eumenes' attending to dying Craterus, but the sympathetic and apologetic portrayal of the Cardian suggests Hieronymus as a source instead; cf. Schäfer 2002, 88.

33. Diod. 18.32.2–4; Nepos. *Eum.* 4.3; cf. Arr. *Succ.* 1.27.

ter Eumenes' battle with Craterus and some after the battle with Neoptolemus ten days earlier. A. B. Bosworth has made the strongest case for the
latter view, but in my opinion W. E. Thompson has successfully challenged
his arguments and shown the greater likelihood of attributing the episode
to Eumenes' second victory.[34] Rather than rehashing these scholars' arguments, I would add my own reservation about one of the key points used
to identify the phalanx with Neoptolemus's veterans. Historians have surmised that the author of the text would not have noted the Macedonian language skills of Xennias, Eumenes' emissary, unless they set him apart from
others in Eumenes' camp, as would have been the case before Eumenes got
Neoptolemus's Macedonians.[35] Yet the choice of a Macedonian speaker bespeaks not a dearth of Macedonians in Eumenes' force but rather his intended audience. Regardless of how many veterans Eumenes had, he picked
a messenger whom the phalanx could comprehend and, he hoped, trust.
Similarly, before the Battle of Gabene in 317/6 between Eumenes and Antigonus, a Macedonian veteran in Eumenes' army was sent to reproach and
discourage the Macedonian troops in Antigonus's line. There is no doubt
that by then there were at least 3,000 Macedonians in Eumenes' camp
(Diod. 19.41.1; cf. Plut. *Eum.* 16.6–8). The scene described in the fragment,
then, best fits the aftermath of the battle with Craterus.[36]

No less important than the context of this episode is the Macedonians'
behavior before and after their agreement with Eumenes. The veterans' disciplined and effective response to the cavalry attacks justified their reputation, which played such an important role in the psychology and the strat-
egies of both sides. It also suggested that they had capable commanders.
Their confidence in the face of Craterus's defeat—Xennias said they perceived themselves as invincible (*amachoi*)—and the fact that Xennias addressed them more than once suggest that they believed at first that they
could extract themselves from their predicament. But even if Craterus's
phalanx and the cavalry attached to it could win a direct confrontation,

34. Bosworth 1978 (whose view appears to be more influential); W. E. Thompson
1984 (cf. Schäfer 2002, 81–84, supporting Bosworth); and Anson 2004, 106nn103, 109
(for the opposite view). All cite earlier scholarship.

35. See Briant 1973b, 223–224n13; Bosworth 1978, 278, 230. For the following cf.
Badian 1982b, 41.

36. Similarly, the fact that, according to the papyrus, Eumenes threatened the phalanx with his cavalry and not with his infantry does not indicate that he lacked Macedonian infantrymen, but rather indicates that the horsemen could carry out his threat
more effectively; cf. Polyaenus 4.6.6.

they had no real answer to the tactics of harassment and food deprivation that Eumenes' superior cavalry could employ against them.

They therefore promised to serve him and confirmed the deal with an oath, receiving in return the right to raid the locals. For Eumenes it was a low-cost solution that also made him their new caretaker. That they were expected to repay him with their loyal service but instead went on to out-trick the trickster Eumenes moved our pro-Eumenes sources to criticize the Macedonians for violating their oath to him (Diod. 18.32.4; Nepos *Eum.* 4.3). No one praised them for sticking with Antipater, because each gen-eral appreciated loyalty only to him and liked treachery in the other camps. Eumenes pursued the veterans both to avenge their "faithlessness" (Diod. 18.32.4) and to prevent them from strengthening the enemy and setting an example for his Macedonians. But why didn't Craterus's phalanx imi-tate Neoptolemus's Macedonians, who moved to Eumenes' side and stayed there?

There were a number of reasons. Unlike Neoptolemus after his first de-feat by Eumenes, Craterus could not be blamed for running away or be-traying his troops. The phalanx that faced Eumenes consisted of Crater-us's veterans but also of new recruits who had been drafted in Macedonia by Leonnatus and Antipater. We do not know how many belonged to the latter category, but they were more attached to, and familiar with, Anti-pater than Eumenes, whom they had never seen before.[37] Therefore it is quite possible that the veterans' decision to flee Eumenes was influenced in part by their younger compatriots. The phalanx's officers (who must have provided the leadership for the armed clash with Eumenes, the negotia-tions with him, and the escape) were also Antipater's and Craterus's men. The fact that Antipater was not far away—no farther than on his way to Cilicia (Diod. 18.29.6, 33.1)—strengthened the impulse to join him and de-terred Eumenes from pursuing the Macedonians any further. In addition, the Macedonians had had enough time to find out that Eumenes was iso-lating Neoptolemus's veterans in his camp and treated them with suspi-cion. Earlier he had created a cavalry force as an *antitagma* (counter-unit) to the same Macedonians. It was a record that did not bode well for the fu-ture of the phalanx in his army. The veterans also saw that Eumenes had re-lied on his local cavalry in both of his battles with Neoptolemus and Cra-terus. Though important for Craterus, who counted on them for victory,

---

37. Neoptolemus's veterans at least shared service with Eumenes during Alexan-der's campaign and possibly in Armenia.

the Macedonians were less vital to Eumenes' strategy, and he was less dependent on them than Craterus was.

Finally, there was a matter of trust. Our sources are impressed by Eumenes' stratagem of concealing the identity of the enemy from his troops. Because he won, his army was probably not upset with him, but one wonders if all observers shared the sources' admiration of his deceit. In any case, Craterus's veterans, who surrendered to Eumenes, had reason to suspect his honesty. They gave him their pledge because that was the only means of creating a solemn pact between a general and his soldiers (cf. Plut. *Eum.* 5.5). But the binding power of oaths went only so far, and the veterans' record of keeping their pledges was not perfect.[38] Conversely, there is an inscription, recording an exchange of oaths between a different Eumenes (I), ruler of Pergamum, and a group of mercenaries sometime between 263 and 241, that shows that the breach of agreement between a leader and his soldiers could go both ways. It records the two parties' pledge that they would not conspire or march in arms against, or betray, one another.[39] There was likely a mutual distrust between the Macedonians and their former enemy, who, even after their agreement, kept them away from his camp. Troops who fled to Antipater, on the other hand, could expect a warm welcome from him. With Craterus gone, the tension that had existed between his veterans and Antipater lost its raison d'être.

Craterus's death provides a convenient breaking place for taking stock of Alexander's veterans. Omitting those who had died, had melted away, or were serving with Polyperchon in Macedonia, there were thousands of veterans in the royal army that made its way from Egypt to Syria, and another large group that marched with Antipater to Cilicia. There were veterans in Eumenes' camp and others who served with Alcetas, whose whereabouts at this point are unknown.[40] The scattering of Alexander's Macedonians that began in 324 with the king's discharge of 11,500 veterans home had led to their service in rival camps. So far, the veterans appeared to have

---

38. For the claim that taking oaths "mercenarized" the army, see Launey 1950, 2:926–927, 938; cf. Briant 1972, 71–73 (repr. 1982, 59–61), on the present case, but also chap. 8, note 40, below. The Roman sources appear to be more attentive than the Greeks to the subject of soldiers' oaths and their violations: e.g., Nepos *Eum.* 10.2; Just. 14.1.10, 4.3. For the veterans' violations of their pledge, see, in addition to this episode, Diod. 18.7.8 (violation of their pledge to the Greek rebels during Pithon's campaign), or Just. 14.4.3 (violation of their pledge to Eumenes in 317/6).

39. *OGIS* 266, vv. 24–64; Austin 2006, 402–405n230.

40. For Alcetas, see chap. 6. Arrian (*Succ.* 1.39) states that he fled following Perdiccas's death, but not whence or where.

been spared fighting each other, but it was just a matter of time before that changed.

Of all the groups of veterans, those who served with Eumenes had potentially the brightest future because of his string of military successes and his office as supreme commander over Asia Minor. Perdiccas's Egyptian fiasco spoiled everything and turned Eumenes into a public enemy. But the effect of his condemnation and outlawing on the Macedonians in his army was minimal, for several reasons. One had to do with Eumenes' control and shaping of the information that reached his camp. Justin reports that Eumenes was concerned that the news from Egypt would alarm his followers. Wishing to know their true feelings, he told them about the decision against him and allowed anyone to leave who wished to do so. Their unanimous answer was to urge him to go to war and to promise that they would overturn the Macedonians' decrees by the sword.[41] Clearly it took more than a briefing and a declaration of a liberal attitude to produce such a show of loyalty. We don't know what else Eumenes told the troops, but this was a good time both to clear himself of the charge of killing Craterus by describing him as his personal friend and to blame Neoptolemus for the conflict. He may also have pledged loyalty to the Argead house and assured the army that he had overcome greater foes.

Especially convincing for his Macedonians were the fresh memories of Eumenes' victories and the lack of viable alternatives to service with him. They could not go to Antipater, now in Cilicia or on his way to Triparadeisus in Syria, or to Antigonus, now in Cyprus or also on his way to Syria. They could possibly go home, but the veterans' record suggests that this was not their preferred choice. They constituted a minority in Eumenes' army and, with little weight to throw around, they likely joined the rest of the troops rather than opposed them. Lastly, the veterans (unlike their modern historians) were not experts in constitutional law or believers in the right of the royal assembly (in Egypt) to speak for all Macedonians. As we shall see, those who insisted on respecting the decisions of the "Assembly of the Macedonians" were not the troops but the generals whose interest was served by its resolutions. Even Eumenes' alleged responsibility for causing a Macedonian civil war had little effect. The veterans' reluctance to fight each other was selective, and I do not know of a single veteran who

---

41. Just. 13.8.10–14.1.5. Justin links Antigonus's mission to fight Eumenes to the decision in Egypt to outlaw him; cf. Plut. *Eum.* 8.4. Even if not anachronistic, Antigonus's mission was taken seriously only after Triparadeisus. For the following see also Anson 2004, 117.

is recorded to have left his general because of the commander's violations of Macedonian solidarity. On the other hand, generals such as Antigonus and Polyperchon were ready to overlook Eumenes' condemnation and record when they invited him to become their ally. The veterans who would serve with him repeatedly chose to ignore urgings to kill him or to desert his camp.[42]

The next reported actions of Eumenes and his Macedonians took place after the meeting of the royal army with Antipater and his forces at Triparadeisus, which we shall now examine.

TRIPARADEISUS

After Perdiccas's assassination, the royal army confirmed his replacement as guardian by Pithon and Arrhidaeus (the general)—probably a temporary appointment until Antipater and Antigonus arrived at Triparadeisus in Upper Syria (Arr. *Succ.* 1.31). It was during the wait for Antipater in Triparadeisus that a dispute broke out between the new guardians and Eurydice-Adea, wife of Philip III/Arrhidaeus. The queen used her Argead lineage and probably her husband's rank to claim the right to approve, and thus also to veto, any decision made by the guardians. The sources disagree on how the crisis evolved. Diodorus says that the guardians resigned and the Macedonians elected Antipater as plenipotentiary guardian before his arrival. Arrian, however, reports that the guardians did not oppose Eurydice at first, but refused to give her the management of public affairs until the arrival of Antipater and Antigonus. When the latter arrived, power passed into Antipater's hands.[43]

What role did the Macedonians play in the affair? The conflict centered on where ultimate power resided, and it played out in front of the veter-

---

42. Charging Eumenes with killing Craterus and civil war: Diod. 18.37.1–2, 62.1–2; 19.12.1–3. 13.1–2; Arr. *Succ.* 1.30; Plut. *Eum.* 8.1–4, 18.1–2; Nepos *Eum.* 5.1; App. *Syr.* 53; cf. Arr. *Succ.* 1.40. See the next chapters for the Macedonians' ignoring charges against Eumenes or rejecting urgings to kill and desert him. Hadley (2001, 21–22) rightly claims that the sources glorify Eumenes by emphasizing the Macedonians' loyalty to him. Yet the fact remains that they stayed with him.

43. Diod. 18.39.2; Arr. *Succ.* 1.31–32. Briant thought that Arrian's version recorded a compromise between the guardians and their opponents that allowed the former to hold power until Antipater's arrival. Such a scenario, however, does not exclude the possibility that the guardians resigned before his arrival; Briant 1973b, 275n8; cf. Billows 1990, 67n30. Errington (1970, 67) prefers Diodorus's version.

ans and with their direct involvement. At first the generals Pithon and Arrhidaeus sought to avoid exacerbating the feud, probably because they saw that the Macedonians supported the queen: Diodorus says that the guardians called an assembly and abdicated because the Macedonians were increasingly obeying Eurydice's commands instead of theirs (Diod. 18.39.2). We can assume that the two generals spoke against her interference in government (Arr. *Succ.* 1.31) and made derogatory remarks about her gender and her Illyrian descent. The Macedonians sided with Eurydice for several reasons. She had been "their queen" since Perdiccas had allowed her to marry Philip III in a concession to their protest against Perdiccas's elimination of her mother, Cynane. In fact, the veterans' record of supporting the Argeads against their adversaries dated from as far back as Babylon. Eurydice, like Cynane, also had a martial appeal: she had been given military training by her mother, and her wearing Macedonian arms and her readiness to meet Olympias in battle in 317 suggest a combative courage that the troops could appreciate (Polyaenus 4.6.4; Duris in Athen. 13.560f.). Nevertheless, the Macedonians did not back Eurydice entirely, not favoring any plan she may have had to abolish or significantly weaken the guardianship. They wanted Antipater to hold this position, probably because they deemed him a more effective leader and patron.[44]

Thus in the triangular relationship among the royal house, the guardians, and the Macedonians, much depended on the balance of power between the first two. Perdiccas and Antipater were strong guardians who could control or intimidate the members of the royal family and thereby prevent the kind of conflict that occurred in Triparadeisus. But the authority of Pithon and Arrhidaeus was evidently weaker, allowing Eurydice to challenge their rule with the help of the army. Triparadeisus was not Egypt, where the commanders were able to tell an impaired and seething army what to do. It was the army's recovery from the Egyptian campaign and a rift within the leadership that enabled the Macedonians and their assembly to exercise power, although only for a time.

A tense situation awaited Antipater in Triparadeisus. Eurydice did not give up, and the Macedonian troops, who gained power and confidence in the course of her feud with the guardians, expected him to yield to their demands—chiefly, according to Arrian, for the payments that Alexander had

---

44. On Eurydice in Triparadeisus, see Carney 1987, 499; 2000b, 132–133. Bosworth (2002, 15) thinks that she incited the Macedonians regarding overdue payments, but the evidence suggests that the dispute was over whose orders to follow, while the issue of payment came up only after Antipater's arrival.

promised them. The veterans likely evoked Alexander's pledge (upon discharging their fellow Macedonians home at Opis in 324) to reward handsomely those who remained with him, a promise never fulfilled, as far we know. The veterans were always sensitive to injustice, especially when it affected them.[45] The sources do not reveal what made the Macedonians suddenly recall Alexander's old promise. They probably compared their experience with that of Craterus's veterans, newly arrived in Antipater's army, whom the king had handsomely rewarded. Eurydice's agitation may also have played a role. Hoping to embarrass and weaken Antipater, she could suggest that her husband, as Alexander's successor, and she, as an Argead, were especially motivated to keep his promise.

Alexander had given more than a talent to each departing veteran, and since the veterans of the royal army in Triparadeisus would have expected no less, the total sum demanded ranged in the thousands of talents.[46] Antipater, and most probably Eurydice, did not have that kind of money, but much depended on how they presented their case. Antipater's reaction, as reported by Arrian, was clumsy at best. The marshal said that he had no money but promised to inspect the royal treasury and other sources and to do all he could in order not to earn the soldiers' reproach. The army was not pleased (Arr. *Succ.* 1.32). This was not the time for delays and carefully worded answers, especially with the royal treasury in their very midst. Veterans with good memory could recall how they had ransacked the treasury with Meleager in Babylon when leadership was similarly unclear.

Eurydice now openly presented herself as an alternative to Antipater's rule, and she had allies among the troops who made accusations against him. One such charge likely recycled rumors of his involvement in Alexander's alleged poisoning.[47] United in their demand for payment and in their sense of being unfairly treated, the veterans had now found willing leadership and were emboldened to put pressure on the marshal in the ways they knew best: by rioting and protesting. All this time Eurydice kept stirring the pot. Her rank, lineage, and forceful personality, along with the current

---

45. The Macedonians' demand: Arr. *Succ.* 1.32. Alexander's promise: Arr. *Anab.* 7.8.1; Hammond 1988 (repr. 1994, 3:143–150).

46. Eurydice's agitation: Diod. 18.39.3; Arr. *Succ.* 1.32. The Macedonians' contrasting themselves with Craterus's veterans: Bosworth 2002, 87n82. Alexander's bonuses: chap. 2 above. The number of veterans in the royal army at this time is a matter of conjecture. Hammond's generous estimate is over 10,000 (1984, 58), but Bosworth cuts the number in half (2002, 84–85).

47. Arr. *Succ.* 1.33; Plut. *Alex.* 77.1–5; Briant 1973b, 277n2.

crisis, legitimized this woman's appearance in the army assembly and her speaking there against Antipater. Photius, Arrian's epitomator, chose to report on who helped her write the speech—Attalus and the secretary Asclepiodorus—though not on its contents. But the identity of Attalus may tell us something about what she said.[48]

This was most likely the Attalus (son of Andromenus) who was Perdiccas's brother-in-law. He commanded the Perdiccan fleet during the Egyptian campaign and took it to Tyre after the murder of his sister and Perdiccas. Although Attalus must have been among those condemned to death in absentia after the regent's assassination, he now joined the royal army in Triparadeisus. His presence there puts in perspective the staying power of popular decisions and the Macedonians' readiness to enforce them. Attalus had two assets that should have endeared him to the troops. One was his brief support of Meleager, the veterans' leader in Babylon, which some troops might have counted to his credit.[49] Much more important, however, were Attalus's deep pockets. When he fled Egypt for Tyre, the local Perdiccan commander handed over the city to him with the 800 talents Perdiccas had left there (Diod. 18.37.3–4). Eight hundred talents were probably insufficient to meet the troops' demand in full, but they could allow Eurydice to draw a contrast between Antipater's real or feigned poverty and the funds that her supporters and (probably) she herself controlled. Eurydice must have inherited the funds of her mother, Cynane, who had enough money to finance their fateful trip to Asia Minor with a military escort.[50] Macedonian noblewomen and wives of men in power also acted as patronesses of the soldiers, paying their expenses, arranging their marriages, and performing other acts that defined a benefactor (*euergetes*). Eurydice seemed to have the financial capacity to play such roles.[51]

---

48. Arrian's description of the assembly makes it look like a trial, with accusations, testimony for and against Antipater, and even a logographer (*Succ.* 1.33); see Briant 1973b, 277. Yet both Arrian and Polyaenus (4.6.4) make it clear that the central issue was money. The speechwriters: Arr. *Succ.* 1.33. Asclepiodorus's identity is uncertain. See Berve 1926, 2:88–89; Heckel 2006, 58n4.

49. Attalus's identity: Diod. 18.37.2–4, 41.7; Arr. *Succ.* 1.39; Briant 1973b, 278n6; Billows 1990, 68n31; Heckel 1992, 182, 381–384. Attalus and Meleager: Just. 13.3.2, 7; Heckel 1992, 381–384. Bosworth (2002, 44n58) believes, however, that Meleager's supporter was a different Attalus. For the following, cf. Errington 1970, 67–68.

50. See Polyaenus 8.60; Carney 2010, 416; cf. Macurdy 1932, 49.

51. Noble Macedonian patronesses: Diod. 19.59.3–6 (Phila, the wife of Craterus and then Demetrius) or Diod. 19.67.1–2 (Cratesipolis, the wife of Alexander, son of Polyperchon).

The sources diverge on what happened next. Diodorus reports on Antipater's conflict with Eurydice and the tumult in camp but then skips to the end of the crisis and Antipater's victory (Diod. 18.39.3–4). Photius's summary of Arrian is more detailed but limits most of the action to the assembly where the queen and marshal clashed (Arr. *Succ.* 1.33). Polyaenus tells about Antigonus's ploy, which rescued Antipater from troops who blocked his way to his camp and threatened to kill him (4.6.4). The following reconstruction tries to reconcile these different accounts.

By all signs, Antipater fled the assembly in question by the skin of his teeth. That he was *reelected* as guardian at the conclusion of the mutiny suggests that the agitated and threatening soldiers had deposed him (Arr. *Succ.* 1.33). An anecdote from Polyaenus's collection of stratagems is best placed in the aftermath of the meeting (4.6.4). It centers on Antigonus, who accompanied Antipater to Triparadeisus. On one side of the river Orontes stood Antipater and Antigonus with like-minded cavalry, and at the other end of the bridge were Macedonians ready to stone Antipater to death unless he paid them on the spot.[52] Antipater was at a loss, but Antigonus came to the rescue, telling him to wait while he crossed the bridge in full armor. The Macedonians, treating him as a man of rank, allowed him to pass through. He divided the phalanx in two, told the divisions to follow him, and then spoke in turn to both, defending Antipater at length, making promises, and speaking words of encouragement and reconciliation. These diversions allowed Antipater and the cavalry to cross the bridge in peace, escaping the danger.

Since Arrian (*Succ.* 1.33) says that both Antigonus and Seleucus barely saved Antipater and themselves from a riotous assembly, it is possible that Polyaenus omitted Seleucus's role in the affair in order to focus on Antigonus. Polyaenus also makes Antipater a foil to Antigonus's resourcefulness by presenting the old marshal as frightened and helpless. But it is the troops' conduct that calls for our attention here. Rarely if ever had the troops threatened to kill their chief commander, but at Triparadeisus there were extenuating circumstances. Both in Babylon and in Egypt the veterans had witnessed, and may even have participated in, the elimination of lesser commanders and their followers. Such experiences—combined with

---

52. Briant (1973b, 276) and Billows (1990, 69) wrongly assume that Antipater's camp was separated from the royal army by a river. In fact, the river ran through the royal camp, and Antipater, who camped separately (Arr. *Succ.* 1.33), shared a riverbank with it. According to Polyaenus (4.6.4), Antipater had to go across a bridge *and* through the rioting Macedonians who camped nearby in order to get to his base.

their frustration with Antipater over their unanswered demands, the agitation of his opponents, and the likelihood that he was no longer protected by his office of guardian—paved the way to their violent threats against him. Among the mutinous Macedonians were the 3,000 Silver Shields, whose joint service as hypaspists in Alexander's army contributed to their unity.[53]

The veterans' readiness to accommodate and hear Antigonus showed at least that they were also looking for a resolution of the crisis. Further influences were his imposing figure, his dress as a man of rank, and his recent success against Perdiccan allies in Cyprus. And if Antigonus lacked authority in the eyes of some—he had left Alexander's campaign to govern Phrygia as early as 333, and so was known to some veterans only superficially or by rumor—he was backed by the familiar figure of Seleucus. This general, who helped in the persuasion efforts either here or earlier in the assembly, had served in the royal army since it had crossed to Asia in 334 and, after the king's death, was Perdiccas's second-in-command, later joining in the plot against him. But once it became clear to the troops that Antigonus, Seleucus, and especially Antipater had no money to offer, and that Antigonus had actually helped Antipater to get away, we can assume that they became even more enraged at Antipater and his friends, both for duping them and for leaving them empty handed.[54]

Photius/Arrian tells us that Antipater retired to his camp and called in the cavalry commanders (hipparchs), adding that the mutiny was put down with difficulty and that Antipater was reelected to the command (Arr. *Succ.* 1.33). Photius's synopsis does not make it clear exactly how the riots were quelled. It has been argued that Antipater managed to split the rebels and to deprive them of leadership by drawing the cavalry of the royal army to his side, but this is uncertain.[55] The source does not identify the cavalry commanders he summoned, yet the description of what looks like a commander's council makes it likelier that they were Antipater's hipparchs. In addition, Polyaenus describes the cavalry that faced the raging crowd at the bridge with Antigonus (and Antipater) as "like-minded men" (*homophronountas*), suggesting that the hipparchs were Antipater's supporters all along (Polyaenus 4.6.4). It is unknown where the Macedonian cavalry of the royal army stood in this conflict, but they may have shared the pha-

---

53. Arr. *Succ.* 1.38 with, e.g., Plut. *Eum.* 13.2–3.

54. Antigonus's and Seleucus's careers up to this point: Billows 1990, 16–69; Grainger 1990, 1–27. There is no evidence to support Briant's claim (1973b, 278–279) that the soldiers wanted to go home or resented Attalus's presence.

55. Briant 1973b, 278; Billows 1990, 69; cf. Kanatsulis 1968, 169; Huss 2001, 117.

lanx's discontent. They too did not receive the reward promised by Alexander, unlike the cavalry that accompanied Craterus to Asia Minor (Diod. 18.16.4).

We do not know the position of Antipater's veterans in the conflict. He camped away from the royal army, but this should not have prevented the mingling of veterans from both camps. The most that can be said about Antipater's or Craterus's Macedonians is that they could not legitimately claim to have been cheated of Alexander's promise. I suspect that they stayed inactive or helped Antipater against their former comrades, because their joining the protest would have made it almost impossible for him to oppose the phalanx. At any rate, the best evidence for Antipater's countermeasures comes from Diodorus, who states that he spoke to the troops and scared Eurydice into silence (18.39.4). He may even have threatened her with his daughter Nicaea, who after Perdiccas's death was eligible to become Philip III's second wife.[56] With the queen cowed and her supporter Attalus on the run, it was clear that the Macedonians had lost their leaders, although Antipater still had trouble restoring order in camp (Arr. *Succ.* 1.33, 39).

The veterans' defeat was sound. Their demands were not met and their dominance in camp lasted but a short time. The army assembly was most powerful when there was a leadership crisis, which forced the contenders to seek the troops' support. Once the struggle was over, with or without the troops' help, the assembly lost its power. The crisis in Triparadeisus, therefore, confirmed that the Macedonian troops could make more trouble than change. Appropriately, the sources make Antipater solely responsible for redistributing commands among the generals in the aftermath of the mutiny, crediting the soldiers with no say about their missions and destinations. One veteran group, however, got a plum assignment. The 3,000 Silver Shields were sent under Antigenes to bring money from Susa. Presumably they were promised a bonus for their efforts.[57]

In addition to a command over the Silver Shields, Antigenes was rewarded with the satrapy of Susiana for being among the first to attack

---

56. Nicaea ended up marrying the Diadoch Lysimachus: Ogden 1999, 57–58. Antipater's older daughter, Phila, also became available for marriage after Craterus's death.

57. Distribution of commands: Arr. *Succ.* 1.34; Diod. 18.39.5–7. Antipater likely consulted other commanders about their missions: Briant 1973b, 255. The Silver Shields' assignment: Arr. *Succ.* 1.38; Bosworth 2002, 87. Waterfield (2011, 68) regards their mission as punitive even though their leader, Antigenes, was rewarded for his part in Perdiccas's assassination: Arr. *Succ.* 1.35.

Perdiccas (Diod. 19.39.6; Arr. *Succ.* 1.34). It was important to reinvigorate the anti-Perdiccan campaign after the resurfacing of Attalus, Perdiccas's brother-in-law, in Triparadeisus and in view of the upcoming war against the remaining Perdiccans in Asia Minor. Antigonus Monophthalmus got the assignment of leading this war, for which he was given the royal army and the satrapies of Greater Phrygia, Lycaonia, Pamphilia, and Lycia (Diod. 19.39.6; Arr. *Succ.* 1.37–38). He took the kings along because they had become inseparable from the royal army and because they legitimized the campaign against the Perdiccans.[58] There is no better evidence for the Argeads' decline than the fact that, unlike earlier warrior kings such as Philip II and Alexander, they did not lead the army but followed it.

The number of the veterans who went with Antigonus was depleted, perhaps to the low thousands. They left without the 3,000 Silver Shields, and there are signs that royal veterans were present in other armies as well. For instance, before Antipater crossed back to Europe, he had to deal with troops who "mutinied again on account of the money" (Arr. *Succ.* 1.44). The recidivist mutineers were most likely Macedonians who had made the same demand in Triparadeisus.[59] In 319, Arrhidaeus, the former guardian and now the satrap of Hellespontine Phrygia, tried to secure his satrapy against Antigonus by taking over the city of Cyzicus. His infantry included 1,000 Macedonians in addition to 10,000 mercenaries and 500 Persian bowmen and slingers. Arrhidaeus had gotten his Phrygian command in Triparadeisus, and with it, it is highly likely, the Persian and the Macedonian troops as well.[60]

Triparadeisus, then, was the last and only possible reunion for Alexander's veterans. Their splitting up into smaller groups and dispersal into various armies was the logical conclusion of the ugly scenes in Triparadeisus. This scattering eliminated the danger that the veterans would ever again fight under a single leader and responded to the generals' competing demands for these experienced warriors, who remained useful despite their unruly conduct. Arrian's statement that everybody commended Antipater

---

58. Errington 1990, 70–71; cf. Grainger 1990, 27.

59. See chap. 6 for this episode and the troops' identity.

60. Diod. 18.39.6, 51.1; Bosworth 1986, 9 with n56 (where he suspects that the veterans were Craterus's); 2002, 104n25; Anson 2003, 386 with n56. In 312 Ptolemy took to the Battle of Gaza 18,000 infantrymen, of whom the Macedonian troops were a minority: Diod. 19.80.4. Perhaps he too got them in Triparadeisus (so Bosworth 2004, 88), but the possibility that they came from Perilaus's army, captured by Ptolemy's admiral Polycleitus in Asia Minor in 315, should not be discounted: Diod. 19.64.5–7. See also Billows 1995, 196.

on his settlement suggests that the military elite was united in its wish to disband Alexander's former army (*Succ.* 1.38).

Although the veterans were desirable recruits, their military record was not unblemished. Between Alexander's death in Babylon and the meeting at Triparadeisus, they had fought victoriously with Pithon against Greek rebels, unsuccessfully with Leonnatus in Greece, victoriously with Perdiccas in Cappadocia and Pisidia (although later unsuccessfully in Egypt), victoriously under Craterus and Antipater in Greece, with unlikely success for Neoptolemus in Armenia, and unsuccessfully with Neoptolemus against Eumenes. Finally they were defeated under Craterus by Eumenes. It was a checkered record at best, and quite poor for an army used to invincibility. It is true that the Macedonians should not be called out for blame or credit in these actions, since the veterans constituted a minority in most of these armies and their commanders were not always up to par. Whatever was responsible for their altered status, however, this was patently clear: the veteran infantry and cavalry could no longer be counted on to win battles on their own. This did not prevent the veterans, their leaders, and other contemporaries from overvaluing their reputation for valor and experience.

CHAPTER 6

THE VETERANS, EUMENES, AND ANTIGONUS IN ASIA MINOR

The history of the Macedonian veterans from the settlement of Triparadeisus (summer 320) to Eumenes' assumption of the command over the Silver
Shields (spring 318) must be reconstructed from highly condensed accounts
and fragmentary or anecdotal evidence. It is by observing the fortunes of
the individual commanders, tied by the sources to those of their troops,
that we shall best be able to follow the veterans' divergent paths.

EUMENES AND THE PERDICCANS

Thanks probably to Hieronymus, our information is most abundant on
Eumenes and his army. Of the different scholarly reconstructions of his
actions, the following sequence appears least controversial. After news of
his condemnation reached his camp, Eumenes turned to raid Hellespontine and western Phrygia. He then met in Sardis with Alexander's sister,
Cleopatra, in a failed attempt to make her his ally. From there he retired to
Celaenae in Cappadocia for the winter of 320/19, a season in which he tried
to form a coalition with other Perdiccan generals. It is highly likely that his
raiding expeditions were extended into that winter.[1]

Eumenes faced significant challenges during this time. After the settlement of Triparadeisus, Antigonus and the royal army were assigned to fight
him and the other Perdiccan generals, further increasing Eumenes' dependence on the goodwill and loyalty of his army. He lacked both the royal
legitimacy and the resources of his enemies, and the prospect of fighting
a much larger army was unnerving. Much of Eumenes' subsequent activity was dominated by his need to alleviate his troops' concerns about all of

---

1. See Bosworth 1992a, 72–75.

these points. We shall discuss Eumenes' efforts to retain his troops' loyalty thematically rather than chronologically.

Eumenes sought to legitimize his position in a variety of ways. One involved inducing his army to make a show of support, as when he told them that he was outlawed in Egypt. In a display of magnanimity and self-confidence, Eumenes released whoever wished to leave the camp, and the soldiers responded with equal generosity by urging him to lead them to battle and promising to abolish the Macedonians' decrees by the sword. In fact, Eumenes' troops had few alternatives to staying in camp, but they needed to hear and see that they were all behind him in spite of his status as an outlaw.[2] Eumenes lacked the legitimacy of Antipater and Antigonus, who had the backing of the two kings and could embarrass Eumenes' Macedonians with charges that they were fighting against their monarchs. It was to correct this disadvantage that Eumenes went to Sardis to see Alexander's sister, Cleopatra. He had supported her candidacy to become Perdiccas's wife in the past and now sought to renew their partnership in the hope that she would strengthen the loyalty of his soldiers, probably by serving as a figurehead for them and possibly for the entire Perdiccan camp. In fact, Justin says that the aim of Eumenes' visit was to make his "centurions" and chief officers loyal to him by virtue of Cleopatra's royal status and kinship to Alexander.[3] Eumenes' concern about the loyalty of his command structure was justified, because mass desertions usually depended on the troops' immediate commanders, who met the soldiers on a daily basis and exerted greater influence over them than did their chief general. He hoped to impress Cleopatra with his military victories, his army, and his successful raiding expeditions in the face of Antipater's inaction, but the princess declined his advances. She was aware that Eumenes' rivals enjoyed greater legitimacy and had more troops and money than he had. Siding openly with a man who had made his reputation defeating and killing Macedonians could earn her the animosity of their compatriots both at home and abroad.[4]

Eumenes could also gain legitimacy and the soldiers' goodwill through

---

2. Just. 14.1.1–5; chap. 5 above.

3. Just. 14.1.7–8. I prefer understanding the text to mean that Cleopatra was intended to reassure Eumenes' commanders rather than confirm them in their posts.

4. Arr. *Succ.* 1.40; Plut. *Eum.* 8.4. See also Briant 1973a, 51n2 (repr. 1982, 63n20). Cleopatra was a sought-after bride (see Meeus 2009a, 245–246; 2009b), but it is both unattested and unlikely that Eumenes asked for her hand (notwithstanding the general statement in Diod. 20.37.4).

raids. Plunder compensated soldiers who were accustomed to late wages and was sure to raise his popularity (Plut. *Eum.* 8.10–11). And the sources suggest that Eumenes did tend to resort to raiding after suffering a setback, such as being outlawed in Egypt (Just. 14.16), failing to secure Cleopatra's public support (Arr. 1.40–41), or failing to set up a Perdiccan coalition (Plut. *Eum.* 8.8–9). Ultimately, however, it was Eumenes' limited resources and lack of access to the royal treasury that moved him to raid territories that were governed by rival satraps and were rich in booty and the possibilities of ransom.[5]

At one point after being outlawed, Eumenes captured horses for his cavalry from the royal herds around Mount Ida in northwestern Asia Minor, afterwards trying to legalize his action by writing down their number and reporting it to the royal overseers (Plut. *Eum.* 8.5). Ostensibly he was acting as a royal official, but not differently from a bandit except in notifying the impotent authorities of his theft, which may have been part of a larger raiding expedition. According to Justin, after the news of his condemnation in Egypt reached his camp (but before his visit to Cleopatra at Sardis), Eumenes raided Aeolia, where he gave cities the choice of paying him ransom or being plundered like enemies.[6] This method of obtaining funds and rewarding soldiers is illustrated in greater detail by a fragmentary account in what is known as the *Gothenburg* (or *Göteborg*) *Palimpsest*. The fragment probably comes from Arrian's history of Alexander's successors, and its mention of Eumenes and Antipater dates the incident to a time when their forces were near one another.[7]

We know that Antipater and Eumenes came close to clashing around Sardis when Antipater came there on his way from Triparadeisus to the Aegean (late 320), but that Cleopatra prevailed upon Eumenes to leave the region. Arriving at Sardis, Antipater charged her (perhaps even in front of the Macedonians) with supporting the Perdiccans, but Cleopatra defended herself successfully and the two were reconciled.[8] Eumenes attacked An-

---

5. For paying through pillaging in Hellenistic times: Launey 1950, II:734–745.

6. Just. 14.1.6. See Bosworth 1992, 72, for the possibility that the raiding of the herds belongs here.

7. Gothenburg Palimpsest of Arrian 72r–73v. For a new reading and additional lines, see Dreyer 2007.

8. Arr. *Succ.* 1.40. Carney (2006, 66) speculates that, as in the case of Cynane, Cleopatra and Antipater competed for influence over the Macedonians and in front of them, and that Cleopatra may have blamed Antipater for Alexander's death. This is possible, although we are ignorant of the troops' reaction, as we are not with the Cynane incident.

tipater's allies in the region sometime during the winter of 320, but before trying to form a Perdiccan coalition. The fragment describes how he came upon a windfall for himself and his soldiers.

We read that Eumenes successfully surrounded Antipater's allies, who were unable to defend themselves against his attacks. The mutilated fragment then lists the distribution of spoils among Eumenes' men by kind and according to rank, mentioning a ransom and what looks like an agreement between Eumenes and the defeated. It appears that Eumenes and his party demanded 1,000 talents for the return of the booty, and received more than 800. The source suggests that although Eumenes did not get all he hoped for, there was no great feeling of disappointment. The money came unexpectedly, easily, and risk-free, making his troops and even those of Antipater think highly of him. The Palimpsest goes on to flatter Eumenes by depicting his enemies as awestruck by his leadership and intelligence, and contrasts their admiration for him with their contempt for Antipater, who led a larger army and camped near the enemy, yet did nothing but watch his foe capture, plunder, and enslave his allies.

The strong pro-Eumenes bias of the account should warn us against placing full confidence in the authenticity of the troops' admiring response to Eumenes' action in both camps. But such a reaction is not implausible in itself. From the perspective of Eumenes' troops, he showed himself a winning general, a good provider, and (no less important) lucky. It is also likely that Antipater's men were displeased with their commander's lack of valor and generalship in abandoning his allies and doing nothing (despite his numerical superiority) in the face of Eumenes' daring (cf. Arr. *Succ.* 1.41). At the same time, the veterans' criticism of Antipater's inaction evinced their readiness to clash with Eumenes' Macedonians and, in general, their limited inhibition against fighting fellow veterans. Antipater's policy, however, was to avoid battle while in Asia Minor. Perhaps he feared Eumenes' cavalry, and he surely did not want to risk solidifying Eumenes' winning reputation by giving him an opportunity to defeat yet another ranking Macedonian, after Neoptolemus and Craterus. In addition, his accusation that Cleopatra had sided with the Perdiccans, as well as Cleopatra's apprehension of being perceived as fomenting war (Arr. *Succ.* 1.40), suggests that Antipater did not want to be blamed for fighting fellow Macedonians. It was the leaders who had to bear the political consequences of answering the veterans' call to arms.

In the meantime, Eumenes tried unsuccessfully to form a pact with other Perdiccan leaders (below). After reporting on this failed attempt, Plutarch describes how Eumenes oversaw the plunder of an unnamed territory. Eumenes' diplomatic failure and the plundering seem connected. Plutarch's statement that Eumenes *regained* the army's favor after the plundering suggests that he had lost it (*Eum.* 8.11), and rewarding the troops with booty certainly made sense after the collapse of the negotiations over a Perdiccan coalition that could have improved their fighting chances against the enemy.[9] The rewards were immediate: Eumenes promised to pay the troops within three days and completely controlled the operation. He knew where the plunderable places were and had the authority to allocate them as well as the siege engines to facilitate the raiding. This allowed him to subcontract the raids, with little risk to himself. He gave siege engines and sold farms and fortresses full of animals and slaves to a commander of a detachment and to a mercenary general, who commanded the plundering operations. Plutarch says that everyone in the army received his due share of the spoils, presumably according to rank, and that Eumenes once again became very popular. While taking credit for the loot, Eumenes also profited by selling it to his subordinates, who had to labor for it along with the troops. There is no word of sympathy for the local inhabitants, whom Plutarch regarded as natural victims, as did Eumenes and his troops.[10]

Eumenes also tried to keep his soldiers loyal by seeking partners for the war against the royal coalition of Antigonus and Antipater. During the winter of 320/19, according to the Gothenburg Palimpsest, Eumenes sent messengers to Alcetas, Attalus, Polemon, Docimus, and other generals who were condemned to death after Perdiccas's fall, with an offer to unite all their armies. His message indicates what commanders thought could move colleagues and soldiers to pick a side in the conflict. Eumenes suggested that the united Perdiccans would have both a large force comparable to their foes' and enough resources to provide for it. By carrying on the war, they would be able to augment their army, presumably with locals and deserters, because Antigonus, Antipater, and their associates were unpopular, had accomplished nothing, and were held in contempt. The enemy, he added, would be weakened because men were continuously leaving them. They would then sue for an agreement that allowed the Perdiccans to keep their territories according to the original (presumably the Babylonian) settlement.

Thus, according to Eumenes' thinking (likely shared by other gener-

---

9. Bosworth (1992, 72–75) thinks that Plutarch places this episode out of its chronological context, but I see no reason it cannot be dated to the winter of 320/19 and after the failed negotiations.

10. Plut. *Eum.* 8.10–11; cf. Gothenburg Palimpsest fr. 72r. For a detailed analysis of Eumenes' plundering scheme see Briant 1973a, 44–55 (repr. 1982, 56–67); Dreyer 1999, 52–56.

als), what drove troops from one camp to another was the respective size of their armies, the ability to provide for them, the parties' visible accomplishments, the military skills and reputation of their generals, and the troops' respect for them. Yet Eumenes, in his effort to sweeten his offer, gave a too-optimistic prediction of their opponents' conduct. While his mention of men who deserted the enemy may refer to the 3,000 Macedonians who left Antigonus's winter camp in Cappadocia to pillage Lycaonia and Phrygia, there is no evidence for similar desertions from Antipater's camp.[11] More importantly, none of those who deserted the enemy joined the Perdiccan camps.

The issue of the supreme command was also problematic. Although Eumenes was discreetly silent on the question of who would lead the joint army, he was clearly a stronger candidate for the position than the other commanders. His army was the largest: when he later met Antigonus in battle, he brought along 20,000 infantry and 5,000 cavalry, while Alcetas and his colleague had 16,000 infantry and 900 horsemen (Diod. 18.40.7, 45.1). Eumenes could also boast two military victories over prominent Macedonian generals, as well as the successful pillaging of enemy territory. He held an appointment from Perdiccas as chief commander in Asia Minor, and he had more Macedonian veterans than the other generals. All of this gave him a significant advantage over his prospective partners, who must therefore have been concerned about his ambitions.

Up to this point, certainly, the records of Alcetas, his colleagues, and their veterans (if they had any) were unremarkable at best. After Perdiccas's death, Alcetas left for Pisidia, where he busied himself in building up local support and raiding enemy territory. There is no mention of his Macedonians, but equally no indication that he lost the ones he had gotten from Perdiccas.[12] Attalus, who had furthered Eurydice's claim to leadership in Triparadeisus, fled the camp, going probably to Tyre and then to Alcetas; the two are found operating together later that year. Unlike Eumenes, however, Attalus had little to show for himself. After his escape he used his financial resources to assemble an army of 10,000 infantry and 800 cavalry. Apparently using what was left of his Perdiccan fleet, he sailed to the Aegean and attacked Cnidus, Caunus, and Rhodes, but was defeated by the

---

11. Desertion of Antigonus: Polyaenus 4.6.6. See below for a discussion of the episode.

12. Diod. 18.44.1, 46.1–2. According to Arrian's order of events, Alcetas and Attalus's victory over Antipater's ally, Asander, followed the aforementioned negotiations with Eumenes: *Succ.* 1.40–42.

Rhodians. If he had any Macedonians, they must have been few in number.[13] Docimus was a Perdiccan governor of Babylon who joined Attalus and then Alcetas, probably after Perdiccas's downfall. There is no record of his exploits and no evidence of his commanding Macedonians. Lastly, Polemon had failed with his brother Attalus to stop the general Arrhidaeus from delivering Alexander's corpse to Ptolemy in 321. He was probably in Attalus's camp when Eumenes' offer reached him, and there are no veterans associated with his name at this juncture.[14] In short, none of the Perdiccan commanders could rival Eumenes' success, and their inferior position made them apprehensive of his intentions. In addition, Alcetas, who had competed with Eumenes in the past for leadership of the Perdiccan camp (Plut. *Eum.* 5.2), surely regarded himself as deserving of supreme command.

Hence when Alcetas heard of Eumenes' plan, he grew excited about the possibility of taking over a joint army. The Gothenburg Palimpsest mentions Macedonian troops among the attractions of Eumenes' army for Alcetas, describing them, probably wrongly, as the majority of Eumenes' force. The Macedonian troops were certainly the best part of his infantry, but they were no more desirable (and probably less effective) than his large cavalry force. At this point the Palimpsest breaks off, but brief notices in Arrian and Plutarch suggest that Alcetas and his associates debated Eumenes' proposal, that the main problem was who would be the lead commander, and that Alcetas eventually decided against cooperation.[15]

The negotiations among the Perdiccan generals directly affected the fortunes of the veterans in Eumenes' and, possibly, Alcetas's armies. Although

13. Alcetas: Arr. *Succ.* 1.39, 42; Diod. 18.44.1. Attalus's navy: Diod. 18.37.4; Simonetti Agostinetti 1993, 91. Bosworth (2002, 87n86) thinks that a portion of Attalus's 10,000 infantry and 800 horses (Arr. *Succ.* 1.39) could be Macedonian. However, Diodorus (18.37.3–4) mentions only Perdiccas's friends among those who had fled to Attalus at Tyre, and Arrian (*Succ.* 139) refers to "those around" Attalus during his Aegean campaign. Both suggest, then, that he was joined by a limited number of high-ranking refugees and, at best, a handful of others in an army made up mostly of mercenaries.

14. Docimus: Arr. *Succ.* 24.3–4; Diod. 18.44.1; Heckel 2006, 114–115. Mehl (1986, 39–40), however, thinks that before arriving in Asia Minor, Docimus went from Babylon to Perdiccas in Egypt. Polemon: Arr. *Succ.* 1.25, 24.1; Diod. 18.45.3; Heckel 2006, 224–225.

15. The Gothenburg Palimpsest's exaggeration of the Macedonians' number: Bosworth 2002, 89n94. The failed negotiations: Arr. *Succ.* 1.41; Plut. *Eum.* 8.7–8. Unless there were several meetings among these generals, Plutarch's suggestion that they met in Celaenae, Eumenes' winter base, cannot be reconciled with the Palimpsest's reports that Eumenes sent them messengers, or with Arrian's implication of a conference in Alcetas's headquarters.

the troops had no say in the debate, the desire to keep or acquire them played an important role in the considerations of their commanders. Nevertheless, Alcetas's decision against uniting the Perdiccan armies suggests that the wish to acquire Macedonian veterans was not compelling.

Eumenes' failure to strengthen his position, along with the likelihood that he would not come to the help of the other Perdiccan generals after the failed negotiations, probably encouraged Antipater to change his hitherto-nonconfrontational policy. He dispatched Asander, the satrap of Lydia, to fight Alcetas and Attalus in Pisidia. The ensuing battle was at first indecisive, but eventually Asander was defeated (Arr. *Succ.* 1.42). Alcetas presumably took his veterans into battle, but unless Antipater assigned Macedonian troops to Asander, which he is nowhere reported to have done, the satrap must have had no veterans, or only very few.

Once again, the post-Alexander Macedonians in opposing camps had managed to avoid fighting each other, intentionally or by coincidence. So far, Eumenes, Alcetas, and their troops had done better than their opponents on the battlefield, despite having inferior numbers and resources: a success that should have contributed to their self-esteem.

ANTIGONUS AND ANTIPATER

Sending Asander against Alcetas was Antipater's main though modest contribution to the campaign against the Perdiccans. Fighting them was properly Antigonus's brief, but hitherto he had done very little in the way of war, partly because his relationship with Antipater had become tense, for the following reason. When Antipater was distributing commands and offices in Triparadeisus, he appointed his son Cassander as chiliarch, that is, commander of a distinguished squadron of cavalry.[16] But Cassander and Antigonus did not get along, and although Antipater would not quarrel with Antigonus for his son's sake, he became suspicious of Antigonus's am-

---

16. Cassander as chiliarch: Arr. *Succ.* 1.38; Diod. 18.39.7; Just. 13.4.18 (in the Babylonian settlement); *Heidelberg Epitome* 1.4. Diodorus says that Antipater attached Cassander to Antigonus to see if the latter was acting in his own interests. Yet Diodorus's account is so condensed that it could have predated both Cassander's suspicion of Antigonus and the latter's plans. See Landucci Gattinoni 2008, xviii–xix, 171–174, for the sources' analysis, but also A. Meeus's review of her book in *BMCR* 2009.03.45. For the narrow interpretation of the chiliarchy as a command over the cavalry, see Heckel 1992, 366–370; Meeus 2009c, esp. 302–303; cf. Collins 2001, esp. 269.

bitions after a meeting with Cassander in (Hellespontine) Phrygia. A later meeting between Antipater and Antigonus helped to iron out their differences. In what looked like a tradeoff, Antigonus gave the kings (and Cassander) to Antipater, who (now reassured of Antigonus's good intentions) gave him in return 8,500 Macedonian infantry, an uncertain number of cavalry, and seventy elephants from the army that had crossed with him and Craterus to Asia. Their mission was to help Antigonus in his campaign against Eumenes, suggesting that one of the reasons Antigonus had been reluctant to face Eumenes was his smaller army.[17]

It appears that there were few if any veterans among the 8,500 Macedonian infantry who now joined Antigonus. In the Battle of Paraetacene between Antigonus and Eumenes about three years later, Antigonus's army had no more than 8,000 Macedonians, identified as those he got from Antipater. These Macedonians were rebuked before the subsequent Battle of Gabene by one of Eumenes' veterans for daring to fight their "fathers," who had fought with Philip and Alexander. The Macedonians that Antigonus got from Antipater, then, were at least one generation removed from Alexander's veterans (Diod. 19.29.3, 41.1).

It has been suggested that the two generals exchanged troops, Antigonus getting young Macedonians from Antipater and giving him veterans in return. Veterans are indeed attested later in Antipater's camp. Before he crossed over to Europe in early 319, his army mutinied and demanded money "again" (Arr. *Succ.* 1.44). The repeated monetary request identifies the mutineers as veterans who had previously demanded money in Triparadeisus, as does Antipater's promise to pay the protesters their "gift" (*dōrea*), which best fits Alexander's unfulfilled promise in Opis to give a bonus to those who stayed with him. Yet the scholarly assumption that Antipater got these veterans from Antigonus in exchange for the younger Macedonians is problematic.[18] No source reports such a transaction, even though the cross-movement of such a large number of troops was not a trivial matter. It is also unlikely that Arrian's epitomator, condensed as he is, chose to report on just one side of the alleged exchange. Much simpler is the assump-

---

17. Arr. *Succ.* 1.43. Most scholars reject Arrian's report that Antipater gave Antigonus 8,500 cavalry as an improbable high, exceeding even Alexander's cavalry: Billows 1990, 72n40 (1,000 cavalry); Bosworth 2002, 92 (half of Antipater's cavalry); Anson 2004, 123n31 (probably less than 2,000).

18. Exchange of Macedonians: Hammond 1984, 59 (repr. 1994, 3, 139); Billows 1990, 72–73; Anson 2004, 123. Bosworth (2002, 91) identifies the protesters as mercenaries, but there is no record of mercenaries' requesting money earlier.

tion that Antipater had had veterans since his Asian expedition or Triparadeisus, where, as we have seen, they and their comrades were distributed
among various commanders.[19]

Antigonus too must have held on to the Macedonians he got at Triparadeisus. At the same time, the veterans of the royal army lost their kings.
They and their monarchs had been inseparable since Babylon, and the
troops' loyalty to the Argead house was above reproach. The kings' presence in camp also distinguished their followers from other veterans and
gave them a sense of continuity, a stable identity, and probably increased
self-importance. Yet these attributes were also threatening to others. The riots in Babylon and the Cynane and Eurydice affairs showed that the veterans' common background and attachment to the royal house could be mobilized against the army's leadership. In addition, Perdiccas had used the
kings and the veterans in his military and propaganda campaigns against
his opponents, as his enemies had done after getting rid of him. This history
must have been on Cassander's mind when he warned his father against letting Antigonus have the kings.[20] Antipater heeded his advice and took the
kings, ensuring that neither Antigonus nor anyone else could use them to
legitimize his military command and a civil war, or to unite the veterans
behind him. Thus the kings' removal helped to weaken the power and solidarity of the royal veterans. More docile, and with reduced numbers, Antigonus's veterans had no alternative but desertion to following their leader
wherever he went.

Although the sources are unclear about the exact whereabouts of Antigonus and his army in the winter of 320/19, it appears that he spent at
least part of it in Phrygia.[21] Polyaenus reports that during this winter,
3,000 Macedonian hoplites rebelled and deserted him, and that they raided
Lycaonia and Phrygia from their mountain strongholds. Antigonus did not
want to destroy them but was also concerned that they might join Alcetas. He sent them one of his commanders, Leonidas, who pretended to join
the rebels and was elected by them as their general. Taking advantage of
their lack of cavalry, Leonidas led them to a plain where Antigonus and his
cavalry captured them together with their leaders, Holcias and two other
commanders. The captives pleaded with Antigonus to spare them, and he

---

19. See below for the possibility that Antigonus's army had an unknown number of
Craterus's veterans after the alleged exchange.

20. Arr. *Succ.* 1.43; cf. W. Heckel 2002, 90.

21. Thus Billows 1990, 74, and Anson 2004, 122–123n27, in spite of their disagreement about details.

agreed to release them if they would return peacefully to Macedonia. He also sent Leonidas with them, ostensibly to escort them safely, but in fact to lead them home (Polyaenus 4.6.6).[22]

It is regrettable that the rebels' background and motives are not reported, yet it is easier to ascertain their identity than their reasons to desert. They could not have come from among the 8,500 Macedonians whom Antipater gave Antigonus, because three years later 8,000 of these Macedonians were still serving with him in Asia. This identifies the rebels as veterans of the royal army, which Antigonus had led since Triparadeisus.[23] But why did they desert? Not, as has been assumed, in order to join Alcetas, or because they wished to go home. Polyaenus reports the option of their joining Alcetas as Antigonus's concern but not as their motive. They might have contemplated going to Alcetas or even to Eumenes, because Leonidas is said to have convinced them not to join anyone. Yet the fact that they preferred to stay in fortified places and raid the countryside shows that joining Antigonus's opponents was not their primary or immediate goal. Nor did they desert in order to return to Macedonia, because their return was actually forced on them by Antigonus. The general wanted both to prevent anyone else from drafting them and to stop their raiding his territory. This is also the reason he conditioned their release on their going to Macedonia quietly, i.e., without leaving a trail of destruction and plunder behind them. Leonidas was assigned to lead them there, thereby ensuring their good behavior

---

22. The exactitude of the figure of 3,000 troops—with occasional qualifiers of "about" or "more than" that number—is a matter of concern because of its too-frequent appearance in different contexts, especially in Diodorus. Besides the 3,000 Silver Shields and the rebels from Antigonus, see, for example, the recurrence of this number in relation to the Macedonian infantry in Pithon's army (Diod. 18.7.3), to the Greek rebel cavalry against him and those who defected to him (Diod. 18.7.2, 5; cf. also the 3,000 Greek rebels who returned to Greece: Diod. 17.99.5–6), to the infantry that deserted Eumenes in Cappadocia (Diod. 18.40.2), to the troops who received Macedonian training in Peucestas's army (Diod. 19.14.5), to Antigonus's infantrymen across the Coprates River (Diod. 19.18.4), to the hypaspists in Eumenes' army (Diod. 19.28.1), to Antigonus's Lycians and Pamphilians in the Battle of Paraetacene (Diod. 19.29.3), and even to the prisoners captured by Demetrius in 307, who fled back to the Egyptian side (Diod. 20.47.4). It is possible that the figure 3,000 stood for three military units (lochoi), regardless of their exact complement. See, generally, Rubicam 1991; 2003.

23. The 8,500 and later 8,000 Macedonians: Arr. Succ. 1.43; Diod. 19.29.3. The rebels' likely veteran status: Hammond 1984, 60 (repr. 1994, 3:140). Billows (1990, 74n42; 1995, 195) has recognized that they came from Perdiccas's army but thinks that Antipater gave them to Antigonus on top of the 8,500 Macedonians. This goes beyond the extant information, and it is simpler to assume that Antigonus had them all along.

and a direct journey home.[24] The most likely reason for the desertion was what the rebels are in fact reported to have done afterward, namely, plundering. They had been familiar with the country and its looting potential from the time they had plundered two cities in Lycaonia during Perdiccas's campaign there in 322 (Diod. 18.22). Rumors about Eumenes' successful raiding of locals could have whetted their appetite too, and the deserters (unlike Eumenes' troops) did not have to share the spoils with their chief commander.[25]

The case of the deserting Macedonians also suggests the nature of the veterans' relationship with their commanders. Of the rebels' leaders, the source names only Holcias, who might or might not have been the Holcias who authored the fictitious will of Alexander and the account of Alexander's last days, in which he gave himself a probably unwarranted prominent role.[26] Whoever he was, he had to accept Leonidas's leadership, or share command with him, after the troops' election of Leonidas as their general. Their semi-democratic act recalls the election of generals by the Greek mercenary army that went with Cyrus the Younger against the Persian king in 400, a force that found itself leaderless in Asia after the death of its employer. Both the Cyreans and the Macedonian deserters had to fend for themselves in a hostile environment and to rely on their group solidarity and leaders for survival. These special circumstances empowered the deserters to pick their own generals, unlike the larger Successor armies, which tended to accept leaders assigned them by the military elite.

The rebels' choice of Leonidas presupposes their familiarity with him, which is understandable if he was the same person who had led Alexander's disciplinary unit (the *ataktoi*).[27] His background, experience, and prominence under Antigonus probably gave him an authority greater than that of Holcias, who is nowhere mentioned in the annals of Alexander's military expedition. In addition, the "conversion" of Leonidas to their cause, which

---

24. Polyaenus's text reads as if the agreement to return quietly involved Holcias and his colleagues, but Leonidas would not have been sent to Macedonia to escort just a few men.

25. The rebels' wish to join Alcetas: Billows 1990, 74n42, 75, 413; cf. Anson 2004, 121–122; or to go home: Briant 1973, 64 (repr. 1982, 76); Hammond 1984, 60 (repr. 1994, 3:140); *contra*: Anson 2004, 122n22. Cf. Bosworth (2002, 90), who thinks that they were resentful of Antipater's failures against Eumenes and uncomfortable fighting his Macedonians.

26. Holcias's conjectured identity: Berve 1928, 2:283n580; Billows 1990, 412–413; Bosworth 2000b, 240–241; Heckel 2006, 140–141.

27. Curt. 7.2.35; Berve 1928, 2:236n470; Heckel 2006, 147.

resembled Meleager's and Attalus's changing sides from the cavalry to the infantry in Babylon (if historical), affirmed for the deserters that they did right to rebel and constituted a victory against Antigonus. Conversely, the fact that Leonidas was able to lead the Macedonians into a trap exemplified the price that troops in the post-Alexander era paid for their trust in, and dependence on, their leaders. Antigonus's stratagem succeeded also because it exploited his advantage in cavalry, which, as was seen in the case of Eumenes and Craterus's veterans, could harass the phalanx to the point of surrender.

Once they were defeated, however, Antigonus's options for dealing with the deserters were limited. Killing so many soldiers of Macedonian nationality was not just "cruel" (so Polyaenus) but also politically out of the question. Another solution was to punish select individuals and to reintegrate the rest into his army. Alexander, Perdiccas, and Eumenes (as we shall see) all took rebels back after punishing their leaders. Antigonus, however, chose to send them all home. He could not risk trusting them, because this was the third time (after Babylon and Triparadeisus) that they had rebelled against authority, even threatening his life in Syria (Arr. *Succ.* 1.33). The reinforcements he got from Antipater also diminished his need for the deserters. Since the troops and their commanders feared his retribution, he could stiffen his magnanimity with an ultimatum. He accepted their supplication but also prevailed on them to leave for Macedonia, where they would be inaccessible to the Perdiccans. He even made them take as their leader the general who had betrayed them.

Antipater too had to deal with dissatisfied soldiers. As noted above, his army mutinied sometime before their crossing to Europe in the spring of 319. The troops again demanded money and prevented Antipater from marching to the coast and then home. The marshal showed that he had learned the lesson of Triparadeisus and could lift a page from Eumenes' book on how to trick one's troops. He did not make the Macedonians an evasive, "I'll-do-my-best" promise as he had done in Triparadeisus, almost losing his life as a consequence. Instead, he gave them a false pledge to pay them all or most of what was owed to them upon reaching Abydus on the Bosporus, thus naming a specific time and place for the reward. This put an end to the mutiny and allowed Antipater to reach Abydus. Using a stratagem again, he and the kings sneaked by night across the straits to Lysimachus, the satrap of Thrace. The soldiers followed him the next day and delayed their demand for money (Arr. *Succ.* 1.45).

The episode, which concludes Arrian's history of Alexander's successors, illustrates the biased perspective of our sources. Mutinying troops were by definition in the wrong, and it was legitimate, even praiseworthy, for a general to cheat them out of their wages. Historians and their readers were expected to appreciate or be entertained by such cunning. The soldiers, naturally, were less amused. The most vocal among them were the veterans of the royal army, who thought that the circumstances favored their demand. The transfer to Antigonus of the Macedonians Antipater had recruited for the Asian campaign left the latter without his core supporters and more vulnerable to pressure. The veterans were also aware that they had more leverage on Antipater in Asia than at home or even in Thrace. But when Antipater and the kings fled, the Macedonians were left without a general, a paymaster, or the crown. Since the Perdiccans were too remote to help, the veterans had little choice but to follow Antipater to Europe in the hope that he would reward them there. It is doubtful that he ever did so, because a failed mutiny also meant that the soldiers lost their best bargaining chip.[28] Antipater died in the summer of that year (319), and the veterans who went home with him disappear from our records.

ANTIGONUS'S WAR AGAINST EUMENES AND THE PERDICCANS

Meanwhile, Antigonus made preparations for a campaign against the Perdiccans that would include an abortive attempt on Eumenes' life. Both Plutarch and Justin report on this incident and its impact on Eumenes' veterans.

According to Plutarch's version, letters from the enemy promising 100 talents and honors to the man who should kill Eumenes were found in his camp. This discovery greatly angered the Macedonians, who passed a resolution that one thousand of their leading soldiers would serve continuously as Eumenes' bodyguard wherever he went and guard his door at night. With this done, they took pleasure in receiving from Eumenes the honors that the Macedonian kings gave their friends, such as purple hats and cloaks, which Eumenes was empowered to grant (Plut. *Eum.* 8.11–12).

While in Plutarch the story, like others, illustrates Eumenes' popularity with the army, Justin's version is more Machiavellian and shows the Cardian's cleverness. According to this Roman epitomator, when Eumenes learned of Antigonus's letters and the offer to kill him, he told the troops

---

28. It did not help that in the winter of 319 Antigonus seized 600 talents destined for Macedonia: Diod. 18.52.7.

that he himself had forged them in order to test their loyalty. The ploy restrained soldiers whose loyalty was wavering and undermined the credibility of future similar attempts against his life. All now competed for the honor of serving as Eumenes' bodyguards (Just. 14.1.9–14).

The theme of Eumenes' cunning dominates other accounts of him, and it likely led Justin, or his source, to rework here a later and much better attested instance of Eumenes' forging letters to save himself from a similar predicament. In 317 he produced false letters from Polyperchon and Olympias that gave him the upper hand in a struggle with a fellow general over the supreme command (Diod. 19.23.1–3). This forgery could easily have inspired the earlier, similar story.[29] Both Justin and Plutarch, however, agree that the invitation to murder was authentic, indicating the existence of channels of communication between the army and the enemy that Eumenes was impotent to block. The accessibility of the troops to enemy overtures and the presence in camp of men friendly to Antigonus—someone had to circulate his letters (Plut. *Eum.* 8.11)—suggest that it was very much in Eumenes' interest to have a bodyguard.[30] In reality, the greatest threat to a general's life came not from his army but from rival or subordinate officers. Such men were Perdiccas's killers, and when Ptolemy and Antigonus tried later to get rid of Eumenes, they first communicated with officers in his army (Diod. 18.62.1–7). The formation of a bodyguard for Eumenes, then, was designed to protect him primarily from his own chain of command.

Plutarch terms the resolution to form a bodyguard a *dogma*, a decree, which suggests that it was moved in the army assembly, probably by one of Eumenes' loyalists.[31] In spite of Plutarch's wish to portray the act as a spontaneous expression of the Macedonians' rage at the attempt to kill their leader, Eumenes was in fact the major beneficiary of their measure, and motions in the assembly tended to originate with the leadership.[32] But

---

29. Rosen's (1967, 72–73) assertion that Plutarch conflated two incidents of subversive letters (the other: Diod. 18.62.3–63.6) seems to have attracted no followers. See also Anson (2004, 117–118n3) against Rosen's postdating Antigonus's letters to Eumenes' stay in Cilicia more than a year later.

30. Anson (2004, 117n2) doubts the story of forged letters on this occasion because there would not be a need for a bodyguard if the letters were proclaimed inauthentic. Justin's suggestion (14.1.13) that there were men in camp who could be tempted to kill Eumenes justifies the need for a bodyguard.

31. Plut. *Eum.* 8.11. Cf. Hatzopoulos 1996, 1:287.

32. Cf. Briant (1973a, 51–55 [repr. 1982, 63–67]), whose suggestion that Eumenes made the soldiers into mercenaries on this occasion overinterprets their oath to him.

there is little doubt that it was warmly supported by the troops, and Plutarch provides a key to understanding their reaction when he ties the story of the assassination attempt to Eumenes' earlier permission to loot enemy territory. The link is thematic because both events relate to Eumenes' popularity. Even if a long period had elapsed between the looting and Antigonus's letters, the call for his murder was badly timed, because the troops were still relatively well off and grateful to their leader. By forming a bodyguard, the Macedonians reciprocated the "favor" and protected their benefactor, but they benefited from it too.

One thousand of them, whom Plutarch identifies as leading soldiers or officers (*hegemonikoi*), became closer to the general in camp and won greater prestige and higher status than other troops in Eumenes' diverse army. Indeed, they appear to have resembled the royal *agēma* of the hypaspists, the elite infantry unit that served as Alexander's military bodyguards and often accompanied him on special missions.[33]

The Macedonians also approved Eumenes' right to distribute royal honors. It goes without saying that the measure increased his stature, but it also answered a popular need, because the power to grant honors was often matched, if not created, by the craving for them. Eumenes' Macedonians were used to receiving honors from royalty, but with the kings now in the enemy's camp, they chose the next-best distributor of honors, a military leader. This served Eumenes' purposes, because the power to honor did not challenge the legitimacy of the Argeads—to whom he always professed loyalty—and because he could expand the distribution of high honors from formerly selected individuals to now a larger group of grateful recipients.[34]

Antigonus sought to get rid of Eumenes by treason because it had worked against Perdiccas, because it was easier than waging a war against him, and because it would have allowed Antigonus to concentrate his efforts on the other Perdiccans. When the attempt failed, he assembled troops from their winter quarters and, in the spring of 319, set out to fight Eumenes in Cappadocia. Diodorus reports in this context that Eumenes suffered a desertion of 3,000 infantry and 500 cavalry, led by the distinguished commander Per-

33. For the hypaspists and the royal infantry *agēma*, see Tarn 1948, 2, 148–154; Milns 1971; Griffith in Hammond and Griffith 1979, 2:414–418; Anson 1985.

34. Plut. *Eum.* 8.12. Bosworth (1992, 72–73), however, denies that Eumenes arrogated royal prerogatives to himself. Following Just. 14.1.1–14, he dates the episode to the aftermath of Eumenes' visit to Cleopatra, and argues that Eumenes honored officers whom he had appointed with Cleopatra's blessing, using her charisma; cf. also Hornblower 1981, 162; Schäfer 2002, 101. But see Anson's counterarguments: 2004, 121n18. For the honors, especially the right to wear the Macedonian hat: Saatsoglou-Paliadeli 1993, esp. 139–140.

diccas (Diod. 18.40.1–4). Although it is tempting to detect the long arm of Antigonus behind their departure, the fact that the deserters neither joined his camp nor were on their way to it suggests that this was not their intention.[35] Diodorus's calling these troops "mutineers" (*synapostantōn*) suggests that they were unhappy with Eumenes for some reason, and perhaps that they were apprehensive of his imminent clash with Antigonus. We can only speculate on their identity. Their commander, Perdiccas, had a good Macedonian name, and Eumenes' later dispersal of them among different units implies their unity of background. Yet these clues are insufficient to identify them as veterans. The 500 cavalry among them are unlikely to have been Macedonians, because Eumenes' cavalry was recruited locally.

Eumenes dealt effectively with the alarming situation. He sent against the deserters a force of 4,000 picked infantry and 1,000 cavalry under the command of Phoenix of Tenedos, the man he had trusted with half of his cavalry in the battle against Craterus. After a quick night march, Phoenix surprised and captured the deserters in their sleep. We don't know if Phoenix took veterans with him, although the description of his infantry as "picked" (*epikleous*) suggests that some may have been veterans.[36] Eumenes executed the rebel leaders but regained the soldiers' loyalty by treating them kindly (i.e., by not punishing them) and by scattering them in his army, thereby eradicating their identity as a rebel group. His different treatment of the soldiers and their commanders was based on several considerations. Obviously, executing a few individuals was more tolerable than killing a crowd of soldiers, and Eumenes needed all the troops he could get for the coming battle with Antigonus. But he had also learned the lesson of the mutiny at Opis, where Alexander showed that the way to regain control over rebellious soldiers started with eliminating their leadership. The troops' immediate commanders could influence them more than their chief general, as in other cases of mass desertion. Lastly, by killing Perdiccas and his fellow officers, Eumenes hoped to deter other commanders from leaving him with their units. As it happened, his countermeasures failed to yield the expected results.

The mutiny against Eumenes followed the desertion of Holcias and his

---

35. Billows (1990, 74), followed by Schäfer (2002, 112), sees here a response to Antigonus's propaganda, while Anson (2004, 127–128) alludes to the power of his purse.

36. Diod. 18.40.2–4. Diodorus's account of Phoenix's operation is somewhat puzzling. Although the deserters camped a three-day journey from Eumenes' camp, Phoenix was able to capture them within hours: after a night march, he reached them in the second night watch, i.e., around midnight. Perhaps by the time Phoenix left, Eumenes' and the deserters' camps had moved closer to one other.

3,000 Macedonians from Antigonus and the riots against Antipater. All three cases of insubordination took place within a relatively short time (late summer to winter 320) and demonstrated the generals' difficulties in keeping their armies disciplined and loyal. But it would be prudent to resist looking for additional common denominators among these incidents. Only two of these revolts certainly involved veterans, and their causes can be gauged only for the mutinies against Antipater (money owed) and Antigonus (probably booty), but not for the one against Eumenes. It is possible that the different groups of rebels inspired each other, but (to borrow Tolstoy's aphorism about unhappy families) each seems to have been unhappy in its own way.

What happened next was a battle on the plain of Orcynia, somewhere in Cappadocia, in which Macedonian veterans in Eumenes' and Antigonus's armies fought each other.[37] Antigonus proved himself the better general, although the odds favored Eumenes, who had an army of 5,000 cavalry and 20,000 infantry against Antigonus's 2,000 cavalry, 30 elephants, and more than 10,000 infantry, half of whom were Macedonians "admired for their manly valor" (Diod. 18.40.6–7). Eumenes aimed to take advantage of his quantitative and qualitative superiority in cavalry, for whose benefit he picked a plain for the battlefield. His plan was sensible but predictable, and Antigonus frustrated it with a combination of trickery and clever use of the terrain. To undermine Eumenes' edge in cavalry, he conspired with Apollonides, Eumenes' cavalry commander, to induce him to desert Eumenes during the battle.[38] He also occupied the foothills on the edge of the plain, which secured him a possible refuge from which to attack Eumenes' weaker rear and capture his baggage (Polyaenus 4.6.12; Diod. 18.40.8).

Polyaenus relates that Antigonus misled the enemy into thinking that his army was more numerous than it really was, first by misinforming them about an alleged arrival of allies and then by thinning and stretching his phalanx line to about twice its normal length. Believing that they faced a large army, Eumenes' troops refused battle and fled.[39] Antigonus could lie convincingly to the enemy about the arrival of reinforcements because his

---

37. Diod. 18.40.5–8; Plut. *Eum.* 9.3; Justin 14.1–2; Engel 1971; Billows 1990, 75–77; Schäfer 202, 110–15.

38. Apollonides' identity is uncertain, but he might be related to Apollonides of Cardia (Eumenes' birthplace), who had received land from Philip II: [Dem.] 7.39.

39. Polyaenus 4.6.19, and see Billows (1990, 75–76) in favor of ascribing this passage to the Battle of Orcynia. The following discussion may answer Anson's reservations about Polyaenus's account: 2004, 129n43.

occupation of the hills prevented Eumenes, who was on the plain, from verifying reports of reinforcements from that direction. By offering battle the very next day, Antigonus did not give Eumenes enough time to assess the situation. Yet the devastating impact his deception is said to have had on Eumenes' troops is questionable, because the thinning of Antigonus's infantry line was less likely to scare them than to invite a counterattack. Diodorus's explanation—that the battle was decided by the desertion of Apollonides and his cavalry in the midst of the fighting—is preferable. By all accounts, Antigonus won a great victory: he killed about 8,000 enemy soldiers and seized their baggage. As a result, most of Eumenes' army joined his side, moved to do so both by their disappointment with their general and by the prospect of regaining their possessions and families.[40]

Few would dispute that Eumenes took Macedonian veterans into battle: they served as his personal bodyguard, and Macedonians are mentioned among those who fled with him (Plut. *Eum.* 8.11–12, 9.7). In contrast, the Macedonians with Antigonus have been identified as nonveterans. Bosworth thought that they came from the 8,500 Macedonians whom Antipater had given Antigonus earlier, depicted as younger than the veterans in the Battle of Paraetacene in 317. Such Macedonians were also the right kind of troops to use against Eumenes' veterans, because they did not share the experience of service with Alexander.[41] But it is too restrictive to identify Antigonus's 5,000 Macedonians at Orcynia only with his younger Macedonians, since at this time his army still included veterans as well. Moreover, Antigonus could ill afford not to use veterans against veterans. A scruple against such use would have disqualified them from military missions not just against Eumenes but also against Alcetas, who had veterans of his own, and scholars have plausibly surmised that, before marching against Eumenes, Antigonus sent the rest of his army to watch the movements of Alcetas and Attalus, who were then in Caria or Pisidia. Besides, Eumenes had no inhibitions about using his veterans in this battle, and there is no reason to assume that Antigonus, with his significantly smaller army, was more considerate or cautious.[42] And the veterans' presence may be trace-

40. Diod. 18.40.8, 41.4; Plut. *Eum.* 9.3, cf. 10.1. The cavalry that deserted Eumenes is unlikely to have been Macedonian: Plut. *Eum.* 4.3; 7.1; Anson 2004, 128n43.

41. Bosworth 2002, 91.

42. Antigonus's dispatching troops against Alcetas and Attalus: Vezin 1907, 60; Engel 1971, 228, with Billows' modifications: 1990, 75n43. See, however, below against Hammond's (1984, 59–60 [repr. 1994, 139–140]) identification of Antigonus's Macedonians only with Craterus's veterans.

able in the outcome of the battle. The elimination of 8,000 enemy troops recalls the brutal scale of killing by other veterans, such as Pithon's Macedonians against the Greek rebels and the Silver Shields against Antigonus's army later in Asia.

Otherwise, the veterans' contribution to the battle was unremarkable. The sources largely ignore the phalanx's performance, but they assign a key role to the non-Macedonian cavalry on each side: either the cavalry who deserted Eumenes or those who captured his baggage.[43] For the record, Eumenes' veterans had found themselves on the losing side at least twice, one against him with Neoptolemus and one on his side against Antigonus. Indeed, there were now fewer and fewer veterans who could rightfully claim to be invincible.

It is likely that many of Eumenes' veterans moved to Antigonus's side, sharing his other troops' disappointment and loss of heart (Diod. 18.40.8, 41.4). A probably smaller number of them stayed with him in his flight (Plut. *Eum.* 9.7). Their loyalty in spite of the devastating defeat and loss of their baggage should puzzle only those who regard all the veterans as slaves to personal gain and to the satisfaction of simple needs. By now, Eumenes' Macedonians had been serving with him for more than three years, and he had labored hard to bind them to him by winning battles, by giving them distinctions, honors, and material rewards, and by keeping them close to him as his bodyguards.[44]

Much of Eumenes' conduct during his flight aimed at snatching crumbs of victory from the jaws of defeat in order to retain the loyalty and boost the morale of those around him. He managed to seize the person who had betrayed him, probably Apollonides, thereby giving a modicum of retributive satisfaction to those distressed by the defeat.[45] Another minor accom-

---

43. It is possible that Hieronymus, the likely source for the battle, tried to excuse Eumenes' loss to a smaller army by foregrounding the treason of the cavalry; see Engel 1971; Schafer 2002, 112–113; Landucci Gattinoni 2008, 188–189. But the desertion, which was hardly unique to this battle, surely contributed to his defeat.

44. Cf. the apt observations of Bennett and Roberts on loyalty as a need: 2009, 2:54.

45. Plut. *Eum.* 9.3 says that Eumenes, while in flight, seized and executed the man who had betrayed him before the latter could join the enemy. He does not name the traitor, but his account seems to contradict Diodorus, who states that Apollonides deserted Eumenes in the midst of battle (18.40.8). Accordingly, some have assumed that Plutarch refers here not to the Battle of Orcynia but to Eumenes' earlier capture and punishment of the deserter Perdiccas (Bosworth 1992, 87n119; Heckel 2006, 293n96). Yet Plutarch clearly puts the story of punishing the traitor in the context of Eumenes'

plishment was burying his dead soldiers after reversing direction to avoid his pursuers and sneaking back to the deserted battlefield. In Greek warfare, possessing the battlefield and burying the dead there were marks of victory, with the victorious side normally surrendering the enemy dead to the defeated army. In the case of Orcynia, however, both sides postponed the ritual in favor of pursuit on one side and flight on the other. Eumenes could not have fooled anyone into believing that his gesture meant that he had won the battle, but it did detract from Antigonus's victory and demonstrate Eumenes' concern for his soldiers, dead or alive. The second-century author Philon of Byzantium advised generals to gain the loyalty of their mercenaries by taking care of their families and the wounded, and by burying their dead (*Mechanica Syntaxis* 5.94.26–29). Eumenes, Antigonus, Antigonus's son Demetrius, and Ptolemy all recognized the benefit that accrued to both victors and vanquished who met this expectation.[46] Eumenes also acknowledged the social and military hierarchy of the army when he made separate pyres for the commanders and the troops. The pyres, or deathbeds, were made of wooden doors, obtained by raiding neighboring villages (Plut. *Eum.* 9.5). (It was common for locals to supply the needs of the troops and of their commander both in life and in death.) Plutarch adds that when Antigonus returned to the battlefield and saw the mounds that Eumenes had heaped over the dead, he admired his adversary's boldness and strength (*Eum.* 9.5). Whether or not this flattering remark is historical, it illustrates the politics of burial for these Hellenistic commanders.

Eumenes' symbolic victories must have had only a limited impact on his companions. A greater reward awaited them in their discovery of Antigonus's baggage, which included many free persons, slaves, and riches accumulated over many wars and raids (Plut. *Eum.* 9.6). I have dealt with this episode in my introduction (above) in order to demonstrate the sources' at-

---

escape from the battle, and it is hard to see why his killing of Perdiccas should preclude his later killing of Apollonides. Moreover, Diodorus does not really say that Apollonides joined Antigonus, only that he deserted Eumenes. Like Leotodorus and the 3,000 troops who deserted the Greek rebels against Pithon in 323, he could have withdrawn to a place away from the battlefield (Diod. 18.7.5–6). It was while fleeing that Eumenes probably chanced upon and killed him. Engel (1971, 229–230), however, thinks that Apollonides pursued Eumenes and fell into his hands by some misfortune. Landucci Gattinoni (2008, 189–190) gives Apollonides a possible extension of life by identifying him with a man later associated with Demetrius.

46. Antigonus and Eumenes (later in Iran): Diod. 19.31.1–4, and see chap. 1 above and chap. 7 below. Ptolemy and Demetrius following the Battle of Gaza: 19.85.1–4. Ptolemy and Perdiccas's dead: chap. 4 above.

titudes toward the veterans. Here I wish to assess its significance for the veterans' history. But before discussing how and why Eumenes prevented his troops from taking the loot, I must first identify its owners.

N. G. L. Hammond asserts that the baggage belonged to Craterus's former veterans, who now served in Antigonus's army, arguing from Diodorus's description of the 5,000 Macedonians who fought with Antigonus at Orcynia as "admired for their valor," and especially from Plutarch's description of Antigonus's baggage as made up of riches accumulated through many wars and raids, which Hammond suggests "can apply only to the veterans who fought with Alexander." Thus Hammond traces their story from Opis up to their (alleged) transfer to Antigonus by Antipater before he returned to Macedonia.[47]

It is likely that Antigonus had an unknown number of Craterus's veterans, but the proof of this is not the baggage, whose history as reconstructed by Hammond is problematic. Diodorus's phrase "being famous for valor" is vague enough to apply to Macedonians and non-Macedonians alike, including Alexander's soldiers even before they became veterans.[48] In order for the baggage to belong to Craterus's veterans, it would have had to travel a very tortuous route that made its survival or opulence questionable. It must have followed the veterans from Opis to Asia Minor, from there to Thessaly, and then home to Macedonia (without being left there?). From Macedonia the baggage would have gone back to Asia Minor, where it supposedly remained with the veterans even though they surrendered to Eumenes and then fled from him. It then would have followed them to Triparadeisus in Syria, from there back to western Asia Minor, and finally to Orcynia, east of Cappadocia. The chances that it remained intact and full of riches after such a journey were not very good.

Finally, limiting the baggage "collected and plundered in many wars" (Plut. *Eum.* 9.6) to Craterus's veterans unjustifiably excludes the possibility that it belonged to other veterans in Antigonus's army (including non-Macedonians), whom Antigonus had inherited from Perdiccas after the Triparadeisus settlement (Arr. *Succ.* 1.38). Indeed, this possibility is suggested by Plutarch's statement that Antigonus's Macedonians were grateful to Eumenes for sparing their children from enslavement and their wives

47. Hammond 1984, 59–60 (repr. 1994, 3:59–60); Diod. 18.40.7; Plut. *Eum.* 9.6, 11.
48. E.g., Diod. 12.62.1 (Spartans); 17.11.5 (both Macedonians and Thebans), 84.3 (Macedonians), and esp. 17.78.2 (Macedonians, in language very similar to that of 18.30.4); 18.7.2 (Greek veterans who rebelled in Asia). Cf. Billows 1995, 196n33.

from shame (Plut. *Eum.* 9.11). Unlike Craterus's veterans, the Macedonians of the royal army did not have to leave their camp families behind.

In any case, the capture of Antigonus's baggage would have enriched Eumenes' troops and compensated them with the recovery of their own lost baggage and families. Eumenes, however, decided to pass on the chance, believing that so much booty would make the soldiers less mobile and more self-indulgent, thus frustrating his plan to win the war against Antigonus over the long run. Accordingly, he kept them away from the baggage long enough to allow his old friend Menander, who was in charge of it, to follow Eumenes' advice to take the baggage to an easily defensible place. Eumenes pretended to be sorry about the news and left the scene with his companions. His action, we are told, earned him the gratitude and favor of Antigonus's Macedonians for not enslaving their children or abusing their wives, but Antigonus dismissed it as self-serving, saying that Eumenes did not want to shackle himself (with the loot) when in flight (Plut. *Eum.* 9.6–12).

The episode demonstrates (once again) Eumenes' ingenuity, which he often used to dupe his troops. The depiction of the Macedonians as lacking in restraint when in sight of the rich loot, as opposed to the controlled and farsighted Eumenes, justifies the deception for the reader, even if his resort to a ruse instead of discipline shows that his authority was weak. Eumenes' dealing with Menander also suggests the existence of a personal network that the military elite used behind the troops' back to, at least in this case, frustrate their wishes.

The tale raises questions about the wisdom of Eumenes' action, however. His concern that the loot would encumber his escape is confirmed both by Antigonus's interpretation and by a fourth-century military manual that recommends attacking troops who are laden with booty and have become undisciplined (Aeneas Tacticus, *Siegecraft* 16.4–8; cf. Menander, *Aspis* 1–65). But there were other considerations that should have tipped the balance in favor of taking the baggage. It would have compensated his soldiers, raised their morale, and given them an incentive to stay with him by reuniting them with their possessions and families. It would also have greatly distressed Antigonus's soldiers and allowed Eumenes to influence their conduct through his possession of their baggage. Finally, how would Eumenes have justified his action to his troops once they learned (by themselves or from their pursuers) that they had lost their baggage and families through his deception? Indeed, Diodorus tells us that Eumenes' plan to escape to Armenia was frustrated by Antigonus and by the desertion of his troops to the enemy, suggesting that Eumenes' soldiers followed their baggage and may have uncovered his ploy (Diod. 18.41.1). It appears that Eumenes' decision about the baggage was a blunder.[49]

The episode has a larger importance, because it touches upon the commanders' use of the troops' baggage and families to shape their relations with their subordinates and peers. The troops' strong attachment to their baggage and camp families was not universal and should not be taken for granted, but there is enough evidence to suggest that the families constituted a vulnerability that the enemy and their commanders exploited.[50] Plutarch reports that in 368/7 the Theban general Pelopidas sought to punish Thessalian mercenaries for deserting him by seizing their possessions, wives, and children. It was only his capture by Alexander of Pherae that prevented him from fulfilling his design (Plut. *Pelopidas* 27).

Control of the troops' families and possessions could be used to punish or deter disloyalty, but also to encourage defection. In 317 the Silver Shields under Eumenes fought Antigonus in the Battle of Gabene but then moved to his side because he had captured their baggage.[51] In 307 Antigonus's son, Demetrius, won a battle in Cyprus against Ptolemy's brother, Menelaus, and captured nearly 3,000 men, whom he absolved from any wrongdoing and distributed among his units. But the new recruits fled back to Menelaus because their baggage, which likely included their families, was left in Egypt. After intercepting the refugees on their way, Demetrius apparently sent them to his father in Syria. Later that year, Demetrius won a naval battle against Ptolemy near Salamis in Cyprus, capturing many of his ships. His take included many servants, friends, and women, as well as 8,000 troops aboard the ships and the ships' crews. He then incorporated them and about 8,000 additional troops into his army.[52] Drafting defeated or captured soldiers into the victorious army was common by now, but Demetrius's ability to enlist Ptolemy's troops without risking their desertion must be largely attributed to his capture of their baggage and families. Ptolemy's bringing the baggage along to Cyprus was perhaps impru-

---

49. See also Schäfer 2002, 114–115; cf. Engel 1971, 230.

50. On the baggage (*aposkeuē*), which included also free and servile attendants, see Holleaux 1942; Launey 1949, 2:785–790; Loman 2005; cf. Heinen 1983; D. Thompson 2006, 101. But see Diod. 18.20.5–6 for a case where the capture of the troops' baggage did not appear to affect their loyalty.

51. See chap. 8 below; cf. Diod. 19.84.5–8 about cavalrymen who left Demetrius for their baggage after his defeat in the Battle of Gaza (312).

52. Demetrius and Menelaus's men: Diod. 20.47.4; Loman 2005, 350. Demetrius and Ptolemy's men: Diod. 20.52.6–53.1; Plut. *Demtr.* 16, 17.5; Billows 1990, 154–155.

dent, but he may have planned a prolonged campaign, and possibly his soldiers refused to leave without it.

Yet some cases of captured baggage also suggest that the leaders made
a distinction between the soldiers' baggage and that of their commanders. Once again Demetrius's career may illustrate the point. After his defeat by Ptolemy and Seleucus at Gaza in 312, the victors restored his baggage, his court attendants, and his friends and their possessions, saying that
they were fighting not for gain but because of Antigonus's unjust treatment of them. Soon thereafter Demetrius responded in kind. Having captured Ptolemy's general Cilles and his rich camp in Syria, he let Cilles and
his friends go with presents, allegedly finding joy not in riches but in the
opportunity to reciprocate Ptolemy's generosity. Demetrius acted similarly
after his victory over a Ptolemaic fleet in the Battle of Salamis, Cyprus, in
306, returning Ptolemy's son, brother, and friends to Ptolemy in Egypt,
with their attendants and possessions.[53] These apparently chivalrous gestures had several effects. Their declared motives were tantamount to claiming that the war was fought for legitimate rather than mercenary reasons.
They showed that generals answered to a higher code of conduct than their
followers, who would not dream of returning the loot. Finally, the acts established or sustained *kharis* (reciprocal favor) and friendly relations between the individual leaders in spite of their rivalry, while at the same time
identifying the victor in the conflict. In contrast, baggage belonging to the
defeated troops was excluded from this transaction and rarely returned to
its original owners, going first to the military leader and then to his victorious army.

The above cases shed additional light on Eumenes' refusal to take Antigonus's baggage. The instances of troops who left or remained with a general because of their baggage show how wrong he was to give up on capturing Antigonus's baggage. Apart from preoccupation with his escape, he
may also have been influenced by the difference in how generals and troops
perceived captured baggage. Unlike the Macedonians, for whom the enemy's baggage was a rich source of income and a chance to regain their
families, Eumenes had friends and resources waiting for him in Armenia
and Cappadocia. On finding Antigonus's baggage he saw an opportunity

---

53. Restoring the baggage to Demetrius after Gaza: Diod. 19.85.3; Plut. *Demtr.* 5;
Just. 15.1.7–8 (the point might also have been to embarrass Antigonus, who refused
to share his booty with the other Successors: Just. 15.1.9). Demetrius and Cilles: Plut.
Demtr. 6. Restoring the baggage after Salamis: Just. 15.2.7; Plut. *Demtr.* 17.1.

to place Antigonus, his general Menander, and Antigonus's soldiers in his debt. Protecting the baggage from his own troops was a form of returning it and resembled the gesture of a victorious general. It also gained him the gratitude of Antigonus's Macedonian veterans and presumably other enemy troops. But Antigonus, by saying that Eumenes had acted selfishly rather than honorably, rejected the defeated general's attempt to project from this gesture.[54]

Eumenes planned to collect men and resources in Armenia, but Antigonus kept him on the run until Eumenes found shelter in the fortress of Nora, probably in Cappadocia. By now most of his army had joined Antigonus. A pro-Eumenes tradition claims that he encouraged many of his fellow refugees to leave him (Nora could accommodate only a limited number of troops).[55] We may trust that the veterans did not wait for Eumenes to explain the situation to them. That he enjoyed limited goodwill, even among those who did not miss their baggage, is suggested by Eumenes' concern that he would be betrayed to the enemy if the siege became difficult to endure (Just. 14.2.3). In addition, after Eumenes' defeat, despite his numerical superiority, it was hard to make a persuasive case for future victory. Of the Macedonians who had pledged to protect Eumenes as his bodyguards, probably only a handful joined the ca. 600 cavalrymen and hoplites who stayed with him at Nora.[56]

Antigonus's siege of Eumenes in Nora lasted from the summer of 319 to the spring of 318. Only one episode of the siege, discussed in an earlier chapter, involves the veterans. Before the siege or in its early stages, Antigonus and Eumenes met in Antigonus's camp. Antigonus hoped to turn Eumenes into an inferior ally in order to avoid fighting him and the other Perdiccans at the same time. Eumenes demanded in return a full restoration of his commands and holdings and the retraction of the charges against him,

---

54. Plut. *Eum.* 9.12. For the practices concerning booty under Alexander and in the Hellenistic world, see Austin 1986, 463–466; Faraguna 1998, 379–386; Préaux 2002, 1:305–309; Chaniotis 2005, 129–137; Juhel 2002.

55. Eumenes' army joining Antigonus: Diod. 18.41.1, 4; Nepos *Eum.* 5.2–3. Eumenes' dismissing his followers: Plut. *Eum.* 10.1; Just. 14.2.3; Bosworth 1992, 79. Nora's exact location is unknown, but it was likely in Cappadocia: Anson 2004, 131n52.

56. Eumenes' force: Plut. *Eum.* 10.1–2 (200 hoplites and 500 cavalry); Diod. 18.41.3 (600 altogether); 18.57.3 (500 men at the siege's end). Anson (2004, 130n50, 154–155) surmises that most of the Macedonians surrendered to Antigonus at the end of the battle, and that Eumenes retained at most a couple hundred of them. But the Macedonians in Diod. 18.63.1 (and 18.62.4) whom Anson identifies with these remnants could very well have been the commanders and members of the garrison at Cyinda.

namely, his condemnation and outlawing by the Macedonians in Egypt after Perdiccas's death.[57] His request for rehabilitation was designed less to affect public opinion than to fend off rival generals' attempts to delegitimize him. The veterans who had fought with him and served as his bodyguards had already shown that the attitude of the Macedonian troops toward him was not universally hostile. In any case, his demand for exoneration was far less problematic than the full restoration of his powers. Antigonus referred the matter to Antipater, showing that he was loyal to the regent in spite of rumors about the former's independent ambitions.[58]

The Macedonians in Antigonus's camp were surely ignorant of these high politics, but when they learned of Eumenes' presence in their camp, according to Plutarch, they rushed eagerly to see the man who, more than any one else, had been the talk of the camp after Craterus's death. They made such a tumult that Antigonus had to push them away with his bodyguards lest they harm Eumenes (*Eum.* 10.7–8). Although Plutarch or his source means to convey the impression of a celebrity mobbed by curious fans, the fact that Antigonus had to protect Eumenes from the Macedonians' violence suggests otherwise. The biographer provides a clue to their motives when he mentions Craterus's death. The men most motivated to harm Eumenes, apparently, were Craterus's soldiers, either his new recruits for the Asian campaign against Perdiccas or the veterans who had served with him since Opis, or both.[59] Yet other veterans did not necessarily share their hostile attitude, because the Macedonians who followed Eumenes up to his defeat and even to Nora appeared to be little troubled by his responsibility for the death of the great marshal. Antigonus had a similar attitude, and his restraint of the Macedonians shows how little their feelings influenced the generals' schemes.

Antigonus would change his mind about making a deal with Eumenes, but only later. Probably in the summer of 319, he led his army to a place near Cretopolis in Pisidia, where he decisively defeated Alcetas and his fellow generals, Attalus, Docimus, Polemon, Antipater (not the regent), and

---

57. The chronology of Nora: Diod. 18.53.5; Nepos *Eum.* 5.7; Boiy 2007, e.g., 118. For the episode, see Plut. *Eum.* 10.3–8; Diod. 18.41.6–7; chap. 1 above.

58. Anson (2004, 131–132n54) rightly notes that the negotiations between Antigonus and Eumenes indicate the impotence of the army assembly, which the generals failed to involve in their discussions. Had the talks been successful, however, Eumenes would probably have asked Antigonus or Antipater to call an assembly to reverse the verdict against him: cf. Diod. 19.51.1–4 on Olympias's attempt to overturn her condemnation.

59. Cf. Anson 2004, 124.

Philotas. The sources on this campaign make no mention of Macedonian troops, and for a reason.[60] Although it is likely that veterans fought on each side, they and their fellow Macedonian infantrymen played only a secondary role in the battle. Both Antigonus and Alcetas relied chiefly on their cavalry (and, in Antigonus's case, on elephants) for victory, while the opposing phalanxes were fairly stationary. Before the battle, Antigonus had occupied the hills, giving himself an advantage over Alcetas's position. Alcetas attacked him there with his cavalry, leaving the phalanx behind to fend for itself, but the attack failed and Alcetas retreated to the phalanx, which was utterly surprised by a counterattack from Antigonus's cavalry and elephants. Alcetas's infantry lost its bearings in spite of his desperate attempts to organize it for defense. Even Antigonus's phalanx, which was superior to Alcetas's in size and "valor," merely helped to encircle Alcetas's infantry by standing above them while Antigonus's elephants and cavalry attacked them from every direction.[61]

Moreover, the veterans' minority status in both armies was more pronounced than ever. Their numbers can only be guessed, but while they might still have made an impact in Alcetas's smaller coalition army of 16,000 infantrymen and 900 cavalry (of which 6,000 were Pisidians), their effect in Antigonus's larger army of 40,000 infantry and 7,000 cavalry bordered on the negligible. This picture did not improve after Antigonus's victory. The defeated veterans who likely joined Antigonus helped to increase their number in his camp but not their ratio in an army that had now grown to 60,000 infantry and 10,000 cavalry. But apart from the ca. 3,000 Silver Shields then in Cilicia, Antigonus's men still constituted the greatest concentration of veterans in Asia at this point.[62]

The defeated veterans fared better than their general Alcetas. The general fled the battle with his hypaspists and Boys (pages), who may have been Macedonians, but who disappear from the record at this point (Diod. 18.45.3). After searching for shelter in Pisidia, Alcetas committed suicide rather than be surrendered to Antigonus by a Pisidian faction. Antigonus mutilated his body for three days before exposing it to the elements. Alcetas's Pisidian friends, however, gave him a magnificent funeral, and a

---

60. Diod. 18.44.1–45.5; 19.16.1; Polyaenus 4.6.7. For Antigonus's campaign, see Engel 1972; Billows 1990, 76–79; S. Mitchell 1994, 130–132; Syme 1995, 146–148.

61. Diod. 18.45.2. Polyaenus 4.6.7 also mentions Alcetas's use of peltasts to occupy a vantage point, but they are unlikely to have included Macedonians.

62. Diod. 18.45.1–5, 50.1–3. For estimates of Macedonians in both armies: Bosworth 2002, 89–90.

relief in Termissus showing a horseman has been identified as his grave marker.[63]

Antigonus treated Alcetas's fellow commanders more humanely, imprisoning them in a fortress, probably in Phrygia. About two years later (317) these resourceful Macedonians succeeded in taking over the fort and held it for sixteen months before a betrayal (by Docimus) regained it for Antigonus's forces. Diodorus says that the daring and skills they had acquired under Alexander enabled them to overcome a guard that greatly outnumbered them (Diod. 19.16.1–5). Their feat confirmed for contemporaries and historians the reputation for military excellence—untarnished by their defeats here and elsewhere—shared by all Alexander's veterans.

When Antipater died in 319, Polyperchon replaced him as the regent of the kingdom, and in the spring of 318 it became clear that Antigonus intended to become the lord of Asia. This made Eumenes, now in Nora, a potential ally to anyone who opposed Antigonus, chiefly Polyperchon and the royal house (with whose opponent, Cassander, Antigonus was now allied) but also other commanders who worried about Antigonus's great ambitions (cf. Diod. 18.51,1, 52.4). Antigonus offered Eumenes his freedom with even more territory and possessions than before. In return Eumenes became his friend, i.e., underling, and gave Antigonus his allegiance. This is largely Diodorus's account, which is preferable to Plutarch's that Eumenes left Nora after persuading the Macedonians in charge of the siege that he would pledge his loyalty not just to Antigonus but also to the kings and Olympias, and to Nepos's story that Eumenes fled the fortress after outwitting the besiegers. Both versions try to whitewash Eumenes' alliance with the greatest rival of the royal house, to which Eumenes had professed his unwavering loyalty.[64] Plutarch's version, however, shows that a profession of loyalty to the Macedonian royal house still served to legitimize one's position in the eyes of peers and troops, although its actual effect on the Macedonians was minimal, because no general at this time had openly thrown off royal authority.

Eumenes went from Nora back to Cappadocia and soon assembled a force of more than 2,000 infantry and 500 cavalry. They included 500 of the

---

63. Diod. 18.47.1–3. Pekridou 1986; Fedak 1990, 94–96.

64. Diod. 18.50.4–5, 53.4–5; Plut. *Eum.* 12.1–4; Nepos *Eum.* 5.7. Justin (14.2.4–5) wrongly ascribes Antigonus's lifting of the siege to Antipater's dispatching reinforcements to help Eumenes. No other source mentions this fact, and Antipater was dead by now. For criticism of Plutarch's and Nepos's reports: Anson 1977; 2004, 136–137; Bosworth 1992, 65–67; Schäfer 2002, 119–120; cf. Hadley 2000, 18–20.

original company of 600 who came with him to Nora, as well as former followers who had not joined Antigonus but were scattered around the country.[65] Diodorus claims that men joined Eumenes because he was well liked,
but the fact that he was now one of Antigonus's "friends" (*philoi*) surely
added to his appeal. He soon received an invitation from Polyperchon and
Olympias to be their general in Asia against Antigonus (see below).

Probably in the winter of 319/8, while the siege of Nora was still going on, another group of veterans fared poorly under Arrhidaeus, the former regent and now the satrap of Hellespontine Phrygia. As with Eumenes,
it was their general's fault that their record was marred by defeat. Becoming worried about Antigonus's growing power and plans, Arrhidaeus decided to consolidate his own position in the region by planting garrisons in
cities that were independent of Arrhidaeus's rule. One such city was Cyzicus on the shores of the Propontis (Dardanelles), which Arrhidaeus hoped
to take by surprise. He marched there with an army of 10,000 mercenaries, 1,000 Macedonians, 500 Persian light-armed troops, and 800 cavalry,
bringing various instruments of war. He had probably gotten his Macedonian and Persian troops, and perhaps even the mercenaries, at Triparadeisus from what used to be Perdiccas's army (see chap. 5). Perdiccas had de-
ployed veterans to assault fortified sites in both Asia Minor and Egypt, and
Arrhidaeus could count on their experience, even though the burden of
fighting fell chiefly on the mercenaries, who constituted the majority of his
the army.

At first things seemed to go well. Arrhidaeus succeeded in surprising the
city and captured many of its residents outside the walls. Thinking that his
success would move the city to accept his garrison, he agreed to its leaders' request for a temporary truce, which they used to prepare Cyzicus for
the siege. Then they took advantage of his lack of ships by using their own
to get provisions and missiles from Byzantium and to bring in people who
had fled to the country. The returnees filled the ranks of the defenders and
allowed them to mount counterattacks. After suffering many losses, Arrhidaeus retreated homeward (Diod. 18.51.1–7; Athen. 11.509a).

We are not told how the veterans performed in this campaign, but they
and their fellow warriors cannot be held accountable for the defeat. His initial success and his alliance with an influential local politician made Arrhidaeus overconfident of his ability to force his terms on the city, and he

---

65. Diod. 18.53.6–7, 59.1; Plut. *Eum.* 12.5–6 (who reports that he had 1,000
horsemen).

made an error of judgment in failing to press on with the attack and allowing the Cyzicans time to recover. He was also wrong to bring no fleet to shut off the city's harbor and to attack it simultaneously from the sea, counting wholly on a surprise attack by land. These mistakes allowed the Cyzicans to import freely the men, armaments, and supplies that were ultimately his undoing.

We hear nothing further of Arrhidaeus's Macedonians. The satrap was soon at war with Antigonus, deploying his troops in garrison duties and in an unsuccessful attempt to free Eumenes from Nora. By the summer of 318, Arrhidaeus and his army had sought shelter in the city of Cius on the Propontis. He was rescued from there by Cleitus, Polyperchon's admiral, who won a naval victory only to lose all his ships and crews to Antigonus shortly thereafter. It is impossible to tell from the sources if Arrhidaeus's veterans took part in these activities, and it is unlikely that they served on Cleitus's ships. Like many other veterans, they melted away or possibly offered their services to Antigonus, who was now the biggest military employer in the region.[66]

During the winter of 319 and the spring of 318, Antigonus was actively fighting in western Asia Minor. He first rushed with selected troops to Cyzicus's aid, and later sent part of his army to check Arrhidaeus's movements. He took the rest of his army to Lydia, where he used force or persuasion to take control over various cities (Diod. 18.52.1–8). He also gave Cassander 4,000 men and 35 ships for his war against Polyperchon (Diod. 18.54.3, 68.1). The sources are silent about the role, if any, of Macedonian troops in all these operations, but one of Antigonus's actions was relevant to their history. While in Ephesus, Antigonus appropriated 600 talents that were being shipped from Cilicia to the kings in Macedonia, claiming that he needed the money for his mercenaries. Diodorus comments that this act showed his independence from, and opposition to, the kings (18.52.7–8). Antigonus's statement also suggests that the mercenaries, rather than his Macedonian soldiers, were the key to his military power. Antigonus's Macedonians, in any case, were unaffected by the political implications of his hijacking the royal money, and they continued to serve him.

There is a measure of irony in how things turned out for both Antigonus's and Alexander's veterans, because the man who now may have had the most veterans at his command was also the one with whom they had

---

66. Arrhidaeus after Cyzicus: Diod. 18.52.1–5, 72.1–9; cf. Just. 14.2.4. For conjectural reconstructions of his later career, see Billows 1990, 375n18; 1993, 256–257; Heckel 2006, 53.

the least in common. Though he shared their Macedonian ancestry and military pursuits, Antigonus had left Alexander and his soldiers for a satrapal position in Phrygia as early as 333, thereby missing most of the king's expedition. In the post-Alexander era he posed the greatest danger to the imperial union of Macedonia and Asia that the veterans had helped to create. With Polyperchon and the kings in the rival camp, he also lacked legitimacy. Indeed, his official authority rested only on Antipater's appointment of him in Triparadeisus as the supreme commander (*strategos autokrater*) of Asia and royal guardian, and on his now-obsolete mandate to fight the Perdiccans.[67] These factors (though hardly alone) may have played a part in Antigonus's later decision not to take veterans on his campaign against Eumenes. Henceforth, the history of the veterans would be dominated by the Silver Shields and their commanders.

---

67. Arr. *Succ.* 1.38; Diod. 18.39.7, 40.1, 50.1; 19.61.3; Just. 14.1.1; App. *Syr.* 53, and, e.g., Engel 1978, 21–28; Billows 1990, 81–82.

CHAPTER 7

EUMENES AND THE SILVER SHIELDS

THE SILVER SHIELDS AND EUMENES IN CILICIA

Shortly after leaving Nora in the spring of 318, Eumenes received letters from the royal guardian, Polyperchon, and Alexander's mother, Olympias. The consequent change in his fortunes delights our sources, who are keen on highlighting the roller-coaster nature of his career. Diodorus and Plutarch summarize and paraphrase the letters, which included an invitation to Eumenes to be the protector of the Macedonian kings (especially Alexander IV), to lead the war against Antigonus, to take money from the Cilician treasury of Cyinda, and to assume command over the Macedonian veterans known as the Silver Shields.[1]

Scholars have persuasively shown that the Silver Shields were originally Alexander's hypaspists—elite units of the Macedonian phalanx. At that time it is probable that they already numbered around 3,000 men, with occasional additions and reductions. They were given the name "Silver Shields" no later than Alexander's Indian campaign. I subscribe to the view that they formed part of the royal army that followed Perdiccas from Babylon to Egypt, and that they played an active role in the riots against Antipater when he arrived at Triparadeisus in 321/0 to become the regent of the kingdom. Antipater sent them with their commander Antigenes, and presumably Teutamus as well, to bring down money from the treasury in Susa.

Their history is uncertain from that point until they met Eumenes in Cilicia in 318 and became a dominant force in his army. They are nowhere attested, as is commonly assumed, to have served as the guardians of the royal treasury at Cyinda in Cilicia (which was well fortified in any case) be-

---

1. Letters to Eumenes: Diod. 18.57.3–58.4; Plut. *Eum.* 13.1–3; Nepos *Eum.* 6.1–5; *Heidelberg Epitome* F 3.2; cf. Diod. 18.53.7. Rosen's reconstruction (1967, 69–71) of Polyperchon's correspondence is too speculative.

fore Polyperchon instructed them to join Eumenes. But it is unknown what they were doing in Cilicia at that time. Perhaps their commanders were waiting for the right opportunity or employer. The Silver Shields certainly became attractive to many generals once Eumenes got them.[2]

In his account of the opposing sides at the Battle of Gabene in 317 between Eumenes and Antigonus, Diodorus describes the Silver Shields as the conquerors of the world under Philip and Alexander and as irresistible because of their experience. He says that their average age was seventy, with some even older, and that the youngest of them were sixty. Plutarch, who gives a very similar description in the same context, calls them "athletes of war, undefeated and unfailing up to this time," thus suggesting a common source, probably Hieronymus.[3] Such elderly gentlemen would have been promising candidates for the role of jurors in Aristophanes' *Wasps* but hardly useful in a force elsewhere described as "the spearhead of the entire army," or as men who were "invincible, and because of their excellence, spread much fear among the enemies."[4] It is equally hard to imagine that the Argyraspides were able to keep their 3,000-member unit intact for such a long time and without supplanting the dead and the disabled with younger warriors. Most of the Silver Shields must have been fit, adult warriors who could sustain the physical demands of marching and hand-to-hand fighting. The old warriors probably constituted a minority among the 3,000 Silver Shields, but they caught the attention of the sources, for whom they represented the golden age of Philip's and Alexander's conquests, anchored in military *aretē* and experience.[5]

---

2. The hypaspists' number: Bosworth 1980–1995, 2:195–199; Heckel, forthcoming. Oddly, scholars' recent interest in the Silver Shields often has focused not on their character but on their number of 3,000, which is used, with other figures, for widely different assessments of the numbers of veterans in the Successors' armies. The Silver Shields' origins and history: Tarn 1948, 2:116–118, 149–153; Anson 1981; 1988b; Heckel 1982; 1992, 307–319; forthcoming (he believes that they followed Craterus to Asia Minor but then joined Perdiccas's campaign; but see Bosworth 1992, 66–67). For the possibility that Alexander modeled the Silver Shields on an Asian unit: Olbrycht, forthcoming. The Cilician treasury: Simpson 1957; Bing 1973. Diodorus's (18.58.1–4) language and timetable give little support to Bosworth's suggestion (1992, 66–67) that they moved to Cilicia only after receiving Polyperchon's directive in 318; see Anson 2004, 144n92.

3. Diod. 19.41.1–2; Plut. *Eum.* 16.6–7. Hieronymus as their source: Bosworth 1992, 62; cf. Hornblower 1981, 193.

4. Diod. 19.30.6, 28.1; cf. Plut. *Eum.* 18.2; Just. 12.4.6.

5. For the Silver Shields' age, see Anson 1981, 199; Hornblower 1981, 193; Billows 1995, 18–19. Diod. 17.27.1–2 reports that during Alexander's siege of Halicarnassus in

Something should be said about the Silver Shields' aura of invincibility. They justified this image in their performance under Eumenes, or more accurately under their direct commanders, in the battles of Paraetacene and Gabene in Iran in 317, showdowns over Alexander's Asian empire in which Eumenes and a coalition of eastern straps fighting in the name of the Macedonian throne clashed with Antigonus. Yet the Silver Shields' record of success was not unblemished, for they probably fought with Perdiccas against Ptolemy in Egypt in 321 and so shared in his failure to capture the Fort of Camels there.[6] Moreover, the experience of service under Alexander was not a guarantee against defeat, as other Macedonian veterans could testify. What distinguished the Silver Shields was their stable leadership, their protracted unity, and especially the fact that they had not been tested in battle since Perdiccas's Egyptian campaign. In other words, by the time they met Eumenes in 318, they had barely had the opportunity to display their qualities or to stain their invincible reputation by suffering defeat, as other veterans had.

Eumenes needed all the help he could get, and he was eager to add the Silver Shields to the force of about only 2,500 men he had assembled in Cappadocia. But what moved them to join him? Diodorus says that Antigenes and Teutamus, the commanders of the Silver Shields, obeyed the letters of Polyperchon, written in the kings' names, that instructed them to help this new commander of Asia, and that the Silver Shields met Eumenes with friendliness and great enthusiasm.[7] Communication in this period was often restricted to members of the military elite, who were inclined to make decisions without consulting the troops. Here, however, the Silver Shields were notified of the royal request, although Diodorus does not explain why they and their commanders decided to honor it.

Part of the answer lay with the letters that Olympias and especially Polyperchon wrote to Eumenes alone, which read like pamphlets designed to promulgate his new role and explain why he should be followed. The propagandist nature of these letters should not add credence to the scholarly

---

334, Philip's brave veterans, who had been discharged from service, turned the fighting around when they joined battle and attacked the enemy; cf. Curt. 5.2.5; 8.1.36. This one-time effort hardly makes them the forerunner of the more durable Silver Shields, who often led Eumenes' army in marching and battle.

6. Diod. 18.33.5–34.5. Hammond (1978, 135 [repr. 1994, 3:210]), who objects to their participation in this operation because they were "invincible," seems to take the epithet too literally. Cf. Bosworth 2002, 87n80.

7. Diod. 18.58.1, 59.3; cf. Plut. *Eum.* 13.1–3; Just. 14.2.6–12.

allegation (based on other considerations) that Eumenes forged them with the help of his friend Hieronymus.[8] Rather, the letters made Eumenes appealing to potential allies and recruits because that was their original intention. They presented Eumenes as a leader and employer who had both the legitimacy and the means needed for a successful war against Antigonus. They legitimized the war by pitting the royal house against the rebel satrap, portraying it as a just and urgent conflict designed to rescue Alexander's defenseless son and mother from their enemies at home and abroad. The letters argued that Eumenes was fit to lead the war because of his steadfast loyalty to the royal house, his status as Olympias's most trusted friend, and his new offices of *strategos autokratōr* (supreme general) of Asia and satrap. Even the option that Polyperchon gave Eumenes of becoming his co-regent in Macedonia added to the Cardian's image as the protector of royalty.[9] To present the war against Antigonus as winnable, the letters declared that Eumenes was about to receive a great deal of money from the royal treasury in Cyinda, that Olympias had instructed loyalist governors to obey him, and that, if needed, Polyperchon would come with the kings and the entire royal army to help him.[10]

There is much in this that the Silver Shields would have found to their liking, but there were also some weighty considerations against following Eumenes. One was that Eumenes had a small army and Antigonus a very large one. The year before, when Eumenes had had the bigger army and the two had met in battle, Antigonus had won decisively. Even now, Eumenes was a man on the run who had just evaded a chase by Antigonus's commander, Menander (Diod. 18.59.1–2). Lastly, the help that Eumenes hoped to get from Polyperchon and friendly satraps was an uncertain prospect. Nevertheless, the Silver Shields and their commanders decided to go with Eumenes. Scholars have suggested variously that they were moved by reverence for and loyalty to Alexander and his house, by Eumenes' military

---

8. The letters: see note 1 above. Forged correspondence (at least in part): Briant 1973a, 75–77 [repr. 1982, 87–89]. *Contra*: Anson 2004, 142–143nn84, 86; cf. Landucci Gattinoni 2008, 243.

9. Diod. 18.57.3. The offer to make Eumenes a co-regent is confusing because it would have taken Eumenes away from the war against Antigonus. But this may have been Polyperchon's concession to Olympias, who initially wanted Eumenes beside her: Plut. *Eum.* 13.1; cf. Nepos *Eum.* 6.3–4. Above all, it was politic to offer Eumenes alternative rewards for deserting Antigonus while making the Asian command more attractive. For additional explanations, see note 8 above, as well as Rosen 1967, 69–71.

10. Diod. 18.57.3–4, 58.1; Plut. *Eum.* 13.1–2; Nepos *Eum.* 6.4. Polyperchon never crossed to Asia.

reputation, or by their earlier ties to Polyperchon.[11] It is true that the Silver Shields, in their former character as hypaspists, had spent many hours in direct contact with Alexander, who had commanded them in person on various occasions. Moreover, the Macedonian veterans in general tended to support the Argead house. But this did not prevent many of the same veterans, earlier and later, from fighting against its representatives. Eumenes' military reputation had a limited attraction, especially after being tarnished by his recent defeat by Antigonus, while the veterans' presumed respect for Polyperchon was surely not an overwhelming factor.

I suggest that in addition to loyalist and moral grounds, the Silver Shields were drawn to Eumenes by the financial incentives (or bribes) that accompanied the royal offer to him. Polyperchon instructed those in charge of the royal treasury in Cilicia to give Eumenes 500 talents for his expenses and a blank check for recruiting mercenaries. It has been conjectured that the treasury at Cyinda, Cilicia, contained nearly 20,000 talents at that time. In addition, Eumenes was given permission to withdraw as much money as he wanted from other royal treasuries. As the history of the events following Alexander's death shows, a general's abilities to provide for his troops and to safeguard their possessions and families were cardinal factors in winning and maintaining loyalty. Eumenes looked very promising in this respect.[12]

The decision of Antigenes and Teutamus, the Silver Shields' commanders, to join Eumenes was similarly but more richly motivated. Information on their careers before their meeting with Eumenes is spotty at best. The better-known Antigenes served in Alexander's campaign but is mentioned only intermittently in its histories. In 331 he came second in a contest of bravery and was awarded the command of a chiliarchy (1,000 men), probably of the hypaspists. In the Battle of the Hydaspes in 326 against the Indian ruler Porus, he commanded a phalanx battalion. His name is associated with veterans for the first time in 325, when Alexander sent him to a rendezvous with the king in Carmania, with Craterus and others as leaders of a force that included veterans from India. In 324, already elderly, Antigenes accompanied Craterus (and Polyperchon) at the head of the discharged veterans on their way home from Opis. But this force remained in Asia Minor, and Antigenes at some point joined Perdiccas, whom he helped to assassinate in Egypt. His reward came in 320 at Triparadeisus, where he

---

11. The Silver Shields' reverence for royalty: Anson 1981, 119–120. Eumenes' reputation and ties to Polyperchon: Bosworth 2002, 100–101.

12. Money for Eumenes: Diod. 18.57.3, 58.1; 19.15.5; Plut. *Eum.* 13.1–2. Twenty thousand talents at Cyinda: Simpson 1957.

got the satrapy of Susiana and the mission to bring money from there to (apparently) Cilicia. Although scholars have dated his command of the Silver Shields to different times before the Triparadeisus settlement, this is the first explicit mention of his leading them (320), and hence the best date for the inception of his command.[13] The sources treat Antigenes more favorably than his colleague, Teutamus, who is nowhere mentioned before the meeting with Eumenes in Cilicia. Diodorus suggests that he held a satrapy, which has been doubtfully identified as Paraetacene.[14]

But despite these generals' less-than-brilliant careers under Alexander, they had something to lose by the time they met Eumenes. Antigonus's plan to replace satraps in Asia with his own friends did not bode well for their future, and it is possible that Antigenes' satrapy, Susiana, was also exposed to the expansionist designs of Pithon, the satrap of Media. This prospect largely explains both their welcome of Eumenes and their promise to cooperate with him fully.[15] Eumenes had once been Perdiccas's most loyal supporter, and Antigenes was known and rewarded for killing the marshal, but it was typical of the age that there were no hard feelings.[16]

The sources say, however, that Eumenes did not trust the Silver Shields and their commanders. In Egypt they had voted for his death, and he worried that they would reject or even kill him before long because of his alien (Greek) origin, their envy, their personal ambitions, and their lack of respect. Eumenes first dealt with this problem by declining the money and denying any desire or fitness for the office he was offered. It was a gambit that seemingly leveled the playing field and placated whoever might have seen himself as worthy of the Asian command or even better qualified for it than Eumenes. He followed it with his well-known "Alexander's tent" show. Eumenes reported a dream of his in which Alexander was sitting on a throne in full regalia, giving orders and exercising his monarchical rule. Eumenes suggested putting up a tent with an empty golden throne and other symbols of royalty, in which all commanders present would offer sacrifices to Alexander and deliberate under Alexander's spiritual guidance

---

13. Antigenes in Triparadeisus: Arr. *Succ.* 1.35, 38. His career: Berve 1926, 2:41–42, 372; Heckel 1982; 1992, 308–316; 2006, 30–31 (rightly rejects Lock's 1977 dating the Silver Shields' origins to Triparadeisus); Bosworth 1992, 66–67; 1980–1995, 2:297–298.

14. Teutamus: Diod. 18.62.6–7; Heckel 1992, 316–319; 2006, 262; Bosworth 1992, 66–67; Heckel, forthcoming.

15. Diod. 18.50.5, 59.3, 62.7; 19.14.1–8; Bosworth 1992, 66–67.

16. *Pace* Grainger 1990, 36.

and in his name. Once this had been done, Eumenes won goodwill with his easygoing ways. He also took the money and assumed command.[17]

In the eyes of the sources, the story substantiates the topos of Eumenes' cunning intelligence. But how was this intelligence directed? In spite of the seemingly universal reservations about his appointment, it appears that Eumenes' main concern—the prime target of the Alexander séance—was not the veterans but their commanders and other officers. Several sources directly link the stratagem to these generals' envy and their refusal to meet in Eumenes' tent or acknowledge his leadership. More significantly, the military masses were excluded from it, as they were from the original Alexander tent. Only the commanders took orders from "Alexander," sacrificed and made *proskynesis* to him, and sat in council in "his" tent.[18] Eumenes would use the same device later in Susiana, with similar actors and audience, when other generals challenged his command. Diodorus says that he then called daily meetings of this council in Alexander's tent, as if in a democratic city.[19] But since there was no popular assembly to discuss the council's motions, the purpose was to reach a consensus of the kind practiced in an oligarchy. Indeed, a story in Plutarch about the Macedonians in Asia clamoring for no one but the ailing Eumenes to lead them into battle suggests that they were dissatisfied with the cooperative spirit of the "Alexander's tent" device, and that it was designed to regulate Eumenes' relationship with the military elite (Plut. *Eum.* 14.4–11). Such a narrow objective and use speak against scholarly interpretations that see here the establishment of a cult for the Macedonian troops or for the entire ethnically diverse army and empire. The problem and the solution concerned Eumenes' control of other commanders.[20]

The generals agreed to participate in the ritual for several reasons. Combined with the shared respect of both commanders and troops for Alex-

17. Diod. 18.60.1–61.3; Plut. *Eum.* 13.4–8; Polyaenus 4.8.2; Nepos *Eum.* 7.1–3 (who postdates the scene to what was actually a reuse of the tent device in Iran).

18. Envy of, and resistance to, Eumenes: Plut. *Eum.* 13.4; Nepos *Eum.* 7.1–3; Polyaenus 4.8.2. Commanders and "Alexander's tent": Diod. 18.60.6–61.2; Plut. *Eum.* 13.4–8; Nepos *Eum.* 7.2–3; Polyaenus 4.8.2.

19. Diod. 19.15.1–4. For different interpretations of this "democracy," see Briant 1982, 80n3, and Rzepka 2005, 138–139.

20. For views that Eumenes' stratagem instituted a military cult for the veterans and the army, see, e.g., Launey 1950, 2:945–947, followed by Picard 1954, 4–7; Anson 2004, 152. Creating an imperial cult common to Macedonians, Greeks, and barbarians: Schäfer 2002, esp. 21–37; *contra* Bosworth 2005, 685–686.

ander, the Macedonians' belief in life after death, as suggested by elite burial sites, supported the fiction that he could rule them from the grave. Eumenes' story about his dream won credence because of his history of communicating with Alexander through dreams.[21] Although some might object that the tent solidified his link to Macedonian royalty on heaven and earth, opposing his idea meant declining the political and even supernatural benefits that Alexander's patronage might entail. No less important was the tent's creation of a seeming equality within the elite, resolving the problem of competing claims to honor while confirming the participants' superior rank in camp.[22]

Of course, the audience of the "Alexander's tent" show included the veterans. Having been at Babylon in 323, the Macedonians in camp were already familiar with the use of Alexander's throne and royal insignia, and even of his body, to obtain the dead king's approval in resolving crises of leadership.[23] It is even possible that Eumenes called the Macedonians together to tell them about his tent proposal, and that they approved it and the expenses it incurred (Polyaenus 4.8.2; cf. Diod. 18.61.1). Yet the veterans played only a secondary role in the affair, because the opposition to Eumenes came mostly from their commanders. The rank and file also seem to have been little troubled by Eumenes' non-Macedonian origin.

About two years later (317), after losing the Battle of Gabene to Antigonus, some Silver Shields called Eumenes a "plague from the Chersonese." But taking this often-quoted abuse out of context does not prove a pervasive contempt for his Greek birth. Those who used it were echoing the propaganda of his enemies and seeking to justify handing him over to Antigonus. Eumenes' origins did not deter the veterans from supporting him strongly, at least until the catastrophic loss of their goods and families at Gabene overwhelmed their loyalty. His problems with his army never stemmed from his Greek ethnicity, but involved obtaining funds and provisions and assuring the troops that he could win military conflicts.[24]

---

21. Macedonian afterlife: Hardiman 2010, 513–520. Eumenes and dreams of Alexander: Plut. *Eum.* 6.8–9; cf. Näf 2004, 68.

22. Diod. 18.61.3; Plut. *Eum.* 13.4–8; cf. Anson 2004, 150.

23. On Ptolemy and Perdiccas in Babylon as Eumenes' inspiration: Errington 1976, 139–140. For the royal throne, see chap. 3 above, note 8.

24. Negative references to Eumenes' ethnicity: Diod. 18.60.1–3; 19.13.1–2; Plut. *Eum.* 8.1; Nepos *Eum.* 3.1, 7.1. But see also Diod. 18.62.7 and Plut. *Eum.* 3.1. Eumenes himself stressed his alien origin when it served his ends: Diod. 18.60.3. "Chersonesan plague": Plut. *Eum.* 18.2; Anson 1980, 56.

This is not to say that the Silver Shields did not require persuasion to join Eumenes: we see here again that the kings' letters or the veterans' respect for Alexander and his house were insufficient to ensure obedience. Justin, who fails to mention the story of Alexander's tent, reports that the Silver Shields' invincible record led them to regard obeying any other leader but Alexander as disgraceful and unacceptable. Eumenes resorted to flattery and supplication. He called the Argyraspides his sole hope, his protectors and comrades in arms during Alexander's campaign. He told them that they were the only troops who had conquered the East, surpassing the feats of Dionysius and Heracles, and that they alone had made Alexander so great and divine. He begged them to accept him not as a leader, but as a colleague and comrade. By giving them individual advice and treating their infractions with leniency, he was able to gradually assume leadership in camp (Just. 14.2.6–12).

Justin's description has its share of problems. It includes rhetorical echoes of Alexander's speech to the restive army on the Hyphasis, which probably go back to his and Curtius's source, Pompeius Trogus. There too the king told the Macedonians that their glory had surpassed human standards, begging them not to desert him but to regard him as a fellow soldier (Curt. 9.2.28).[25] In addition, the Silver Shields' alleged refusal to obey anyone but Alexander is belied by their long service with their immediate commanders, Antigenes and Teutamus, and by their obedience to superior commanders such as Perdiccas and even Antipater after the settlement of Triparadeisus. Eumenes' persuasive stratagem also fits the commonplace of his outsmarting any opposition, and is informed by the elitist presumption that the vain, simple-minded veterans could be easily bamboozled by flattery and supplication. In fact, as Justin himself reports, though flattery helped Eumenes over their initial opposition, he attained leadership only after creating a network of personal relationships and a reservoir of goodwill. Yet Eumenes' attribution of Alexander's success and his glory to the Silver Shields makes rhetorical and historical sense. As we shall see, they also demanded and obtained sole credit, at the expense of other units, for Eumenes' later victories against enemy infantry. Undoubtedly these veterans had a high opinion of themselves and appreciated those who confirmed it for them. Their respect for Alexander's memory was, to a significant degree, an exercise in self-admiration.

---

25. This is a case of rhetorical borrowing rather than of *Alexandri imitatio*, which never included self-abasement.

THE MARCH TO IRAN

In addition to ingratiating himself with the veterans, Eumenes dispatched his friends with bags full of money to recruit mercenaries in Pisidia, Lycia, Coele Syria, Phoenicia, and Cyprus: all territories under the nominal control of his enemies, Antigonus and Ptolemy. The offer of good wages attracted men even from Greece, enabling Eumenes to add more than 10,000 infantry and 2,000 cavalry to the 3,000 Silver Shields, 2,000 infantry, and 500 horses he had brought with him from Cappadocia. His totals of 15,000 infantry and 2,500 cavalry, however, made a force smaller than the 20,000 infantry and 5,000 cavalry he had taken to his defeat at Orcynia (Diod. 18.61.4–5, 40.6–7). The size of his army explains, in part, why he sought to avoid confronting Antigonus militarily. It also meant that the Silver Shields found themselves in the same minority status occupied by other veterans in the Successors' armies. They now constituted about one-fifth of Eumenes' infantry—a ratio that was bound to become even smaller. Nevertheless, as a cohesive military and ethnic group with key leaders and claims to a long record of invincibility, they enjoyed a preferred status in camp.

Eumenes was becoming a force to be reckoned with, and his recruiting activity in Ptolemy's sphere of influence spurred the satrap of Egypt into action. He took a fleet to Zephyrium, a port near Cynda, and set about undermining the Silver Shields' support of Eumenes and his access to the Cyindan treasury, two principal foundations of his power. Ptolemy sent messages to the Silver Shields' commanders urging them to disengage from Eumenes, a man condemned to death by all Macedonians. He also rebuked the commanders of the garrisons in Cyinda for giving money to Eumenes and gave them assurances of safety (Diod. 18.62.2).

According to Diodorus, these efforts got Ptolemy nowhere, because the kings, Polyperchon, and Olympias had instructed all these generals to obey Eumenes fully as the supreme commander of the kingdom (18.61.1–2). Certainly Ptolemy's authority was weaker than theirs. In the murky waters of Macedonian "constitutionalism" and legitimacy, a recent edict issued by the kings and their regent, and endorsed by Alexander's mother, carried more weight than a disinterred resolution of the Macedonian assembly sanctioned by the same kings. (I note that the strongest advocates for the authority of Macedonian popular will were not the Macedonians but their leaders.) Yet there were additional reasons for Ptolemy's failure. His appeal to the commanders alone was based on the common assumptions that ordinary troops had no say in choosing sides in the conflict, and that they would normally follow their commanders anywhere. Incidents of mass desertions led by unit commanders justified such an outlook, but the Silver Shields were different. Their first encounter with Eumenes made clear the necessity of addressing them directly. Nor does Ptolemy appear to have backed up his offer with adequate incentives or threats. Ensconced in well-fortified Cyinda, the men to whom he appealed had little to fear from his fleet.[26]

Antigonus too became alarmed by Eumenes. The royal point man against him in Asia now had money and troops that made him a significant ally of the regent Polyperchon. Because Antigonus was busy with operations in Greece, Thrace, and western Asia Minor, he resorted once again to fomenting treason. But he had learned the lesson of his (and probably of Ptolemy's) past failures, and he did not content himself with circulating letters calling for Eumenes' murder or communicating with the command structure alone. Along with a letter calling for Eumenes' elimination, Antigonus sent men to speak personally with the Silver Shields, their commanders, and other Macedonians (probably the commanders and members of the guard at the treasury).[27] It appears that he planned to rely first on inducements and then, if these proved unsuccessful, on intimidation. His emissaries promised rewards to the commanders and the Macedonians for killing Eumenes. When this failed, they produced his letter, which threatened to punish those who refused (Diod. 18.62.3–63.2).

Antigonus's delegation to the veterans' camp was led by one of his friends, Philotas, and included thirty Macedonians with persuasive skills that earned them Diodorus's unkind descriptors of "busybodies and talkative."[28] They promised Antigenes and Teutamus, the Silver Shields' commanders, large gifts and greater satrapies in return for their plotting against Eumenes. Spreading his net wide, Antigonus also instructed his men to seek out acquaintances and compatriots among the Silver Shields and to bribe them to do the same.[29]

Antigonus targeted the Silver Shields because they could easily eliminate Eumenes and because they were the weakest link in his army. While

---

26. Cf. Meeus (2009, 240), who emphasizes the Macedonians' loyalty to the royal house.

27. Rosen (1967, 72) rightly notes that Antigonus's letter addressed the entire army (Diod. 18.63.1).

28. Diod. 18.16.4: *periergōn kai lalōn*. The terms and the combination, *hapax legomena* in Diodorus, may come from Hieronymus. For Philotas, see below.

29. Diod. 18.62.3–4, 63.1–2. For the meaning of *politai* as compatriots, cf. Diod. 18.50.4. Briant (1973, 57n1 [repr. 1982, 69n1]) finds in the term a reference to regional recruiting of soldiers.

the majority of Eumenes' troops were hard-core supporters from Cappadocia and mercenaries in his pay, the Macedonians formed a unified group
of independent-minded men. And by notifying the troops as well as the
commanders of his offer, Antigonus made sure that the latter would not be
able to decline it on their own. The men he sent to Cyinda were qualified
for the job. Philotas's identity cannot be surely determined, because there
are a number of known Macedonians of that name. But if he was, as generally agreed, a commander of an infantry battalion under Alexander and
a satrap of Cilicia in 323, ousted from office by Perdiccas as Craterus's ally,
there was enough in his background and rank to appeal to Antigenes, Teutamus, and their troops, including those who still cared about Craterus's
death by Eumenes' hands.[30] The identity of the other thirty Macedonians
is unknown, but their having acquaintances among the Silver Shields made
them likely to be fellow veterans who had either followed Antigonus from
Triparadeisus or served in the armies of Eumenes and other Perdiccans before joining him. Like the Macedonian Xennias, whom Eumenes sent to
Craterus's veterans to dissuade them from fighting him (chap. 5 above),
they spoke the veterans' language and could create an easy rapport based
on a shared background and personal relationships at home and in Asia.
The service they rendered Antigonus shows how wrong it is to regard Alexander's veterans as cut from one cloth, even in their devotion to the Argead house.

Antigonus's scheme yielded better results than Ptolemy's, but not good
enough. According to Diodorus, Teutamus succumbed to the envoys' corrupting influence and asked Antigenes to join him in the plot. But Antigenes refused, earning the source's compliments on his intelligence and
fidelity in persuading Teutamus to stick with Eumenes. He proved to Teutamus that his best interest lay with the Cardian, pointing out that Antigonus
had his own friends to take care of, and that he would reward these friends
with Antigenes' and Teutamus's satrapies once their service had made him
stronger. In contrast, Eumenes was a non-Macedonian, with no ambitions
or agenda beyond his present office. Hence he would treat them as friends,
protect their satrapies, and even augment them (Diod. 18.62.6–8).

It is hard to trust this story fully, if only because Antigenes sounds like
Eumenes or his spokesman. He replicates the Cardian's earlier description

---

30. Philotas: Billows 1990, 423–424n95; Heckel 1992, 328–330; 2006, 219n6. His
Cilician background could have come in handy in negotiations with the garrison's commanders. If he was Philotas Augaeus, who was appointed by Alexander to a hypaspists'
chiliarchy in Sittacene in 331, he also shared service with the Silver Shields: Curt. 5.2.5.

of himself to the Silver Shields as a selfless, duty-bound general whose non-Macedonian origin proves his lack of ambition (Diod. 18.60.1–3). Antigenes even anticipates Eumenes' later warning to the Silver Shields that Antigonus would go back on his promises the minute he got what he wanted (Diod. 19.25.6–7). And the negative portrayal of the corrupt Teutamus may derive from his later negotiations with Antigonus after the Battle of Gabene, which resulted in Eumenes' capture and death and in Antigenes' horrific punishment (Plut. *Eum.* 17.1–2). I suggest that Hieronymus heavily reworked the consultation between Antigenes and Teutamus; although they may indeed have chosen to stick with Eumenes out of concern for the fate of their satrapies and hope of greater rewards, it is hard to ascertain their motives.[31]

The decision of Antigenes and Teutamus to stay loyal to Eumenes did not put an end to the affair, because the Silver Shields had yet to be persuaded. Accordingly, Antigonus's emissary, Philotas, seems to have initiated a meeting that was attended by all Macedonians but not by Eumenes. Philotas then produced Antigonus's letter accusing Eumenes (probably in relation to his outlawing in Egypt), inviting the army to murder him, and warning that, if disobeyed, Antigonus would come in full force and punish those who rejected his demand. Diodorus then says that the commanders and the troops were at a loss: siding with the kings would bring retribution from Antigonus, but obliging him meant a reproach from Polyperchon and the kings. It was at this crisis point that Eumenes showed up. After reading the letter, he called upon the Macedonians to obey the kings instead of a rebel, and he discussed other (unspecified) matters. The result was an increase both in the assembly's good opinion of him and in his power (Diod. 18.63.1–6).

For Diodorus (or his source, Hieronymus), the episode illustrates Eumenes' survival skills. Depicting the Macedonians as torn between fear of Antigonus and loyalty to the kings also justifies Eumenes' cause. Diodorus shows them choosing between a royalist by conviction and appointment, who influenced people by advocating obedience to the kings, and a renegade who corrupted and bullied them (Diod. 18.62.3–63.5). Yet the Macedonians' indecision means that they seriously considered killing Eumenes. In

---

31. See chap. 1 above, and the use of *ideoparagein* (to work in one's interest) in Diod. 18.62.7, which reflects Hieronymus's fondness for utilitarian motives. Significantly, Antigenes does not justify supporting Eumenes on moral or legal grounds. Antigonus's hatred of Antigenes (Diod. 19.44.1) could have originated with this incident, but see Schäfer (2004, 127), who thinks that it had earlier grounds.

other words, there were limits to the effectiveness of his advantage in legitimacy, his cultivation of personal ties with the Silver Shields, and his "Alexander's tent" production. Readers may be also justified in asking where
Eumenes was or what he was doing before he came to the Macedonians' assembly, because he seemed to learn of Antigonus's letter only in this meeting (Diod. 18.63.4). Even if we assume that the Silver Shields camped separately from his headquarters, we may wonder how a large delegation from
his enemy could have discussed his assassination unhindered (in private or
public), or how the Macedonians and the commanders met separately to
do the same, all in his absence. Whether Eumenes was ignorant of Antigonus's initiative or (as is more likely) impotent to stop it, the affair exposes
the weakness of his leadership and of his control over the veterans. It is no
wonder that he soon took his army to Phoenicia, away from Antigonus's
threats and promises.

Diodorus must have significantly abbreviated the speech of Eumenes to
the Macedonians that convinced them to stay with him and made him even
more powerful, according to the historian. He mentions only Eumenes' appeal to heed the kings' instructions rather than those of a rebel (18.63.4–
6). The veterans were surely inclined to fight for kings and legitimate rule
rather than their opposites, but there must have been additional factors that
influenced the veterans' decision. The commanders of the Silver Shields
supported Eumenes, and their support carried weight with their followers. The fact that Eumenes, unlike Antigonus, was there to persuade the
crowd in person also helped his cause. It is likely that he warned the veterans that Antigonus should not be trusted, as Antigenes is said to have
warned Teutamus.

In any case, Eumenes' tangible financial resources, which enabled him
to compensate the troops on the spot, were more attractive than Antigonus's future and conditional rewards. If, as is equally likely, Eumenes also
told them of his intention to leave Cilicia and of Polyperchon's plan to fight
Antigonus in Asia (Diod.18.63.6), Antigonus's threat to go to war against
them would have looked less alarming. Finally, the courting of the Silver
Shields and their commanders by both Antigonus and Eumenes was proof,
if proof was needed, of the unit's desirability and power. But the realists
among them knew that they had much greater leverage on Eumenes than
on Antigonus.

In the autumn of 318, Eumenes took his army to Phoenicia, whence
he helped Polyperchon with ships and money (Diod. 18.63.6; Polyaenus
4.6.8). The veterans surely shared Eumenes' hope that Polyperchon would
use the aid and his own forces to gain control over the Aegean and then

cross to fight Antigonus in Asia. But Antigonus won decisively against the royal fleet near Byzantium, and therefore could direct his attention toward Eumenes, marching against the Cardian with a mobile, picked force of 20,000 infantry and 4,000 cavalry.[32]

Here the sources lose sight of Antigonus until the winter of 317, which he spent in Mesopotamia. The army he assembled there must have consisted of his original force and substantial reinforcements (Diod. 19.13.5, 15.6). By all signs, Antigonus did not take with him any meaningful number of Alexander's veterans. According to Diodorus, his army at the Battle of Paraetacene in the autumn of 317 included "no more than 8,000 Macedonians, whom Antipater had given him when Antipater became the royal guardian," and in the subsequent Battle of Gabene these Macedonians are described as younger than the Silver Shields by a generation (Diod. 19.29.3, 41.1; Plut. *Eum.* 16.8). It is unknown what Antigonus did with his veterans. He may have assigned them to garrison duties in Asia Minor, placed them in colonies, or even discharged them, because some of them were getting too old for what was expected to be an arduous campaign. (The suggestion that he did not wish to use troops who would be reluctant to fight their brothers-in-arms in Eumenes' army is inconsistent with Antigonus's record of using veterans against veterans in his wars with the Perdiccan generals.) Antigonus's renewed campaign against Eumenes thus marks the end of the history of Macedonian veterans in his service.[33]

Eumenes' stay in Phoenicia was not free of worries. In spite of his financial resources and vigorous recruiting, his army of more than 15,000 infantry and 2,500 cavalry was still smaller than Antigonus's, with its 20,000 infantry and 4,000 cavalry. It was also expected that Ptolemy would arrive to reclaim control over the region.[34] Finally, Polyperchon's defeat significantly

---

32. Antigonus's victories: Diod. 18.72.5–9; Polyaenus 4.6.8. I shall not discuss the political and military conflicts in Greece and Macedonia involving Polyperchon, Cassander, Olympias, and others, because the sources fail to mention the participation of veterans in them. Antigonus's force against Eumenes: Diod. 18.73.1.

33. Antigonus's reluctance to use veterans: Bosworth 2002, 92n104. Bosworth (2002, 119–120n87) suspects that Antigonus took more than the 8,500 Macedonians he got from Antipater but that only 8,000 survived. If this is true, the additional Macedonians were as young as the survivors, because it is unlikely that only veterans perished on the way.

34. Eumenes' army: Diod. 18.61.5. In late 317, after suffering losses in Mesopotamia, Eumenes crossed to Iran with 15,000 infantry and 3,300 cavalry: Diod. 18.73.2–4. He got his additional recruits either in Phoenicia or, as argued by Anson (2004, 158n33), in Mesopotamia.

reduced the chances of his helping Eumenes against Antigonus. For the veterans and their leader, it meant that they would have to be on the run until Eumenes became strong enough to face the enemy or Antigonus caught up with him. These unfavorable circumstances increased Eumenes' dependence on the veterans, on their commanders, and on royalist satraps in the east. He and his army marched in the direction of Susiana, which was Antigenes' satrapy and had a rich treasury at Susa, as well as being a good rallying point for prospective allies from the upper satrapies in central Asia.[35]

From the extant sources it is not easy to reconstruct the story of Eumenes' march eastward. Diodorus's two separate accounts of it (Diod. 18.73.2–4; 19.12.1–13.5), although largely overlapping, are not fully compatible, and each has its own deficiencies. In addition, the so-called *Chronicle of the Successors*, a fragmentary record written by Babylonian priests, dates to 317/6 events that could be relevant to the march. The text mentions royal troops along with *Hanu* (probably Greek soldiers) and the local satrap, all of whom were involved in fighting at Babylon and the capture of the palace there. Although some historians have interpreted the Babylonian record as referring to Eumenes' fighting in (and even temporarily taking) Babylon, wide scholarly disagreements over the reading of the text and the identity of the fighting parties, and even Diodorus's silence about such a significant event, advise against speculating on its exact meaning. Without insisting on the following reconstruction of events, my description of Eumenes' march relies chiefly on Diodorus, focusing on the veterans' participation.[36]

To reach Susiana from Phoenicia, Eumenes had to travel through the satrapies of Mesopotamia and Babylonia, governed by Amphimachus and Seleucus, respectively. He marched through Coele Syria to Amphimachus's satrapy of Mesopotamia (Diod. 18.73.2), where his forces were probably well received, because Amphimachus (who might have been the half-brother of king Philip III, on whose behalf Eumenes was fighting) is later mentioned as a cavalry commander in Eumenes' army.[37] We then learn that Eumenes wintered in Babylonia at a place called the "Carians' Vil-

---

35. Diod. 18.73.1–4; 19.12.3, 48.7–8. Diodorus (18.73.1–2) links Eumenes' departure to Antigonus's mobilization of a force against him, and suggests that his stay in Phoenicia was short. But see Anson 2004, 155n25, in favor of a longer stay.

36. The Babylonian text and its different interpretations: *ABC* 10, obv. 14–18 = *BCHP* 3, obv. 33–37; Smith 1924, 131–132; Hornblower 1971, 112–113; Grayson 1975, 116; Del Monte 1997, 184–189; van der Spek; Boiy 2010. Eumenes in Mesopotamia: Bosworth 2002, 103–114; Schäfer 2002, 131–135; Anson 2007, 195–197.

37. Amphimachus: Arr. *Succ.* 1.35; Diod. 18.39.6; 19.27.4; Schober 1981, 79–80; Bosworth 2002, 113; Anson 2004, 158, but also Heckel 2006, 22.

lages," whose exact location is unknown but was probably north of Babylon. Although Diodorus mentions only Eumenes, Antigenes, and the Silver Shields as camping there, he means the entire army, having inherited Hieronymus's preferential attention to these elements at the expense of others.[38] From his winter camp, Eumenes sent envoys to Seleucus, the satrap of Babylonia, and to Pithon, the satrap of Media (who had stayed with Seleucus), asking them to join him. Pithon was a veteran Macedonian general who had put down a Greek rebellion in the upper satrapies in 323. He was instrumental in the killing of Perdiccas in Egypt, and consequently got the royal guardianship until Antipater assumed the office in Triparadeisus, where Pithon was given the satrapy of Media and the office of general of the upper satrapies. His superior authority, combined with his expansionist designs and violent ways, led the governors of these satrapies to unite against him. Pithon was defeated in battle and went to seek aid from Seleucus for a second round.[39]

At this point, Eumenes' envoys arrived at Seleucus's headquarters to ask both satraps to join the war on behalf of the kings and against Antigonus (Diod. 19.12.1). Seleucus rejected the invitation, saying that he was ready to serve the kings but would not obey Eumenes, whom the Macedonians had condemned to death. His manifesto-like statement was followed by long deliberations over Eumenes' proposal, but Diodorus gives no information about their contents (Diod. 19.12.2). Perhaps Pithon needed some persuading that Eumenes was bound to strengthen Pithon's enemies with 3,300 cavalry and 15,000 infantry, including the renowned Silver Shields. In fact, the Cardian had already sent the upper satraps a letter from the kings, requesting their full cooperation.[40] Seleucus's view prevailed in the end. The

---

38. Diod. 19.12.1. Diod. 19.12.3 rules out the possibility that only Eumenes and the Silver Shields wintered at the Carian Villages. See below for other places where Eumenes' "Macedonians" stand for the entire army. Boiy (2007, 55n122) identifies the Carian Villages as a military colony since Achaemenid times.

39. Pithon's career: chaps. 4 and 5 above; Diod. 19.14.1–3. For the legality of his superior command in Asia, see Schober 1981, 74–78 (by usurpation), but more likely: Bosworth 2002, 104–105n27; Anson 2004, 160–161n39 (by authorization).

40. Diodorus (19.13.7) does not clearly date the dispatch of the letter, but it must have been before Eumenes reached Babylonia. Scholars suggest that it was sent from Phoenicia (e.g., Schäfer 2002, 132n5) or even Mesopotamia (Vezin 1907, 86). Generally overlooked is the fact that the royal letter to the governors was sent not by the kings or Polyperchon, but by Eumenes; cf. Diod. 19.15.5. In a conference on the Diadochi (La Coruna, 2010), Alexander Meeus suggested that Diodorus neglected to mention this letter in his report on Polyperchon's correspondence with Eumenes in spring

two satraps had a reasonable chance of adding Eumenes' army to theirs if they could eliminate him by treason or in combat, and Antigonus's independent policy, successful military record, and larger army made him the more attractive and intimidating leader. Therefore they decided to send to Eumenes' camp an envoy who would urge the Silver Shields and their commanders to overthrow Eumenes, probably replicating Seleucus's justification for rejecting Eumenes' request.[41]

For the Silver Shields, a message from Seleucus and Pithon carried the authority of men who had served with them in their command structure during Alexander's campaign and its aftermath. Seleucus could even boast of having led the veterans in person as a hypaspists' commander (as could Antigenes and quite a few others), and both he and Pithon had plotted against the hated Perdiccas.[42] Their appeal to the Silver Shields to get rid of Eumenes relied, like earlier attempts, on the supposed anomaly of the Macedonians being led by a man whom they themselves had outlawed. It was another example of generals' reminding the Macedonians to honor their own decisions, which the Macedonians tended to ignore as easily as they made them. Seleucus, in particular, was fond of using the Macedonians' popular decisions and his services to the Macedonian monarchy to justify his positions, as he did both here and later, when he refused on similar grounds to give an account of his revenues to Antigonus (Diod. 19.55.3; cf. 19.56.1). In fact, both satraps had nothing better to use against Eumenes' greater legitimacy as the kings' appointee and savior. Hence, in order to undermine the identification (fundamental to Eumenes' power and propaganda) of loyalty to the kings with loyalty to Eumenes, they told the Silver Shields that they shared their goal of helping the kings, but that the veterans should depose Eumenes as the enemy of the Macedonians (cf. Diod. 19.13.1). They did not even ask the veterans to stop the campaign against the rebel Antigonus. The veterans rejected the offer. Eumenes' authority was better founded, and he had a larger army than Seleucus's, along with better prospects of augmenting it (and his financial resources) in Susiana. Antigenes very likely used his influence in the Cardian's favor as well.

Seleucus and Pithon's attempt thus resembled similar appeals to the Sil-

---

318 (18.57.3–58.1). Also possible is that the Cardian used an open letter that called on local commanders to obey him, or the one that was addressed to him; see above about Polyperchon's letters to Eumenes.

41. Diod. 19.12.2. For additional explanations of Seleucus and Pithon's response, see Mehl 1986, 43–49; Grainger 1990, 35–38.

42. See Hornblower (1981, 192), who overrates the impact of Seleucus's hypaspist command.

ver Shields to rid themselves of Eumenes, based on the belief that they would be most receptive to the rhetoric of legitimacy and national identity. Neither these satraps nor Antigonus and Ptolemy thought that the veterans should decide who got or lost a military command, but the result of their appeals (and of Eumenes' and even Polyperchon's) was to make the Macedonians the arbiters of authority and offices, certainly in their own minds. The veterans believed they deserved this privilege because they were Macedonians with an exemplary record of fighting and conquest. Antigenes made this point later in Susiana when, amid contesting claims to the supreme command, he argued that only his Macedonians were entitled to select the man for this office (Diod. 19.15.2). The claim was self-serving but relied on the perception that in a diversified army, the Silver Shields alone had the right to allocate power. Furthermore, the repeated failure to incite the Silver Shields against Eumenes reaffirmed and even strengthened their bond to him and habituated the veterans to resist future similar attempts. Diodorus says that Eumenes thanked the Silver Shields for ignoring Seleucus and Pithon's call to disobey him (19.12.3). Paradoxically, he should have been grateful to these satraps too.

This was not, however, the end of Seleucus's military and diplomatic offensive, in the face of which Eumenes decided to keep moving toward friendlier Susa. At some point in Babylonia his army suffered losses in a night attack by locals near the River Tigris (Diod. 18.73.3). There was also a problem with supplies, because the land west of the river had been plundered by Eumenes' men, or by Seleucus, or by both (Diod. 19.12.3). The need to provide for the army drove Eumenes to try crossing the river to get to Susiana at a time and (probably) place not of his choosing. He camped near the western bank of the Tigris at a distance of 300 stades (ca. 55 km) from Babylon and began assembling vessels to transport his men across the river.

In a second attempt to unseat him, Pithon and Seleucus arrived with troops aboard two triremes and smaller vessels from a fleet that Alexander had constructed in Babylonia in 324–323. They addressed Antigenes and the Silver Shields, probably from the height of a trireme's deck, wisely speaking in person rather than (as earlier) attempting to persuade the veterans through an envoy and presumably a communiqué.[43] They also shifted the reasoning for betraying Eumenes somewhat, from legal to ethnic grounds, claiming that it was the veterans' patriotic duty to rebel against an alien and killer of many Macedonians. Once again, the Silver Shields rejected

---

43. See also Schäfer 2002, 134.

the call to change sides (Diod. 19.12.3–13.1). They were as good Macedonian patriots as the satraps, but they readily followed a non-Macedonian commander into battle, even against their compatriots, while letting the generals wave the banner of Macedonian nationalism.[44]

Diodorus is silent on Eumenes' role in the encounter on the river, and it is likely that he had none. He could not prevent the satraps from speaking even if he wanted to, and the Silver Shields had grown accustomed to being courted directly. They did not let Eumenes down, but their presumed ability to decide the fate of the entire campaign by themselves gave them power and status in inverse proportion to their number.

Encouraging betrayal was the easy way of stopping Eumenes and his army. When this failed, Seleucus proceeded to clear an old canal that could be used to flood Eumenes' camp. After a day of hesitation, it appears that Eumenes' troops used vessels to transport the "strongest part of the army" to the other bank, without interference from Seleucus (his cavalry was inferior to Eumenes'). But when night approached, Eumenes became concerned about the baggage left behind. He ferried back the troops, or a number of them sufficient for his purposes, and moved to a higher mound. Relying on local intelligence, he found a place to dig and diverted the canal.[45]

Scholars, however, have claimed that Eumenes was forced to return and save the baggage under pressure from his men, especially the Silver Shields, and that he showed a generally cavalier attitude toward the troops' baggage, indicating that he misunderstood their aspirations. Yet the Silver Shields should not be singled out for credit, or Eumenes for blame. In fact, Diodorus explicitly states that rescuing the baggage was Eumenes' initiative. Moreover, it is true that Diodorus calls the troops whom Eumenes transported back "Macedonians," but a close reading of Diodorus's text shows that he uses the appellation "Macedonians," both here and elsewhere, not in its narrow ethnic sense but to describe Eumenes' army as a whole. On the Tigris, then, Eumenes saved the baggage of the entire army, and without being compelled to do so by the Silver Shields.[46]

---

44. Mehl's assertion (1986, 48) that the attempt failed because only money could influence the soldiers echoes our sources' elitist outlook. It is likely that Seleucus, Pithon, and the satraps of the upper provinces had Macedonian veterans too, yet none equaled the Silver Shields in numbers or prestige.

45. Diodorus describes this event twice, once in an abbreviated form and later in greater detail, but the descriptions are not entirely similar or clear: Diod. 18.73.3 (wrongly locates the crossing on the Euphrates); 19.13.2–5.

46. The Silver Shields' pressuring Eumenes: Vezin 1907, 88; Bosworth 2002, 111. Eumenes' underappreciation of the baggage's significance: Billows 1990, 102n26. He was certainly protective of his own baggage: Plut. *Eum.* 2.4–5, 3.11. Eumenes' initiative:

Seleucus allowed Eumenes a free passage after he had failed to stop him by intrigue or by unleashing the forces of nature. But the satrap also allied himself firmly with Antigonus, then in Mesopotamia, urging him to come quickly with his army before the armies of the upper satraps should come over (Diod. 19.13.5). This was hardly good news for Eumenes and his army, who had additional reasons to be discontented. The troops, including the Silver Shields, had not been paid for quite some time—it was only after reaching Susa in late winter 317 that Eumenes gave them six months' pay (Diod. 19.15.5)—and they had to contend in Babylonia with loss of men, lack of food, and the danger of flood. The crossing into Susiana brought little improvement. To facilitate the search for markets and plunderable places, Eumenes divided the army into three separate columns, enabling the soldiers to acquire plenty of sesame, dates, and rice, but not the grains that were their traditional and preferred staple at home and on the march.[47]

CONTESTS OF LEADERSHIP

Knowing all this, we may imagine that when Eumenes' army later joined the armies of the upper satrapies, not all of troops were in a good mood. They cheered up, however, when they saw the number, the equipment, and the elephants of their allies (Plut. *Eum.* 13.9).

The meeting took place on the road to Susa and resembled Eumenes' first encounter with the Silver Shields in its progress from (presumably) initial welcome to rivalry over leadership and finally to an unstable resolution. The satraps and other generals led forces from (in west-to-east order) Persis, Carmania, Aria and Drangiana, Arachosia, Paropanisadae, Bactria, and India, with the most important contingents coming from Persis under Peucestas and from India under Eudamas. Eudamas arrived with just a few hundred infantry and cavalry, but his prize possession was 120 elephants. These terrifying beasts could potentially decide a contest between Eumenes and Antigonus, making Eudamas an important ally for any satrap who craved Eumenes' overall command against Antigonus (Diod. 19.14.5–8, 15.5; cf. Plut. *Eum.* 16.3).

The chief contender for this office was Peucestas, the satrap of Persis,

---

Diod. 19.13.2, 4; cf. 18.73.3; 19.15.6. Macedonians tantamount to the entire army: Diod. 19.13.2, 4; 18.73.3. Cf. 19.15.6, where once again the Macedonians stand for the whole army. Diod. 19.18.3–7 may be another example.

47. Diod. 19.13.6; Engels 1978, 123. The fact that the armies of the satraps' coalition assembled in Susiana put additional strain on local supplies.

who had excellent credentials. He was a noble Macedonian and widely known for his courage and loyalty to Alexander from the time he and Leonnatus had protected the almost fatally wounded king in an Indian town in 326. Alexander rewarded him with inclusion in the exclusive circle of his bodyguards and with the satrapy of Persis. Peucestas was by now a veteran governor and very popular with his local subjects, whose customs he readily adopted. He had also successfully led the recent satrapal war against Pithon and had the largest contingent in the coalition army, including 10,000 Persian archers and slingers, 3,000 troops of different backgrounds who were trained in Macedonian warfare, 600 Thracian and Greek cavalry, and more than 400 Persian cavalry.[48]

Soon Peucestas and other commanders began to question Eumenes' right to the leadership of the combined army. The contest took place in front of a common assembly that probably consisted of any troops who cared to come (not just the Macedonians), as the speakers' arguments indicate. Peucestas claimed that he should have the overall command because of the many men who fought on his side, and because he was deemed eminent by Alexander. Peucestas's contingent was in fact smaller than Eumenes' army, but perhaps he referred to the number of troops in the satrapal coalition army that he had led against Pithon. In any case, it is doubtful that he or others in attendance bothered to produce statistical tables. Antigenes countered Peucestas's motion with a no-less-self-serving proposal that the Silver Shields should decide who got the office. Thus both men seem to have acknowledged the presence of a diversified army in the assembly, one in an effort to obtain its approval, and the other in order to curtail its power.[49]

Where did the Silver Shields stand on the issue of leadership? Their attitude toward Peucestas must have been ambivalent. His Macedonian origin, martial courage, closeness to Alexander, and high rank under him gave Peucestas an advantage over Eumenes. Before becoming Alexander's favorite and the satrap of Persis, Peucestas was also a hypaspist, just like the veterans. But he was also known to be an avid follower of Alexander's "orientalism." The Macedonian-style warriors in Peucestas's army might once

---

48. Diod. 19.14.4–5. Peucestas: Billows 1990, 417–418n90; Heckel 2006, 203–205n2.

49. The contest over leadership: Diod. 19.15.1; Plut. *Eum.* 13.9–13 (apparently conflating this episode with later events); Nepos *Eum.* 7.1. The combined armies of Eumenes and the satraps totaled 33,500 infantry and 7,900 cavalry: Diod. 18.73.4; 19.14.6. See also note 51 below for the troops' figures. Acoustic considerations and perhaps even space worked against effective attendance of all troops.

have been Epigoni—the troops so resented by the veterans—and surely resembled them. For the veterans, Peucestas and his troops recalled the situation at Opis, where the Macedonians saw that they could be replaced by Asian troops and that the king and his loyal satrap were taking to Persian ways.[50] Peucestas's motion to grant the supreme command to the general with the most troops similarly undermined the Silver Shields' special status, influence, and power in an army of which they comprised around one-fourteenth of the entire combined force. It is safe to assume that they did not favor his suggestion to turn the assembly into a general electorate.[51]

Despite their presumably strong feelings, the Silver Shields were dragged into the debate rather than taking an active part in it. The man who took up their cause was Antigenes, whose advocacy of their political entitlement to select a commander was based on conviction and self-interest. He justified giving the veterans this privilege on the grounds that they were Macedonians who had conquered Asia under Alexander and that they were undefeated because of their valor (*aretē*; Diod. 19.15.2). His reasoning echoed Eumenes' praises of the Silver Shields when he first encountered them, and restated their claims to special identity and preferential treatment based on their ethnicity, military accomplishments, and status as victors—in short, on all the qualities that the other units lacked (cf. Just. 14.2.7–10). Such politization of the veterans' identity recurred elsewhere, but here it was primarily designed to help Eumenes and Antigenes.[52]

The next attested speaker was Eumenes. Fearing that the dispute would weaken the anti-Antigonus front, he suggested that the commanders meet together in front of the throne in Alexander's tent instead of deferring to a single leader. All agreed, and Eumenes called them daily to a council

---

50. Peucestas the hypaspist: Arr. *Anab.* 1.11.7–8, 6.9.3; Diod. 17.99.4. Alexander's orientalism: Arr. *Anab.* 7.6.3. For the possibility that the Macedonian-trained troops were former Epigoni, see the forthcoming third volume of Bosworth's commentary on Arrian's *Anabasis*; cf. 2002, 84–86.

51. After listing the individual figures of each satrap's army, Diodorus (19.14.5–8) gives their total as more than 18,700 infantry and 4,600 cavalry (with 120 elephants). In fact it is lower: 18,500 infantry and 4,200 cavalry. For different attempts to bridge the gap, see Hornblower 1981, 110n14; Anson 2004, 158n33, 164n51; Bosworth 2002, 106–107n35. Eumenes had 15,000 infantry and 3,300 cavalry (18.73.4). Therefore the 3,000 Silver Shields can be said to have comprised less than one-fourteenth of the combined army of 33,500 infantry and 7,900 cavalry.

52. Diod. 19.15.1–2; Nepos *Eum.* 7.1. Antigenes' agenda: Billows 1990, 90 (*pro se*); Schäfer 2002, 137 with n30 (*pro Eumene*). Antigenes' and Eumenes' later cooperation (Diod. 19.17.4) seems to give favor to the latter view.

that was "like one in a democratic city" (Diod. 19.15.3–4). Diodorus, likely following Hieronymus, places Eumenes in the familiar role of a clever problem-solver, whose reemployment of the "Alexander's tent" device unselfishly served the common interest. But it was not just foresight and the spirit of reconciliation that guided Eumenes' steps.

Both Peucestas's and Antigenes' criteria for choosing a leader showed a disregard of the royal appointment of Eumenes as the leader of the campaign, which was stated in the letters to him and the satraps. Apparently this authority alone also failed to persuade the troops to support Eumenes. Deprived of his major asset in the rivalry over the command, Eumenes was forced to recognize others' right to it. The tent stratagem worked because it was based on what the generals had in common, namely, Antigonus as an adversary, Argead loyalty (cf. Diod. 19.61.4), and Alexander as a former king who provided both legitimacy and talismanic powers. Its major appeal, however, was that it did not decide the competition over leadership but only postponed it. Diodorus's assertion that the commanders' gathering resembled the council of a democratic city was at best only partially correct. The satraps were not elected to office, and although Diodorus describes them and the commanders as men who had been selected by army (Diod. 19.15.3), the selection likely referred to mid-level commanders or to the confirmation of already-made appointments, as was the case with the distribution of commands and governorships in Babylon or Triparadeisus.[53] This "democracy" was for the commanders alone, and even for them it was not a council of equals, since Eumenes, Antigenes, and Peucestas must have dominated the discussion. There were also signs of Eumenes' future prominence. It was he who chose to share Alexander's tent and regalia with the others, who had his own tent closest to Alexander's, and who probably called the daily meetings and controlled the rituals associated with the tent.[54]

The army's role in the entire affair was limited. Peucestas's suggestion to link leadership to the size of a commander's army, Antigenes' motion to limit the vote to the Macedonians, and Eumenes' delegation of power to

<hr />

53. See, however, Hammond 2000, 147n21. Unless the evidence is at fault, not a single general mentioned in the coalition army appeared to hold a command over troops whom he did not have before.

54. Diod. 19.15.4; Nepos *Eum.* 7.3; Polyaenus 4.8.2. Briant (1973a, 68n3 [repr. 1982, 80n3]) thinks that Diodorus's (or Hieronymus's) description of the council as democratic was not complimentary, but see Haatzopoulos 1996, 1:344–345, as well as Rzepka 2005, 138–139.

the generals' council all showed that the authority of the general assembly was ill defined and could be expanded or restricted almost at will. It was the military leaders who called the meeting, spoke in it, and eventually resolved the controversy. The blame for this state of affairs rested primarily with the soldiers. If in Babylon the Macedonians took advantage of the split within the elite to make their voice heard and to influence events, in Persis neither the entire army nor the veterans seemed to be interested in pressing their point. They must have supported Antigenes' position, but they also approved Eumenes' proposal because they preferred a united over a divided leadership and because they knew they would be impotent once the elite had resolved its differences. Generally, when the troops wanted their opinion heard (usually when they were dissatisfied), they resorted not to voting but to acts of indiscipline, vocal protests, and mutinies.

Arriving at Susa, Eumenes gave a royal letter to officials, including Xenophilus, commander of the citadel and treasury there, instructing them to open their coffers to him. No doubt following Hieronymus, Diodorus states that only Eumenes had such an authorization, and the treasurers' obedience confirms for the reader the Cardian's right to lead the war (Diod. 19.15.5, 17.3, 18.1). Antigenes, the satrap of Susiana, who had already taken money from Susa with the Silver Shields sometime after Triparadeisus, must have helped in the persuasion. Using his newfound wealth, Eumenes paid his troops their wages for six months. This generosity likely scored points with them against his main competitor, Peucestas, whose payment of *his* troops depended on revenues from his more distant satrapy. Eumenes was certainly aware that he would lose his financial edge once he had left Susa and had spent the money from the treasury.[55]

It is possible that Eumenes' payment to his soldiers triggered a reaction in kind from other commanders. Plutarch's depiction of a massive corruption campaign by Eumenes' competitors may belong in this context. The biographer, who is short on specifics but generous with moralistic condemnations, describes how the satraps flattered the Macedonians, entertained them, and threw money at them. The camp became a place of unrestrained

---

55. Antigenes and the treasury after Triparadeisus: Arr. *Succ.* 1.38; cf. Grainger 1990, 36. Eumenes' payments: Diod. 19.15.5. Although Diodorus called the recipients of the payments "Macedonians," he must mean the entire army: see 19.15.6 for the synonymy. The other beneficiary was Eudamas, the elephants' master, who got from Eumenes the hefty sum of 200 talents. The treasury would become inaccessible to Eumenes once Antigonus besieged it, and in Persis Eumenes had to borrow money from his colleagues: Diod. 19.18.1, 24.2–3, 48.6.

festivity and the army a mob induced to vote for generals as if in a democracy. Plutarch adds that the Macedonians took gifts from these corrupting agents and waited at the doors of leaders who had bodyguards and wanted to be generals.[56]

Part of Plutarch's account may be an expanded embellishment of a later episode in Persis, where Peucestas used his wealth to court the Macedonians (see below). But the biographer may be right to date to a period of relative quiet, such as in Susa, an intense competition for the goodwill of the Silver Shields, who were valuable for their military reputation and political significance. Although Antigenes failed to secure for them the sole power to select the high commander, his idea could be resurrected by anyone who thought that the Macedonians owed him a favor. For the Silver Shields, then, these were good times, in which their skills and status finally and literally paid off. What Plutarch describes as corrupting gifts from generals were popular entertainment, free food, and a source of livelihood. Becoming a bodyguard would have given the individual Macedonian a higher rank and probably a steadier income than serving in the phalanx. Nevertheless, the veterans did not follow their purses, and all the attention paid to them failed to have an impact on their loyalty to Antigenes and Eumenes.[57]

The busy political activity in camp may explain why Eumenes and his colleagues lost the military initiative to Antigonus. After the arrival of reinforcements in infantry and cavalry as well as elephants, Antigonus set out from Mesopotamia to meet Seleucus and Pithon in Babylonia, where the three generals agreed to cooperate. Around June 317, Antigonus and his new allies crossed the Tigris. Eumenes and the satraps decided not to oppose them there but retreated toward the Pasitigris River, a four-day march from Susa. They planned to use the river as a line of defense and to attack Antigonus at the crossing.[58]

---

56. Plut. *Eum.* 13.9–14.2. Plutarch's hostile attitudes toward radical democracy: Aalders 1982, 28–29; cf. Hornblower 1981, 188.

57. Plutarch (*Eum.* 13.12–13) links this episode to Eumenes' stratagem of taking loans from his rivals in order to turn them into creditors who would be reluctant to plot against him. I prefer to follow Diodorus's dating of the ploy to later in 317, when the army was in Persis: 19.24.2–3.

58. Diod. 19.15.6, 17.2–3, 18.2, 27.1; Anson 2004, 166–167. Diodorus errs twice: he calls the river where the allies made their camp the Tigris instead of the Pasitigris, and he locates it one day's march from Susa instead of four. He got the distance right in 17.67.1–2; see Hornblower 1981, 109. The size of Antigonus's army at this point is unknown. After suffering heavy losses but also receiving reinforcements, he marshaled 28,000 infantry, 10,500 cavalry, 65 elephants, and many light-armed troops for the Battle of Paraetacene in the autumn of that year (317): Diod. 19.27.1, 29.1–7.

Although our sources shine the light almost exclusively on Eumenes, Peucestas soon showed how significant his contribution was. The coalition army needed men to guard the river's eastern bank, because it was unknown exactly where Antigonus would cross the Pasitigris or if he would cross in more than one place. Eumenes and Antigenes asked Peucestas to bring over 10,000 Persian bowmen, who could inflict heavy damage on the enemy at the vulnerable stage of crossing. The sources depict a dilatory Peucestas, torn between resentment of Eumenes and fear of Antigonus until he finally decided to provide the reinforcements in the hope that having many soldiers would get him the chief command. The attribution of selfish and calculating motives to the satrap grossly misrepresents his full cooperation with Eumenes and Antigenes and his increasing contribution to the war. It is also likely that the (prompt) arrival of the Persian reinforcements allowed Eumenes to take the risk of attacking Antigonus before the latter reached the river. The point of recalling the entire episode, then, was to malign Peucestas.[59]

Before arriving at the river, Antigonus, Pithon, and Seleucus entered undefended Susa, where Seleucus stayed to besiege the citadel and its treasury. Antigonus and his army continued their march in the scorching heat of June, which exacted a heavy toll in men and beasts. Eumenes learned that Antigonus was crossing the Coprates River, a tributary of the Pasitigris about 15 km from Eumenes' camp on the Pasitigris. Rushing to the scene with 4,000 infantry and 1,300 cavalry, Eumenes surprised those of Antigonus's troops who had already crossed, taking advantage of their shortage of boats, which prevented Antigonus from rescuing or reinforcing the men across the river. These included 6,000 scattered foragers, 3,000 infantry, and 400 cavalry who were building and securing a defensible location for the entire army. Eumenes easily overcame them with his numerical superiority. Among the many who fled the scene were Macedonians, if Diodorus uses the term in its ethnic sense (19.18.5). Four thousand enemy troops chose captivity over death by drowning or by offering resistance.[60]

It is doubtful that the Silver Shields participated in Eumenes' attack. We do not know how far exactly the opposing sides were from each other, but Eumenes' forced march had to cover a considerable distance in order to reach and pursue the enemy, and his surprise attack relied on speed and

59. Diod. 19.17.4–7, 18.4, and see chap. 1 above for this episode. Plutarch (*Eum.* 14.1–2) exaggerates the dependence here of the troops and their commanders on Eumenes, the only "real general."

60. Diod. 19.18.1–7; Plut. *Eum.* 14.2, who confuses the Coprates with the Pasitigris.

agility. Alexander's younger hypaspists could have done it, but probably not the veterans.[61] Nevertheless, Eumenes' convincing victory should have strengthened the Silver Shields' trust in his leadership and recalled his earlier successes against Neoptolemus and Craterus. For Eumenes, the victory was especially sweet because he had won it against a general who had defeated him in the past and was now leading an even larger army.

After the battle, Antigonus marched north to Pithon's satrapy of Media in order to recover from the battle and to invade the upper satrapies from there. His soldiers paid dearly for his decision to take the shorter rather than the longer but safer way. The heat continued to claim lives, there was little food, and Antigonus's insistence on forcing rather than paying his way through the tribal territory of the Cossaeans cost him many men and horses (Diod. 19.19.1–8). When he reached the part of Media that was under Pithon's control, his soldiers voiced their dissatisfaction. Antigonus failed to meet their primary expectations of a general: he fared miserably against his enemies (and the elements), he could not provide for the army, and he was responsible for their losses. Yet Antigonus was a seasoned general who knew how to deal with a failure that he could not blame on others. Like Perdiccas at the beginning of the Egyptian campaign, he placated the soldier's anger through displays of kindness and affability. He also made sure that they were well provided for, and after Pithon came back from a successful recruiting and supply mission in Media, Antigonus gave horses to the cavalrymen and pack animals to the soldiers to replace those lost on the march. It is also likely that some of the 500 talents that Pithon brought with him trickled down to the rank and file. These compensations, and the troops' lack of alternatives in their isolation, enabled Antigonus to regain their favor.[62]

The departure of the common enemy Antigonus to Media exposed anew the fissures in the coalition of Eumenes and his allies. We hear of a debate on the banks of the Pasitigris among Eumenes, Antigenes, and "all those who had marched up from the sea"—presumably the other commanders in Eumenes' army, who wanted to return west, and the governors of the upper satrapies, who sought to protect their territories from Antigonus and

---

61. The distance between the camps could be 15 km or longer: Diod. 19.18.3. For the geography and distances, see also Diod. 17.67.1–2; 19.17.3; Strabo 15.3.5–6; Vezin 1907, 93; Bosworth 2002, 116n74; Anson 2004, 166n56, 168–69n65.

62. Diod. 19.20.1–4. Billows (1990, 93) thinks that the 500 talents brought by Pithon were for the soldiers' pay, but Antigonus is attested to have given away only horses, beasts of burden, and provisions.

Pithon. It is a piece of brazen favoritism on the part of Diodorus, and likely his source Hieronymus, to charge the satraps but not Eumenes with acting in self-interest (Diod. 19.21.1).

The historian does not report how Eumenes and Antigenes justified their wish to return. They may have argued that this was an opportune time to attack Antigonus's home base in Asia Minor, and that such an attack would draw Antigonus away from the region or compel him to split his forces. But to the satraps (and the unbiased reader) it looked as if Eumenes, who was responsible for bringing Antigonus and his huge army to their country, was going to leave them in the lurch. Diodorus says that when the quarrel intensified, Eumenes decided to go with the satraps, thinking that no party would be able to contend with the enemy on its own (19.21.2). Once again we are encouraged to appreciate Eumenes' logic and to contrast his unselfish ways with the self-interest of the satraps (cf. Diod. 18.62.7; 19.15.3). Yet Eumenes gave up because he saw that the satraps were not going to help him or the kings regain power in western Asia before their satrapies were secured; they might even reach an agreement with Antigonus. Returning west, then, depended on a victory over Antigonus in Iran. The Silver Shields likely supported their commanders' wish to go back, but they too were forced to realize that their future depended on cooperation with the satraps. Eumenes and Antigenes' failure to have their own way suggested also the limits of the veterans' power to influence such important decisions.[63]

The coalition army marched from Pasitigris toward Persepolis in Peucestas's satrapy of Persis. After traversing a valley under hot temperatures and with no provisions, they reached a higher and cooler ground with streams, shade and fruit trees, and royal parks, of which the soldiers took full advantage. Ever since the army's stay in Susiana, the business of providing for the troops' needs and comfort had been highly politicized, and in Persis Peucestas had a clear advantage in this regard. In addition to allowing the soldiers to enjoy themselves in his satrapy, he distributed local herds among them. Diodorus's comment that the local inhabitants were very warlike suggests that Peucestas encountered some resistance in gathering supplies for such largesse (19.21.2–3). The historian also remarks unkindly that the satrap was aiming for popularity with the troops, as if Eumenes' and Antigonus's goals were different.

---

63. For different suggestions concerning Eumenes' aims and reasoning, see Billows 1990, 93; Schäfer 2002, 140; Bosworth 2002, 120–121; cf. 150.

Eumenes, in any case, was in a tough spot. After losing the debate over the direction of the campaign, he had now to respect Peucestas's exclusive right to plunder his own subjects. But Peucestas might have been looking beyond popularity and the wish to weaken Eumenes' position. There was a need to prove to troops such as the Silver Shields, who had been disappointed by the decision not to go west, that going in the opposite direction had its rewards.

Peucestas also took great care to entertain the army on a royal scale when it arrived in Persepolis. He brought so many animals to the city that he could give every soldier an animal to sacrifice, along with decorative rugs. He also provided whatever else was needed for a huge-scale banquet in Achaemenid or Alexander's style, during which the army was seated in four concentric circles that reflected its hierarchy of honor. At the center were altars to the gods and to Alexander and Philip, surrounded by a circle of reclining generals, cavalry commanders, and the most distinguished Persians. In the second circle reclined secondary commanders, friends, generals who had no combat unit, and the cavalry. The third circle included the Silver Shields and "companions [*hetairoi*] who had fought with Alexander," probably veteran infantry (*pedzhetairoi*) who served in the satraps' retinues. The last and widest circle consisted of mercenaries and allied troops.[64]

Peucestas, the most Medized of Macedonian satraps, played to both the local and the Macedonian audiences on this occasion. It could very well be that the seating arrangement followed a Persian protocol and that the gods honored at the center of the spectacle included Persian deities.[65] For status-sensitive veterans, however, the message was mixed. They were honored more than the crowd (*plēthos*) of mercenaries and allies in the last circle, but less than the cavalry, the officer class, and the eminent Persians. They had also suffered a decline in rank from Alexander's days. After the mutiny at Opis (324), Alexander sacrificed and threw a banquet (whose memory Peucestas might have been trying to evoke), at which the great king sat surrounded first by his bodyguards and then by Macedonians, Persians, and

---

64. The banquet: Diod. 19.22.1–3; cf. Plut. *Eum.* 14.4. The *hetairoi* could hardly be veterans of Alexander's cavalry Companions, whose natural place was in the second circle with the cavalry. Nor were they the "so-called *hetairoi*," also cavalry, who are mentioned in Eumenes' right wing in the Battle of Paraetacene. See Diod. 19.28.3 (cf. 19.29.4); Anson 1988, 132n10; Bosworth 2002, 121.

65. So Weisehöfer 1994, 53; Spawforth 2007, 97–102 (although, *pace* p. 103, Arrian 7.11.8–9 does not describe guests sitting in concentric circles). Goukowsky (1978–1981, 1:98), however, believes that Peucestas was courting primarily the Silver Shields.

other nationalities, ranked by honor. On the occasion of the Susa weddings (324) and whenever he gave a formal audience, the king was surrounded first by his bodyguards, then by 500 Silver Shields followed by other units, including 1,000 Macedonians.[66] At Persepolis the Macedonian troops were still ranked above their Asian counterparts, but had been pushed back from the front to the third circle. This was hardly a proper place for men to whom Antigenes wished to give the exclusive right of picking the chief commander. The Macedonians also appeared not to have the privilege of reclining, which was reserved for the cavalry and the officer class, with the men of the first circle enjoying the additional distinction of reclining in booths decorated with rugs and tapestries.[67] Diodorus says that the circles were well separated from each other to prevent crowdedness and to allow access to the provisions (19.22.3). The separation also prevented the mixing of honors, but at least the seating in a circle equalized those who were included in it.

The veterans could find even greater solace in the worship of Philip and Alexander. With a huge mass of Asians behind them, and in a city heavy with Persian religious and national symbols, they needed such an affirmation of their own identity and heritage. Philip and Alexander also stood for conquest and invincibility, which were the foundations of the Silver Shields' reputation and were now inseparable from Macedonian identity at large. Finally, the Argead kings linked them to other Macedonian troops and commanders in the audience and served as divine patrons.

It has been claimed that Peucestas's intention was to upset Eumenes' use of the tent. As a rival to Eumenes' Alexander-centered cult, Peucestas established a new cult that added Philip to Alexander. He also eliminated Eumenes' privilege of having his own tent closest to Alexander's tent, placing every commander's tent or hut close to the altars.[68] But Peucestas had no reason to oppose a cult that centered on Alexander. He owed his fame to saving the king's life in India and to serving as his bodyguard, and thus had a better claim to Alexander's memory than Eumenes, who for his part had no reason to oppose Philip's inclusion. Moreover, there is nothing in Diodorus's description of the feast to suggest that Peucestas intended to institu-

---

66. The Opis banquet: Arr. *Anab.* 7.11.8–9; Briant 1973, 68n4 (repr. 1982, 80n4); Schäfer 2002, 142. Alexander's audience: Phylarchus in Athen. 12.539d–f; Aelian *VH* 9.3; Polyaenus 4.3.24; and see, e.g., Roisman 2003, 301; Bosworth 2002, 121n92.

67. For Diodorus 19.22.3 and the meaning of *klisia* (booth, hut), see Schäfer 2002, 141–142.

68. Schäfer 2002, 141–143.

tionalize it as a permanent cult or to make it, like Eumenes' tent, a site for the commanders' council.

The importance of these arrangements should not be overstated, because they reflect chiefly on their organizer, Peucestas, and his perspective on distributing honor in camp. The satrap's considerable investment in the banquet was designed to foreground his status and to gain respect and goodwill from officers and troops alike (cf. Diod. 19.24.4). Yet there is no need to follow the sources who suggest that he was looking for a showdown with Eumenes. Judging by the Cardian's actions, it was he who pushed for confrontation with Peucestas, interpreting the satrap's increased authority and popularity as a threat to his own power (Diod. 19.23.1; cf. Polyaenus 4.8.3). Unlike Peucestas, whose seating of all the high commands in a circle suggests an attempt to equalize them, Eumenes was never happy with partners in command.

The Cardian could not compete with Peucestas in resources and hospitality, but he knew that winning the war ultimately meant more to the commanders and the troops than gifts and honors (cf. Diod. 19.23.1). To make this point and to regain the army's support, he resorted to a ruse: fabricating a letter from Orontes, the strap of Armenia, stating that Olympias and her protégé, Alexander IV, had gained control over Macedonia after eliminating Antigonus's ally Cassander. This turnabout restored Eumenes' friends to power and allegedly freed Macedonian resources for the war against Antigonus. Indeed, the letter added that Polyperchon had crossed over to Asia to fight Antigonus with the best part of the royal army and with elephants, and that he was already around Cappadocia.[69] The document appeared genuine because it was written in Aramaic script and purported to come from Orontes, who was geographically closer to the events it described than were the forces in Persepolis, and who was known as Peucestas's friend, a man with no obvious interest in helping Eumenes. Like many other successful deceptions, the letter mixed truth with lies. Olympias had indeed gained control of Macedonia after overcoming Eurydice and Philip, who were allied with Cassander. But Cassander was very much alive, and Polyperchon had taken no army to Asia.[70] Eumenes' agents went

---

69. The forgery required some groundwork, and although Eumenes' previous role as a secretary equipped him to forge letters in foreign languages (Schäfer 2002, 144n64), a credible messenger had to be produced as well. It is unknown if Eumenes said that he received or intercepted the letter.

70. The events in Greece and Macedonia and their disputed chronology have little relevance to our subject; see, e.g., Anson 2004, 172–174. For a similar rumor about

around the camp and showed the letter to commanders and to many soldiers (probably in that order), winning numerous adherents.

Ostensibly, the courting and persuading of the army suggest the troops' power to make a general into a chief commander. In fact, the episode shows how easy it was to manipulate the soldiers and their immediate commanders. In any case, Eumenes took advantage of his renewed popularity to change the rules of the game. Up to this time, he, Peucestas, and other generals had used persuasion and positive reinforcement to garner support. Now Eumenes turned to intimidation. He targeted Sibyrtius, the satrap of Arachosia, who had three things against him: his refusal to follow Eumenes' orders, his friendship with Peucestas, and his own ambitions of high command, or so Eumenes thought. Accordingly, Eumenes brought Sibyrtius to trial on unknown charges, perhaps for treason. Eumenes also sent a cavalry unit to Arachosia to capture Sibyrtius's baggage. The satrap managed to escape, but this was only a minor setback, because Eumenes' goal was to use the army and its institutions to eliminate or scare off the opposition, especially Peucestas. Diodorus's statement that the assembly would have condemned Sibyrtius to death if he had not escaped shows that the results of the trial were predetermined and that his case was not a good example of the army's judicial discretion.[71]

Eumenes' forged letter was bound to reinforce his hold over the Silver Shields. The return of Olympias to Macedonia as Polyperchon's ally to watch over Alexander IV strengthened the ties among Eumenes, the veterans, and the regime in Macedonia, all connected through Alexander the Great. More important for the veterans was the promise of cooperation between Eumenes and Polyperchon's army. Lacking in political will, the Macedonians left power machinations largely to the generals.

Having cowed the opposition, Eumenes could afford to be lenient with Peucestas. With Antigonus's army refreshed and reinforced in Media, both commanders realized that their best chance of survival lay in cooperation, and Peucestas agreed to be Eumenes' second-in-command. Diodorus generously describes this concession as showing goodwill toward Eumenes and enthusiasm in fighting for the kings.[72] But it did not mean an end to the ri-

---

Polyperchon's defeating and capturing Cassander: Theophrastus, *Characters* 8.5.

71. Diod. 19.23.1–4; Polyaenus 4.8.3. Sibyrtius's forces were transferred to one Cephalon, but after Antigonus's victory over Eumenes, the satrap was reinstated in his post: Vezin 1907, 99; Billows 1990, 432–433n106; Bosworth 2002, 122.

72. Diod. 19.24.1, 6. After Olympias had eliminated Philip III and Eurydice in Oct.–Nov. 317, there was only one king, the minor Alexander IV: Diod. 19.11.5;

valry over leadership, and especially not to Eumenes' suspicion that others coveted it. It was also possible that the army would discover his deception and realize that no royal army had crossed to Asia. These were the circumstances surrounding a massive loan of 400 talents from fellow commanders to Eumenes. The official explanation was that he (or, in formal terms, the crown) was short of funds. The real reason, say the sources, was to enforce loyalty and prevent conspiracies and desertions by the lenders, who would now have a clear interest in sticking with Eumenes and keeping him alive.[73]

The sources' fascination with Eumenes' cleverness makes them ignore the question of why men who presumably wanted Eumenes dead would agree to loan him money and provide him with this kind of life insurance. The sources also underestimate the commanders' ambitions and other considerations that ranked above financial losses. It could be that Eumenes strong-armed the commanders into giving him the money, or that the lenders were interested not so much in his safety as in the success of a campaign fought to protect their rule as well as his.[74] It is no less likely that Eumenes and his historian, Hieronymus, saw plots even where they did not exist. They present a transaction that actually put Eumenes in other people's financial and moral debt as an ingenious scheme based on an appeal to their self-interest. In any case, the troops, who had no surplus money to give, played no part in these transactions except to soon become the beneficiaries of Eumenes' sudden enrichment.[75]

Eumenes began borrowing at the end of summer 317, after it was known that Antigonus was marching on Persis. Eumenes took the army to meet Antigonus, stopping on the second day for a mass sacrifice and costly feasting (Diod. 19.24.4–5), paid for almost certainly from the recently collected 400 talents. There was more than one reason for the halt. The army's morale needed boosting before what promised to be a decisive battle. By pre-

---

Gullath and Schober 1986, 377–378. But it is likely that the news had not yet reached Persis.

73. Diod. 19.24.1–3; Plut. *Eum.* 13.12–13; cf. 16.2, which wrongly predates the episode to Susiana.

74. For the first possibility: Bosworth 2002, 123; for the second: cf. Schäfer 2002, 146 with n73.

75. Plutarch (*Eum.* 16.2) states that Eudamus, the elephants' master, and one Phaedimus informed Eumenes later of a plot against his life in order to protect their investment. Yet the informants were unlikely to admit that losing money was their motive, and Eudamas is attested not as a lender but as a recipient of Eumenes' generosity: Diod. 19.15.5. Cf. Anson 2004, 183n114.

siding over the public sacrifice and royal-scale entertainment, Eumenes showed the troops that he was now their patron as well as their undisputed general. We can imagine that the generals whose loans helped to finance the festivities were pained to see their money squandered, and even more worried about its political impact on the army.

Eumenes himself became a casualty of the revelry when he fell ill after excessive drinking.[76] The hard-drinking Macedonians probably found his carousing charming, if not reminiscent of their dead king Alexander, but the sources say they were mostly terrified by his sickness. This was the occasion when the Silver Shields, sighting Antigonus's army in a plain, refused to march on unless Eumenes, who was being carried on a litter at a distance, came to lead them in person into battle.[77] We have discussed this episode, the elitist depiction of the troops, and the reasons behind their reaction, which were no less pragmatic than emotional, in chapter 1. The incident suggests that the Silver Shields were leaders in the army as a whole, which also stopped marching and asked for Eumenes in imitation. The veterans were self-assured enough to tell their commanders not to move or begin fighting before Eumenes showed up. One wonders if their conduct pleased their general Antigenes, who with Peucestas led the army during Eumenes' convalescence.

As in Babylon or elsewhere, the veterans articulated their sentiments through shouting and with weapons. To show that they were unwilling to advance, they grounded their arms, and to express their joy at seeing Eumenes and their readiness for battle, they saluted him in Macedonian, banged their spears against their shields, and challenged the enemy to fight (Plut. *Eum.* 14.8–11). Their enthusiasm soon subsided. Antigonus refused battle, and the veterans again faced the hunger and inaction that they knew so well. They would get their wish to meet the enemy, but more by force of circumstance than by design. The next chapter investigates the Silver Shields' conduct on the battlefield and away from it, along with the ultimate ineffectiveness of their military fame and performance.

---

76. To be sure, his guests made him do it: Diod. 19.24.5. Plutarch (*Eum.* 14.4) passes in silence over the cause of the illness.

77. Plut. *Eum.* 14.4–15.3; Diod. 19.24.5–25.1.

CHAPTER 8

THE SILVER SHIELDS IN BATTLE
AND EUMENES' DEATH

In previous chapters we have discussed the relationships between the Silver Shields and their commanders, along with the unit's role and status in the Successors' armies. Oddly, and in spite of the veterans' formidable military reputation, the ancient accounts barely refer to their performance on the battlefield after they joined Eumenes. This picture changes, however, when the sources come to describe the battles between Eumenes and Antigonus in Iran and their aftermath.

After Eumenes' recovery from his illness, he and Antigonus stood with their massive armies one day's march apart, probably somewhere around Yezd-i-Khast, south of Esfahan.[1] Each general took a defensive position and stationed his army behind a river and a ravine in expectation of an attack that never came, because of the difficult terrain. The stalemate encouraged the commanders to narrow the gap between the armies to about half a kilometer, but skirmishing was the only result. It was a dearth of supplies that ended their inaction, since such large forces could not remain immobile and be fed by plunder. (The borrowed 400 talents by Eumenes could have bought him supplies and staying power, but he had spent much of it on the politics of feasting.) After five days of impasse, Antigonus tried to defeat Eumenes by betrayal, sending envoys to Eumenes' camp and inviting the satraps and the Silver Shields to join him. He promised the governors to keep them in their posts and offered the veterans grants of land (apparently in his settlements), a return home with honors and gifts, or suitable employment in his army. Diodorus says that the assembled Macedonians refused to listen to the envoys and even threatened them (Diod. 19.25.1–4).[2]

---

1. Diod. 19.25.1–2. For the location, the topography, and Antigonus's march to this point, see Bosworth 2002, 124–129. For the size of the armies, see below.

2. Antigonus did not control Macedonia, but his promise to send veterans home meant that he would allow them to go there in peace.

Antigonus had already attempted and failed to entice the Macedonians to betray Eumenes. This time he asked them to desert rather than to kill the Cardian, and his envoys seem not to have asked Antigenes and Teutamus to change sides, although Antigonus's promise to keep the satraps in their commands must have applied to these generals too. But as in his earlier attempts at subversion, he offered to reward the Macedonians, who were free to meet his envoys and to discuss their options independently of Eumenes. Diodorus suggests that Eumenes arrived at the scene only after the Macedonians had already rejected the invitation to desert him (Diod. 19.25.4).[3]

Clearly, Antigonus courted the Macedonians because of their military skills, and because, as a rebel against the Argead throne, he needed the legitimacy that men who were intimately identified with Philip and Alexander could give him (cf. Diod. 19.41.1–2). Although his appeal suggests their power to change the course of the campaign and to choose their own supreme commander, the Silver Shields failed to realize this potential. A number of reasons may have moved them to reject his offer. There were probably men in their midst who spoke for Eumenes. His recent victory over both Antigonus on the field and Peucestas in camp, as well as his consequent cooperation with Peucestas, had helped to consolidate Eumenes' position. Previous failures to draw the Macedonians away from him, and even his illness, had also strengthened the veterans' attachment to him. And the timing of the offer was bad. The troops suffered from a lack of supplies, but they had been recently pampered by both Peucestas and Eumenes, and therefore had greater confidence in these men's ability to take care of them than in Antigonus's. Considerations of legitimacy also favored the loyalist Eumenes and the satraps over the rebel Antigonus.

Antigonus's offer of land, a return home, or service in his army showed the limited options that awaited the Macedonians if they left their general, but it is doubtful that they declined them because they did not like the choice. As Eumenes would soon tell them, Antigonus's offer could very well be an empty promise. And even if Antigonus was sincere, the veterans would have to fight for the rewards against Eumenes and Polyperchon, whom they believed was coming to help the Cardian. Finally, the record of the veterans shows that they changed sides only after losing something that already belonged to them, such as their possessions and families, rather than when they had something to gain—differing in this tendency from other deserters, who normally changed sides to improve their lot. In sum,

---

3. Indeed, Bennett and Roberts's claim (2009, 2:62) that Eumenes protected Antigonus's envoys from the Macedonians expects too much of him.

staying with Eumenes and (they hoped) defeating Antigonus struck them as the better prospect. Apparently the satraps thought so too, because not one of them deserted to Antigonus.

When Eumenes showed up in the Macedonians' assembly, he merely put the finishing touch on the decision not to desert him. According to Diodorus, he praised the veterans and told them the following parable. A lion fell in love with a maiden and asked her father for her hand. When the father expressed concern that the lion might lose its temper and kill her, the lion yanked out his own claws and teeth. The father then took a club and killed the lion. Eumenes explained that Antigonus would keep his promises until he became the master of the army, and then he would execute their leaders. The crowd approved and shouted "Right on!" (Diod. 19.25.4–7).

This story well illustrates the elitist outlook of the sources that has been a theme of this book: the leader expresses himself in a speech and the troops exclaim approval. The elite often used fables to support the existing power structure or its own supremacy. Indeed, Eumenes' tale told the rank and file that they were powerless and vulnerable without their general, and the soldiers' applause suggests their concurrence with this view. After this happy conclusion, Eumenes dismissed the assembly before the troops could change their minds.[4]

Indeed, there was a danger that the hardships of the waiting period could move some of the troops to reconsider their options. The two huge armies had exhausted their provisions, and the general who was the first to reach the well-supplied and easily defensible region of Gabene could attract hungry soldiers. Antigonus tried to steal a march on his adversary, but Eumenes learned about his move and caused him to stop midway to Gabene by misinforming him through deserters that he would come under attack. The ploy earned Eumenes' army no more than a few hours (two night watches) of quick march toward Gabene, which was three days away. When Antigonus learned Eumenes' position, he took his cavalry in hot pursuit and told Pithon to follow him with the rest of the army at a slower pace. He presented himself from afar to Eumenes, who stopped to prepare his army for battle, mistakenly thinking that Antigonus had come with his entire army. Though Diodorus compliments both generals on outwitting each other, it was Antigonus who came out on top. He prevented Eumenes from reach-

---

4. *Pace* van Dijk 1997, 283. For other versions of the tale: van Dijk 1997, 281n71. Fables and elite: Dubois 2003, 170–188, esp. 174, 183–186. Aristotle, *Politics* 3.8 (1284a10–17) cites a fable about a lion that mocks democracy and democratic decision-making by apparently referring to the participants' lack of claws and teeth; cf. Aesop, *Fables* 241.

ing Gabene ahead of him, and even if Antigonus's cavalrymen and their horses needed rest, which they got, Eumenes' army had to face battle after a hurried night march and only a light meal (Diod. 19.26.1–10).

This race for food and shelter resulted in the Battle of Paraetacene (417/6), one of the largest military encounters of ancient times, fought to decide who would rule Alexander's Asian empire. The principal source is Diodorus, who provides an unusually detailed account (likely from Hieronymus) of how the opposing armies were composed and arrayed. He is somewhat less informative, however, about the battle itself (Diod. 19.27.1–30.10; cf. Nepos *Eum.* 8.1). Our interest in the Silver Shields will lead us to focus on their place in the battle and their contribution to it.

In brief, Eumenes put his elephants and light-armed troops in the front and, like Alexander, his cavalry on his right and left wings, with the infantry at the center. Antigonus arranged his troops similarly. In the battle, cavalry fought cavalry and infantry fought infantry, fairly independently of each other. The fighting began when Pithon, on Antigonus's left, used his mounted archers to attack the elephants on Eumenes' right, inflicting much damage on the enemy. Eumenes charged back and pushed Pithon to the hills. As this was going on, the two phalanxes fought each other for a long time, with the Silver Shields defeating anyone who was in their way and, with the rest of the phalanx, routing the enemy, who fled to the hills. Their advance created a gap, which Antigonus exploited to attack and defeat Eumenes' left wing. Both generals then recalled their armies. The battle thus ended indecisively.

Assessing the Silver Shields' role in the battle is not easy. Diodorus focuses much of his description on the cavalry, both because it was led by Eumenes (his sources' prime interest) and because, from the time of Alexander, the cavalry had traditionally delivered the main blow to the enemy—a plan of battle now followed by Eumenes, as in the past. Before his meeting with the Silver Shields, he relied chiefly on his cavalry in both defeat and victory, and not because he trusted the loyalty of his infantry less. In the Battle of Orcynia in 319, which he lost to Antigonus, Eumenes had 5,000 cavalry against Antigonus's 2,000 and 20,000 infantry against Antigonus's 10,000. His infantrymen even included Macedonian veterans, who fully supported him. But Eumenes pinned his hopes on the cavalry, which deserted him during the battle.[5] He continued to rely on cav-

---

5. The Battle of Orcynia and the size of the armies: esp. Diod. 18.40.5–8 and chap. 6 above.

alry, as well as on elephants, after he had incorporated the Silver Shields into his forces, probably because Antigonus enjoyed a significant numerical advantage in infantry but less of one in cavalry. In the Battle of Paraetacene, Antigonus's phalanx numbered 28,000 and Eumenes' only 17,000 (both generals also had many light-armed foot soldiers). The gap in cavalry was less pronounced: Antigonus had 8,500 horsemen and 65 elephants against Eumenes' 6,300 horsemen and 114 elephants (see below). Diodorus says that Eumenes' right wing, which the general himself commanded, had the best of the cavalry, and that he trusted these forces the most (19.29.1). It appears, then, that Eumenes had lower expectations of his phalanx, including the Silver Shields. The planning and outcomes of his battles suggest that the Silver Shields were neither able nor expected to decide a battle on their own.

In the battle, Eumenes' phalanx soundly defeated Antigonus's phalanx. Diodorus gives credit for this result to the Silver Shields alone, saying that they were "more than 3,000 men, invincible, and, because of their excellence, spread much fear among the enemies" (19.28.1). He reports that the opposing phalanxes fought each other for a long time, with many falling on both sides, but that no one could face the Silver Shields, who excelled in daring and skill because of their long service. Even though they numbered only 3,000, they became the edge, or spearhead (*stoma*), of the entire army. In this battle, Antigonus lost 3,700 infantrymen to Eumenes' 540. The historian's accolades deserve scrutiny.[6]

At Paraetacene, Eumenes arranged the phalanx as follows. Next to his stronger right cavalry wing, which he commanded himself, he put more than 3,000 hypaspists, and next to them more than 3,000 Silver Shields. These last two units were led by Teutamus and Antigenes, probably respectively. Next to the Silver Shields, Eumenes placed an ethnically mixed force of 5,000 troops with Macedonian equipment, and he completed the phalanx's line with more than 6,000 mercenaries, who stood next to his weaker left wing, composed of cavalry.[7] Generals placed their best troops where they expected the brunt of the battle, traditionally on the right of the phalanx. This was where Eumenes' hypaspists stood, but not the Silver Shields.

---

6. Diod. 19.30.5–6. For the expression "spearhead of the army," see Hornblower 1981, 193; Bosworth 2002, 139 with n151. Losses: Diod. 19.31.5; see Bosworth (2002, 119n87, 139n152) against Billows's (1995, 92n20) questioning of their credibility.

7. Diod. 19.27.2–6. See the figure on page 217, which focuses on the infantry in this battle. Diodorus's totals of troops do not always tally with the figures he gives for individual units. I follow the latter.

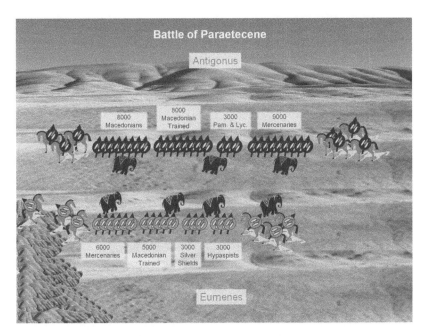

The infantry in the Battle of Paraetacene (317 BCE). Source: Diod. 19.27–32.

Eumenes' Forces

Right wing, cavalry (*from left*): 800, 900, 300, 300, 100, 200, 300 (subtotal: 2,900); 40 elephants with light-armed troops.

Center, infantry (*from left*): 6,000 mercenaries, 5,000 Macedonian-trained troops, 3,000 Silver Shields, 3,000 hypaspists (subtotal: 17,000); 40 elephants with light-armed troops.

Left wing, cavalry: 50, 50, 100, 950, 600, 600, 500, 500 (subtotal: 3,350); 45 elephants with light-armed troops.

(Diodorus's total: 35,000 infantry, 6,100 cavalry, 114 elephants.)

Totals of individual units: 125 elephants; 6,300 cavalry, 17,000 infantry (with probably 18,000 light-armed troops).

Antigonus's Forces

Right wing, cavalry (*from left*): 500, 1,000, 500, 1,000, 300, 3 servile squadrons (150?), 3 squadrons (150?), 100 (subtotal: 3,400 cavalry + 6 squadrons [300?]); 30 elephants with light-armed troops.

Center, infantry (*from left*): 9,000 mercenaries, 3,000 Lycians and Pamphylians, 8,000 Macedonian-trained troops, 8,000 Macedonians (subtotal: 28,000); most other elephants (30?).

Left wing, cavalry: 1,000, 200 (emended no.), 1,000, 1,500, 400, 1 squadron, 800 (subtotal: 4,900+); few elephants.

(Diodorus's total: 28,000 infantry, 8,500 cavalry, 65 elephants.)

Totals of individual units: 28,000 infantry; cavalry: 8,300 + 6 squadrons; elephants: 30 + unspecified number.

Eumenes here followed Alexander, who in all of his major battles positioned the hypaspists on the right of the phalanx and next to the cavalry. I agree with scholars who regard Eumenes' hypaspists as his own creation. Our information on his army up to this battle precludes the identification of most of these hypaspists with Macedonian veterans.[8]

To ascertain which of Antigonus's infantry the Silver Shields and the hypaspists faced, it is best to begin reconstructing the opposing phalanxes from the hills on Eumenes' left, which can serve as an anchor point. Eumenes arranged his left wing of 3,300 horsemen from high ground in the hills. The mercenaries, the Macedonian-equipped troops, the Silver Shields, and the hypaspists were stationed next to them, from left to right. Antigonus drew up his lines after observing Eumenes' battle order. This meant that the right end of his right wing paralleled the left corner of Eumenes' left wing and could not extend beyond it to outflank Eumenes on the right, since the hills acted as a barrier.[9] Antigonus's right wing had about 3,600 cavalry, which only slightly overlapped Eumenes' 3,300 horsemen. We can therefore assume that the opposing phalanxes, arranged next to their respective cavalry, stretched to the left from roughly parallel starting lines. As shown in the figure on p. 217, this meant that the Silver Shields faced Antigonus's 8,000 Macedonian-equipped troops, while the hypaspists faced the same troops and 3,000 Lycians and Pamphylians.[10]

This picture would not be very different even if Eumenes had thinned and stretched his infantry lines, because Antigonus advanced with his right and told the rest of his troops to form an oblique line with him (Diod. 19.29.7). This movement put the forces facing the Silver Shields and the

---

8. *Contra*: Bennett and Roberts 2009, 2:9–10. Hypaspists in Alexander's major battles: Arr. *Anab.* 1.14.2 (Granicus); 2.8.3 (Issus); 3.11.9, 13.6 (Gaugamela); 5.13.4 (Hydaspes). Eumenes' hypaspists: Tarn 1948, 2:152–153; Anson 1988, 132; Bosworth 2002, 83–84.

9. The hills were also protected by a cavalry force: Diod. 19.27.2. Cf. Diod. 19.30.4, where Eumenes' pursuit of Pithon's cavalry stops at the high ground. In the past Antigonus had successfully repelled from the hills Alcetas's charge: Diod. 18.44.2–5. Sabin's (2009, 146) denial of the existence of hills at Antigonus's rear does not agree well with Diod. 19.30.4, 7–8, 10.

10. The battle lines: Diod. 19.27.1–29.1. The hills: Diod. 19.27.3; cf. Vezin 1907, 144. Antigonus's observing Eumenes' order: Diod. 19.29.1. For other reconstructions of the battle, see Devine 1985b, 75–86, esp. 85; Schäfer 2002, 149–154, esp. 151; Bosworth 2002, 127–141; Anson 2004, 176–181; Sabin 2009, 145–148. Both Devine and Schäfer have Eumenes and Antigonus placing cavalry and elephants left off the high ground, presuming an unlikely attack by Antigonus's forces through the hills. See Bosworth 2002, 132n129.

hypaspists farther away and to the right. Richard Billows's suggestion that Eumenes compensated for his numerical inferiority by lengthening his lines with many light-armed troops between the heavy infantry units is unattractive. The only attested light-armed troops in this battle order were those placed alongside the elephants, and filling gaps between various heavy infantry units with light-armed troops would have weakened Eumenes' front considerably. Indeed, forming a close line provided protection against a numerically superior phalanx.[11]

If the above reconstruction is correct, it appears that the hypaspists occupied the most dangerous position in the phalanx, because they were exposed to an attack from Antigonus's 9,000 mercenaries and probably from the additional troops who overextended Eumenes' phalanx. This situation required that they either hold off the line or attack a much more numerous enemy, at the risk of being outflanked. It was to the hypaspists' credit that Eumenes trusted them with such an important and vulnerable position, on the principle of using better troops in (relative) proximity to the general and where the hardest fighting was expected.

The same principle seems to have informed Antigonus's line, where the Macedonians were placed on the right side of his phalanx. Brian Bosworth has argued that Antigonus deliberately avoided setting Macedonians against Macedonians, both because they might not fight each other and because they were too precious to waste. But Macedonians had fought Macedonians on previous occasions, and by all indications Paraetacene was fought as a decisive battle rather that an engagement in which to be sparing or cautious. Antigonus's dispositions, like Eumenes', were guided by the rule of putting strong units against the weaker units of the enemy. With the hypaspists at their side, it was easy for the Silver Shields to lead the attack and function as the "spearhead" of the phalanx. Yet their charge cannot have been devastating, because, by Diodorus's own account, the opposing phalanxes fought each other "for a long time" (19.30.5). In any case, Eumenes seemed to have relied on the hypaspists no less than on the Silver Shields to overcome or repulse Antigonus's phalanx. Clearly, the hypaspists'

---

11. Billows 1990, 96–97. Light-armed troops' position: Diod. 19.28.2, cf. 30.4 (joining the cavalry in pursuit). Compare Alexander's close formation against a numerically superior enemy in Gaugamela. Kahnes and Kromayer (1931, 4:391–446, 412–413) speculate that Eumenes mixed the depth of his infantry to prevent outflanking, and Sabin (2009, 147) says that Antigonus's ranks were 16 deep, while Eumenes' Silver Shields and his hypaspists were 8 deep. It would be more reassuring if the sources suggested these scenarios.

performance in this battle (along with that of Teutamus, if he led them) has not been properly recognized.[12]

Equally neglected is the contribution of Eumenes' mercenaries on his left. We do not know at exactly what point the infantry fighting began, but if Antigonus's line advanced obliquely while Eumenes' phalanx held or advanced in a straight line, the first of Eumenes' infantry to engage would have been the mercenaries, who had to fight Antigonus's Macedonians. I suspect that the reason for the silence about the hypaspists and the mercenaries is Hieronymus's focus on Eumenes and the Silver Shields. As we shall see, the accounts of the Battle of Gabene reflect the same narrow perspective.[13]

This is not to argue that the Silver Shields did not excel in fighting, but rather that the sources, and probably Hieronymus, unduly privilege their performance. There was more than one reason for this preferential treatment. The Silver Shields symbolized the glorious Macedonian past of uninterrupted victory and conquest. They were highly vociferous in demanding attention to their wishes, reputation, and special status in camp. They also stood for the Macedonian authority and legitimacy so important to their employer. Lastly, the sources show practically no interest in troops that were not Macedonian. Asian troops and mercenaries stood low in the social and military hierarchy of the coalition army, and I suspect that the historian and his readers cared little about their accomplishments.

Soon, however, the Silver Shields and the non-Macedonian troops were to unite in a protest against Eumenes. Following the inconclusive battle, the opposing armies reorganized and marched in parallel lines at a distance of about 120 meters in an apparent attempt to outflank each other or to force the enemy to open a gap in its lines.[14] By midnight, after marching for several hours, the armies had gone nearly five kilometers from the battlefield. The soldiers had had enough; tired and hungry, they let their generals know that they wanted to go back to their camps. Realizing that

---

12. Bosworth 2002, 134. In private correspondence Bosworth has modified his reconstruction of the battle, tentatively placing the Silver Shields against Antigonus's Lycians, Pamphylians, and mercenaries. My reconstruction would place the Silver Shields against Antigonus's Macedonian-style troops. Macedonians fought Macedonians in Babylon in 323, as well as in Antigonus's campaigns against the Perdiccans in 320–319.

13. The elephants' contribution might have been underestimated as well. For their conjectural role: Kahnes and Kromayer 1931, 4:418 with n1, but also Bosworth 2002, 138–139.

14. Diod. 19.31.1–2. Attempt at outflanking: Bosworth 2002, 140, although such a plan would have exposed Eumenes' rear to attack from Antigonus's larger army.

there was not going to be a second battle, each of the two generals moved to claim victory in order to score points both at home and abroad. In truth, Eumenes won the battle, inflicting many more losses on the enemy and later taking the prize of Gabene while Antigonus went back to Media.[15] But since Antigonus won on his wing, and Eumenes had to recall his army from its pursuit, the Cardian's victory was flawed.

To settle the point, the two generals competed for possession of the battlefield and the privilege of burying the dead, which constituted a claim to victory. Antigonus won that race because Eumenes' army refused to return to the battlefield and shouted that they wanted to go to their baggage. The biased depiction of the troops' insubordination and their good reasons for it have been discussed in a previous chapter.[16] Although Diodorus does not single out the veterans from the other protesting soldiers, theirs was likely a leading voice. Their attachment to their baggage and families went back to Alexander, and their status in camp and performance in the battle added authority to their demands. Diodorus asserts that Eumenes gave up because he could not discipline the soldiers in view of the threat to his leadership from competing generals (19.31.2–4). But the sources suggest that this threat had diminished significantly since Persepolis, and in the Battle of Paraetacene Eumenes had enjoyed the satraps' full cooperation. The truth was that Eumenes failed to assess his troops' condition correctly, while his reluctance to antagonize them made him the first attested Successor who was forced by his soldiers to abort a mission. Probably encouraged by the success of their indiscipline, the troops would soon disobey Eumenes again when he asked them to camp around him in Gabene.

Antigonus, in contrast, marched unopposed to the battlefield, buried his dead, and declared himself the victor—a claim publicly acknowledged by Eumenes' dispatch of an envoy with a request to bury *his* dead. Yet Antigonus's army needed to recover too, and he took it to an unplundered region in Media. The sources report that he concealed from Eumenes' envoy either his hasty retreat by night or the number of his fallen soldiers.[17] Along with illustrating Antigonus's cunning, the story suggests that Eumenes was the true victor, though he knew better than to pursue Antigonus with his mal-

---

15. Nepos *Eum.* 8.1. Losses: see above. Antigonus's retreat and loss of Gabene: Diod. 19.34.7; Polyaenus 4.6.11, cf. 4.6.10; Vezin 1907, 110. It is equally likely, however, that Antigonus gave up on Gabene, because he could get both supplies and troops from friendly Media: Diod. 19.32.2, 40.1.

16. Chap. 1 above.

17. Respectively, Diod. 19.32.1–2 and Polyaenus 4.6.10.

nourished and agitated army. Instead Eumenes took the battleground unopposed and declared victory by giving the dead a magnificent burial. If the interpretation offered elsewhere in this book is correct, the sources use this occasion to criticize the soldiers' refusal to bury the dead in the first place.[18] The troops, however, took full part in the rituals. Before the dead Indian general Ceteus and his living widow went up in flames on his funeral pyre, the entire army marched in arms around it three times. It was an impressive spectacle, although some soldiers must have chafed at having to wait their turn in an army of about 36,000 infantry, 6,000 cavalry, and more than 100 elephants.[19]

Eumenes' army went from the battlefield to winter in Gabene, where the bountiful province was a great improvement over the difficult terrain and lack of food at Paraetacene (317). Eumenes would have preferred the troops to stay in and around his headquarters, where he could muster them quickly when needed. But the soldiers, including the Macedonians, disobeyed both him and his lieutenants Antigenes and Teutamus, dispersing over a distance of about 185 km in search of provisions and shelter. The sources, who reflect the high command's perspective, harshly criticize their conduct, but how else could so many soldiers have found food and accommodations? Moreover, when Eumenes called them back to fight against Antigonus, they all showed up on time.[20]

Sometime during the winter, Antigonus led his army over a desert road in an attempt to capture Eumenes unprepared. Eumenes was warned of the march and sent men to light fires on high ground, fooling Antigonus into believing that Eumenes was waiting for him with an army. Antigonus changed direction toward more hospitable terrain, giving Eumenes time to muster his troops. Antigonus also failed to intercept Eumenes' elephants after Eumenes sent cavalry and light-armed troops to their rescue. The Silver Shields seem to have played no part in these events; at most, they could have helped Eumenes in tricking Antigonus with the bonfires.[21]

Despite its failure, Antigonus's surprise march gave Hieronymus an opportunity to malign Peucestas once again. We hear that when the satrap heard of Antigonus's approach, he panicked and wanted to flee to a faraway place, where he could wait for the coalition army to assemble. Only

---

18. Diod. 19.32.3–34.7; chap. 1 above.
19. Apparently the army's circling of the pyre was a Greek modification of the Indian practice, by which only the widow performed this ritual: Szczurek 2009, 128.
20. Nepos *Eum.* 8.1–4; Plut. *Eum.* 15.4; chap. 1 above.
21. Diod. 19.37.1–39.6; Plut. *Eum.* 15.4–13; Polyaenus 4.6.11, 8.4.

Eumenes' promise that he would be able to stall Antigonus convinced Peucestas to stay where he was. This portrayal of the satrap is unfair, at the least. The sources suggest that many other generals shared Peucestas's concern, and there was nothing wrong in regrouping at a remoter place and giving the coalition force more time. Moreover, both here and on the Pasitigris River, where Peucestas fulfilled Eumenes' request for many archers, his actions belied his alleged intentions or character. The satrap went nowhere, staying with Eumenes to fight Antigonus.[22]

Plutarch provides exclusive information on a plot against Eumenes on the eve of the Battle of Gabene (Plut. *Eum.* 16.1–6). He reports that when the army assembled, the troops admired Eumenes' intelligence and urged him to command them alone. This evoked the envy of Antigenes and Teutamus, the Silver Shields' commanders, who called many of their fellow generals together and plotted to kill Eumenes after using him in battle. Eumenes learned of the plot from Eudamus, the elephants' master, and a certain Phaedimus, both of whom did not want to lose the money they had loaned him (cf. Plut. *Eum.* 13.12–13). The Cardian told his friends that he was surrounded by animals, wrote his will, destroyed sensitive documents, and, after contemplating his options, prepared the army for battle.

The story has several problems, including Eumenes' resignation in face of the conspiracy. The general showed in Persis that he knew how to deal with Sibyrtius and Peucestas, whom he considered rivals, but here he did nothing to punish, deter, or break up the alliance against himself, even though his life was said to be in danger. In addition, the record of Teutamus and Antigenes shows that the latter, at least, was consistently loyal to Eumenes. And if Eumenes were to win the upcoming battle against Antigonus, as his recent successes against Antigonus suggested he would, how could the conspirators explain to the army the killing of their victorious general? Similar questions and others have led scholars to reject the story altogether or to accept only its gist.[23]

While the historicity of the plot is open to doubt, there is nothing implausible in Eumenes' surge of popularity among the soldiers, or in its up-

---

22. Peucestas's fear: Diod. 19.38.1–2; Plut. *Eum.* 15.7–9; Nepos *Eum.* 9.2; cf. Bosworth 2002, 145. Peucestas also was the man who informed Eumenes of Antigonus's approach: Polyaenus 4.8.4; Plut. *Eum.* 15.7–8; cf. Diod. 19.37.6–38.1.

23. Rejection or postdating the plot to after the battle: Schäfer 2002, 158. Accepting its gist or elements of it: Heckel 1992, 314; Bosworth 1992, 68–70; 2002, 143n160; Anson 2004, 185–186 with n132. See also chap. 7, note 75 above, for doubts concerning the informants.

setting effect on other commanders. The troops liked a winning general such as Eumenes, who had proved himself, both on his wing in Paraetacene and more recently in preventing Antigonus's surprise attack and in rescuing Eudamus's elephant unit. Their request that Eumenes lead them alone evinced their wish to fight in a united rather than a coalition army and to answer directly to him instead of to their generals. It is likely that the Silver Shields clamored for Eumenes with the rest of the troops, for they had already shown that they wanted only the ailing Eumenes to lead them in battle. It is significant that the commanders of the army column at that time were Peucestas and Antigenes, who can hardly have been pleased to hear that the Macedonians lacked confidence in their leadership (Plut. *Eum.* 14.7–11; Diod. 19.24.6). Over the winter in Gabene the veterans had refused to camp next to Eumenes, disobeying orders both from Eumenes and from their direct commanders (Nepos *Eum.* 8.2; Plut. *Eum.* 15.4). Therefore Antigenes and Teutamus had reasons to worry that they were losing their grip on the veterans. At the same time, no display of enthusiasm for a successful general was sufficient to overcome the army's internal division, and Eumenes knew better than to undermine the generals' command and loyalty on the eve of the battle. Thus we find Antigenes commanding the Silver Shields in Gabene as he had done in the past (Diod. 19.41.1).

Following his source, or abbreviating it eclectically, Diodorus gives a less-detailed account of the battle lines at Gabene than of those at Paraetacene. He does show, however, that Eumenes and Antigonus did not change their basic setup of putting the infantry at the center, the cavalry on the flanks, and the elephants and light-armed troops in the front. The generals also did not change their plan of deciding the battle with the cavalry, aided by the elephants. The differences between the battles lie in the size of the opposing armies and in Eumenes' decision to move with the strongest part of his army from right to left. Thus, at Gabene, Antigonus's infantry had been reduced from 28,000 to 22,000 men, while Eumenes presumably retained his phalanx of 17,000 men and even increased his light-armed force by about 1,700 men to a total of 36,700. In cavalry, Antigonus augmented his force from 8,500 to 9,000, while Eumenes had 300 horsemen less than at Paraetacene, bringing his total to 6,000. The number of their elephants remained unchanged: 65 for Antigonus and 114 for Eumenes.

Not surprisingly, Antigonus intended to win the battle with his numerically superior cavalry and with his elephants. Eumenes too pinned his hopes for victory on his cavalry and elephants, though at Paraetacene his phalanx had won a convincing victory over the enemy phalanx, while his cavalry's record was mixed. In that earlier battle, Eumenes won with his cavalry on the right against Pithon, but Eudamus (who had to give some of his cavalry to Eumenes) fled Antigonus's charge on the left, and the contribution of Eumenes' elephants was negligible. Nevertheless, Eumenes did not change his tactics at Gabene, but continued to rely on both his cavalry and elephants, even though the size of the opposing phalanxes was more balanced in his favor, and though he had the best infantry unit in the Macedonian world. He also did not lead the Silver Shields in person, but left the task to their commanders. Despite the Silver Shields' excellence and their celebrity in the sources, neither they nor the entire phalanx were believed capable of deciding the battle.[24]

Eumenes' arrangement of the phalanx is also informative. At Paraetacene he led the right wing against Antigonus's weaker left, but at Gabene he strengthened the cavalry on the left wing, which he commanded, in order to meet Antigonus and Demetrius's best cavalry on their right wing.[25] Eumenes' movement from right to left was followed by the hypaspists, who were now stationed next to his cavalry and formed the left end of the phalanx. Next to them stood the Silver Shields, then the mercenaries, and finally the Macedonian-trained troops, who stood beside the cavalry on the right wing (Diod. 19.40.2–4). Once again, the hypaspists, but not the Silver Shields, were placed where the hardest fighting was expected. Yet they are completely ignored in the accounts of the infantry battle, which concentrate entirely on the Silver Shields.

The veterans are (re)introduced to the reader even before the fighting starts. Diodorus says that as the troops were standing in battle formation, Antigenes sent to Antigonus's Macedonian phalanx a Macedonian horse-

---

24. The Battle of Gabene: Diod. 19.40.1–43.9; Plut. *Eum.* 16.6–10; Polyaenus 4.6.13. Still valuable is Kahnes and Koromayer 1931, 4: esp. 426–432 (391–446), and see also Devine 1985a; Bosworth 2002, 127–129, 142–157; Schäfer 2002, 155–164; Anson 2004, 184–188; Bennett and Roberts 2009, 2:76–88. The figures for Eumenes' cavalry in Paraetacene represent the sum of Diodorus's individual units. The total of Antigonus's cavalry replicates Diodorus's totals, for which see Bosworth 2002, 134n135. It is likely that Antigonus had additional light-armed troops in both battles, but their number is unknown.

25. Bosworth (2002, 143, 148–151) thinks that political considerations guided Eumenes' order of battle at both Paraetacene and Gabene. He argues that in Gabene, Eumenes moved the satraps to his wing after separating them from the bulk of their forces, because he distrusted their loyalty and wanted to supervise their movements. Diodorus (19.40.2–4), however, suggests that the division of the satraps' forces between the stronger left wing and the weaker right was done on the basis of their quality. Eumenes' considerations were chiefly military, because the satraps normally led their best units, which Eumenes placed in his wing: Diod. 19.40.2.

man to abuse and rebuke them for going against their fathers, who had conquered the world under Philip and Alexander. The messenger added that they would soon see how worthy the veterans were of the kings and of their previous battles. Diodorus then digresses to describe the Silver Shields' advanced age and celebrated skill and experience in battle. Plutarch's similar combination of the story with a digression on the Silver Shields suggests that both accounts derive from Hieronymus, who participated in this battle.[26] Perhaps Antigenes remembered how the older veterans persuaded Perdiccas's men to desist fighting over Alexander's body in Babylon (Curt. 10.7.18; chap. 3 above). Alternatively, he may have gotten the idea of communicating with Antigonus's Macedonians from Eumenes, who after his victory over Craterus in Asia Minor had sent a Macedonian-speaking man to dissuade Craterus's Macedonians from opposing him (*PSI* 12: 1248). The Macedonian horseman at Gabene cited collective martial pride, like Eumenes' envoy, but claimed it exclusively for his side. He also proclaimed the legitimacy of fighting for the kings and raised the specter of a Macedonian civil war against Antigonus's Macedonians.

For a moment it looked as if the shaming salvo had worked: Antigonus's Macedonians, who seemed for the most part to be of a younger generation than the veterans, expressed their annoyance at having to fight their kin and elders, while the troops around Eumenes cheered him on and urged him to quickly lead them into battle, which he did (Diod. 19.41.2–3). In actuality, the moment did little but add drama to the scene. Antigonus's Macedonians, annoyed as they may have been with fighting "their fathers," nevertheless followed him to battle, while the Macedonian horseman and his fellow cheerleaders were already eager to fight, even against their figurative sons. For obvious reasons, the messenger did not mention Eumenes' Greek origin, but neither did the opposition, because his ethnicity mattered much less to the troops than to their generals. In the end, both sides let reality rather than slogans dictate their moves. Because the sources do not say how Antigonus positioned his infantry units, it is unknown if the opposing Macedonians actually fought each other. If he replicated his order of battle at Paraetacene, as is commonly assumed, his Macedonians could have faced Eumenes' hypaspists and the Silver Shields.

---

26. Plut. *Eum.* 16.6–8; Diod. 19.41.1–3. Diodorus describes the messenger as a member of the Macedonian cavalry. It is conceivable that he was a veteran cavalryman, and perhaps from Antigenes' cavalry *agēma*: Diod. 19.28.3. However, Plutarch's attribution of the rebuke of Antigonus's Macedonians to the Silver Shields, and the possibility that the herald used the horse only as a vehicle and podium, make it no less probable that he was a veteran infantryman.

As at Paraetacene, each group—cavalry, infantry, and elephants—fought its counterpart. Eumenes hoped to win the battle with his strengthened cavalry on the left, and told his right wing under the veteran commander Philip to hold the line.[27] But Eumenes was defeated by the superior generalship, cavalry, and luck of Antigonus. The armies fought on a salty, arid plain, and the movements of men and beasts raised a cloud of dust that Antigonus used to conceal a cavalry unit sent to seize the baggage of Eumenes' army, a little less than a kilometer away. The captured baggage would later induce the Silver Shields to go over to Antigonus's side and thus end Eumenes' campaign, but here Antigonus was more lucky than wise: most sources suggest that he realized this value of the booty only when the veterans approached him with a request to recover their baggage.[28]

What decided the battle, however, was the defeat of Eumenes' wing by Antigonus and Demetrius's elephants and superior cavalry, and their effective use of the dust to screen their attack. It is hardly surprising that the sources blame Peucestas for the result. Peucestas's behavior in Gabene fits his biased portrait elsewhere as a mirror image of Eumenes, who fought honorably, nobly, and loyally for the kings when engaging Antigonus with his cavalry, but whose zeal (*prothymia*) was overcome by numbers. Peucestas, in contrast, panicked on seeing the attack of Antigonus's many cavalrymen and retreated with his cavalry and 1,500 other horsemen. It is difficult to assess exactly why Peucestas retreated and if his action was indeed solely responsible for the collapse of his wing. Antigonus may have aimed his punch where Peucestas stood with others, causing them to give up because of their numerical inferiority.[29] When Antigonus's elephants defeated those of Eumenes, the latter general rode to his right wing in the hope of employing both his (weaker) forces there and the cavalry around Peucestas for a second round. But Peucestas withdrew even farther, to a river, and Eumenes, who was running out of options and daylight, had to join him and the other satraps (Diod. 19.42.5–7, 43.2–3).

These events affected the Silver Shields only later. Diodorus is more ex-

---

27. For Philip, see Hornblower 1981, 123–134; Billows 1990, 422. Eumenes' battle plan: cf. Sabin 2009, 150. I cannot concur with Sabin's stepped arrangement of the opposing units, both here and at Paraetacene, in his figs. 23–24.

28. Plut. *Eum.* 16.9–17.1; Polyaenus 4.8.13; Just. 14.3.3–11, and below. Diodorus (19.42.2), however, ascribes to Antigonus the (false) hope that the capture of the baggage would produce an effortless victory (reading *akonēti* as the more common *akoniti*).

29. Peucestas at Gabene: Diod. 19.42.4, 43.2–3; Plut. *Eum.* 16.9; cf. Just. 14.3.2. Bosworth (2002, 15) suggests that Peucestas and others satraps preplanned their withdrawal in order to leave Eumenes unassisted. It seems from our sources that not even the hostile Hieronymus made such a claim.

pansive about this unit at Gabene than at Paraetacene, partly because its
role at Gabene better deserved such attention, and partly to give credibility to Eumenes' subsequent assertion that their victory justified renewing the battle against Antigonus. Much of Diodorus's description of their
fighting is an extended compliment, relating how the Silver Shields closed
their ranks and charged the enemy, proving so far superior to their adversaries that they killed 5,000 enemy troops and defeated a 22,000 man–
strong phalanx all by themselves, without losing a man.[30] Antigonus's phalanx, depleted after Paraetacene, may have included unskilled troops, and
the whole unit's morale must have been affected by its defeat and the Silver Shields' performance in that earlier battle. Yet for 3,000 troops to defeat seven times their number, including 8,000 Macedonians, was a feat
that even the Silver Shields could not have accomplished on their own. Evidently the historian and his source ignored the contribution of other infantry units. It is worth reiterating that the Silver Shields' spectacular victory
had no impact on the final outcome of the battle.[31]

These reservations should not detract from the Silver Shields' excellence,
which they showed even in retreat. Their flanks and rear were exposed to
enemy attacks by their advance, by Eumenes' defeat on the left, and by the
apparent lack of action on his right wing. Antigonus accordingly ordered
Pithon to lead a cavalry force to attack them. The Silver Shields formed a
square, a common Macedonian formation whose effectiveness is illustrated
by a similar deployment of the Macedonian phalanx in the Battle of Magnesia between the Seleucid and the Roman armies (190). There the phalanx
formed a tight square bristling with sarissas and feigned charges against
the attacks of Roman light cavalry, who threw javelins and shot arrows at
them from a safe distance. When forced to retreat, these latter Macedonians moved back in good order, breaking into disorderly flight only when
the elephants they protected became unruly (Livy 37.40–43). It is to the Silver Shields' credit that they accomplished their retreat without losing their
order, and even more so if, as is likely, their square protected cavalry, light-
armed troops, and maybe even elephants.

---

30. Diod. 19.43.1; cf. Plut. *Eum.* 16.8; Polyaenus 4.6.13; Just. 14.3.5.

31. See also Bosworth 2002, 154 with nn199, 200. Diodorus's description of the Silver Shields' fighting, poor in substance though it is, has not discouraged questionable reconstructions of the phalanx's movement: e.g., Devine 1985b, 92. It would not
be beyond Hieronymus to exaggerate the Silver Shields' prowess in order to show that
Eumenes' later call for a second engagement with Antigonus could have resulted in victory had they not rejected it.

Some veterans may even have cheered up when they saw Pithon approaching. After disobeying him in the campaign against the Greek rebels, opposing his guardianship at Triparadeisus, and rejecting his invitation to desert to him in Babylonia, they now recognized an opportunity to humiliate him again. Apparently unharmed, the veterans retreated all the way to the river where Peucestas and other generals had regrouped. Diodorus says that they blamed Peucestas for the cavalry defeat (Diod. 19.43.4–5), a charge which, coming from such brave warriors, added weight to his culpability. Yet defeats naturally provoke recriminations, and it is hard to believe that Peucestas was singled out for them in this case. Justin's admittedly problematical account actually names Eumenes as responsible for the defeat (14.3.3–9). But by any reckoning, the Silver Shields had earned the right to be upset. They had excelled in battle and routed the enemy, but their reward was the loss of everything dear to them. It was also the second battle in a row in which they won a victory only to see it made hollow by others. It is no wonder that they rejected Eumenes' request to renew the fighting.

Eumenes tried to resume the battle twice, the first time after riding with his remaining cavalry to take command of his right wing and hearing about the loss of his baggage. He resolved to reengage Antigonus's cavalry in the hope of retrieving the baggage and perhaps of capturing Antigonus's baggage too. For this task he needed the cavalry of the satraps, who had withdrawn to a place not far from the battleground. Diodorus suggests that Eumenes went there and tried to convince Peucestas and the other commanders, and possibly their cavalry, to join the battle, but Peucestas would not listen to Eumenes and retreated even farther, to a river (19.43.2–3). This made Peucestas responsible for spoiling the prospect that Eumenes might change the fate of the campaign and his own. In fact, the satrap's and the other commanders' retreat suggests that they shared with the Silver Shields (who arrived later on the scene) a dim view of Eumenes' chances. It was also hard for him to make a strong case for victory when they could see Antigonus and apparently the better part of his cavalry just waiting for them to make a move (Diod. 19.43.3–4).

When all his forces had regrouped after the battle, Eumenes spoke once again in favor of renewing the fighting. Diodorus says that while the satraps favored a hurried retreat to their upper satrapies, Eumenes urged them to fight again, claiming that the enemy phalanx was destroyed and the two opposing cavalry forces were well matched. By emphasizing the phalanx's victory and misrepresenting the opposing cavalry forces as equal, Eumenes seems to have aimed his persuasion especially at the Silver Shields, who had won their share of the battle but were not well informed about the enemy cavalry. The Macedonians, however, refused to entertain any of these options, because they were concerned about their lost baggage (Diod. 19.43.5–7).

Justin's account of the meeting is more detailed than Diodorus's, but it too presents difficulties. According to the epitomator, Eumenes highlighted the superior valor of his army and promised that the enemy would sue for peace once the fighting resumed. He also belittled the loss of the baggage, saying that it consisted of a mere 2,000 women and a few children and slaves, who could more easily be recovered by fighting than by forfeiting victory. This contemptuous downplaying of the Silver Shields' losses made rhetorical sense, but Eumenes was too smart to be so tactless. The Silver Shields' response in Justin is only slightly more credible: they said they would not fight or leave without their families, but then lamented that they had been on the brink of retiring home with their spoils to live in peace when Eumenes came (to Cilicia) to deceive them with empty promises into following him to a ceaseless war. Because of Eumenes, they had suffered defeat and losses, and would now have to spend their remaining years in poverty (Just. 14.3.1–10).

Justin's rendering of the Silver Shields' reaction bespeaks a drastic abbreviation of his source and a wish to introduce pathos into the scene. He tells about the Battle of Gabene and its aftermath immediately after describing Eumenes' first meeting with the Silver Shields in Cilicia, leaving out what happened in between. This sequence leads him to create causal and thematic links between the two episodes, e.g., by stating that the veterans had lost their glory, which a few lines earlier (14.2.9–10, 3.3) Eumenes had praised in Cilicia. The "veterans" themselves keep referring back to Eumenes' tempting them to follow him on that occasion. Moreover, in order to make the Silver Shields' complaints bitter and heart wrenching, Justin incorporates incorrect information into them: that they were about to be discharged in Cilicia, that they were "on the threshold of their fatherland," and that Eumenes made them promises that even Justin fails to record. The soldiers' alleged longing for Macedonia is not mentioned in other sources, and for a reason. Apart from the troops that returned with Antipater, the veterans went anywhere but home before or after serving Eumenes and even Antigonus.[32] Such misinformation does not make Justin's account wholly worthless. It includes details corroborated by other sources and it certainly captures the spirit of the moment. It is likely that the veterans did indeed blame Eumenes for their misfortune. Yet it is a pity that

---

32. *Pace* Briant 1973a, 65–66 (repr. 1982, 77–78).

when the troops, to whom the sources rarely allow more than a few words, are finally allowed to speak at length, their speech is essentially a literary construct.[33]

The sources' descriptions of subsequent events are dominated by the theme of the Silver Shields' ugly betrayal of Eumenes. The accounts differ in detail, but the following summary will perhaps not be controversial. The Macedonians, we are told, rejected both the satraps' suggestion of a retreat to their upper satrapies and Eumenes' exhortation to renew the fighting. Headed by their commander, Teutamus, they sent envoys to Antigonus, who agreed to restore their baggage if they delivered Eumenes to him. Plutarch and Justin report that before he was led in shackles to Antigonus, Eumenes made a speech to the Silver Shields in which he chastised them for shamefully surrendering their general, for violating their oaths of loyalty to him, and for conceding defeat. He then asked them to allow him to kill himself. The Macedonians refused this request, hurled abuse and countercharges at him (according to Plutarch), and took him to Antigonus, who put him under arrest.

Antigonus first had some of Eumenes' cohorts executed, ordering Antigenes to be burned alive in a pit, and then, after consultations, had Eumenes killed as well. The Silver Shields got back their baggage and joined Antigonus's army. Later Antigonus sent many of them to serve with Sibyrtius, the satrap of Arachosia, and on various garrison duties. According to Diodorus, he even instructed Sibyrtius to get rid of them. Both Diodorus and other sources treat their new assignments as divine retribution for their betrayal of Eumenes.[34]

I have omitted from this synopsis the many dramatic devices used by the sources to highlight the despicable treachery of the Silver Shields.[35] This attitude dominates the ancient accounts and consequently much of the modern scholarship, illustrating the elitist approach to history discussed in this book.

Let us try to examine what happened from the Silver Shields' point of

---

33. Plutarch (*Eum.* 18.2) too has the Silver Shields complaining that Eumenes lost them their wages in old age, but he cites the complaint in justification of their betrayal of Eumenes, dating it to that later event; cf. Vezin 1907, 123n4.

34. Diod. 19.43.1–44.3; Plut. *Eum.* 17.1–19.3; Nepos *Eum.* 10.1–12.4; Just. 3.1–4.21; Polyaenus 4.6.13. The Silver Shields' later assignment: Diod. 19.48.3–4; Plut. *Eum.* 19.3; Polyaenus 4.6.15; cf. Just. 14.4.14; and see chap. 1 above.

35. Esp. Plut. *Eum.* 17.1–18.2; Nepos *Eum.* 10.2, 11.5, 13.1; Just. 3.11, 14.4.1–16, and see also Diod. 19.43.8–9, 48.4; *Heidelberg Epitome* 3. Plutarch, however, also criticizes Eumenes for not dying nobly: *Eumenes and Sertorius* 2.4; cf. 18.7–9; Nepos *Eum.* 11.3–5; Bosworth 1992, 60–61.

view. Although they had won a great victory over the enemy phalanx, the loss of everything that was dear to them—their savings, their loved ones, and their other noncombatant dependents—marginalized for them any other considerations, such as the future of the Macedonian empire or of their general. The satraps proposed retreating east, which meant leaving the baggage train behind in Antigonus's hands. Eumenes' call to fight Antigonus again was motivated by his own desperate need for victory, on which his leadership depended, rather than by the troops' plight or interest. The history of the Macedonian veterans shows a close relationship between their loyalty and discipline on the one hand and the winning record of their general on the other. It also shows that pitched battles were decided not by the phalanx, however excellent, but by the cavalry—and it looked unlikely that Eumenes would be able to call on the satraps' cavalry in a new battle. Even if he could, the veterans were well aware that he had lost the Battle of Gabene with the cavalry's support. In any case, Eumenes' fate probably ran a distant second in the Silver Shields' minds (if they even considered it) to their concern about their baggage. It is our sources, rather than his soldiers, who focus on him.[36]

Polyaenus writes that the Silver Shields offered Antigonus their services in return for their baggage.[37] In our sources, whenever troops act in their own interests rather than those of their generals, they are called mutinous, undisciplined, or (as in this case) treacherous. The Macedonian veterans often depended on their leaders for initiative or communication with outsiders, but Antigenes was not involved in the negotiations. His horrible later fate suggests a strong enmity with Antigonus (perhaps because he had frustrated Antigonus's earlier attempt in Cilicia to draw the Silver Shields away from Eumenes), and he apparently sided either with Eumenes or the satraps in the debate over the future of the campaign. Teutamus, however, sent envoys to Antigonus to discuss the baggage, showing that he was more attentive to the soldiers' concerns than was Antigenes, who has generally enjoyed better press among both ancients and moderns.[38] Eumenes probably

36. For the Silver Shields' losses cf. Launey 1949–1950, 785–790; Billows 1990, 102n26; Anson 2004, 253–255. The troops' loyalty and winning record: see the preceding narrative and cf. Briant 1982, 53–61. Troops, baggage, and loyalty: see chap. 6 above.

37. Polyaenus 4.6.13, and see also Diod. 19.43.8; Plut. *Eum.* 17.1–2.

38. Antigenes' foiling Antigonus's attempt: Diod. 18.62.4–7. The veterans' general reliance on their commanders for communication makes Plutarch's version (*Eum.* 17.1) naming Teutamus as the negotiator preferable to Justin's claim (14.3.11) that they contacted Antigonus without their commanders' knowledge. Teutamus's image: Diod.

protested his surrender, and some Silver Shields, troubled in conscience and wishing to curry favor with Antigonus, may have responded with counter-charges. The rest of them were glad to get their property and families back, as well as to have a new employer.

But this is hardly how the sources see things. Plutarch and Justin al-low the shackled Eumenes to take the high ground, topographically and morally, and to denounce the Silver Shields for breaking their oath of loy-alty to him.[39] In Justin's version, Eumenes even reminds them that they had taken the oath three times during "this year," and Nepos too mentions their triple oath (Just. 14.4.3; Nepos *Eum.* 10.2). Justin's epitomizing makes his chronological references uncertain, but if the oaths were taken within a year from Gabene (winter of 317), and not since the Silver Shields made a pact with him (spring of 318), likely occasions would be after Eumenes' prevailing over Peucestas in their contest over leadership, after Antigonus's last attempt to draw the Silver Shields away from Eumenes, and (in an at-tempt to ensure their return) before the dispersal of the troops to their win-ter quarters in Gabene.

More telling, however, is Eumenes' citing of repeated oaths. The ev-idence for the period shows that troops normally took an oath to make common cause with a *new* king or general, at the time when such a leader assumed authority over them. Eumenes, however, was unique in renewing the troops' vow more than once, revealing his shaky hold on leadership.[40] Our pro-Eumenes sources gloss over this insecurity. For them, the troops who broke their word and abandoned Eumenes should have been ashamed of caring more about their possessions and safety than about honor and victory—that is, about their general's ambitions and career.

18.62.5; Vezin 1907, 122 ("the worst agitator"); Bosworth 1992, 70; Heckel 1992, 315–316; Schäfer 2002, 125; cf. Hadley 2001, 14.

39. Plut. *Eum.* 17.5–18.1; Just. 14.4.1–14; cf. Diod. 19.43.9. Bosworth (1992a, 63–64) identifies a common source behind Eumenes' speeches in Plutarch and Justin; cf. Simpson 1959, 375.

40. Making an oath to a new leader or king: e.g., Curt. 10.7.9 (the army to Alexan-der's heirs); Plut. *Eum.* 12.1–7 (Eumenes to Antigonus and the kings, although histor-ically questionable); Plut. *Eum.* 5.5 (Neoptolemus's troops to Eumenes); Diod. 18.32.4 (Craterus's veterans to Eumenes); Just. 13.2.14 (the generals to the new guardians in Babylon); *OGIS* 266, 17–23 (mercenaries to Eumenes I of Pergamum, mid–third cen-tury); cf. Plb. 15.25.11; Just. 14.1.10. The evidence, especially Curt. 7.1.29, fails to support Briant's view that the oath signaled a transition from a national army to a personal, mercenary-like army: Briant 1973a, 59–61, 80 (repr. 1982, 71–73, 92). See also Ham-mond 2000, 148.

What is puzzling about the Macedonian veterans is not that they chose baggage over honor, but that the sources (and probably Hieronymus) present them in a somewhat paradoxical manner. On the one hand, they privilege the veterans' story and accomplishments and praise them as the embodiment of military excellence. They also portray them as men who loved, admired, and needed Eumenes. On the other hand, they depict them as perfidious and self-centered for sacrificing their commander to his enemy. What can explain the contradiction?

One answer is to assume that Hieronymus was a straightforward historian who praised or condemned people as they deserved. Yet his consistently favorable depiction of Eumenes and his very hostile portrayal of Peucestas sufficiently suggest that Hieronymus was no stranger to bias and even distortion.[41] I believe that his elitist attitudes may account for his inconsistent portrayal of the Silver Shields. For him, what counts are the ambitions and actions of great generals and kings. Within this framework, the Silver Shields have one major role that justifies his praises and bestowal of a privileged status: to fight for their general and to serve his needs. As long as they fulfill this function, they deserve accolades and exclusive credit for the victories of Alexander or of Eumenes' phalanx. But when they look out for themselves rather than their commander, they become petty-minded, selfish, and even cowardly men who trade victory and glory for baggage.

To what extent were the Macedonians really responsible for Eumenes' fate? In the first place, they were not the only ones who lost their baggage and wanted it back. Nowhere is it said that Antigonus captured only the Macedonian baggage. According to Polyaenus (4.6.13), Antigonus's proclamation that he would restore the soldiers' possessions for free affected both the Macedonians and the satrap Peucestas with his 10,000 Persians. This is not to deny that the Silver Shields led the movement over to Antigonus's camp. After all, their possessions had been accumulated since Alexander's campaign, while other troops had less baggage or no families at all. Yet it is clear that they did not have to force their views on the others. Eumenes' arrest seems to have triggered no protest beyond his own.

The sources also indicate that not all the Macedonians were of one mind on this issue. According to Justin, Eumenes tried to shame the Macedonians into fighting Antigonus again by defining their loss as consisting "merely" of 2,000 women and a few children and slaves (14.3.6). If Eumenes' count

---

41. For Eumenes, Peucestas, and Hieronymus, see, besides this book, Hornblower 1981, esp. 5–11, 151, 196–211; Schäfer 2002, 156; Anson 2004, 9.

was accurate, it implied that not all of the ca. 3,000 Silver Shields had the strong incentive of a family to induce them to give him up. It is also conceivable that not all the Macedonians cared to the same extent about their possessions or dependents. Plutarch reports that before Eumenes became Antigonus's prisoner, some Macedonians lamented the loss of their baggage, some told him not to lose heart, and some blamed other commanders for the defeat. It is true that the biographer presents these different reactions as a ploy to lull Eumenes into a false sense of security and capture him off guard. But it could be that some of the veterans were genuinely surprised by their comrades' decision to give Eumenes up.[42] Last, Diodorus says that Antigonus sent the most troublesome Silver Shields away to Arachosia (Polyaenus gives their number as 1,000), including those who had betrayed Eumenes (Diod. 19.48.3–4; Polyaenus 4.6.15). This implies that not all of the Macedonians were active in, or agreed about, the surrender of Eumenes.

More significantly, there was no certainty that Eumenes would be put to death. His warning to the Macedonians that he would be killed is included among the elements that constitute his address to the troops in our sources; even if authentic, it was a piece of rhetoric designed to deter them from surrendering him. His execution was certainly an option, but it is worth recalling that, although Antigonus had in the past called upon the Macedonians to kill Eumenes, he refrained from such an exhortation both on the eve of Paraetacene and now. In the Silver Shields' negotiations with Antigonus, it is not unlikely that the general promised not to kill Eumenes, or did not exclude the possibility that he might be imprisoned (as had been done with Alcetas's generals) or offered a position in his army—or even a generous release.[43]

In fact, the sources report that Antigonus hesitated about what to do with his captured friend Eumenes, that he protected Eumenes from lynching when he was brought to his camp, that there were conflicting opinions in Antigonus's council about Eumenes' fate, and that Eumenes himself raised the possibility of his release as well as of his death. It would have been a coup for Antigonus to have Eumenes, the royally appointed chief general of Asia, at his side. But in the end, like many other single rulers, Antigonus yielded to fear, to distrust, to the pressures of his oligarchy (that

---

42. Plut. *Eum.* 17.3; cf. Heckel 1992, 315.

43. Eumenes' warnings: Plut. *Eum.* 17.8–11; Just. 14.4.5–6. Antigonus's imprisonment of Alcetas's commanders: Diod. 18.45.3; 19.16.1.

is, his friends), and to his troops. In short, the sources' condemnation of the deadly treachery of the Silver Shields was an effect of hindsight.[44]

Hindsight seems also to have been responsible for the moralistic interpretation of the Silver Shields' later assignments as just deserts for their betrayal of Eumenes, a view that probably goes back to Hieronymus.[45] It was more likely that Antigonus sent them to the Arachosian satrap Sibyrtius to help him against Chandragupta, who was expanding his realm in the Indus basin at the time.

At the same time, Antigonus had several reasons for dispensing with the services of the Silver Shields. Some veterans may have been upset about the killing of Antigenes, and many about the loss of the power and prestige they had enjoyed under Eumenes. Their Argead sympathies and their cohesive, independent solidarity were also troublesome, and they included elderly soldiers of doubtful usefulness. Therefore Antigonus broke them up into smaller units and sent them away, just as Antipater had done when he sent them from Triparadeisus to fetch money from Susa in 321/0 (Arr. *Succ.* 1.35, 38). But this did not mean that Antigonus distrusted them. The Silver Shields he sent on garrison duties were entrusted with the same duties that other garrisons in occupied lands were expected to perform: representing the ruler and his interests and helping him keep the local population in check.[46] For the Silver Shields in Arachosia or in territories under Antigonus's control, however, his assignments were also the end of the road. There would be no new Eumenes to offer them a second chance.

---

44. Antigonus's wavering (and distrust of Eumenes): Diod. 19.44.1–2; Plut. *Eum.* 18.3–6; Nepos *Eum.* 10.3–11.2, 12.1–3; Jacoby 1913, 1541. Eumenes' expecting death or release: Plut. *Eum.* 18.4; Nepos *Eum.* 11.3. The time separating Eumenes' arrest from his execution ranges from "many days" (Plut. *Eum.* 18.6) to eleven days (Nepos *Eum.* 11.3–12.4). Brown (1947, 687) doubts Antigonus's hesitations, and Billows (1990, 104n29) thinks that Hieronymus tried in this way to exonerate Antigonus. But both Diodorus (19.44.2) and Plutarch (*Eum.* 19.1) are clear about Antigonus's responsibility for his death.

45. See note 35 and chap. 1 above.

46. Cf. Chaniotis 2002, 102, 106–108.

CONCLUSION

The Silver Shields were the last of Alexander's veteran infantrymen to leave an impression on the histories of the period. Faint traces of their existence after they moved to Antigonus's side may be found in his colonies. When Seleucus returned to Mesopotamia in 312, he drafted Macedonian settlers in Carrhae into his force. A. B. Bosworth has identified them as the Silver Shields whom Antigonus is said to have used for garrison duties.[1] The suggestion is attractive but not without problems. Polyaenus (4.6.15) reports that their garrison duty was performed in "strong and impassable" places, a description that does not fit Carrhae. In addition, Seleucus's use of the Silver Shields five years after Gabene does not cohere with Polyaenus's assertion that they all quickly disappeared once Antigonus got rid of them. The advanced age of many surviving Silver Shields at this point is another reason for doubting their identification, as is the possibility that these settlers may have been other Macedonians, domiciled there after Triparadeisus by Amphimachus, the satrap of Mesopotamia (Arr. *Succ.* 1.35; Diod. 18.39.6).

These reservations sufficiently illustrate the difficulties of ascertaining the post-Gabene career of the Silver Shields or other veterans of Alexander's armies. Without ignoring such obstacles, I would nevertheless suggest that some of these veterans settled in what would later become the city of Nicaea in Bithynia. Traditions regarding the foundation of cities tend to be inconsistent and heavily manipulated. In the case of Nicaea, however, there is both explicit and implicit evidence of its being settled by Alexander's veterans. Nicaea was originally founded by Antigonus Monophthalmus, perhaps around 309.[2] Antigonus renamed a local city called Ancore or Helicore (or less reliably, Olbia) after himself, calling it Antigonea. Later, probably

---

1. Bosworth 2002, 234–235. Silver Shields as garrisons: Polyaenus 4.6.15. Seleucus in Carrhae: Diod. 19.91.1.

2. Billows 1990, 145, 304–305, although an earlier date is no less likely.

after Antigonus's death in the Battle of Ipsus in 301, the city was taken by the Diadoch Lysimachus, who renamed it Nicaea after his wife. There were also the expected local traditions ascribing the foundation to more heroic figures, such as Dionysus or Heracles. The most informative source for the men who settled the city is Memnon of Heraclea Pontica, a Greek historian of the Roman period (*FGrHist* 434 F 28). Memnon says that Nicaea was established after Alexander's death by men who had fought with him. The author then recounts a myth about Dionysus, who seduced the nymph Nicaea and fathered a son by her, adding that the men who founded Nicaea came originally from the city of Nicaea in Locris, destroyed by Phocis, presumably in the Third Sacred War, around the middle of the fourth century. But the Byzantine lexicographer Stephanus (s.v. *Nicaea*) says that the settlers came originally from Bottiaea in Macedonia.

Scholars have rejected the tradition of the city's foundation by Alexander's veterans because the great king was never in the region.[3] This unjustly excludes the possibility that the settlers were veterans of Alexander's whom Antigonus settled in the city. We know that Antigonus employed such veterans in Asia Minor against the Perdiccans, and that he later commanded the Silver Shields. It is therefore possible that he settled them in Antigonea before its refounding as Nicaea. The veterans could have been Greeks from Locris or Macedonians originally from Bottiaea, and they probably included both: the Roman-era orator Dio Chrysostom mentions both Greeks and Macedonians in the city (39.1). Moreover, local traditions indicate a clear link to Alexander, who by now formed an inseparable part of the veterans' and other Macedonians' identity. Nicaean coins from the imperial period carry Alexander's image.[4] Even the stories of the city's founding by Dionysus or Heracles must have resonated strongly with Alexander's veterans, evoking the intimate and special link between those heroes and the dead king. The city itself was situated on a lake in a fertile region, surrounded by hills and, from Hellenistic times, by an impressive wall. It was not a bad refuge for weary troops who had been used and reused by Alexander and his successors.

Archaeological evidence for Alexander's veterans is elusive. Macedonian tombs from around the last quarter of the fourth century contain precious metals and martial themes that have been ascribed to veterans laden with Asian wealth. But scholars disagree about the dates of the tombs and the

---

3. Tcherikover 1927, 46–47; Cohen 1995, 398–399.
4. See note 3 above.

possibility that their wealth was of local origin. Even if their occupants were veterans, they seem to have been members of the elite rather than the common soldiers who are my subject.[5]

Thus a retrospective look at the history of Alexander's Macedonian veterans is likely to provoke sad reflections about their lot. Their mistreatment begins with the sources, especially their main ancient historian, Hieronymus of Cardia, the most likely chief informant of our extant sources about the veterans, who regularly ascribes their conduct to such disreputable motives as greed and self-service. He sometimes uses their behavior as a foil to the commanders' more honorable actions, and sometimes to flatter the leader with their displays of admiration for him. Verbal exchanges between leaders and the Macedonian soldiers consist of noise from the latter and long, clear, effective speeches from the former. Tricking troops out of their due payments is considered creditable in a commander. The sources underplay the veterans' contribution to the shaping of historical events, presenting their cause as less worthy or legitimate than that of their general. The troops' dissatisfaction with a general unwilling or unable to meet their justified demands and expectations is unsympathetically characterized as indiscipline or a dangerous attempt to introduce radical democracy into the military. The result is an elitist, distorted portrait, which the present work has aimed to correct.

For powerful individuals such as Alexander's successors, the post-Alexander era was a time of great opportunities and self-fulfillment. They endured considerable personal risk in contests for power and territory, but the winner could reap unprecedented gains. It was also a time when ambition and violence paid off: the exploits of Alexander's former generals testify to his ability to control lieutenants whose talents, aspirations, and destructive energy dominated the period after his death. The stakes for the veterans were smaller and their options more limited, consisting of continuing military service, voluntarily or involuntarily transferring to a rival army, settling down on land provided by their commander, or going home to Macedonia. The evidence for their preference is sketchy, but it appears that returning home was their least favored choice.

The veterans' options often reflected their strong dependence on their general, which encompassed almost all facets of their lives. The commander decided how and where they fought, thereby determining their chances of

---

5. Macedonian tombs and veterans: Themelis and Touratsoglou 1997, esp. 222–223. *Contra*: Hatzopoulos 2008, 112; cf. Barr-Sharrar 1999, 108; 2008, 3.

survival. He was their chief provider, responsible for the welfare of their baggage and families, and even the focus of their emotional needs. The scenes of the soldiers seeking reconciliation with Alexander in India or in Opis, or of the Silver Shields calling upon the sick Eumenes to lead them to battle (and later venting their frustration at him after his defeat and the loss of their families at Gabene), illustrate the mixture of their practical with their sentimental dependence. That the soldiers' families represented a particular vulnerability in this regard is shown by Alexander's retention of the veterans' Asian children for military training, and by other commanders' use of captured families to control the veterans' loyalty. But the imbalance in the relationship between the veterans and their general could be dangerous for the latter as well, leading at times to excessive self-confidence and to a failure on his part to read the troops' mood correctly. Alexander made this mistake in India, Susa, and Opis, as did Eumenes after Paraetacene. On such occasions the soldiers resorted to acts of indiscipline, riots, and mutinies (or even communal weeping) in their plea for understanding, sympathy, and redress.

It is because our sources privilege the role and the outlook of the general that we have a skewed view of the veterans' needs and goals. Naturally the soldiers sought material gain and booty, and there is much evidence of their protesting against late wages or nonpayment of promised bonuses. But to explain their conduct solely on these grounds is to echo the sources' elitist reduction of their motives to greed. The veterans had a developed sense of what was just, were loyal to the Macedonian royal house, and were willing to stand up for these causes. They showed their displeasure when such leaders as Meleager, Alcetas, or Perdiccas used them in personal power struggles. They were not averse to fighting or splitting from fellow Macedonians—sometimes willingly opposing their compatriots on the battlefield, but needing legitimate reasons for doing so, and listening readily to accusations that a general was responsible for a civil war.

Macedonian solidarity or patriotism was a limited motive for the veterans, whose first loyalty was to their immediate commanders: the officers who stood between the army chief and the troops, facilitating the communications between them and helping the leader to assert his control. United opposition from these subordinate officers and the troops was the worst possible threat to a general. This happened to Alexander on the Hyphasis and to Perdiccas in Egypt, where he lost his life to such a defection. On some occasions, commanders deserted with entire units. It was to avoid this kind of disaster that generals such as Eumenes tried to establish direct channels of communication with their soldiers.

The loyalty given to a general depended on his ability to meet his troops' expectations of him, which included winning battles and taking care of his soldiers in life and in death. (Unlike kingship, anchored in office and lineage, the authority of military leaders was notably vulnerable to defeats and other failures.) But material rewards alone were insufficient to engender loyalty. Eumenes' competitors for chief command could not win the veterans to their side by showering them with gifts and honors. The veterans were not mercenaries.

Indeed, the veterans usually supported their leader in his military and political conflicts because they were satisfied with his record of success and with his services to them, because they respected his superior rank, because they were attached to him personally, and—no less important—because the alternative was worse. The veterans were also invested in their general's success, rank, and prestige, feeling that these qualities of his defined their own status. Equally relevant was the Macedonians' wish to curry favor with their general, even by flattery, and to be genuinely liked by him—desires just as strong as their tendency to riot when he disappointed them. By ascribing all such behavior to a leader's manipulative skills, the sources and their modern followers fail to recognize the soldiers' desire to play along.

In politics, the veterans' power was negligible against a united chain of command. The army became a political player only when the military elite was fractured and its members sought the troops' support against their rivals, as in Babylon after Alexander's death, in Triparadeisus before Antipater resumed control, and in Eumenes' camp when his leadership was challenged. Otherwise, with very few exceptions, the army took no political initiative. It was difficult for the veterans to unite independently around anything but common discontent, because they knew better what they did not want than what they wanted. They also failed to develop authentic leaders from their ranks. Political leaders such as Meleager or even Eurydice came from the established elite and command, and only through such figures could the veterans make a difference. The spontaneous and futile Macedonian gathering against Antipater at the bridge in Triparadeisus well illustrates their impotence.

The power of the army assembly depended not on its alleged constitutional role to decide policy and appoint officeholders, but on its usefulness to the elite. When the generals were of one mind, they ignored the assembly or allowed it a passive role at most. But when there was conflict among the leaders, they solicited opinions and decisions from the assembly—opinions that would become largely irrelevant once the conflict was settled. In fact, the Macedonians were most influential outside the assembly and when they backed their wishes with their spears: for example, when Pithon tried to prevent them from getting the reward they were promised on a campaign against Greek rebels in 323.

Of all the veterans, the Silver Shields enjoyed the greatest influence. Despite their minority status in the army, they constituted a dominant force because of their military skills and experience, their group solidarity, their stable military command, and their identity as Alexander's veterans, as Macedonians, and as conquerors. All these attributes endeared them to Eumenes and to the commanders who wished to take them away from him. The competition over their services also gave them power to confer legitimacy on a leader or a cause. But this was an ephemeral and rarely realized privilege that disappeared entirely after Eumenes lost the war against Antigonus.

While the Silver Shields left their strongest impression on the battlefield, they never decided a battle, unlike the cavalry. They also seemed to claim and get credit for victory at the expense of other units, such as non-Macedonian hypaspists or the mercenaries. To some degree, this was their reaction to the realities of war in the post-Alexander era. The Successors continued Alexander's policy of increased reliance on mercenary, Asian, and other non-Macedonian troops. For the veterans of Alexander this represented an *antitagma* policy, the creation of a counter-unit to balance their influence. In their resentment, they loudly claimed a privileged status on the basis of their Macedonian origin, their status as conquerors, and their service under Alexander.

Service with Alexander thus attained a special meaning, although its uses varied. For generals such as Neoptolemus, Peucestas, and Seleucus, a command under Alexander was a claim to valor that conferred the right to rule over troops and territories.[6] For other veterans, both Macedonian and non-Macedonian, service with Alexander was a source of pride and self-importance. Epigraphic evidence shows that Macedonians (or their families) advertised their campaigns with the king; in Amphipolis, Antigonus son of Callas styled himself a companion of Alexander's. The following (likely) Macedonians are also mentioned as participants in Alexander's campaign: Arrhidaeus son of Alexander in Eretria; Philip and Iolaus in Athens; and Aneitus of Rhodes in Athens, who served with Alexander "no-

---

6. Neoptolemus: Plut. *Eum.* 1.2–3; Peucestas: Diod. 19.14.4–5; Seleucus: Diod. 19.55.2–5.

bly and honorably."[7] Fighting under Alexander stood for military experience against enemies ranging from the Greek rebels in the upper satrapies to Damis, the expert in fighting elephants, who helped the city of Megalopolis against Polyperchon (Diod. 18.7.2, 71.2). For the Macedonian veterans in particular, experience with Alexander conferred the additional reputation of invincibility and the privileges that went with it (Diod. 19.41.2; cf. 19.90.3). Their defeats after Alexander's time were insufficient to undermine their fame or self-esteem, which rested on the undying (and cultivated) memory of the king himself.

The Silver Shields left a checkered impression on history. Ancient historians describe them as proud Macedonians who excelled in battle, but also as men who sold out their general. Their reputation seems to have survived this blemish, and although there were no known Silver Shields in Hellenistic Macedonia or Egypt, perhaps because the original *argyraspides* fought and settled in Asia, an elite infantry unit of about 10,000 in the Seleucid army took their name. The Seleucid Silver Shields were probably included in the royal guard of the Syrian kings and fought in the ways of the Macedonian phalanx, whatever their ethnic origin may have been. But they were not worthy heirs of their famous namesakes. There are only two battles in which their participation is explicitly attested—at Raphia in 217 between Antiochus III and Ptolemy IV, and at Magnesia in 190 between the same Antiochus and the Roman army—and both ended in their crushing defeat. About four centuries later (231–232 CE), the emperor Alexander Severus fared better against the Persians with his Silver and Gold Shields, whom he recreated in imitation of Alexander. The emperor's intended homage, however, was much more to the great king than to his soldiers.[8]

---

7. Antigonus: *ISE* no. 113; Arrhidaeus: *IG* XII 9.212; Philip and Iolaus: *IG* II² 561; Billows 1990, 395–396, 421–423; Aneitus: *SEG* 21: 310. See also cavalrymen from Orchomenus: *IG* VII 3206; cf. Philonides, son of Zotes, a Cretan runner and a surveyor for Alexander: *Sylloge Inscriptionum Graecarum*³ no. 303. See also Billows 1995, 34; Meeus 2009, 243. Cf. Pachidis 2006, 258–259, for prominent Macedonians who were possibly veterans.

8. The Seleucid Silver Shields: Plb. 5.79.4; 30.25.5; Livy 37.40.7; App. *Syr.* 32 (who give the name to a cavalry unit); Bar Kochva 1989, 414–429. Bar Kochva argues for their Greco-Macedonian origin, but his efforts to deny them an Asian or mixed origin are not persuasive; cf. Launey 1949–1950, 313; Foulon 1996, 60–62 (who too readily identifies them with peltasts and other units). The Seleucid army had also a unit of Gold Shields, who appear to have enjoyed a higher status: Plb. 30.25.5 (a problematic text); cf. Pollux 1.175. Alexander Severus: *Historia Augusta* "Alexander Severus" 50.

This book has tried to tell the story of Alexander's veterans. In Juan José Saer's novel *The Investigation*, an old soldier, who knows the Trojan War from his personal, dreary experience as a camp dweller, converses with a newly arrived soldier, who knows the war from heroic tales told about it back home. "The old soldier has the truth of experience and the young soldier, the truth of imagination." These truths, the author observes, are never the same, but there are times when they are not necessarily contradictory. I hope this book has not missed the genuine and imaginary truths of the veterans' actual experience.

BIBLIOGRAPHY

Note: Throughout the book, names of journals are abbreviated as in *L'Année Philologique*.

Aalders, G. J. D. 1982. *Plutarch's Political Thought*. Amsterdam.

Adams, W. L. 1986. "Macedonian Kingship and the Right of Petition." *Ancient Macedonia* 4:43–52.

Anson, E. M. 1977. "The Siege of Nora: A Source Conflict." *GRBS* 18:251–256.

———. 1980. "Discrimination and Eumenes of Cardia." *AncW* 3:55–59.

———. 1981. "Alexander's Hypaspists and the Argyraspides." *Historia* 30:117–120.

———. 1985. "The Hypaspists: Macedonia's Professional Citizen-Soldiers." *Historia* 34:246–248.

———. 1988a. "Antigonus, the Satrap of Phrygia." *Historia* 37:471–477.

———. 1988b. "Hypaspists and Argyraspides after 323." *Ancient History Bulletin* 2:131–133.

———. 1990. "Neoptolemus and Armenia." *AHB* 4:125–128.

———. 1991. "The Evolution of the Macedonian Army Assembly (330–315 B.C.)." *Historia* 40:230–247.

———. 1992. "Craterus and the Prostasia." *CP* 87:38–43.

———. 2003. "The Dating of Perdiccas' Death and the Assembly at Triparadeisus." *GRBS* 43:373–390.

———. 2004. *Eumenes of Cardia: A Greek among Macedonians*. Boston.

———. 2007. "Early Hellenistic Chronology: The Cuneiform Evidence." In W. Heckel, L. Trittle, and P. Wheatley, eds., *Alexander's Empire: Formulation to Decay*, 193–198. Claremont, CA.

———. 2008. "Macedonian Judicial Assemblies." *CP* 103:135–149.

———. 2009. "Philip II, Amyntas Perdicca, and Macedonian Royal Succession." *Historia* 58:276–286.

Aperghis, G. G. 1997. "Alexander's Hipparchies." *AncW* 28:133–148.

Asheri, D. 2006. "Hieronymus of Cardia c. 364–?260 B.C." In N. Wilson, ed., *Encyclopedia of Ancient Greece*, 359–360. New York.

Ashton, N. G. 1991. "Craterus from 324 to 321 B.C." *Ancient Macedonia* 5:125–131.

Atkinson, J. E. 1998–2000. *Q. Curzio Rufo Storie di Alessandro Magno*. Trans. V. Antelami and M. Giangiulio. 2 vols. Milan.

———. 2000. "Originality and Its Limits in the Alexander Sources of the Early Empire." In A. B. Bosworth and E. J. Baynham, eds., *Alexander the Great in Fact and Fiction*, 307–325. Oxford.

Atkinson, J. E., and J. C. Yardley, eds. 2009. *Curtius Rufus, Histories of Alexander the Great, Book 10.* Oxford.

Austin, M. M. 1986. "Hellenistic Kings, War, and the Economy." *CQ* 36:450–466.

———. 2003. "Alexander and the Macedonian Invasion of Asia: Aspects of Historiography of War and Empire in Antiquity." In I. Worthington, ed., *Alexander the Great: A Reader*, 118–135. London. Reprint of Austin in J. Rich and G. Shipley, eds., *War and Society in the Greek World* (London, 1993), 197–223.

———. 2006. *The Hellenistic World from Alexander to the Roman Conquest.* 2nd ed. Cambridge.

Badian, E. 1958. "Alexander the Great and the Unity of Mankind." *Historia* 7:425–444.

———. 1961. "Harpalus." *JHS* 81:16–43.

———. 1964. *Studies in Greek and Roman History.* Oxford.

———. 1965. "Orientals in Alexander's Army." *JHS* 85:160–161.

———. 1968. "A King's Notebooks." *HSCP* 72:183–204.

———, ed. 1976. *Alexandre le Grand: Image et réalité.* Geneva.

———. 1982a. "Eurydice." In W. L. Adams and E. N. Borza, eds., *Philip II, Alexander the Great, and the Macedonian Heritage*, 99–110. Washington, D.C.

———. 1982b. "Greeks and Macedonians." In B. Barr-Sharrar and E. N. Borza, eds., *Macedonia and Greece in Late Classical and Early Hellenistic Times*, 33–51. Washington, D.C.

———. 1985. "Alexander in Iran." In I. Gershevitch, ed., *Cambridge History of Iran* 2:420–501. Cambridge.

———. 1987–1988. "The Ring and the Book." In W. Will and J. Heinrichs, eds., *Zu Alexanders d. Gr. Festschrift G. Wirth zum 60. Geburtstag am 9.12.86* 1:605–625. Amsterdam.

———. 2000. "Conspiracies." In A. B. Bosworth and E. J. Baynham, eds., *Alexander the Great in Fact and Fiction*, 50–95. Oxford.

Bagnall, R. S. 2006. *Hellenistic and Roman Egypt: Sources and Approaches.* Leiden.

Bar Kochva, B. 1989. *Judas Maccabaeus: The Jewish Struggle against the Seleucids.* Cambridge.

Barr-Sharrar, B. 1999. "Macedonian Metal Ware: An Update." In *International Congress on Alexander the Great: From Macedonia to Oikoumene, Veria 27–31.5.1998*, 97–112. Veria.

———. 2008. *The Derveni Krater.* Princeton.

Bauman, R. A. 1990. *Political Trials in Ancient Greece.* London.

Bennett, B., and M. Roberts. 2008. *The Wars of Alexander's Successors, 323–281 B.C.,* vol. 1: *Commanders and Campaigns.* Barnsley.

———. 2009. *The Wars of Alexander's Successors, 323–281 B.C.,* vol. 2: *Battles and Tactics.* Barnsley.

Beresford, A. G., P. J. Parsons, and M. P. Pobjoy. 2007. "No. 4808. On Hellenistic Historians." *The Oxyrhynchus Papyri* 71:27–36.

Berve, H. 1926. *Das Alexanderreich auf prosopographischer Grundlage.* 2 vol. Munich.

Billows, R. A. 1990. *Antigonus the One-Eyed and the Creation of the Hellenistic State.* Berkeley.

———. 1993. "*IG* XII 9.212: A Macedonian Officer at Eretria." *ZPE* 96:249–257.

————. 1995. *Kings and Colonists: Aspects of Macedonian Imperialism.* Leiden.

————. 2000. "Polybius and Alexander Historiography." In A. B. Bosworth and E. J. Baynham, eds., *Alexander the Great in Fact and Fiction*, 286–306. Oxford.

Bing, J. D. 1973. "A Further Note on Cyinda/Kundi." *Historia* 22:346–350.

Bingen, J. 2007. *Hellenistic Egypt: Monarchy, Society, Economy, Culture.* R. S. Bagnall, ed. Edinburgh.

Boiy, T. 2007. *Between High and Low: A Chronology of the Early Hellenistic Period.* Bonn.

————. 2010. "Royal and Satrapal Armies in Babylonia during the Second Diadoch War. The *Chronicle of the Successors* on the Events during the Seventh Year of Philip Arrhidaeus (=317/316 B.C.)." *JHS* 130:1–13.

Bosworth, A. B. 1978. "Eumenes, Neoptolemus, and *PSI* XII 1284." *GRBS* 19.3:227–237.

————. 1980. "Alexander and the Iranians." *JHS* 100:1–21.

————, ed. 1980–1995. *A Historical Commentary on Arrian's History of Alexander.* 2 vols. Oxford.

————. 1986. "Alexander the Great and the Decline of Macedon." *JHS* 106:1–12.

————. 1988a. *Conquest and Empire: The Reign of Alexander the Great.* Cambridge.

————. 1988b. *From Arrian to Alexander: Studies in Historical Interpretation.* Oxford.

————. 1992a. "History and Artifice in Plutarch's *Eumenes*." In P. A. Stadter, ed., *Plutarch and the Historical Tradition*, 56–89. London.

————. 1992b. "Philip III Arrhidaeus and the Chronology of the Successors." *Chiron* 22:55–81.

————. 1993. "Perdiccas and the Kings." *CQ* 43:420–427.

————. 2000a. "A Tale of Two Empires: Hernán Cortés and Alexander the Great." In A. B. Bosworth and E. J. Baynham, eds., *Alexander the Great in Fact and Fiction*, 23–49. Oxford.

————. 2000b. "Ptolemy and the Will of Alexander." In A. B. Bosworth and E. J. Baynham, eds., *Alexander the Great in Fact and Fiction*, 207–241. Oxford.

————. 2002. *The Legacy of Alexander: Politics, Warfare, and Propaganda under the Successors.* Oxford.

————. 2003. "*Plus ça change* . . . Ancient Historians and Their Sources." *CA* 22:167–198.

————. 2005. Review of C. Schäfer. 2002. *Eumenes von Kardia und der Kampf um die Macht im Alexanderreich* (Frankfurt am Main). *Gnomon* 77:684–688.

Briant, P. 1972. "D'Alexandre le Grand aux Diadoques: Le cas d'Eumene de Kardia (1er article)." *REA* 74:32–73.

————. 1973a. "D'Alexandre le grand aux Diadoques: Le cas d'Eumene de Kardia (Suite et fin)." *REA* 75:43–81.

————. 1973b. *Antigone le Borgne.* Paris.

————. 1982. *Rois, tributes et paysans.* Paris.

————. 2002. *From Cyrus to Alexander: A History of the Persian Empire.* Trans. P. T. Daniels. Winona Lake, Indiana.

————. 2003. *Darius dans l'ombre d'Alexandre.* Paris.

Brown, T. S. 1947. "Hieronymus of Cardia." *AHR* 52:684–696.

Brunt, P. A. 1963. "Alexander's Macedonian Cavalry." *JHS* 83:27–46.

————, ed. 1976–1983. *Arrian: History of Alexander and Indica.* 2 vols. LCL. Cambridge, MA.

Carney, E. D. 1987. "The Career of Adea-Eurydice." *Historia* 36:496–502.

———. 1988. "The Sisters of Alexander the Great: Royal Relics." *Historia* 37:385–404.

———. 1995. "Women and *basileia*: Legitimacy and Female Political Action in Macedonia." *CJ* 90:367–391.

———. 1996. "Macedonians and Mutiny: Discipline and Indiscipline in the Army of Philip and Alexander." *CP* 91.1:19–44.

———. 2000a. "Artifice and Alexander History." In A. B. Bosworth and E. J. Baynham, eds., *Alexander the Great in Fact and Fiction*, 263–285. Oxford.

———. 2000b. *Woman and Monarchy in Macedonia*. Norman, OK.

———. 2001. "The Trouble with Philip Arrhidaeus." *AHB* 15:63–89.

———. 2004. "Women and Military Leadership in Macedonia." *AncW* 35:184–195.

———. 2006. *Olympias: Mother of Alexander the Great*. New York.

———. 2010. "Macedonian Women." In J. Roisman and I. Worthington, eds., *A Companion to Ancient Macedonia*, 409–427. Malden, MA.

Cartledge, P. 2004. *Alexander the Great: The Hunt for a New Past*. New York.

Chaniotis, A. 2002. "Foreign Soldiers—Native Girls? Constructing and Crossing Boundaries in Hellenistic Cities with Foreign Garrisons." In A. Chaniotis and P. Ducrey, eds., *Army and Power in the Ancient World*, 99–114. Stuttgart.

———. 2005. *War in the Hellenistic Age: A Social and Cultural History*. Oxford.

Cohen, G. M. 1995. *The Hellenistic Settlements in Europe, the Islands, and Asia Minor*. Berkeley.

Collins, A. W. 2001. "The Office of the Chiliarch under Alexander and the Successors." *Phoenix* 55:259–283.

Davidson, J. N. 1997. *Courtesans & Fishcakes: The Consuming Passions of Classical Athens*. New York.

Del Monte, G. F. 1997. *Testi dalla Babilonia Ellenistica*, vol. I: *Testi Cronografici*. Pisa.

Depuydt, L. 1997. "The Time of Death of Alexander the Great: 11 June 323 B.C. (–322), ca. 4.00–5.00 P.M." *Die Welt des Orients* 28:117–135.

Devine, A. M. 1985a. "Diodorus' Account of the Battle of Gabiene." *AncW* 12:87–96.

———. 1985b. "Diodorus' Account of the Battle of Paraitacene (317 B.C.)." *AncW* 12:75–86.

Dijk, G. J. van. 1997. *AINOI, LOGOI, MYTHOI: Fables in Archaic, Classical, and Hellenistic Greek Literature*. Leiden.

Dmitriev, S. 2004. "Alexander's Exiles Decree." *Klio* 86:348–381.

Dreyer, B. 1999. "Zum ersten Diadochenkrieg: Der Göteborger Arrian-Palimpsest (ms Graec 1)." *ZPE* 125:39–60.

———. 2007. "The Arrian Parchment in Gothenburg: New Digital Processing Methods and Initial Results." In W. Heckle, L. Tritle, and P. Wheatley, eds., *Alexander's Empire: Formulation to Decay*, 245–263. Claremont, CA.

Dubois, P. 2003. *Slaves and Other Objects*. Chicago.

Ducrey, P. 1999. *Le traitement des prisonniers de guerre dans la Grèce antique des origins à la conquête romaine*. Rev. ed., Paris.

Dudley, J. P. 1998. "Reports of Carnivory by the Common Hippo Hippopotamus Amphibius." *South African Journal of Wildlife Research* 28:58–59.

Echoles, E. C. 1953. "Crossing a Classical River." *CJ* 48:215–224.

Ellis, W. M. 1994. *Ptolemy of Egypt*. London.

Engel, R. 1971. "Anmerkungen zur Schlacht von Orkynia." *Museum Helveticum* 28:227–231.

———. 1972. "Zum Geschichtsbild des Hieronymos von Kardia." *Athenaeum* 60:120–125.

———. 1974. "Zwei Heersversammlungen in Memphis." *Hermes* 102:122–124.

———. 1978. *Untersuchungen zum Machtaufsteig des Antigonos I. Monophthalmos.* Kallmünz.

Engels, D. W. 1978. *Alexander the Great and the Logistics of the Macedonian Army.* Berkeley.

Errington, D. M. 1970. "From Babylon to Triparadeisos: 323–320 B.C." *JHS* 90:49–77.

———. 1976. "Alexander in the Hellenistic World." In E. Badian, ed., *Alexandre le Grand: Image et réalité,* 137–179. Geneva.

———. 1977. "Diodorus Siculus and the Chronology of the Early Diadochi, 320–311 BC." *Hermes* 105:478–504.

———. 1978. "The Nature of the Macedonian State under the Monarchy." *Chiron* 8:77–133.

———. 1990. *A History of Macedonia.* Berkeley.

———. 2008. *A History of the Hellenistic World, 323–330 B.C.* Malden, MA.

Erskine, A. 2002. "Life after Death: Alexandria and the Body of Alexander." *G&R* 49:163–179.

Faraguna, M. 1998. "Aspetti amministrativi e finanziari della monarchia macedona tra IV e III sec. A.C." *Athenaeum* 86:349–395.

Fedak, J. 1990. *Monumental Tombs of the Hellenistic Age.* Toronto.

Flower, M. A. 1994. *Theopompus of Chios: History and Rhetoric in the Fourth Century B.C.* Oxford.

———. 2000. "Alexander the Great and Panhellenism." In A. B. Bosworth and E. J. Baynham, eds., *Alexander the Great in Fact and Fiction,* 96–135. Oxford.

Fontana, M. J. 1960. *Le lotte per la successione di Alessandro Magno dal 323 al 315.* Palermo.

Foulon, É. 1996. "Hypaspistes, peltastes, chrysaspides, argyraspides, chalcaspides." *RÉA* 98.1–2:53–63.

Franz, D. 2009. "Kriegsfinanzierung Alexanders des Grossen." In H. Müller, ed., *1000 & 1 Talente: Visualisierung antiker Kriegskosten. Begleitband zu einer studentischen Ausstellung,* 115–150. Gutenberg.

Fraser, P. M. 1996. *Cities of Alexander the Great.* Oxford.

Fredricksmeyer, E. 2000. "Alexander and the Kingship of Asia." In A. B. Bosworth and E. J. Baynham, eds., *Alexander the Great in Fact and Fiction,* 136–166. Oxford.

Garland, R. 1985. *The Greek Way of Death.* Ithaca, NY.

Geiger, J. 1995. "Plutarch on Hellenistic Politics: The Case of Eumenes of Cardia." In I. Gall and B. Scardigli, eds., *Teoria e Prassi Politica Nelle Opere di Plutarco,* 173–185. Naples.

Goukowsky, P., ed. 1978. *Diodore de Sicile. Bibliothèque historique Livre XVIII.* Paris.

———. 1978–1981. *Essai sur les origines des mythe d'Alexandre: 336–270 av. J.C.* 2 vols. Nancy.

von Graeve V. 1970. *Der Alexandersarkophag und seine Werkstatt.* Berlin.

Grainger, J. D. 1990. *Seleukos Nikator: Constructing a Hellenistic Kingdom.* London.

———. 2007. *Alexander the Great Failure: The Collapse of the Macedonian Empire.* London.

Grayson, A. K. 1975. *Babylonian Historical-Literary Texts.* Toronto.

Green, P. 1990. *From Alexander to Actium: The Historical Evolution of the Hellenistic Age*. Berkeley.

————. 1991. *Alexander of Macedon, 356–323* >B.C.: *A Historical Biography*. Berkeley.

————. 2003. "Occupation and Co-existence: The Impact of Macedon on Athens." In O. Palagia and S. V. Tracy, eds., *The Macedonians in Athens, 322–229 B.C.*, 1–7. Oxford.

————. 2006. *Diodorus Siculus, Books 11–12.37.1: Greek History 480–431 B.C., the Alternative Version*. Austin, TX.

Greenwalt, W. S. 1984. "The Search for Arrhidaeus." *AncW* 10:69–77.

Griffith, G. T. 1935. *The Mercenaries of the Hellenistic World*. Cambridge.

————. 1963. "A Note on the Hipparchies of Alexander." *JHS* 83:68–74.

Gullath, B., and L Schober. 1986. "Zur Chronologie der frühen Diadochenzeit die Jahre 320 bis 315 v. Chr." In H. Kalcyk, B. Gullath, and A. Graeber, eds., *Studien zur alten Geschichte. Siegfried Lauffer zum 70. Geburtstag am 4. August 1981 dargebracht von Freuden, Kollegen und Schülern*, 329–378. Rome.

Habicht, C. 1973. "Literarische und epigraphische Überlieferung zur Geschichte Alexanders und seiner ersten Nachfolger." *Vestigia* 17:367–377. Munich.

Hadley, R. A. 2001. "A Possible Lost Source for the Career of Eumenes of Kardia." *Historia* 50:3–33.

Hamilton, J. R., ed. 1969. *Plutarch's Alexander: A Commentary*. Oxford.

————. 1987. "Alexander's Iranian Policy." In W. Will and J. I. Heinrichs, eds., *Zu Alexander dem Grossen. Festschrift Gerhard Wirth zum 60. Geburtstag am 9.12.86*, 467–486. Amsterdam.

Hammond, N. G. L. 1978. "A Cavalry Unit in the Army of Antigonus Monophthalmus." *Asthippoi. CQ* 28:128–135. Repr. 1994 in *Collected Studies* 3:203–210.

————. 1980. "Some Passages in Arrian Concerning Alexander." *CQ* 30:455–476. Repr. 1994 in *Collected Studies* 3:65–86.

————. 1983a. "The Meaning of Arrian VII, 6, 2–5." *JHS* 10:139–144. Repr. 1994 in *Collected Studies* 3:87–92.

————. 1983b. *Three Historians of Alexander the Great: The So-Called Vulgate Authors, Diodorus, Justin, and Curtius*. Cambridge.

————. 1984. "Alexander's Veterans after His Death." *GRBS* 25:51–61. Repr. 1994 in *Collected Studies* 3:131–141.

————. 1988. "An Unfulfilled Promise by Alexander the Great." In W. Will and J. Heinrichs, eds., *Zu Alexander dem Grossen: Festschrift Gerhard Wirth zum 60. Geburtstag am 9.12.86*, 1, 627–634. Amsterdam. Repr. 1994 in *Collected Studies* 3:143–150.

————. 1989a. "Aspects of Alexander's Journal and Ring in His Last Days." *AJP* 110:155–160.

————. 1989b. "Casualties and Reinforcements of Citizen Soldiers in Greece and Macedon." *JHS* 109:56–68.

————. 1989c. *The Macedonian State: Origins, Institutions, and History*. Oxford.

————. 1993. *Sources for Alexander the Great: An Analysis of Plutarch's Life and Arrian's Anabasis Alexandrou*. Cambridge.

————. 1994. *Collected Studies*. 3 vols. Amsterdam.

————. 1996. "Alexander's Non-European Troops and Ptolemy I's Use of Such Troops." *BASP* 33:99–109.

————. 1998. "Cavalry Recruited in Macedonia down to 322." *Historia* 47:404–425.

——. 1999. "The Speeches in Arrian's *Indica* and *Anabasis*." *CQ* 49:238–253.

——. 2000. "The Continuity of Macedonian Institutions and the Macedonian Kingdoms of the Hellenistic Era." *Historia* 49:141–160.

Hammond, N. G. L., G. T. Griffith, and F. W. Walbank. 1972–1988. *A History of Macedonia.* 3 vols. Oxford.

Hardiman, C. I. 2010. "Classical Art to 221 *B.C.*" In J. Roisman and I. Worthington, eds., *A Companion to Ancient Macedonia*, 505–521. Malden, MA.

Hatzopoulos, M. B. 1996. *Macedonian Institutions under the Kings.* 2 vols. Athens.

——. 2008. "The Burial of the Dead (at Vergina) or The Unending Controversy on the Identity of the Occupants of Tomb II." *Tekmeria* 9:91–118.

Hatzopoulos, M. B., and P. Juhel. 2009. "Four Hellenistic Funerary Stelae from Gephyra, Macedonia." *AJA* 113:423–437.

Hauben, H. 1977. "The First War of the Successors (321 *B.C.*): Chronological and Historical Problems." *Anc. Soc.* 8:85–120.

Heckel, W. 1982. "The Career of Antigenes." *Symbola Osloenses* 57:57–67.

——. 1983–1984. "Kynnane the Illyrian." *RSA* 13/14:193–200.

——. 1992. *The Marshals of Alexander's Empire.* London.

——. 2002. "The Politics of Distrust: Alexander and His Successors." In D. Ogden, ed., *The Hellenistic World: New Perspectives*, 81–95. London.

——. 2006. *Who's Who in the Age of Alexander the Great.* Malden, MA.

——. 2008. *The Conquest of Alexander the Great.* Cambridge.

——. Forthcoming. "The Vicissitudes of the Three Thousand: The History of Alexander's Infantry Guard." *Oxford Handbook on Greek and Roman Warfare.* Oxford.

Heckel, W., and R. Jones. 2006. *Macedonian Warrior: Alexander's Elite Infantryman.* Oxford.

Heckel, W., and J. C. Yardley. 1981. "Roman Writers and the Indian Practice of Suttee." *Philologus* 125:305–311.

Heinen, H. 1983. "Zum militärischen Hilfpersonal in P. Med. Inv. 69.65." In E. van't Dack, P. van Dessel, and W. van Gucht, eds., *Egypt and the Hellenistic World*, 129–142. Studia Hellenistica 27. Leuven.

Herman, G. 1980. "The Friends of the Early Hellenistic Rulers, Servants or Officials?" *Talanta* 12–13:103–149.

Högemann, P. 1985. *Alexander der Grosse und Arabien.* Munich.

Holleaux, M. 1942. "'Ceux qui sont dans le begage.'" *Études d'épigraphie et d'histoire grecques* 3:15–26.

Holt, F. L. 1982. "The Hyphasis 'Mutiny': A Case Study." *AncW* 5:33–59.

——. 1988. *Alexander the Great and Bactria: The Formation of a Greek Frontier in Central Asia.* Leiden.

——. 2000. "The Death of Coenus: Another Study in Method." *AHB* 14:49–55.

——. 2005. *Into the Land of the Bones: Alexander the Great in Afghanistan.* Berkeley.

Hornblower, J. 1981. *Hieronymus of Cardia.* Oxford.

Huss, W. 2001. *Ägypten in hellenistischer Zeit, 332–330 v. Chr.* Munich.

Jacoby, F. 1913. "Hieronymos von Kardia." *RE* 8, no. 10:1540–1560.

——. 1929–1930. "Hieronymos von Kardia." *FGrHist* IIB: 544–547; IID: 829–835.

Juhel, P. 2002. "'On Orderliness with Respect to the Prizes of War': The Amphipolis Regulation and the Management of Booty in the Army of the Last Antigonids." *ABSA* 97:401–412.

Kahnes, E., and J. Kromayer. 1931. "Drei Diadochenschlachten." In J. Kromayer, ed., *Antike Schlachtfelder, Bausteine zu einer antiken Kriegsgeschichte* 4:391–446. Berlin.

Kanatsulis, D. 1968. "Antipater als Feldherr und Staatsmann nach dem Tode Alexanders des Grossen." *Makedonika* 8:121–184.

Kebric, R. B. 1977. *In the Shadow of Macedon: Duris of Samos.* Stuttgart.

King, C. J. 2010. "Macedonian Kingship and Other Political Institutions." In J. Roisman and I. Worthington, eds., *A Companion to Ancient Macedonia,* 373–391. Malden, MA.

Landucci Gattinoni, F. 1997. *Duride di Samo.* Rome.

———. 2003. *L'arte del potere: Vita e opere di Cassandro di Macedonia.* Stuttgart.

———. 2005. "La tradizione su Seleuco in Diodoro XVIII–XX." In C. Bearzot and F. Landucci Gattinoni, eds., *Diodoro e l'altra Grecia: Macedonia, Occidente, Ellenismo nella biblioteca storica,* 155–181. Milan.

———. 2008. *Diodoro Siculo. Biblioteca storica Libro XVIII.* Milan.

———. 2009. "Cassander's Wife and Heirs." In P. Wheatley and R. Hannah, eds., *Alexander & Successors: Essays from the Antipodes,* 261–275. Claremont, CA.

Lane Fox, R. 1974. *Alexander the Great.* London.

Lateiner, D. 2009. "Tears and Crying in Hellenic Historiography: Dacrylogy from Herodotus to Polybius." In T. Fögen, ed., *Tears in the Greco-Roman World,* 105–134. Berlin.

Launey, M. 1949–1950. *Recherches sur les armées hellénistiques.* 2 vols. Paris. Repr. with addenda by Y. Garlan et al. 1987.

Lehmann, G. A. 1988. "Hieronymus von Kardia und der 'lamische Krieg.'" In W. Will and J. Heinrichs, eds., *Zu Alexander d.Gr.: Festschrift G. Wirth zum 60. Gerurtstag am 9.12.86.* 2:745–764. Amsterdam.

Lendon, J. E. 2005. *Soldiers and Ghosts: A History of Battle in Classical Antiquity.* New Haven.

Le Rider, G. 2007. *Alexander the Great: Coinage, Finance, and Policy.* Trans. W. E. Higgins. Philadelphia.

Lianou, M. 2010. "The Role of the Argeadai in the Legitimation of the Ptolemaic Dynasty: Rhetoric and Practice." In E. Carney and D. Ogden, eds., *Philip II and Alexander the Great: Father and Son, Lives and Afterlives,* 123–134. Oxford.

Lock, R. 1977. "The Macedonian Army Assembly in the Time of Alexander the Great." *CP* 72:91–107.

Loman, P. 2005. "Mercenaries, Their Women, and Colonisation." *Klio* 87:346–365.

Lush, D. 2007. "Body Armour in the Phalanx of Alexander's Army." *AncW* 38:15–37.

Macurdy, G. H. 1932. *Hellenistic Queens.* Baltimore.

Manni, E. 1949. "Tre note di cronologia ellenistica." *RAL* 4:53–85.

———, ed. 1953. *Vita Demetrio Poliorcete.* Florence.

Markle, M. M. 1982. "Macedonian Arms and Tactics under Alexander the Great." In B. Barr-Sharrar and E. N. Borza, eds., *Macedonia and Greece in the Late Classical and Early Hellenistic Age,* 87–111. Washington, DC.

Martin, T. R. 1983 [1987]. "Quintus Curtius' Presentation of Philip Arrhidaeus and Josephus' Accounts of the Accession of Claudius." *AJAH* 8:161–90.

McKechnie, P. 1999. "Manipulation of Themes in Quintus Curtius Rufus Book 10." *Historia* 48:44–60.

Meeus, A. 2008. "The Power Struggle of the Diadochoi in Babylon, 323 B.C." *Ancient Society* 38:39–82.

———. 2009a. "Alexander's Image in the Age of the Successors." In W. Heckel and Trittle, L., eds., *Alexander the Great: A New History*, 235–250. Malden, MA.

———. 2009b. "Kleopatra and the Diadochi." In P. van Nuffelen, ed., *Faces of Hellenism: Studies in the History of the Eastern Mediterranean (4th Century B.C.–5th Century A.D.)*, 63–92. Studia Hellenistica 48. Leuven.

———. 2009c. "Some Institutional Problems Concerning the Succession to Alexander the Great: 'Prostatia' and Chiliarchy." *Historia* 58:287–310.

Mehl, A. 1986. *Seleukos Nikator und seine Reich*. Leuven.

Merker, I. L. 1988. "Diodorus Siculus and Hieronymus of Cardia." *AHB* 2:90–93.

Millett, P. 2010. "The Political Economy of Macedonia." In J. Roisman and I. Worthington, eds., *A Companion to Ancient Macedonia*, 472–504. Malden, MA.

Milns, R. D. 1968. *Alexander the Great*. London.

———. 1970. "The Hypaspists of Alexander III: Some Problems." *Historia* 20:186–195.

———. 1976. "The Army of Alexander the Great." In E. Badian, ed., *Alexandre le Grand: Image et réalité*, 87–136. Geneva.

Mitchell, L. 2007. "Born to Rule? Succession in the Argead Royal House." In W. Heckel, L. Tritle, and P. Wheatley, eds., *Alexander's Empire: A Formulation to Decay*, 61–74. Claremont, CA.

Mitchell, S. 1994. "Three Cities in Pisidia." *AS* 44:129–148.

Mooren, L. 1983. "The Nature of Hellenistic Monarchy." In E. Van 'T Dack, P. van Dessel, and W. van Gucht, eds., *Egypt and the Hellenistic World*, 205–240. Studia Hellenistica 27. Leuven.

Mossé, C. 1998. "Le procès de Phocion." *Dike* 1:79–85.

Müller, S. 2003. *Massnahmen der Herrschaftssicherung gegenüber der makedonischen Opposition bei Alexander dem Grossen*. Frankfurt am Main.

Näf, B. 2004. *Traum und Traumdeutung im Alrtertum*. Darmstadt.

Nagle, D. B. 1996. "The Cultural Context of Alexander's Speech at Opis." *TAPA* 126:151–172.

Niese, B. 1893. *Geschichte der griechischen und makedonischen Staaten seit der Schlacht bei Chaeronea*. Vol. 1. Gotha.

Ober, J. 1996. *The Athenian Revolution: Essays on Ancient Greek Democracy and Political Theory*. Princeton.

———. 1998. *Political Dissent in Democratic Athens: Intellectual Critics of Popular Rule*. Princeton.

O'Brien, J. M. 1992. *Alexander the Great: The Invisible Enemy. A Biography*. London.

Ogden, D. 1999. *Polygamy, Prostitutes, and Death: The Hellenistic Dynasties*. London.

Olbrycht, M. J. 2009. "Curtius Rufus, the Mutiny at Opis, and Alexander's Iranian Policy." In J. Pigon, ed., *The Children of Herodotus: Greek and Roman Historiography and Related Genres*, 231–252. Newcastle.

———. Forthcoming. *Iranians in Alexander the Great's Army and Iranian Influence on His Warfare*.

Orth, W. 1993. *Die Diadochenzeit im Spiegel der historischen Geographie*. Wiesbaden.

Pachidis, P. 2006. "The Interpenetration of Civic Elites and Court Elite in Macedonia." In A.-M. Guimier-Sorbets, M. B. Hatzopoulos, and Y. Morizot, eds., *Rois, Ci-*

tés, Nécropoles: Institutions, Rites et Monuments en Macédoine, 251–268. Actes de colloques de Nanterre (Decembre 2002) et d'Athenes (Janvier 2004). Athens.

Palagia, O. 2000. "Hephaestion's Pyre and the Royal Hunt of Alexander." In A. B. Bosworth and E. J. Baynham, eds., *Alexander the Great in Fact and Fiction*, 167–206. Oxford.

Parke, H. W. 1933. *Greek Mercenary Soldiers from the Earliest Times to the Battle of Ipsus*. Chicago.

Paspalas, S. A. 2005. "Philip Arrhidaios at Court—An Ill-Advised Persianism? Macedonian Royal Display in the Wake of Alexander." *Klio* 87:72–101.

Pekridou, A. 1986. *Das Alketas-Grab in Termessos*. Tübingen.

Picard, C. 1954. "Le trône vide d'Alexandre dans la cérémonie de Cyinda et le culte du trône vide à travers le monde gréco-romain." *Cahiers Archéologiques* 7:1–17.

Potts, D. T. 1990. *The Arabian Gulf in Antiquity: From Alexander the Great to the Coming of Islam*. Vol. 2. Oxford.

Préaux, C. 2002. *Le monde hellénistique: La Grèce et l'Orient de la mort d'Alexandre à la conquête romaine de la Grèce, 323–146 av. J.-C.* 5th ed. 2 vols. Paris.

Pritchett, W. K. 1971–1991. *Greek States at War*. 5 vols. Berkeley.

Proctor, D. 1971. *Hannibal's March in History*. Oxford.

Rathmann, M. 2005. *Perdikkas zwischen 323 und 320: Nachlassverwalter des Alexanderreiches oder Autokrat?* Vienna.

Redfield, J. R. 1975. *Nature and Culture in the Iliad: The Tragedy of Hector*. Chicago.

Rogers, G. M. 2004. *Alexander: The Ambiguity of Greatness*. New York.

Roisman, J., ed. 2003a. *Brill's Companion to Alexander the Great*. Leiden.

———. 2003b. "Honor in Alexander's Campaign." In J. Roisman, ed., *Brill's Companion to Alexander the Great*, 279–321. Leiden.

Roisman, J., and I. Worthington, eds. 2010. *A Companion to Ancient Macedonia*. Malden, MA.

Rosen, K. 1967. "Political Documents in Hieronymus of Cardia (323–302 B.C.)." *Acta Classica* 10:41–94.

Rubicam, C. 1991. "Casualty Figures in the Battle Descriptions of Thucydides." *TAPA* 121:181–198.

———. 2003. "Numbers in Greek Poetry and Historiography: Quantifying Feeling." *CQ* 53:448–463.

Rutz, W. 1983. "*Seditionum procellae*: Livianisches in der Darstellung der Meuterei von Opis bei Curtius Rufus." In E. Lefèvre and E. Olshausen, eds., *Livius: Werk und Rezeption. Festschrift für Erich Burck zum 80. Geburtstag*, 399–409. Munich.

Rzepka, J. 2005. "*Koine Ekklesia* in Didorus Siculus and the General Assemblies of the Macedonians." *Tyche* 20:119–142.

———. 2008. "The Units of Alexander's Army and the District Divisions of Late Argead Macedonia." *GRBS* 48:39–56.

Saatsoglou-Paliadeli, C. 1993. "Aspects of Ancient Macedonian Costume." *JHS* 113:122–147.

Sabin, P. 2009. *Lost Battles: Reconstructing the Great Clashes of the Ancient World*. London.

Sacks, K. S. 1990. *Diodorus Siculus and the First Century*. Princeton.

Schachermeyer, F. 1954. "Die lezte Pläne Alexanders." *JÖAI* 41:118–140.

———. 1970. *Alexander in Babylon und die Reichsordnung nac seine Tode*. Vienna.

Schäfer, C. 2002. *Eumenes von Kardia und der Kampf um die Macht im Alexanderreich.* Frankfurt am Main.

Schmitt, O. 1992. *Der Lamische Krieg.* Bonn.

Schober, L. 1981. *Untersuchungen zur Geschichte Babyloniens und der Oberen Satrapien von 323–303 v. Chr.* Frankfurt am Main.

Schom, A. M. 1997. *Napoleon Bonaparte: A Life.* New York.

Schubert, R. 1914. *Die Quellen zur geschichte der Diadochenzeit.* Leipzig.

Schwahn, W. 1930. "Die Nachfolge Alexanders des Grossen." *Klio* 23:211–238; 24 (1931): 306–332.

Seibert, J. 1969. *Untersuchungen zur Geschichte Ptolemaios I.* Munich.

———. 1983. *Das Zeitalter der Diadochen.* Darmstadt.

Sekunda, N. V. 2010. "The Macedonian Army." In J. Roisman and I. Worthington, eds., *A Companion to Ancient Macedonia,* 446–471. Malden, MA.

Sharples, I. 1994. "Curtius' Treatment of Arrhidaeus." *Mediterranean Archaeology* 7:53–60.

Simonetti-Agostinetti, A., ed. 1993. *Flavio Arriano: Gli eventi dopo Alessandro.* Rome.

———. 1997. "Geronimo di Cardia: Storico di parte o equilibrato narratore della storia del suo tempo?" *MGR* 21:209–226.

Simpson, R. H. 1957. "A note on Cyinda." *Historia* 6:503–504.

———. 1959. "Abbreviation of Hieronymus in Diodorus." *AJP* 80:370–379.

Sisti, F., and A. Zambrini, eds. 2001–2004. A. *Arriano, Anabasi di Alessandro.* 2 vols. Milan.

Smith, S. 1924. *Babylonian Historical Texts Relating to the Capture and Downfall of Babylon.* London.

Sordi, M. 2002. *Scritti di storia greca.* Milan.

Spann, P. A. 1999. "Alexander at the Beas: Fox in a Lion's Skin." In F. B. Titchener and R. J. Moorton, Jr., eds., *The Eye Expanded: Life and the Arts in Greco-Roman Antiquity,* 62–74. Berkeley.

Spawforth, T. 2007. "The Court of Alexander the Great between Europe and Asia." In A. J. S. Spawforth, ed., *The Court and Court Society in Ancient Monarchies,* 82–120. Cambridge.

Spencer, D. 2002. *The Roman Alexander: Reading a Cultural Myth.* Exeter.

Sprawski, S. 2008. "Leonnatus's Campaign of 322 B.C." In E. Dabrowa, ed. *Studies on Greek and Roman Military History,* 9–31. Electrum 14. Krakow.

Stewart, A. 1993. *Faces of Power: Alexander's Image and Hellenistic Politics.* Berkeley.

Syme, R. 1995. *Anatolica: Studies in Strabo.* Oxford.

Szczurek, P. 2009. "Source or Sources of Diodorus' Accounts of Indian Suttee (Diod. Sic. 19.33–34.6)?" In J. Pigon, ed., *The Children of Herodotus: Greek and Roman Historiography and Related Genres,* 119–143. Newcastle.

Tarn, W. W. 1948. *Alexander the Great.* 2 vols. Cambridge.

Tcherikover, V. 1927. *Die hellenistischen Städtegründungen von Alexander dem Grossen bis auf die Römerzeit.* Leipzig.

Themelis, P. G., and J. P. Touratsoglou. 1997. *Hoi Taphoi tou Derveniou.* Athens.

Thompson, D. J. 2006. "The Hellenistic Family." In G. R. Bugh, ed., *The Cambridge Companion to the Hellenistic World,* 93–112. Cambridge.

Thompson, W. E. 1984. "*PSI* 1284: Eumenes of Cardia vs. the Phalanx." *ChrEg* 59:113–120.

Trittle, L. A. 1988. *Phocion the Good*. London.

Van der Spek, B. The Diadochi Chronicle. http://www.livius.org/cg-cm/chronicles/bchp -diadochi/diadochi_01.html.

Vezin, A. 1907. *Eumenes von Kardia: Ein Beitrag zur Geschichte der Diadochenzeit*. Münster.

Volkmann, H. 1990. *Die Massenversklavungen der einwohner eroberter Städte in der hellenistisch-römischen Zeit*. 2nd ed. Stuttgart.

Walsh, J. 2009. "Historical Method and a Chronological Problem in Diodorus, Book 18." In P. Wheatley and R. Hannah, eds. *Alexander and His Successors: Essays from the Antipodes*, 72–87. Claremont, CA.

Waterfield, R. 2011. *Dividing the Spoils: The War for Alexander the Great's Empire*. Oxford.

Weisehöfer, J. 1994. *Die 'dunklen Jahrhunderte' der Persis: Untersuchungen zu Geschichte und Kultur von F_rs in frühhellenistischer Zeit (330–140 v. Chr.)*. Munich.

Wheatley, P. V. 1998. "The Chronology of the Third Diadoch War, 315–311 B.C." *Phoenix* 52:257–281.

Will, É. 1984. "The Succession to Alexander." In *CAH*, 2nd ed., 7.1:23–61.

Wilson, N. G. 1994. *Photius. The Bibliotheca*. London.

Wirth, G. 1967. "Zur Politik des Perdikkas 323." *Helikon* 7:281–322.

———. 1984. "Zu einer schweigenden Mehrheit: Alexander und die griechischen Söldner." In J. Ozols and V. Thewalt, eds., *Aus dem Osten des Alexanderreiches: Völker und Kulturen zwischen Orient und Okzident: Iran, Afghanistan, Pakistan, Indien. Festschrift zum 65. Geburtstag von Klaus Fischer*, 9–31. Cologne.

Worthington, I. 2004. *Alexander the Great: Man and God*. Harlow, Eng.

Wüst, F. 1953–54a. "Die Rede Alexanders des Grossen in Opis: Arrian VII 9–10." *Historia* 2:177–188.

———. 1953/54b. "Die Muterei von Opis (Arrian VII, 8; 11.1–7)." *Historia* 2:418–431.

Yardley, J. C., and W. Heckel, eds. 1984. *Quintus Curtius Rufus: The History of Alexander*. London.

———, eds. 2003. *Justin Epitome of the Philippic History of Pompeius Trogus. Books 11–12: Alexander the Great*. Vol. 1. Oxford.

INDEX